Teaching Today

An Introduction to Education

Sixth Edition

David G. Armstrong
The University of North Carolina at Greensboro

Kenneth T. Henson
Eastern Kentucky University

Tom V. Savage
California State University, Fullerton

Upper Saddle River, New Jersey
Columbus, Ohio

Library of Congress Cataloging-in-Publication Data

Armstrong, David G.
  Teaching today: an introduction to education / David G. Armstrong, Kenneth T.
Henson, Tom V. Savage.– 6th ed.
    p. cm.
  Includes bibliographical references and index.
  ISBN 0-13-022680-7
    1. Teaching–United States. 2. Education–Study and teaching–United States.   3.
Teaching–Vocational guidance–United States. I. Henson, Kenneth T. II. Savage, Tom
V. III. Title.

LB1775.2.A75 2001
371.102'0973–dc21

99-088678

Vice President and Publisher: Jeffery W. Johnston
Editor: Debra A. Stollenwerk
Developmental Editor: Gianna M. Marsella
Editorial Assistant: Penny S. Burleson
Production Editor: Mary Harlan
Design Coordinator: Diane C. Lorenzo
Photo Coordinator: Sandy Lenahan
Production Coordinator: Amy Gehl, Carlisle
    Publishers Services

Text Design: Carlisle Publishers Services
Cover Designer: Ceri Fitzgerald
Cover Art: Kenneth A. Henson, 1999
Production Manager: Pamela D. Bennett
Director of Marketing: Kevin Flanagan
Marketing Manager: Amy June
Marketing Services Manager: Krista Groshong

This book was set in Schneidler and Humanist by Carlisle Communications, Ltd. It
was printed and bound by R. R. Donnelley & Sons Company. The cover was printed by
Phoenix Color Corp.

Earlier editions, entitled *Education: An Introduction,* © 1993, 1989, 1985, 1981 by
Macmillan Publishing Company.

Photo Credits: The U.S. National Education Association of the United States, 1; Anthony
Magnacca/Merrill, 7, 36, 47, 157, 168, 222, 240, 251, 255, 275, 279, 296, 338, 367, 370, 428;
Anne Vega/Merrill, 19, 136, 146, 183, 343, 397, 401, 439; Scott Cunningham/Merrill, 22, 63,
66, 95, 104, 130, 186, 192, 205, 236, 291, 434; Used with Permission, 53; Charles
Arbogast/Merrill, 81; Corbis-Bettmann,107, 312, 318, 350; Andy Brunk/Merrill, 115; Jeff
Atteberry/Indianapolis Star/SIPA Press, 170; KS Studios/Merrill, 283, 407; Courtesy of the
Library of Congress, 321; Mary Kate Denny/Photo Edit, 363; Michelle Bridwell/Photo Edit,
384; Cartoons by Randy Glasbergen.

Merrill
Prentice Hall

10 9 8 7 6 5 4 3 2 1
ISBN 0-13-022680-7

What is wrong with today's schools? How can they be made better? At various periods in our national life, these questions have been answered in quite different ways. If you review what educational reformers were saying in the 1960s, you will find comments such as the following:

- Schools are inhumane places that fail to acknowledge the dignity of learners.
- Learners' individual development suffers because all are subjected to a common curriculum.
- Administrators and teachers exercise too much authority over what learners study in school.
- Many more "electives" and other kinds of learning options should replace curricula that are too narrow in scope.
- There is far too much use of standardized testing.

Certainly not all critics of school practices in the 1960s agreed with these statements, but these opinions were common during this period of our history. Now contrast these views with what many critics of educational practices are saying as we enter the new century:

- School curricula often are too fragmented; it is better for learners to study fewer subjects in more depth.
- Standardized testing of some kind is needed so that meaningful comparisons can be made among different schools.
- More academic rigor is needed in school curricula, and it is the responsibility of administrators and teachers to ensure this happens.
- The primary purpose of schools is to focus on learners' academic development.

By no means do all present-day proponents of educational reform agree with these propositions. However, these ideas are widespread, and actions of school districts throughout the country to emphasize school accountability, rigorous testing of learners, and strong academic programs attest to their potency.

We draw the contrast between these prescriptions for "making the school better" to make the point that you will be entering a profession where today's received wisdom may be tomorrow's discarded, stale news. To be happy in education, you must embrace change as a given. Better yet, you need to be energized by your participation in a public debate that will be a career-long shaper and reshaper of your professional life.

Education today demands smart, altruistic people. If school districts were to put up signs to attract the kinds of people they want to hire, the signs might well read: "Wanted: Teachers Who Lead." If you seek a career free from the confrontations of contemporary life, choose another line of work. You will be expected to function as a proactive leader. The trend is toward involving teachers more and more in decisions about budgeting, management, and many other areas that go well beyond their traditional concerns for instructional planning. The level of involvement you can have as a teacher will give you an opportunity to assume significant responsibilities and make a difference soon after beginning your career.

In preparing the sixth edition of *Teaching Today,* we have sought to provide you with an explanation of topics relevant to the world you will enter as a classroom teacher. These relate to the nature of the profession; special characteristics of learners; theories and research associated with instruction, management, and evaluation; the social, historical, and philosophical foundations of the profession; issues associated with school reform and curriculum patterns; and common organizational arrangements of schools. In addition, you will find material designed to help you analyze, reflect, and decide. You can expand your understanding of these issues by going beyond the text to pursue information at a number of World Wide Web sites that we recommend. You also will find useful an extensive glossary of specialized terms.

We hope this book will help you develop your ability to think carefully about educational issues and to grasp key characteristics of teaching and schooling. Welcome to the profession!

ORGANIZATION OF THIS TEXT

Earlier editions of *Teaching Today* have been used both by undergraduate and graduate students. We have prepared the book for use in introduction to education classes, introduction to teaching classes, foundations of education classes, school curriculum classes, issues in education classes, and problems in education classes. This edition organizes content under five major headings. The title of each provides a context for the chapters it includes.

Part I is titled "The Profession Today." Chapter 1 emphasizes the changing nature of the profession. To illustrate teachers' many responsibilities, there is a useful description of a teacher's typical day. Chapter 2 introduces the phases in a teacher's professional development, including continued development once initial preparation has been completed. The chapter also briefly introduces roles in education other than classroom teaching. Chapter 3 explores the numerous legal issues affecting teachers today.

Part II focuses on "Learners and Their Diverse Needs." Chapter 4 explores issues associated with multiculturalism. Specific examples of programs that have well served culturally diverse young people are introduced. Chapter 5 considers legal requirements and instructional approaches relevant to appropriately serving learners with special needs and special talents. Chapter 6 focuses on legal aspects of learners' rights and responsibilities. The chapter includes an extensive discussion of relevant court cases.

Part III centers on "Teaching in Today's Classrooms." Chapter 7 emphasizes direct instruction and includes information related to such issues as active teaching, program planning, teacher questions, homework, and teacher-learner observation instruments that can be used in the classroom. Chapter 8 focuses on the important issue of classroom management and discipline. Specific suggestions are included for a scaled series of teacher responses that vary according to the seriousness and frequency of the disruptive behavior. Chapter 9 describes approaches to assessment, measurement, evaluation, and grading. In addition to more traditional approaches, there is extensive treatment of portfolios.

Part IV focuses on "Influences on Teachers and Learners." Chapter 10 explains how learners' membership in schools, families, religious and social organizations, and certain ethnic and cultural groups influences their patterns of behavior in the classroom. Chapter 11 traces important historical roots of American education. Chapter 12 introduces information that illustrates how varying philosophical perspectives influence attitudes toward specific curricula and instructional practices.

Part V considers "Contexts of Teaching." Chapter 13 focuses on school reform and includes such topics as systemic reform, INTASC standards, the National Board for Professional Teaching Standards, school choice options, school-business partnerships, and full-service schools. Chapter 14 addresses issues associated with curriculum, with particular attention to curricula based on needs of learners, curricula based on academic subject matter, and curricula based on the needs of society. Chapter 15 describes patterns of school funding, staffing, and organization.

At the end of the book, you will find a complete glossary in which all terms introduced in the text are defined.

SPECIAL FEATURES OF THIS TEXT

Features of the sixth edition of *Teaching Today* include the following:

- **Bulleted objectives** at the beginning of each chapter draw students' attention to important chapter content.
- **Graphic organizers** *(NEW!)* at the beginning of each chapter provide a convenient graphical summary of chapter content.
- **Introductions** at the beginning of each chapter set the stage for information to be presented.
- **Links to the companion website,** *(NEW!)* located at http://www.prenhall. com/armstrong, are integrated throughout each chapter and embedded in most feature boxes.
- Two **Following the Web** features *(NEW!)* in each chapter provide opportunities for students to enrich their understanding of new content by going to selected sites on the World Wide Web.
- **Critical Incidents** in each chapter provide students opportunities to engage in higher level thinking as they reflect on situations faced by teachers today.
- **What Do You Think?** features in each chapter ask readers to examine their personal convictions and consider alternate perspectives so they can better relate to colleagues and students in their classrooms.
- **Video Viewpoint** features *(NEW!)* in every chapter connect segments on the accompanying video, *Critical Issues in Education,* to chapter content and provide classroom opportunities for lively discussions and self-reflection.

- **Cartoons** that appear periodically illustrate educational issues and help convey to the students that, while education is serious business, it need not be grim.
- **Figures** in each chapter provide opportunities for students to reflect on issues that are introduced.
- **Key Ideas in Summary** sections at the end of each chapter facilitate content review by drawing students' attention to important ideas.
- **Reflections** materials at the end of each chapter prompt students to engage in critical thinking about various issues that have been raised.
- **Field Experiences, Projects, and Enrichment** sections at the conclusion of the chapters provide opportunities for students to extend their understandings by engaging in appropriate application activities.
- **References** at the end of each chapter direct students to source materials used by the authors.

NEW TO THIS EDITION

- A new introductory chapter titled **"Teaching in an Age of Change"** (Chapter 1)
- A new chapter titled **"Becoming a Professional Educator"** (Chapter 2)
- A new chapter titled **"Exceptional Learners"** (Chapter 5)
- A new chapter titled **"Assessing Learning"** (Chapter 9)
- A new chapter titled **"Challenges of School Reform"** (Chapter 13)
- A comprehensive **glossary** of concise definitions for terms introduced in the chapters
- Several useful and appealing new chapter features, including graphic organizers, **Following the Web,** integrated links to the companion website, **Video Viewpoints,** and **What Do You Think?**, as well as a number of new **Critical Incidents**
- Much additional content related to the important issue of **reflective teaching**
- Broadened and updated coverage of issues related to **multicultural education**
- Greatly expanded coverage of the use of **portfolios**, both to assess learners and as an evidentiary base for the evaluation of teachers
- Greatly expanded coverage of **school funding** issues in a chapter titled "School Funding, Staffing, and Organization" (Chapter 15)
- Updated content on important **legal issues** facing learners and teachers
- Continued broad and updated coverage of **management and discipline** issues
- Exciting new supplements, including a **video library, a companion website,** and **acetate transparencies**

USING THE TEXT

We believe that schoolteachers should take personal control over the instructional process. They should not feel obligated to follow the numerical order of chapters in their texts. Similarly, we encourage instructors who use this text to follow this logic and to assign students to read chapters in an order that makes sense in light of how they have designed their courses. We have written chapters in this book to be "free-standing." That is, no chapter has content that is prerequisite to that introduced in any other chapter.

SUPPLEMENTS TO THE TEXT

All supplements are available free of charge to instructors who adopt this text. To request any of the following supplements, contact your Prentice Hall representative or visit our website at http://www.merrilleducation.com. (If you do not know how to contact your local sales representative, please call faculty services at 1-800-526-0485 for assistance.)

Instructor's Guide
The **Instructor's Guide** provides professors with a variety of useful resources, including chapter overviews, teaching strategies, and ideas for classroom activities, discussions, and assessment.

Computerized Testbanks
Customizable **test banks** on disk are available for both Macintosh and Windows users to assist in the preparation of classroom assessments.

Acetate Transparencies
A packet of **acetate transparencies** featuring figures and other important material from the text is available to assist in delivering lectures and presentations on chapter topics.

Video Library
The video library, entitled **Critical Issues in Education,** contains 15 segments—one for each chapter—drawn from ABC News programming such as Nightline, 20/20, and Good Morning America. Video segments cover a variety of topics and vary in length for maximum instructional flexibility. The Video Viewpoint in each chapter can be used to link the video segment to the text and to promote thoughtful classroom discussion of critical—and sometimes controversial—issues in education.

Companion Website
Located at **http://www.prenhall.com/armstrong,** the Companion Web site for this text includes a wealth of resources for both students and professors, including:

- The **Syllabus Manager** enables professors to create and maintain the class syllabus online while also allowing the student access to the syllabus at any time from any computer on the Internet.

- **Chapter Objectives** help students review chapter content.
- Students can test their knowledge by taking interactive **Self Tests**—multiple-choice quizzes that provide immediate feedback with a percentage score and correct answers.
- Additional assessment opportunities are provided by the **Reflections** and **Critical Incidents** modules, where students can submit essay-style answers to instructors or study partners via e-mail.
- The **Following the Web** feature assists students in using the web to do additional research on chapter topics and key issues.
- Both the **Message Board** and **Live Chat** features encourage student interaction outside of the classroom.
- In addition, the **Glossary** module provides a convenient online reference for students familiarizing themselves with key vocabulary.

ACKNOWLEDGMENTS

Some fine professionals participated in the development of the sixth edition of *Teaching Today*. We gratefully acknowledge the contributions of the following individuals who reviewed preliminary versions of the chapters: Rose Adesiyan, Purdue University—Calumet; Richard N. Avdul, University of Saint Francis (Fort Wayne, Indiana); Hugh Campbell, Concord College; Carolyn J. Kelley, The University of Central Arkansas; and Janis E. Murphy, Murray State University. In addition, we especially commend the attention that Debbie Stollenwerk, our editor at Merrill/Prentice Hall, devoted to this project. Her excellent suggestions contributed importantly to the substance of the final version. Finally, we wish to extend a special "thank you" to our spouses for their unwavering support during the time we were working on this revision.

DISCOVER THE COMPANION WEBSITE ACCOMPANYING THIS BOOK

The Prentice Hall Companion Website:
A Virtual Learning Environment

Technology is a constantly growing and changing aspect of our field that is creating a need for content and resources. To address this emerging need, Prentice Hall has developed an online learning environment for students and professors alike—Companion Websites—to support our textbooks.

In creating a Companion Website, our goal is to build on and enhance what the textbook already offers. For this reason, the content for each user-friendly website is organized by chapter and provides the professor and student with a variety of meaningful resources. Common features of a Companion Website include:

For the Professor—

Every Companion Website integrates **Syllabus Manager**™, an online syllabus creation and management utility.

- **Syllabus Manager**™ provides you, the instructor, with an easy, step-by-step process to create and revise syllabi, with direct links into Companion Website and other online content without having to learn HTML.
- Students may logon to your syllabus during any study session. All they need to know is the web address for the Companion Website and the password you've assigned to your syllabus.
- After you have created a syllabus using **Syllabus Manager**™, students may enter the syllabus for their course section from any point in the Companion Website.
- Clicking on a date, the student is shown the list of activities for the assignment. The activities for each assignment are linked directly to actual content, saving time for students.
- Adding assignments consists of clicking on the desired due date, then filling in the details of the assignment—name of the assignment, instructions, and whether it is a one-time or repeating assignment.
- In addition, links to other activities can be created easily. If the activity is online, a URL can be entered in the space provided, and it will be linked automatically in the final syllabus.
- Your completed syllabus is hosted on our servers, allowing convenient updates from any computer on the Internet. Changes you make to your syllabus are immediately available to your students at their next logon.

For the Student—

- **Chapter Objectives:** outline key concepts from the text
- **Interactive self-quizzes:** complete with hints and automatic grading that provide immediate feedback for students

After students submit their answers for the interactive self-quizzes, the Companion Website **Results Reporter** computes a percentage grade, provides a graphic representation of how many questions were answered correctly and incorrectly, and gives a question by question analysis of the quiz. Students are given the option to send their quiz to up to four E-mail addresses (professor, teaching assistant, study partner, etc.).

- **Message Board:** serves as a virtual bulletin board to post—or respond to—questions or comments to/from a national audience
- **Chat:** real-time chat with anyone who is using the text anywhere in the country—ideal for discussion and study groups, class projects, etc.
- **Web Destinations:** links to www sites that relate to chapter content
- **Additional Resources:** access to chapter-specific or general content that enhances material found in the text

To take advantage of these and other resources, please visit the *Teaching Today* Companion Website at:

www.prenhall.com/armstrong

Contents in Brief

Contents

PART I
The Profession Today   1

PART II

Learners and Their Diverse Needs   95

6 **Learners' Rights and Responsibilities**   **152**

PART III

Teaching in Today's Classrooms   **183**

7 **Effective Instruction**   **184**

8 Classroom Management and Discipline   216

9 Assessing Learning   246

PART IV

Influences on Teachers and Learners   **279**

PART V

Contexts of Teaching   *363*

Special Features

Critical Incidents

Following the Web

Video Viewpoint

What Do You Think?

Part One

The Profession Today

CHAPTERS

1

Teaching in an Age of Change

OBJECTIVES

This chapter will help you to

- describe how changes in society influence education.
- state alternative views concerning needed reform of schools.
- describe how changes in the learner population are leading to changes in education.
- state alternative views relating to multicultural and bilingual education.
- explain what is meant by "standards-based education."
- point out some implications of "constructivism" for educational practice.
- explain what is meant by "multiple intelligences."
- identify some factors that contribute to the complexity of teaching.

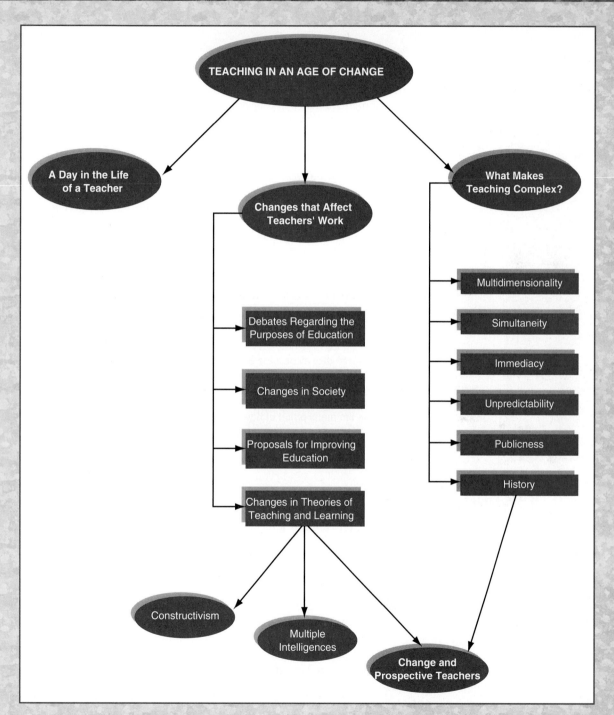

FIGURE 1.1 Teaching in an Age of Change

Critical Incident

Let Me Teach!

Laura Jacobs is a college senior. She has been frustrated in her attempts to fit in all of the requirements for graduation due to the extra courses required for her teaching certificate. Until yesterday, she had reconciled herself to spending at least one extra semester to meet all of the requirements. She brightened last night when she saw the headline, "Governor Proposes Change in Teacher Education," in the local paper.

The article described the governor's frustration with the low scores of public school students on the most recent administration of standardized tests. She said the "obvious remedy" was putting teachers in the classroom who had more academic preparation in the subjects they were teaching. The governor then noted recent cutbacks in the defense and aerospace industries. There were, she claimed, a large number of individuals with a rich background in math and science who could make an excellent contribution to solving the current education crisis. The governor fumed that present regulations would require any of these people who might be interested in teaching to go back to college to take a lot of "meaningless education courses." The governor announced that she was sending the legislature a proposal to scrap many course-related requirements for teacher certification—a move, she said, that would get some "really high-quality people in our classrooms in a hurry."

Laura put down the paper and thought to herself:

> That really makes sense. I hope the legislators will move on this idea in a hurry. It would really help me. I don't need to take all of these education courses. I *know* how to teach. In fact, I've known how for years. I've always watched my favorite teachers carefully, and I'm sure I can do what they did. I especially remember Ms. Edwards. When I was in high school, she really turned me on to academics and got me interested in learning. Thanks to her, I went on to college, and I'm pretty proud of how well I've done. I know I've learned information far beyond what elementary kids will need to know.
>
> Friends who are teaching tell me that wonderful teachers' guides are provided with all of the textbooks. They should help me plan. In addition, I've had lots of experience work-

INTRODUCTION

With the arrival of the 21st century, education has moved to the top of the American political and social agenda. A rapidly changing, technology-oriented society depends on a highly educated citizenry for its survival. Today, some people fear that American schools are not adequately preparing young people for the challenges they will face as adults.

Discussions about how to change education are so widespread that you will almost certainly witness important changes during your years in the profession. Many of them will relate to what you do in the classroom. Increasingly, people who have studied education recognize that the key to educational improvement is the teacher.

As a teacher, you will be a role model who can have an influence on learners that will last a lifetime. What you do can help young people face the future confident in their abilities to succeed. Similarly, poor teaching can enhance learners' anxieties and undermine their confidence to cope with the complexities of modern life. To serve young people well, you will be called upon to use your intellect, creativity, compasing at the YWCA, and I've done lots of baby-sitting. What more do I really need? How hard can it be to teach kids that two times two is four or that "cat" is spelled c-a-t? I feel I'm ready to go to work right now. These education courses are only going to waste my time. Maybe there are some people who need them, but I don't. I want to get out there and start teaching. I hope the governor's idea becomes law so I can avoid these required courses, go to work, and finally start making some money.

. . .

What are some assumptions the governor makes about characteristics of good teachers? How realistic are these? If the governor's proposals become law, what are the prospects that high numbers of talented new people will enter the teaching profession? On what do you base your conclusion?

What is your reaction to the points Laura makes? Is there specialized knowledge needed by people who are preparing to teach? Do you think most people have had so much experience as learners themselves that they already know how to teach? What assumptions is Laura making about the role of a teacher? Do you think that reducing requirements for certification would be an incentive for academically talented individuals to enter teaching? How do you react to her modeling her teaching after a favorite teacher in the past? Does Laura seem to be inferring that the challenges of teaching are constant and do not change over time? What general advice would you give to Laura?

ℂ𝕎 To respond to this Critical Incident online, and to save or submit your response electronically, visit the companion Web site, located at *http://www.prenhall.com/armstrong*. Select Chapter 1 from the front page of the Web site, then choose the Critical Incidents module on the navigation bar on the left side of the page. Instructors and students may also wish to use these scenarios as discussion topics on the Message Board for the companion Web site.

sion, and patience. You may find these challenges exciting, rewarding, humbling, and frustrating. However, we suspect that you will rarely find them dull.

As you develop as a professional educator, you need to consider these questions:

- What is the good society, and how does education contribute to that society (philosophical foundations)?
- How does education affect different segments of society, and how do proposed changes influence different groups (social foundations)?
- From where did present school practices and traditions come, and are they still important (historical foundations)?
- Who has the power to decide priorities and influence how the schools will operate (political foundations)?
- What is taught, and why is it taught (curriculum foundations)?
- What are the important components of good teaching (instructional foundations)?
- What are your legal and ethical rights and responsibilities as a teacher (legal foundations)?

Keep these questions in mind as you consider teaching as a career and as you progress through this text. These questions are central to discussions about educational change, and answers will help you better evaluate the merit of specific school-improvement proposals.

A DAY IN THE LIFE OF A TEACHER

What is teaching really like? You have spent thousands of hours as a student in classrooms, and you may have spent some time observing teachers. As a result, you may think you have a good, clear grasp of the role of a teacher. However, you may have a false sense of understanding. Like many skilled professionals, excellent teachers are so good at what they do that their work often looks easy to outsiders. They move smoothly through the curriculum, their learners do their work, and the day is punctuated by few disruptive or otherwise dramatic moments.

What outsiders often fail to see is the thinking and decision making that has gone into lesson preparation. Similarly, small but important adjustments good teachers make as they do their work may be difficult to observe. Often these involve teachers' reactions to subtle cues that only experienced professionals recognize. Teachers' responsiveness to them often prevents potential problems. Thus, what appears to be an effortless activity in reality is a complex interplay of actions and interpersonal communications.

The apparent ease with which experienced teachers discharge their responsibilities may lead to the conclusion that good teaching requires little preparation. For example, a student with whom we worked some years ago commented, "All you need to know to be a teacher is how to read the teachers' guide!" Not surprisingly, this person did not have a successful student-teaching experience.

The unobserved aspects of the public performance of fine teachers may be only one of the surprises you will encounter as you start your work in the profession. We have often heard former students say, "There is so much I didn't know." Many people are surprised at how much time is taken up by activities that do not involve direct work with learners. Among them are responsibilities associated with

- planning lessons;
- record keeping and other administrative duties;
- participating in special school events such as "back-to-school" nights;
- attending faculty meetings;
- serving on committees of various kinds;
- participating in activities of professional groups; and,
- communicating with parents or guardians.

The types of activities you will be involved with will vary according to the age level of your learners and nature of the school and the district. What might be an issue in one place may not be an issue in another. For example, the special characteristics of your school may make it essential that you quickly come to understand its internal political climate. This kind of information may be much less critical in an-

Teachers often spend time communicating with parents or guardians.

other setting. If you teach at the secondary level, you may be expected to serve as an adviser or sponsor of a school organization or to assist at athletic events or social activities. If you teach in an elementary school, you may spend some of your time monitoring learners on the playground or in the lunchroom.

There are no "ordinary" days in teaching, and there are no "typical" schools. No two days are alike, and no two learners are alike. Young people in the same classroom may react differently to the same lesson. This lack of excessive predictability appeals to many teachers and may have influenced you to pursue a career in teaching. You might find these differences and lack of predictability to be stimulating.

Place-to-place and day-to-day differences make it difficult to describe the "reality" of a day in the life of a teacher. However, we thought it worthwhile to make the attempt. We observed a randomly chosen elementary teacher for a single day. We make no claim that this scenario necessarily generalizes to this teacher's other days or to teachers in other settings. Our purpose in providing this information is not to suggest that this day is "typical." Rather, our intent is to prompt you to consider aspects of teaching that you may not have considered.

J. D. Smith's Day at School

Pupils at J. D. Smith's elementary school are expected to arrive by 8:30 A.M. However, the day for J. D. and the rest of the teachers begins much earlier, as school regulations require teachers to be present no later than 8:00 A.M. Many teachers are in the building by 7:30 A.M. or earlier working on room decorations, preparing lessons, copying handouts for learners, taking care of administrative work, and preparing for the instructional day. On this morning, J. D. spends time completing paperwork from the district personnel department relating to validation of summer-term courses taken at a local university.

J. D. learns that a parent has called the school. Her child is ill and will miss school for several days. J. D. has been asked to prepare assignments the parent can pick up and use with the child at home. The parent does not want her son to fall behind. Another surprise event this morning is the unexpected arrival of a parent of one of J. D.'s pupils. The parent is concerned about the youngster's progress, so J. D. and the parent spend some time discussing the situation. Phone calls from parents, unexpected arrivals, and other early-morning events are typical of what J. D. encounters each morning. On some days, there are scheduled early-morning meetings of the entire faculty. What all of this means is that there are few days when J. D. has uninterrupted time in the early morning to work alone in the classroom.

We are visiting J. D. in early fall. This is the time of year when the district regularly schedules its annual Back-to-School Night. During this event, each teacher gives parents an overview of the curriculum and teacher expectations. J. D. knows that this explanation will need to be repeated at least twice so that parents with more than one youngster in school can visit at least two classrooms. On the other hand, J. D. does not have to engage in as much repetition as the secondary school teachers in the district who must prepare a brief overview for every period of the day. J. D. is expected to pay careful attention to the public relations' importance of the Back-to-School event, and extra time will have to be spent making the classroom attractive. J. D. begins this before the start of the instructional day by putting up a bulletin board with samples of learners' work.

The children arrive, and things begin to move quickly. During the first part of the morning, J. D. moves the class smoothly through the topics taught. Class members stay on task, and things go well. Recess time arrives, and learners quickly exit the room. J. D. gathers up materials that have been used and puts them away. Then, after a quick check to make sure that the material needed for the rest of the morning is ready, it is time for a quick trip to the lounge for a cup of coffee and some conversation with other teachers.

Recess time passes quickly. J. D. and the other teachers position themselves in the hall outside their doors to monitor learners as they file back into the rooms. Several problems have occurred during the recess period. One of J. D.'s youngsters has a skinned elbow that needs attention, so J. D. sends this child to the office. In times past, the school nurse would have handled this situation, but because of budget cuts, a nurse is available in the building only a few hours each week. In the absence of the nurse, the school secretary calls the parent and gets permission to bandage the elbow.

J. D. also has to deal with a complaint brought by several children who claim that others were not behaving properly on the playground during recess. J. D. informs them that the matter will be addressed. These assurances satisfy them, and J. D. quickly puts the class to work. While some learners work independently, J. D. holds a brief conference with those who were involved in the recess incident. A warning in a firm tone of voice seems to achieve the desired outcome.

As the morning passes, some members of the class experience difficulty staying on task. Their attention span shortens as the day passes. In response to this situation, J. D. moves around the room working with different groups and refocusing attention on what they are supposed to be doing. Lunch comes as a welcome break.

The lunch period begins with a trip to the cafeteria. J. D. briefly enjoys some light conversation and joking with other teachers. Then there is a trip to the mailbox where there are announcements about Back-to-School Night that need to be sent home that afternoon. J. D. finishes the lunch break by gathering equipment that will be needed for this afternoon's science lesson. As usual, several needed items are missing. This prompts a quick search and some adjustments in the original plan.

J. D. arrives back to the classroom before it is time for class members to return. Materials that are still out from the morning's work are cleaned up. J. D. spends a few minutes reviewing plans for the afternoon. Materials are organized, and J. D. makes a few additional notes in the lesson plan book as reminders of things that need to be re-taught or reviewed tomorrow.

J. D. is still making preparations for the afternoon as the bell rings and learners line up outside the classroom. The youngsters are still excited from lunch and the few minutes they have been on the playground. They are talking loudly. To calm them, J. D. asks them to go quickly to their seats and sit quietly. Then, J. D. takes a children's book from the desk and reads a few pages aloud. This is high-interest material, and there are some groans when the reading stops.

It is time for the next lesson. This lesson and those that follow go reasonably well, but the time from lunch until the close of the school day seems to pass slowly. The class is more restless and less attentive. J. D. knows this is a typical pattern, and many of the afternoon lessons feature active learner participation in the hope that this will keep them focused and involved. A few minutes before the dismissal bell, J. D. stops instructional activities. Pupil workers are asked to perform their duties. Books are replaced in the bookshelves, and papers are collected. J. D. takes time to make last-minute announcements and to give reminders about homework. Papers that need to be sent home are distributed, and J. D. dismisses the class.

Today, J. D. has bus duty. After a hurried walk to the bus loading zone, J. D. monitors the behavior of learners who ride buses and prepares to handle any problems. Once the buses leave, J. D. heads back to the classroom.

Back in the classroom, the first order of business is to gather the papers that need to be corrected. They are placed in a bag to be taken home. Next, J. D. begins to prepare for tomorrow by reviewing the sequence of lessons for the next day and jotting reminders about what is to be done tomorrow in the margins of the daily plan book. Then, it is time to create, gather, and organize supplementary material that will be used. Some materials for tomorrow will require more time to develop, and these are moved into the "take-home" bag. Over an hour has passed since the last child boarded the bus. Finally, it is time for J. D. to lock the door and head home, carrying papers to be graded and lessons to be planned.

Following the Web 1.1

New Teachers and General Information

An important way for you to extend your learning and to find more information on topics of interest to you is through the World Wide Web. Throughout this text we will be providing you with some Web sites that will allow you to learn more about topics that may interest you. The following are some general education sites that you may find useful.

For hot links to these sites, visit the companion Web site, located at *http://www.prenhall.com/armstrong*. Select Chapter 1 from the front page of the Web site, then choose the Following the Web module on the navigation bar on the left side of the page.

Recruiting New Teachers

- *http://www.rnt.org/*

  This is a good place to begin. It is the home page of Recruiting New Teachers, Inc. This nonprofit group provides a variety of information for prospective teachers including supply and demand statistics, information on certification, salaries, and insights on current issues and trends. You might be particularly interested in downloading a copy of the group's electronic newsletter, *Future Teacher*.

The New Teacher Page

- *http://www.new-teacher.com/*

  This is an excellent resource for new teachers or individuals who are interested in teaching. You will find specific information related to topics such as finding a job, substitute teaching, and becoming a professional in the classroom. There are also links to other relevant education-related topics.

Education Week on the Web

- *http://www.edweek.org*

  This is the home page for the Web version of a publication that provides weekly information about a variety of education issues. It is a particularly useful source of

Teachers' Very Full Days

Each day in the life of a teacher is a busy one. You will find that you cannot simply arrive at school and start teaching. You will need to commit time to planning and preparing lessons. Although experienced teachers may not write out the complete lesson plans needed by beginners, successful teachers spend a considerable amount of time thinking about and planning their lessons. In addition, you will have papers to grade, reports to complete, records to keep, faculty and committee meetings to attend, and special problems to address. You may become somewhat frustrated by the need to deal with these "extras," because they will take time away from tasks more closely associated with instruction. To gain adequate time for activities more closely tied to planning and teaching, you will need to develop excellent organizational skills.

information about emerging trends and about the politics of education. Coverage is national in scope.

School.Net—Best Links

- *http://k12.school.net/links*

  This site, which is maintained by School.Net, includes an extensive list of excellent links to many education-related materials. Information is divided into three broad categories: (1) Places to Start (includes links to such sources as the Cisco Educational Archive and the Vose School of Education Resources), (2) Issues and Topics (includes links to such sources as Children Now, Engines for Education, World Education Exchange, and School Psychology Resources), and (3) Products and Services (includes links to such sources as Apple Education, Electronic Learning, Turner Adventure Learning, and Knowledge Adventure).

Teachers and Teaching in the Southeast

- *http://www.columbiagroup.org/report.htm*

  In some parts of the United Sates, people in individual states and regions have studied issues related to teacher recruitment and retention in their part of the country. The Columbia Group, a South Carolina-based organization, has compiled information at this site. You will find information here about many issues related to teacher recruitment and teaching in the Southeast.

[Note: Web addresses change frequently. If you are unable to locate one of these sites using the listed URL, try putting the site name in a standard search engine.]

WHAT MAKES TEACHING COMPLEX?

As you review the day described, consider the variety of things to which J. D. had to attend. As a teacher, you will do much more than teach lessons. You may find yourself emotionally stretched as you learn to cope with these many responsibilities. Walter Doyle (1986) suggested that the following features combine to make the teacher's role particularly complex:

- multidimensionality;
- simultaneity;
- immediacy;
- unpredictability;
- publicness; and
- history.

Video Viewpoint

Teacher Shortage

WATCH: In this ABC News video segment, Bob Chase, President of the National Education Association, and Vicki Rafel of the National Parent Teacher Association discuss several reasons for the current teacher shortage in America, including low teacher salaries and lack of mentoring and support for inexperienced teachers. Other factors not discussed include an aging teacher workforce, a growing student population, and school reforms that dictate lower teacher-student ratios.

THINK: With your classmates, or in your teaching journal, consider these questions:

1. How does society view teachers? What can be done to improve the general public's estimation of teachers?
2. What are some ways to expand the pool of prospective teachers? What are some advantages and disadvantages of the alternative certification movement mentioned in the video?
3. What teacher training, recruitment, and professional development programs could help solve the teacher shortage?

LINK: How might students benefit from changes enacted to solve the teacher shortage problem?

Multidimensionality

Teachers must accomplish many individual tasks. In addition to delivering instruction, these include diagnosing learning difficulties, grouping learners, monitoring learners' progress, making instructional adjustments, responding to unanticipated events, administering standardized tests, participating in meetings, keeping records, following a schedule, relating to parents, and creating and managing materials. When you observe a good teacher in action, you may be prompted to ask, "How do you do all of that and still teach?"

Perhaps the largest challenge you will face as a teacher is responding adequately to learners with different backgrounds, motivations, aspirations, needs, abilities, and learning styles. Some of them will have the prerequisite skills and abilities to achieve success on the assigned task; some will not. It is probable that at least a few of your learners will have limited English proficiency. Quite a few may come from cultural backgrounds that differ from your own. Some of your learners will come to school eager to learn, and others will not. Some come to school as cheerful, well-rested individuals, while others may be tired and angry. While many learners are likely to see you as a caring and supportive mentor, a few may see you as a threatening adult who cares little for things they deem important.

Simultaneity

It is probably not a revelation to you that many things are happening at once in the classroom. When in front of the class, you need to watch for indications of learner comprehension, interest, and attention. Learner answers and questions need to be attended to carefully for relevance, correctness, misconceptions, and signs of confusion. When you provide assistance to one learner, you also must monitor others in the class. You need to deal efficiently with interruptions and inappropriate behavior while, at the same time, monitoring the time so you do not lose too much instructional time. As you develop as a teacher, you will grow in your ability to respond immediately to multiple stimuli. Inattention to any of them can be disastrous.

Immediacy

Not only do many things happen at the same time, but many classroom events demand an immediate response. You usually do not have the luxury of placing things on hold to be dealt with later. When an event requiring action occurs, you cannot defer action until you have thought through a well-considered response. The need to act quickly in complex situations places great stress on teachers. This kind of stress is particularly acute among newcomers to the profession who worry whether their decisions have been appropriate.

The immediacy feature of classrooms requires you to develop good judgment. This is not something that you can learn from reading a book. However, you can prepare yourself by reflecting on the kinds of situations that might develop in the classroom and by thinking about what your responses might be. This kind of preparation can help you make better decisions when circumstances arise that require you to make a quick decision.

As you develop as a teacher, you will get better at making good decisions quickly. As you become more proficient in handling multiple interactions in the classroom, your confidence in your abilities will increase. A growth in confidence often is accompanied by reduced levels of emotionally draining stress.

Unpredictability

Classrooms are filled with young people whose reactions are not always predictable. Humans are not programmable computers who respond in consistent ways to similar situations. This is part of what makes teaching interesting. Individual learners and classes respond to the same stimuli in different ways. You need to be prepared to accept that a lesson that is successful with some learners may not succeed well with others.

Not only are learner responses unpredictable, but distractions and interruptions occur with considerable frequency. An unexpected visitor, a call over the intercom, a fire drill, or a sudden change in the daily schedule are events that you will find happening all too often just as you are trying to clinch an important point in your lesson.

How do individual teachers respond to unpredictable events? Their responses tend to be conditioned by the teachers' individual philosophies and orientations to the profession. In other words, different teachers respond to similar situations in various ways. For example, an unexpected response by learners might be interpreted by one teacher as an act of defiance that must be dealt with firmly, whereas another teacher might interpret the event as a lack of understanding that needs to be dealt with through communication and discussion.

"In an increasingly complex world, sometimes old questions require new answers."

How do you respond to predictability? Do you need to have things flow smoothly from point to point? While you probably will work hard to ensure that your classroom runs smoothly, occasional unpredictable events are certain to upset your plans. You need to be prepared for this reality. If you are uncomfortable in a working environment where there is little or no predictability, you may be well advised to consider a career other than teaching.

Publicness

When you teach, you will be operating in a kind of public arena where learners will closely observe everything you will do. Young people are keen observers, and it will take them only a few days to make personal decisions about what you are "really like." The enthusiasm you display for the subject you are teaching, the way you treat people in your classroom, and the approaches you take in handling unexpected events communicate your values and priorities to a very aware learner audience.

You need to know that a "ripple effect" will follow your actions in the classroom. In other words, your actions will have consequences that go beyond the immediate situation. As a result of what you do, learners will form conclusions about your values and priorities that will affect their own patterns of behavior. Much of classroom life features this interplay between teacher action and learner reaction.

History

The interaction you have with members of your class over a semester or an entire academic year is accompanied by the development of a class "history" or "culture." The manner in which you relate to learners, plan instruction, and react to events and problems communicates your expectations to members of your class. In time, these experiences impart a unique character to each class—a character that is the result of patterns of interactions between you and those you teach.

Differences in particular class histories explain why apparently similar behaviors by different teachers do not always produce similar results. For example, one teacher may find that a quiet word to the class stops inappropriate behavior, while another teacher may find this approach does not work at all. You need to develop your own pattern of productive interaction with learners. Simply trying to mimic what another teacher does will not work. Your learners will have a class history that may be quite different from that of the teacher you are trying to emulate and, as a result, your learners may not respond in ways consistent with your expectations.

CHANGES THAT AFFECT TEACHERS' WORK

Because of the importance of education for the vitality of any community and nation, educational issues frequently feature prominently in policy debates. Many of these discussions center on issues concerning teachers and the roles they play. The following subsections illuminate some issues that are being debated today.

Debates Regarding the Purposes of Education

In part, debates about what teachers should be doing result from a lack of consensus regarding the purposes of education (Clinchy, 1998). Different people often give different answers to questions such as:

- What should our schools be achieving?
- Should we be producing academically proficient individuals ready to enter higher education?
- Should the schools be producing students with marketable vocational skills?
- To what extent should the schools be developing ethical and moral behavior?
- Are the schools the place where social ills need to be addressed and prevented?
- Should schools be directed toward developing the unique potential of each person or toward standardized expectations for all learners?

Because different people answer these questions in varying ways, proposals to "improve" education reflect a tremendous diversity. As a professional, you will have an especially keen interest in suggestions for making the schools better. When you evaluate a specific proposal, one of the first things you need to do is to determine the particular purpose of education it implies. In doing so, you need to consider how the suggested improvement plan would respond to these questions:

- What objectives would be served by the plan?
- Which kinds of learners would benefit the most? How would they benefit?
- What kinds of learners might be worse off? Why?
- What educational "ends" might not be well served?

Standards-Based Education

The lack of consensus regarding the purposes of education is not the only problem you have to consider in weighing the worth of a specific reform proposal. Another problem concerns the difficulty of measuring educational outcomes. Frustrations associated with this problem have led to an interest in organizing school programs and assessments in ways that allow for more accurate measures of learner progress. These concerns have been behind recent attempts to make *standards-based education* more widespread.

Standards-based education is an attempt to develop clear, measurable descriptions of what learners should know and be able to do as a result of their educational experiences. These descriptions typically take the form of goals to be reached or levels of proficiency to be attained (Noddings, 1997). There are several different types of standards. *Performance standards* identify levels of proficiency that a given group is expected to attain. For example, a performance standard in reading might state that all pupils will be reading at or above the grade-level norms for their grade.

Content standards describe what teachers are supposed to teach and what young people are to learn (Noddings, 1997). Though establishing specific content standards has prompted considerable debate, the approach has gained momentum in recent years. For example, many national subject-area organizations have developed a set of content standards defining what the organizations believe to be essential learning outcomes for their subjects. National content standards have been developed for such subjects as mathematics, English-language arts, history, civics and government, science, and geography. In addition, many states have developed content standards that are to guide curriculum development and assessment of learners' academic progress.

Eisner (1999) notes that one of the motivations behind the standards-based movement is the desire to hold the schools accountable. Accountability is facilitated when common standards are in place that allow schools, classrooms, teachers, and learners to be compared. Proponents of clearly defined content standards believe that once standards are clearly specified, measurements can be taken that will provide clear data that can guide decisions directed at improvement. For example, information of this kind can be used to identify educational priorities when scarce resources are allocated. Proponents argue that these measurements can also provide the public with information about the relative excellence of individual teachers and schools.

Not everyone agrees that standards-based education is a good idea. Elliott Eisner (1999), for example, suggests that this approach is based on a faulty understanding of the educational process. He argues that proponents of standards-based education inappropriately view schooling as something like a horse race or an educational Olympics that emphasizes competition among individuals rather than as an enterprise designed to develop children's distinctive talents and abilities.

The focus on standards can provide you with some important benefits when you begin teaching. For example, national standards for history may help you develop an understanding of the purposes of history that goes beyond the memorization of names and dates. The focus on standards can help you orient your instruction toward important educational outcomes.

On the other hand, you should also know that some people have raised concerns about the development and implementation of standards. This trend represents a fundamental shift in some traditional ways educational decisions have been made in this country. It represents a particular challenge to the principle of local control. Local control ordinarily has meant that school improvement efforts have usually been decentralized and have sought a match between what teachers want to teach and what communities want taught (Stake, 1999). Standards that are applied across a state or the entire nation effectively remove control of the curriculum from the local school authorities. Stake argues that whole states and the entire nation do have a legitimate interest in what every child is learning. However, he argues, this does not mean that each child should learn exactly the same content.

This raises the critical question of who should determine what the content standards ought to be for schools? Should a group appointed by politicians such as Congress, the President, or a state governor decide them? Should they be decided by business leaders or perhaps by academic professors from higher education? At times in recent years, members of each of these groups have been involved in attempting to define content standards for education. You might want to reflect on how content standards established by varying groups might be different and on the possible consequences for teachers and learners of following the kinds of standards likely to be favored by each group.

In practice, efforts to establish standards have often led to divisive debates. For example, when national standards for history were first proposed, there was widespread support for the project. However, when the original standards were first published, many conservatives, even those who had originally supported the project, quickly rejected them as too multicultural and unpatriotic. Hence, the seemingly logical and innocent idea of clearly defining expectations for learners can quickly assume political overtones.

In another instance, when science standards were proposed in California, a group of Nobel Prize winners criticized them and proposed their own set of standards. Because of their high profile, the media disseminated their views widely, and soon the debate was underway. Critics pointed out that a Nobel Prize does not necessarily confer on the winner a store of validated knowledge about what is appropriate for young people to learn at different grade levels. Others attacked the apparent assumption of the Nobel Prize winners that *every* public school learner should master science content at a level of sophistication necessary to qualify for admission to the most selective universities.

One of the more significant changes brought about by standards-based education is an emphasis on testing. Once standards are established, then it is possible to develop assessment tools for measuring the attainment of the standards. There has been a large increase in the volume of assessment, and in almost every grade level and in nearly every subject, learner achievement is being assessed (Stake, 1999). In addition, more of this assessment is what can be labeled *high stakes* assessment. (For more discussion of assessment, see Chapter 8.) This means that the results of the assessment have important consequences. They may influence promotion and graduation of learners, funding of the school, evaluation of teachers, and the autonomy of the local school. Because of the high stakes associated with assessment, you probably will spend more of your instructional time preparing learners for testing than would have been the case had you entered the profession 10 or 20 years ago. This emphasis may encourage you to spend more instructional time on kinds of content to be tested than on other types of information. People who have studied this trend point out that the spread of high stakes testing has tended to remove control from the teacher over what is taught and has given control to those who develop the tests.

Changes in Society

With the beginning of the new century, you will find yourself in a world where the rate of change is accelerating. Political challenges, both foreign and domestic, confront many traditional assumptions about the world. Breaks with familiar patterns and shattering of traditional assumptions have important social consequences. In this country, traditional institutions such as the family are at risk. Today, about half of all marriages end in divorce. Changes have led to reconsideration of what constitutes morality and how we should define right and wrong. These changes have led to great social stresses, and it has become increasingly difficult to find consensus on critically important issues. Some people believe there is more social fragmentation in the United States than at any time in the nation's history. This situation is reflected in increasing incidences of terrorism, gang violence, and a general rise in levels of incivility.

One of the most significant changes in society has been an increased diversity of school learners. Population mobility and international interdependence assure that you will have many young people from diverse cultures in your classroom. Population diversity is not just confined to the large urban centers but can be found throughout America in both urban and rural centers. The significance of this change has not been grasped by many adults and policy makers. They have yet to understand that the characteristics of the learners you will serve in the schools vary in important ways from the young people who were enrolled a decade or two ago.

A Changed Population of Learners

Today's schools enroll many learners from homes where the primary language spoken is not English. For example, one quarter of the learners enrolled in California schools in a recent year had limited English proficiency (Schnalberg, 1995). As a teacher, you will face tremendous challenges in providing an environment where these learners can achieve success and where there are open lines of communication between the school and parents and guardians of these young people.

Attempts to respond to this diversity in the classroom have led to several important changes. Many schools have bilingual programs where learners are taught in their native language for at least a portion of the day. There has also been a major emphasis on multicultural education that stresses the cultural heritage of a variety of groups, not just that of White Americans. Both of these trends have resulted in heated debates about the appropriateness of teaching in languages other than English and about including multicultural content in the curriculum. (For more information about multicultural and bilingual education, see Chapter 3.)

You will probably encounter learners in your classes whose first language is not English. Young people whose first language is not English are increasing as a percentage of the total school population.

James Banks (1994), a leading expert on multicultural education, points out that the growing ethnic diversity of the nation requires rethinking school curricula. He believes that all learners should develop multicultural perspectives. This will require a curriculum that accurately describes how different cultural groups have interacted with and influenced Western civilization. If you accept this view, you need to be prepared to teach your learners that knowledge is a social construction that reflects the biases and perspectives of the people who construct it. Thus, rather than a place where the perspectives and knowledge of some groups are excluded, the classroom becomes a place where multicultural debates about knowledge occur.

Multicultural education has had considerable impact on education. Most textbooks now include multicultural content, and many states mandate the inclusion of multicultural content in the curriculum. However, not everyone supports the idea that more multicultural perspectives should be provided to school learners.

Critics of multicultural education worry that, at best, the multicultural content replaces important substantive content in the curriculum or, at worst, tears down the basic values of our national heritage and leads to national disunity (Schlesinger, 1995). They fear that traditional Western writers such as Shakespeare will be eliminated from the curriculum and the teaching of history will be distorted.

Bilingual education also has its supporters and critics. Advocates contend that learners' education should not be delayed until they acquire English language proficiency.

The Bilingual Education Act of 1968 was developed as a program to help learners begin their study of major subjects in languages other than English (Ravitch, 1995). Another argument for bilingual education is that learning in one's primary language improves the feeling of self-worth and helps to develop an understanding of one's own culture (Macedo, 1995).

Critics contend that the effectiveness of bilingual education has not been validated (Ravitch, 1995). They believe that language is an important means by which national unity is maintained. The high costs of bilingual education are cited, and it is claimed that the educational opportunities of those who are not English language proficient are harmed by delaying their learning of English. Many critics of bilingual education suggest that the most effective language instruction programs are total immersion programs (Ravitch, 1995). The controversy over bilingual education has given rise to an effort to have English declared to be the official language of the United States. Some supporters of this idea would like to take money currently spent on bilingual education and reallocate it to pay for total immersion programs for learners who do not speak English.

Another type of diversity relates to the inclusion of learners with a range of mental and physical challenges in the typical classroom. For many years, the traditional practice was to separate these learners in special education classrooms. A concern about the appropriateness of this approach led to legislation mandating the mainstreaming of some of these learners into regular classrooms. In recent years, this has led to what is termed *full inclusion,* which virtually eliminates separate special education classrooms and places all learners in regular classrooms. Special education teachers work with the regular teachers in designing and delivering instruction to these learners. (For additional information about special learners, see Chapter 4.)

Advocates of full inclusion claim benefits for all learners. They assert that full inclusion is basically a moral issue. Disabled learners have the right to "belong" and be educated with others (Arnold & Dodge, 1995). Segregating them into special education classes is an immoral practice that leads to exclusion and feelings of inferiority. On the other hand, when all learners are in the regular classroom, those without disabilities develop an understanding and appreciation for individuals with disabilities.

Others, however, argue that the regular classroom does not provide an environment that benefits all disabled learners (Kauffman, Lloyd, Baker, & Riedel, 1995). They point out that, ideally, the resources should follow the fully included youngster into the classroom and provide services that will help the learner. However, full inclusion may become a way for school districts to save money by cutting those resources (Shanker, 1995). In addition, learners with severe behavior problems can disrupt the learning of other learners in the classroom. At a time when schools are being challenged to increase the achievement of all learners, some question whether full inclusion is compatible with this goal (Shanker, 1995).

As contemporary social problems continue to mount, people look to the schools for help. Unfortunately, there is little agreement regarding what schools should do. Because of this division of opinion, you can expect numerous proposals for change during your years in the profession.

Proposals for Improving Education

Recommendations for "improving" education have come from many different groups within society. These range from proposals advocating a return to the kinds of schools that existed years ago to suggestions for scrapping the present system and creating something unique to replace it. People who believe schools were better in the past ascribe a number of social ills to schools' deviation from past practices and their alleged willingness to embrace ill-considered educational fads. When considering proposals to "make the schools more like they used to be," some people forget that schools in the so-called "good old days" were also criticized (Coontz, 1992).

It is probably true that more people interested in school reform today want to make schools more attuned to changing modern conditions instead of wanting them to return to the educational practices of yesteryear. Many of these critics are distressed that too many schools continue to base their practices on what the critics believe to be an out-of-date industrial or factory model.

The *factory model of education* is based on an efficiency scheme developed to improve assembly-line production (Levin, 1994). Standardization is a defining feature. Schools were standardized so that learners could move from one school to another with little or no difficulty. They were organized into same-grade-level or same-subject classes. The curriculum was very similar in most schools, all classrooms used the same textbooks, and standardized achievement tests were used to make sure learners had mastered the content of the curriculum before they moved on. The assumption was that if the raw materials (learners) were subjected to the same treatment (curriculum and instruction), the result would be a standardized product that would meet quality control standards (a good test score).

Learners were given little or no input into the educational process, because they were simply raw materials to be molded into an appropriate form. Overseers (school administrators) were there to manage and observe the practices of the workers (teachers) to ensure that they were following accepted procedures. This approach assumed a consensus regarding what the final product should be and that standardized tests were valid measures of that product.

This model never worked well. Not all learners learned the same content at the same pace or had the same motivations. In education, there is a problem defining "raw material" and who is "producing." Are the learners the raw materials being processed, or are they the workers producing learning? Today, there is broad recognition that young people play a much more important role than simply serving as raw material to be transformed. If any transformation is to take place, learners must be involved in the process and must choose to make the transformation. Thus educational production is far different than factory production (Levin, 1994). Learners have individual differences in motivations, aspirations, and abilities. They are not the same, and the same type of process will not transform all of them in the same way.

Another problem relates to determining the outcomes of the process. An assumption that guided much past educational practice was that the "product" of public schools should be learners prepared for entry into college; however, the majority of the young people graduating from the public school system did not enter college.

In many places, learners today take more standardized tests than they used to. Some critics allege that too much standardized testing interferes with schools' obligations to develop learners' more sophisticated thinking skills.

Many of those who did not have college as a goal or who had learning difficulties either dropped out or were forced out. The public's fascination with efficiency and standardized production often blinded policy makers to these problems.

As it became clear that society could no longer afford to allow large numbers of young people to drop out of school or fail, some of these questions were raised:

- What should be the purpose of education?
- Should the purpose of education be to prepare individuals for college, for a vocation, or for their roles in a democratic society?
- Who should be educated? Should all learners be required to attend the same type of schools?
- Who should have control over the conduct of the schools?
- What quality standards should be applied to judge the success of the system?

Because people have answered these questions in different ways, not surprisingly, various proposals for change have emerged. Some proposals reflect an acceptance of the factory model and call for changes that would lead to more standardization. Examples of these are calls for national curriculum standards, national accreditation standards, and standardized tests that all learners must pass in order to be promoted or graduate (Cohen, 1995; Jennings, 1995).

Others think this is the wrong approach (Moffett, 1994; Eisner, 1995; Smith, 1995; Kelly, 1999). These people have a completely different set of recommendations concerning what needs to be done to improve education. They are concerned that basing current practices on a faulty model of education will lead to more serious problems rather than solutions.

Critics of basing educational practices on the old industrial model point out that this is an approach that even modern business no longer accepts. Today, the most successful enterprises organize in ways that emphasize employees' problem-solving, critical-thinking, and teamwork skills. This implies a need for schools to emphasize cooperative activities, higher level thinking skills, and participatory decision making.

Today, large numbers of educators understand that learners are not simply raw materials to be shaped in predetermined directions. As you begin your career, you probably will find other teachers generally committed to the idea that each learner brings a prior set of understandings and unique abilities and motivations to the classroom. Education is not a set of "truths" that can be stamped into the minds of learners. Individuals process information and construct their own meaning of the information based on prior experience. Even if you set out to subject all learners to the same set of instructional experiences, it is almost certain that they will differ markedly in the understandings and values they take away from your instruction.

Changes in Theories of Teaching and Learning

How learning takes place has been a topic of interest for centuries. There is still much that we do not know about the human brain and what causes learning to occur. In recent years, new perspectives on how individuals learn and the nature of intelligence have influenced educational practice. As you begin your career in education, you are especially likely to encounter instructional approaches associated with (1) constructivism and (2) multiple intelligences.

Constructivism   *Constructivism* is based on the principle that individuals cannot simply be given knowledge. Rather, learners must construct knowledge through interacting with the world around them. Their constructions of knowledge are rooted in their prior knowledge. Knowledge grows as people compare new information to what they already know. The theory holds that the mind constantly looks for patterns and tries to resolve discrepancies. The social and cultural context within which learning takes place also plays an important part in what is constructed or learned.

There are several important implications of constructivism. One is that the conditions that best facilitate learning are what might be described as "top-down" (Slavin, 1994). This means that, as a teacher, you need to provide learners with complex, complete, and "authentic" problems. Once you do this, then you proceed to help the learners gain knowledge needed to solve the problem. This contrasts with more traditional approaches that introduce learners to small pieces of information that, in time, are put together into more meaningful wholes.

For example, a traditional approach to teaching elementary children arithmetic emphasizes lessons requiring them to memorize multiplication tables. The expectation is that this information will prove useful to learners at a later time when they have a need to apply these skills to solve problems that are important to them. By way of contrast, a constructivist approach to teaching multiplication tables begins by presenting learners with a problem that requires multiplication skills for its solution. The teacher and learners together consider what is needed to solve the problem, and the teacher works with class members as they begin noting patterns and developing a generalized understanding of how multiplication processes work. The idea is to teach multiplication in the context of "real" problems when the skill is needed by the learner.

In the same vein, constructivist approaches to teaching topics such as punctuation and spelling are embedded within larger, story-writing activities that provide learners with a real need to have mastered this kind of content. This general approach has led to a technique that is commonly referred to as *whole language* instruction, which features lessons in which reading, writing, speaking, and listening are taught as a whole process to be learned together. Youngsters in the earliest grades write stories using "invented spelling" and then read them to others. The focus is on encouraging learners to use language, to look for patterns, and to learn writing conventions as they are needed.

Another assumption of constructivism is that the learners need to be actively involved in the learning process. They must actively seek solutions and share ideas. Because the social and cultural context is important, and because it is not likely that any one individual can find a solution working alone, learners often work in pairs or small groups. As a result, lessons built around constructivist principles feature considerable noise and movement.

Constructivism has also changed the way educators think about assessment. Rather than giving a standardized test designed to measure how well learners can repeat what they have been told, new assessment procedures actively involve the learners in solving problems, sharing and discussing what they have discovered and learned.

Multiple Intelligences   Another important thrust that has changed the approaches teachers take to their work is based on new research on the nature of intelligence. Throughout history, there have been debates focusing on the question of whether intelligence is a single ability or many separate abilities (Woolfolk, 1995). Traditionally, many educators have viewed intelligence as a single trait that can be measured by an IQ test. If you accept this view, for example, it implies that you believe someone you have determined to be "intelligent" has potential for success in dealing with most academic situations.

In recent years, there has been growing support for the view of *multiple intelligences.* Howard Gardner (1993) has proposed that there are at least nine distinct and separate kinds of intelligences:

What Do You Think?

Are There Multiple Intelligences?

Not everyone agrees with the concept of multiple intelligences. Critics of the idea point out that although there are individual differences in ability, people who tend to be good in one area are usually talented in other areas as well. This, they argue, is an indication that there is a single, common factor of intelligence. They are also concerned that mixing dimensions such as emotions with intelligence will have the effect of making anything acceptable in the curriculum. This has the potential to reduce the demands of a challenging curriculum designed to increase the academic achievement of gifted learners.

What Do You Think?

1. Do you agree or disagree with the idea of multiple intelligences?
2. What evidence or experiences do you have to support your view?
3. How do you think the curriculum would need to change in order to support multiple intelligences?
4. Do you think that having multiple intelligences means that individuals who are gifted in one area should be allowed to focus on that area and not work in areas where they are not gifted?
5. How do you think schools and society would be different if everyone accepted the idea of multiple intelligences?

- logical-mathematical;
- linguistic;
- musical;
- spatial;
- bodily-kinesthetic;
- interpersonal;
- intrapersonal;
- existential; and
- naturalist.

Thus, an individual who is gifted in the area of logical-mathematical intelligence quickly discerns logical and mathematical patterns. On the other hand, a person gifted in the area of interpersonal intelligence recognizes and responds appropriately to the moods, temperaments, and motivations of others. If you accept this view, then a person who has a high degree of intelligence within one of these areas may not necessarily have a high degree of intelligence within one of the others.

Another influential theorist in the area of multiple intelligences is Robert Sternberg (1990), who has proposed a *triarchic theory of intelligence*. The three types of intelligences he espouses are:

- componental;
- experiential; and
- contextual.

Following the Web 1.2

Multiple Intelligences

In recent years, interest in the theory of multiple intelligences has been growing. You will find numerous sites on the World Wide Web with information related to this topic. We have selected a few you might wish to visit.

  For hot links to these sites, visit the companion Web site, located at *http://www.prenhall.com/armstrong.* Select Chapter 1 from the front page of the Web site, then choose the Following the Web module on the navigation bar on the left side of the page.

Multiplying Intelligence in the Classroom

- *http://www.newhorizons.org/art_miclsrm.html*

  Sometimes it is difficult to find information about how a theory such as multiple intelligences can be used to organize instruction in ways that are consistent with what the theory says. The material prepared by Bruce Campbell, written for the electronic journal *New Horizons for Learning,* addresses this need. Campbell provides practical examples of how learning centers were used in a third-grade classroom for the purpose of engaging learners in all nine of Howard Gardner's types of intelligence.

The First Seven . . . and the Eighth: A Conversation with Howard Gardner

- *http://www.ascd.org/pubs/el/sept97/gardnerc.html*

  Educational Leadership, an important professional journal, recognized the broad interest in multiple intelligences by devoting an entire issue of the publication to the subject. At this Web address, you will find the interview with Howard Gardner that appeared in this issue.

Variations on a Theme: How Teachers Interpret MI Theory

- *http://www.ascd.org/pubs/el/sept97/campbell.html*

  At this site, you will find another article from the issue of *Educational Leadership* that was devoted to multiple intelligences. As the title suggests, this article by

Componential intelligence refers to the ability to acquire information by separating the relevant from the irrelevant, to think abstractly, and to determine what needs to be done. *Experiential intelligence* refers to the ability to cope with new experiences by formulating new ideas and combining unrelated facts to solve new problems. There are two major characteristics of experiential characteristics. They involve (1) having insight or the ability to deal effectively with novel situations and (2) having *automaticity,* the ability to quickly turn new solutions into routine procedures (Woolfolk, 1995). *Contextual intelligence* refers to the ability to adapt to new experiences and to solve problems in a specific situation or context.

Yet another dimension to the notion of multiple intelligences has been added by Goleman (1995). Goleman defines what he labels *emotional intelligence* as the ability to exercise self-control, remain persistent, and be self-motivating. Goleman contends

Linda Campbell suggests how teachers have adapted Gardner's theory to their own work in the classroom.

Multiple Intelligences Schools

- *http://pzweb.harvard.edu/Research/MISchool.htm*

  Project Zero at Harvard has initiated a number of studies focusing on the impact of Gardner's Multiple Intelligences theory. Material at this Web site describes how implementation of the theory has helped schools.

Multiple Intelligences: Theory and Practice in the K-12 Classroom

- *http://www.indiana.edu/~eric_rec/ieo/bibs/multiple.html*

  At this site, you will find an extensive list of abstracts focusing on multiple intelligences that has been compiled by the Educational Resources Information Center (ERIC) at Indiana University. There are also links to other sources of information related to multiple intelligences.

Developing Higher Order Thinking Skills and Multiple Intelligences

- *http://www.metronet.com/~bhorizon/teach.htm*

  At this site, you will find some useful explanations of each type of intelligence identified by Howard Gardner. In addition, there are useful suggestions for incorporating the theory of multiple intelligences into instructional plans.

[Note: Web addresses change frequently. If you are unable to locate one of these sites using the listed URL, try putting the site name in a standard search engine.]

that what people normally think of as intelligence is of little benefit if emotions are uncontrolled.

Views related to multiple intelligence have several important implications for you as a teacher. Perhaps the most important is the need to avoid labeling learners according to their IQ scores. You need to understand that there may be numerous ways that individuals can be "gifted." Another implication is that the school curriculum needs to be varied in order to excite and challenge the different types of intelligences. The possibility of different types of intelligences has implications for the way material is presented to learners. Learning tasks you design for members of your class should not focus just on the acquisition of information but should also provide opportunities for them to use creativity when solving new problems and adapting to different situations. Finally, you may need to broaden your view of what makes individuals "smart" to include information about their emotions, persistence, self-control, and empathy for others.

EXAMPLES OF CHANGES THAT HAVE BEEN IMPLEMENTED

Interest in improving education and a growing body of new knowledge about teaching and learning have led to many changes in school practices. Some reflect the movement toward a more standardized, centralized approach that reflects the efficiency of the factory and ties resources (tax money) to production (learning). Perhaps the most significant of these is the application of standards-based education, as discussed in the previous section.

Other changes have rejected the centralization associated with standards-based education. Some districts, notably in some large urban areas, have encouraged the development of smaller, more autonomous schools. These schools have been given great freedom to innovate and be different.

In numerous places around the country, curriculum revisions are placing more emphasis on thinking and problem solving than on rote memorization. Learners are being challenged to share their understanding and knowledge constructions rather than being called on to repeat conclusions of others. In general, programs featuring active learning are being implemented in the schools. Often, these allow learners to develop and share their unique talents and abilities in cooperative group.

New electronic technologies such as computers are providing learners with opportunities to gather and use information in creative ways. Assessments of learner achievements are beginning to turn away from standardized assessments and toward alternative forms of assessment such as performance assessments and portfolios whereby learners have more choice in sharing what they have learned and what they think is important.

Proposals for change include school-choice options such as charter schools, voucher plans, open-enrollment plans, and magnet schools. One variation of the magnet school concept has been the *fundamental school.* Fundamental schools attempt to implement a back-to-basics approach to education. These special kinds of magnet schools have proven to be popular in school districts that have adopted them.

CHANGE AND PROSPECTIVE TEACHERS

The reality that change is a companion of educators' lives underscores the need for you to commit to lifelong learning. A staggering number of changes already are affecting school curricula, instructional practices, and organizational patterns. Pressures for additional changes continue. All of these mean that you need to be well informed and eager to accept life in a rapidly changing profession. We hope that you will recognize that the controversies swirling around education seek a good end . . . better preparation of young people. We hope that you, similar to many others in the profession, will find these debates energizing.

Key Ideas In Summary

- Because education is viewed as such an important societal institution, it is the subject of much debate and numerous proposals for change. Because there is no national consensus regarding the goals and purposes of education, there is no consensus regarding proposed changes.

- Schools exist as a part of society, and as society changes, so do views regarding the role of education in society. There are those who are quick to blame schools for contributing to societal problems. Some see the problem as too much change, whereas others criticize school changes as moving too slowly.

- Some reformers are challenging the industrial model as a useful model for education to follow. They believe that many of the basic assumptions that guide educational practice need to be challenged.

- The characteristics of the learner population have changed dramatically in the past several decades. It is common to find classrooms with a diverse learner population that may include learners from a variety of cultures, learners who come from homes with primary languages other than English, and disabled learners.

- There continue to be changes in theories of teaching and learning. Especially important for the teacher is the development of the constructivist theory of learning. This theory has several profound implications for planning instruction and delivering content to learners.

- The notion that there are multiple intelligences rather than a single intelligence factor also has important implications for teaching. These implications have particular importance for teachers who wish to develop instructional strategies that respond to individual intelligence types.

- Individuals preparing to teach often think they understand precisely what knowledge and abilities are necessary to be a teacher. They are often shocked to discover that teaching is much different than they expected. Some of the factors that make teaching more complex than many realize are its multidimensionality, simultaneity, immediacy, unpredictability, and publicness. Differing histories of individual classes also contribute to the complexity of the school environment.

- Because there are great differences in schools from place to place and by different levels, there is no one reality of teaching. However, observing the daily activities of a teacher can help individuals capture some of the feelings of what it means to be a professional educator.

Chapter 1 Self Test

To review terms and concepts in this chapter, take the Chapter 1 Self Test on the companion Web site, located at *http://www.prenhall.com/armstrong*. Select Chapter 1 from the front page of the Web site, then choose the Self Test module on the navigation bar on the left side of the page. Feedback for the Self Test is immediate. You can keep track of your Self Test scores yourself, or you can choose to submit your scores via e-mail to your instructor.

Reflections

To respond to these questions online, and to save or submit your response electronically, visit the companion Web site, located at *http://www.prenhall.com/armstrong*. Select Chapter 1 from the front page of the Web site, then choose the Reflections module on the navigation bar on the left side of the page. Instructors and students may also wish to use these questions as discussion topics on the Message Board for the companion Web site.

1. What is your view on change in education? Do you think the schools have changed too fast or too slowly?

2. What are examples of the industrial model as applied to education? Do you think this model is appropriate or outdated? Are there some aspects of this approach that can be salvaged, or does it represent too poor a fit with present realities to have any further use as a way of organizing schools and instruction?

3. Which proposals for change in education would you support? Which ones would you oppose?

4. How is today's learner population similar or different from what you experienced when you were in school?

5. What is your position on multicultural education and bilingual education? Are the benefits associated with these approaches worth the costs? Why or why not?

6. Why is it so difficult for an individual teacher today to know what people want from good teachers? How is it possible that there can be so many views regarding what should be occurring in our schools?

7. What are the basic points of constructivist learning theory? In what ways would lessons developed according to a constructivist approach differ from those developed according to a more traditional planning scheme? What do you think about this theory?

8. What do you see as the implications of the multiple intelligence theory for teachers?

9. What are the dimensions of classroom teaching that make it so complex?

10. Which of the dimensions concern you most? Why?

Field Experiences, Projects, and Enrichment

1. Review the popular media for articles on education. What general patterns do you notice concerning proposed changes in education? With which proposals do you agree and why?

2. Research the pro and con arguments related to one of the changes mentioned in the chapter, such as school choice, full inclusion, bilingual education, or multicultural education. Present your findings in a report to your class.

3. Interview a teacher and ask about the factors of multidimensionality, simultaneity, unpredictability, immediacy, and so forth. Ask

how these factors influence this person's teaching. What advice does the teacher have for beginners who will be confronting these challenges for the first time?

4. Spend a day observing a teacher. Try to record the flow of activities and events in the classroom. If possible, choose a second teacher in a different school and at a different grade or subject. Compare the accounts. What patterns do you notice? What differences did you find?

5. Educators and others interested in the schools often make predictions about what teaching and learning will be like in the

future. Look at some articles printed in professional journals such as *Phi Delta Kappan* between 1955 and 1965. What changes for the future were predicted in articles published during those years? How accurate were these predictions? Present your findings in a short speech to your class, and develop some tentative explanations for predictions that failed to come true.

References

Arnold, J., & Dodge, H. (1995). Room for all. In J. Noll (Ed.), *Taking sides: Clashing views on controversial educational issues* (8th ed., pp. 200–204). Guilford, CT: Dushkin.

Banks, J. (1994). *An introduction to multicultural education.* Boston: Allyn and Bacon.

Clinchy, E. (1998). The educationally challenged American school district. *Phi Delta Kappan, 80*(40), 272–277.

Cohen, D. (1995). What standards for national standards? *Phi Delta Kappan, 76*(10), 751–757.

Coontz, S. (1992). *The way we never were.* New York: Basic Books.

Doyle W. (1986). Classroom organization and management. In M. Wittrock (Ed.), *Handbook of research on teaching* (3rd ed., pp. 392–431). New York: Macmillan.

Eisner, E. (1995). Standards for American schools: Help or hindrance. *Phi Delta Kappan, 76*(10), 758–764.

Eisner, E. (1999). The uses and limits of performance assessment. *Phi Delta Kappan, 80*(9), 658–660.

Gardner, H. (1999). *Intelligence reframed: Multiple intelligences for the 21st century.* New York: Basic Books.

Goleman, D. (1995). *Emotional intelligence: Why it can matter more than IQ.* New York: Bantam Books.

Jennings, J. (1995). School reform based on what is taught and learned. *Phi Delta Kappan, 76*(10), 765–769.

Kauffman, J., Lloyd, J., Baker, J., & Riedel, T. (1995). Inclusion of all learners with emotional or behavioral disorders? Let's think again. *Phi Delta Kappan, 76*(7), 542–546.

Kelly, T. (1999). Why state mandates don't work. *Phi Delta Kappan, 80*(7), 543–546.

Levin, B. (1994). Improving educational productivity: Putting learners at the center. *Phi Delta Kappan, 75*(10), 758–760.

Macedo, D. (1995). English only: The tongue-tying of America. In J. Noll (Ed.), *Taking sides: Clashing views on controversial educational issues* (8th ed., pp. 249–258). Guilford, CT: Dushkin.

Moffett, J. (1994). On to the past: Wrong-headed school reform. *Phi Delta Kappan, 75*(8), 584–590.

Noddings, N. (1997). Thinking about standards. *Phi Delta Kappan, 79*(3), 184–89.

Ravitch, D. (1995). Politicization and the schools: The case of bilingual education. In J. Noll (Ed.), *Taking sides: Clashing views on controversial educational issues* (8th ed., pp. 240–248). Guilford, CT: Dushkin.

Schlesinger, A. (1995). The disuniting of America. In J. Noll (Ed.), *Taking sides: Clashing views on controversial educational issues* (8th ed., pp. 227–236). Guilford, CT: Dushkin.

Schnalberg, L. (1995, August 2). Board relaxes bilingual-ed. policy in California. *Education Week,* p. 1.

Shanker, A. (1995). Where we stand on the rush to inclusion. In J. Noll (Ed.), *Taking sides: Clashing views on controversial educational issues* (8th ed., pp. 205–211). Guilford, CT: Dushkin.

Slavin, R. (1994). *Educational psychology: Theory and practice* (4th ed.). Boston: Allyn and Bacon.

Smith, F. (1995). Let's declare education a disaster and get on with our lives. *Phi Delta Kappan, 76*(8), 584–590.

Stake, R. (1999). The goods on American education. *Phi Delta Kappan, 80*(9), 668–672.

Sternberg, R. (1990). *Metaphors of mind: Conceptions of the nature of intelligence.* New York: Cambridge University Press.

Woolfolk, A. (1995). *Educational psychology* (6th ed.). Boston: Allyn and Bacon.

2

Becoming a Professional Educator

OBJECTIVES

This chapter will help you to

- identify stages associated with teachers' professional development.

- point out relationships of components of preservice teacher-preparation programs.

- describe ways that new teachers deal with challenges they face during their initial years in the profession.

- point out roles of such national professional groups as the National Education Association (NEA) and the American Federation of Teachers (AFT).

- explain the kinds of ethics classroom teachers are expected to have.

- describe the kinds of information that might be found in a teaching portfolio.

- recognize the diversity of career options that are potentially open to people who have completed teacher-preparation programs.

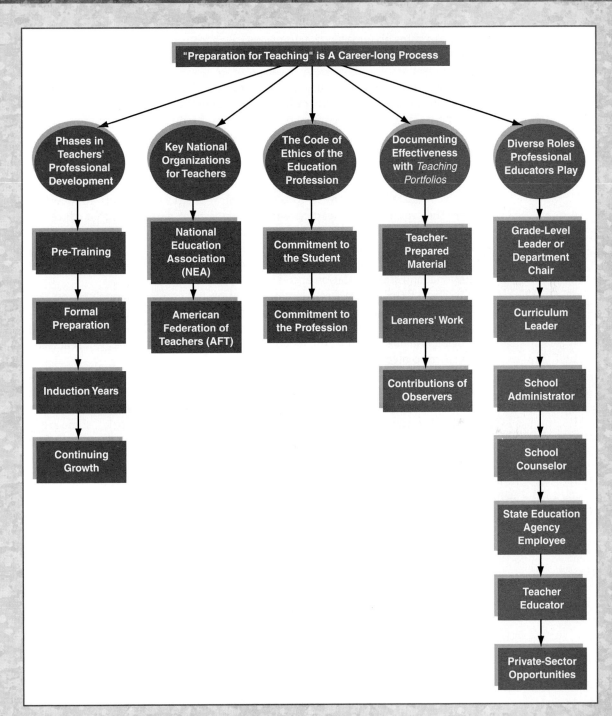

FIGURE 2.1 Becoming a Professional Educator

33

INTRODUCTION

You need to think about what the word *preparing* means in the phrase "preparing for teaching." When you learned to ride a bicycle, you reached a point where someone let you go and you could confidently ride. A profession does not work this way. You do not wake up one day shouting, "Eureka! I know all I need to know about this business." Professionalism is a deliberative, developmental experience. When you "prepare for teaching," you develop a commitment to career-long growth. Your initial preparation program helps you to start learning the kinds of things necessary to continue learning.

Members of individual professions share common values and perspectives. For example, there are ethical standards to which members of the teaching profession subscribe. A shared commitment to certain ethical practices, a concern for development of the capacities of all learners who come to school, and a sense that education should be a high-priority concern for the entire society have led educators to band together in large and powerful organizations. These include the National Education Association (NEA) and the American Federation of Teachers (AFT). These groups help set national and state education agendas.

In recent years, public discussion of education has focused increasingly on performance of both learners and teachers. As a new teacher, you will be entering a profession that attracts much public scrutiny, and it is probable that you will be asked to provide evidence that documents your performance. In many places, teachers are being asked to prepare *teaching portfolios* for this purpose.

As you begin work as an educator, you will probably be surprised by the diversity of the field. People who begin as classroom teachers have knowledge and skills that equip them to pursue many interesting career paths. Some of these options exist within formal education systems and related governmental agencies; some are in the private sector. These options provide you with a wonderful opportunity to find a role in education that fits you well.

PHASES IN PROFESSIONAL DEVELOPMENT: PRE-TRAINING

Your personal experiences and the attitudes you developed before enrolling in any formal teacher-preparation courses reflect the impact of the *pre-training phase* of your professional development. Attitudes of your family members may have influenced you. In addition, your attitudes toward teaching may have been affected by teachers who taught you, the kinds of people who were in your classes, and other experiences you had when you were in elementary, middle, and high school. Influences of your own schooling experiences are to be expected, given that the typical high school graduate has spent more than 10,000 hours in K–12 classrooms.

Memories of your own school days may not be as helpful as you think. Schools and learners today are tremendously diverse. You may find that the schools you see during your preparation program are quite different from those you attended. The young people, too, may differ from those with whom you went to school, and you may find that some instructional techniques that your favorite teachers used (and that you liked) do not work well with other learners in other settings. You must keep an open mind about what constitutes "good teaching" and recognize that practices that are enthusiastically received by learners in some places may not be appropriate for learners in others.

PHASES IN PROFESSIONAL DEVELOPMENT: FORMAL PREPARATION

Since you are using this text, you are probably in the *formal preparation phase* of your professional development. Though there are some differences from institution to institution, there are common features in most teacher-preparation programs. In part, these common features have been developed in response to guidelines of state and national accrediting bodies such as the National Council for Accreditation of Teacher Education (NCATE). Preparation programs often have these three basic parts:

- core studies,
- teaching specialization(s)/academic major(s), and
- professional education.

Core Studies

In addition to the specific content areas you will be expected to teach, you are expected to have some familiarity with information that is generally known by educated adults. The core-studies component of college and university programs for prospective teachers is designed to accommodate this need. Typically, core-studies requirements ask students to take a specified number of content courses from mathematics, the sciences, the liberal arts, and the fine arts. These courses tend to constitute about 30 to 40% of a typical bachelor's degree program.

Teaching Specialization(s)/Academic Major(s)

If you are majoring in elementary education, you will be expected to teach information from a variety of content areas. You may also have a particular teaching specialization such as reading or mathematics that you have studied in some depth as part of your preparation program.

Prospective middle school teachers may have teaching specializations or formal academic majors, and future senior high school teachers almost always have an academic major. If you are preparing to teach in high school, you probably intend to teach courses in your academic major, though often it is also possible for you to be assigned to teach at least a few courses in other subject areas. (Requirements related to teaching outside of the academic major vary greatly; however, a certain minimum number of college or university courses are often required.)

Present-day teacher preparation programs place prospective teachers in real school classrooms for extended periods. These practical experiences provide them with practical experiences in dealing with learners and in coping with other aspects of the teacher's role.

Professional Education

The professional-education component of your preparation program seeks to give you the expertise needed to deliver instruction and manage learners. In recent years, there has been a trend toward having more of this component of the preparation program offered at field sites located in K–12 schools. Prospective teachers today spend much more time in the schools than was the case 10 or 20 years ago. The goal is to smooth the transition from the world of the college or university to the world of the K–12 school. Many programs today provide opportunities for prospective teachers to engage in some supervised instruction of learners in the schools at various stages throughout their preparation program. The traditional pattern that featured virtually no direct contact with K–12 schools until a capstone student-teaching experience at the end of the student-teaching program is rapidly disappearing.

You may have already had some experience teaching K–12 students as part of your own preparation program. If not, chances are that you will soon have an opportunity to do so. Successes you experience will be confidence builders. They can also broaden your appreciation of the many kinds of learners in the schools, and they can challenge your capacity for honoring and responding professionally to the diversity you will probably encounter. Work in the schools, particularly when it is approached seriously, can be a wonderful beginning to a successful career in teaching.

Video Viewpoint

What Makes a Great School?: Mentoring New Teachers

WATCH: In this ABC News video segment, we learn about the mentoring program for new teachers at Malden Catholic High School in Massachusetts. Rookie teacher Joe Laferlita explains how his mentor helped him deal with a few students who weren't doing their homework, and mentor Rick Mazzei explains that he benefits from the process too.

THINK: With your classmates, or in your teaching journal, consider these questions:

1. How would you benefit from having a mentor assigned to you during your teacher training and certification program?
2. How is a mentor-mentee relationship like or unlike a teacher-student relationship?
3. Once you are a classroom teacher, what types of problems or questions would you take to your mentor, and which ones would you choose to try to solve or answer yourself?
4. What might your mentor learn from visiting your classroom?

LINK: How might students benefit when mentoring programs among teachers are established?

PHASES IN PROFESSIONAL DEVELOPMENT: INDUCTION YEARS

The first years in teaching are sometimes called the *induction years*. This term implies that no one assumes you will arrive on the job fully formed as a professional educator. It is another recognition that professionals are involved in a process of career-long development and that the early years are times of particularly intense learning. Much learning during the first few years of teaching centers on adapting to the special characteristics of the school—the learners, the surrounding community, the prescribed curriculum, the available resources, the interpersonal relationships among the teachers, and so forth.

Even new teachers from the finest preparation programs experience stress during the initial years of teaching. One concern is that the kind of support provided by university supervisors and supervising teachers during the preparation program is not as readily available. Many school systems recognize this problem, and some respond by assigning experienced mentor teachers to work with newcomers. In a few places, districts make arrangements with education professionals at local colleges and universities to provide modest levels of continued support.

Much discussion about challenges facing newcomers to the profession used to focus on the first year of teaching. Today, there is recognition that beginners take several years to settle comfortably into their new roles. Increasingly, school leaders are thinking about ways to provide special assistance during the first 2 to 4 years of teachers' professional service.

PHASES IN PROFESSIONAL DEVELOPMENT: CONTINUING GROWTH

As you seek to grow and learn as a professional educator, you will find a number of alternative approaches available to you. These include

- staff-development opportunities,
- college and university courses, and
- work associated with professional organizations.

Staff-Development

You may find yourself employed in one of the many school districts that organize extensive staff-development activities for teachers. Districts commit funds to these activities as part of their efforts to enhance the overall quality of instruction. The term *inservice education* often is applied to these efforts. Often these feature special sessions to introduce new teaching techniques, well-known educational speakers, workshops to prepare materials or modify curricula, or "share" sessions where participants exchange materials and ideas.

It is probable that you will be required to attend some staff-development sessions; others may be optional. In some districts, teachers receive staff-development credits, and when they have accumulated enough credits, they qualify for higher salaries.

College and University Courses

You may elect to take college and university courses to build your professional knowledge base. Many institutions offer night courses so teachers may take them during the school year. It is very common for colleges and universities to have extensive summer-session offerings for teachers. Often college and university courses can be used to fulfill requirements for an advanced degree. Frequently, increases in salary are offered to teachers who complete specified courses or fulfill advanced-degree requirements.

As you think about possible courses you might take during your first years in the classroom, think first about taking those that will help you meet specific challenges you might be facing in the classroom. Initially, you should focus on selecting courses that will directly help you with your work rather than those designed to meet advanced-degree requirements. You may be in the profession for a long time. There will be plenty of time to complete an advanced-degree program after you have addressed some more pressing gaps in the knowledge you need to succeed in the classroom.

Work Associated with Professional Organizations

You will find that many professional organizations sponsor meetings that include sessions designed to improve teachers' expertise. These may take the form of workshops or more formal sessions where individual presenters share their ideas. Joining a professional group such as an organization of reading professionals gives you an opportunity to meet with people with shared interests. Members often find they take away productive new ideas from even casual conversations with others in the group. Many professional organizations sponsor the publication of journals that often feature excellent, practical how-to-do-it articles.

MAJOR PROFESSIONAL ORGANIZATIONS: THE NEA AND AFT

In addition to many specialty organizations that serve teachers with particular grade-level or subject-area interests, two national organizations represent the more general interests of the teaching profession. (See the Appendix for a listing of specialty organizations.) These organizations are:

- the National Education Association (NEA) and
- the American Federation of Teachers (AFT).

There has been much discussion about merging the two organizations. A recent decision to do so was supported by leadership of both the NEA and the AFT. However, the proposal did not win necessary support from the membership, and the issue continues to be discussed.

Professional organizations perform many services for their members. They help to explain what members do to the public at large. They engage in lobbying activities for the purpose of seeking legislation thought to advance the interest of their members and to oppose legislation thought to have negative implications for members. They provide opportunities for members to keep abreast of new knowledge as it relates to their professional development and practice. They also often specify standards of appropriate or ethical practice.

The National Education Association (NEA)

The NEA is the larger of the two major teachers' organizations. Though today the NEA does recognize the strike as one legitimate weapon that teachers can use as they seek improved conditions of practice and better salaries, in general, the organization conceives of teachers as members of learned professions such as law and medicine. Since these professionals have a long tradition of self-governance, the NEA has had a tradition of supporting policies that give teachers more control over their professional lives. This implies a role for teachers in such areas as preparation of teachers, qualifications for hiring of teachers, appropriate content of courses, selection of learning materials, and identification of instructional methods.

The NEA, an organization run by and for teachers, has an active publications unit, a legal-services operation, and a research division. For further information, write to:

National Education Association
1201 16th Street, NW
Washington, DC 20036

What Do You Think?

Teacher's Strikes

Should teachers go on strike? This question often leads to heated exchanges between supporters and opponents of strikes. People opposed to strikes often argue that they undermine teachers' images. They fear that strikes will alienate middle- and upper-class citizens who traditionally have been among public education's strongest supporters. Disgust with strikes could lead them to oppose needed funding for the schools.

Supporters of the strikes often observe that people in general are simply unaware of the pressures teachers face. For example, they point to obligations many state legislatures have placed on teachers to raise learners' achievement levels in the absence of any new commitment of state revenues to help them get the job done. Proponents of strikes contend that people may "talk a good line" about the need to improve schools, but little real action is likely without pressure such as can be exerted by a strike.

What Do You Think?

1. Do strike actions threaten teachers' credibility with parents and other influential members of the community? Why, or why not?
2. Should the question of whether or not teachers should strike be answered "yes" in some instances and "no" in others? If so, in what kinds of instances might strikes be appropriate? Where might they be inappropriate?
3. Have you or any of your family members been involved in a strike, particularly one involving schools? If so, what were the reactions of various groups of people who had a stake in the outcome?
4. How do you personally feel about strikes by teachers? Are there personal experiences you have had that have led you to your position on this issue?

The American Federation of Teachers (AFT)

The AFT, a union affiliated with the AFL-CIO, views teachers as occupying positions similar to those of employees of large corporations. The AFT points out that teachers, unlike such professionals as lawyers, rarely are self-employed. Nearly all of them work for institutions (school districts), which creates a situation where many teachers work at sites distant from the lead administrators in their districts. In the view of the AFT, this creates a condition where teachers need a strong organization to counter the possibility that distant administrators may make decisions that disadvantage teachers and learners.

The AFT has long embraced the strike as a legitimate bargaining tool. It seeks negotiated decisions that maximize teachers' benefits and restrict arbitrary exercise of administrative power. Negotiated agreements tend to specify in considerable detail specific responsibilities and rights of both teachers and administrators. When there are differences of interpretation related to these agreements, an arbitration system is followed that is similar to traditional labor-management practices.

Following the Web 2.1

The NEA and AFT

Home pages of both the NEA and the AFT feature information about many topics related to education. You will find these sites are helpful in locating education-related articles, specific information about successful classroom practices, details about policies, and many other issues.

For hot links to these sites, visit the companion Web site, located at *http://www. prenhall.com/armstrong*. Select Chapter 2 from the front page of the Web site, then choose the Following the Web module on the navigation bar on the left side of the page.

Here are the relevant URLs:

- *National Education Association—http://www.nea.org/*
- *American Federation of Teachers—http://www.aft.org/index.htm*

[Note: Web addresses change frequently. If you are unable to locate one of these sites using the listed URL, try putting the site name in a standard search engine.]

For further information about the AFT and its programs, write to:

American Federation of Teachers
555 New Jersey Avenue, NW
Washington, DC 20001

THE CODE OF ETHICS OF THE EDUCATION PROFESSION

More than professionals in many other fields, teachers are subjected to high levels of public scrutiny. There are several reasons for this. First of all, teachers work with children, who are widely acknowledged to be among the most vulnerable of "clients." Second, teachers are numerous, and they are represented in virtually every neighborhood in the country. Hence, they are highly visible professionals. Finally, they work in environments that are familiar to the adult population. Adults, as former learners in the schools, have a strong sense about what kind of teacher behavior is right and proper.

Because of their own concerns about what constitutes "appropriate" practice and because of public demands that teachers meet high behavioral standards, national organizations of teachers have long been interested in promoting ethical practices. In response to this concern, the Representatives Assembly of the National Education Association adopted a "Code of Ethics of the Education Profession" in 1975. (See Figure 2.2.)

TEACHING PORTFOLIOS: DOCUMENTING PERFORMANCE

Interest is increasing in gathering and packaging more complete information about teachers' instructional performances than can be generated by traditional observation procedures. This collection of information is often called a *teaching portfolio*. A portfolio "... documents the teacher's accomplishments attained over a period of time, across a variety of contexts, and provides evidence of his/her effectiveness" (Hom, 1997).

Preamble

The educator, believing in the worth and dignity of each human being, recognizes the supreme importance of the pursuit of truth, devotion to excellence, and the nurture of democratic principles. Essential to these goals is the protection of freedom to learn and to teach and the guarantee of equal educational opportunity for all. The educator accepts the responsibility to adhere to the highest ethical standards.

The educator recognizes the magnitude of responsibility inherent in the teaching process. The desire for the respect and confidence of one's colleagues, of students, of parents, and of the members of the community provides the incentive to attain and maintain the highest possible degree of ethical conduct. The Code of Ethics of the Education Profession indicates the aspiration of all educators and provides standards by which to judge conduct.

The remedies specified by the NEA and/or its affiliates for the violation of any provision of this Code shall be exclusive and no such provision shall be enforceable in any form other than the one specifically designated by the NEA or its affiliates.

PRINCIPLE I

Commitment to the Student

The educator strives to help each student realize his or her potential as a worthy and effective member of society. The educator therefore works to stimulate the spirit of inquiry, the acquisition of knowledge and understanding, and the thoughtful formulation of worthy goals.
In fulfillment of the obligation to the student, the educator—

1. Shall not unreasonably restrain the student from independent action in the pursuit of learning.
2. Shall not unreasonably deny the student's access to varying points of view.
3. Shall not deliberately suppress or distort subject matter relevant to the student's progress.
4. Shall make reasonable effort to protect the student from conditions harmful to learning or to health and safety.
5. Shall not intentionally expose the student to embarrassment or disparagement.
6. Shall not on the basis of race, color, creed, sex, national origin, marital status, political or religious beliefs, family, social or cultural background, or sexual orientation, unfairly—
   a. Exclude any student from participation in any program
   b. Deny benefits to any student
   c. Grant any advantage to any student

FIGURE 2.2   Code of Ethics of the Education Profession*

If you decided to construct a portfolio, one of the key components would be evidence of such professional work as instructional units you developed, tests and other materials you prepared for learners, and examples of assignments. You probably would also include samples of papers, projects, and other work prepared by members of your class. You also would include information and comments of any people who observed your work and prepared formal assessments of your teaching. Typically, your portfolio would also include some of your own written reflections. Material in this section of the portfolio gives you an opportunity to think about what went well (and why) and to consider possible modifications to what you might do if you find yourself not satisfied with certain aspects of the instructional actions you are reviewing.

7. Shall not use professional relationships with students for private advantage.
8. Shall not disclose information about students obtained in the course of professional service unless disclosure serves a compelling professional purpose or is required by law.

PRINCIPLE II

Commitment to the Profession

The education profession is vested by the public with a trust and responsibility requiring the highest ideals of professional service.

In the belief that the quality of the services of the education profession directly influences the nation and its citizens, the educator shall exert every effort to raise professional standards, to promote a climate that encourages the exercise of professional judgment, to achieve conditions that attract persons worthy of the trust to careers in education, and to assist in preventing the practice of the profession by unqualified persons.

In fulfillment of the obligation to the profession, the educator—

1. Shall not in an application for a professional position deliberately make a false statement or fail to disclose a material fact related to competency and qualifications.
2. Shall not misrepresent his/her professional qualifications.
3. Shall not assist any entry into the profession of a person known to be unqualified in respect to character, education, or other relevant attribute.
4. Shall not knowingly make a false statement concerning the qualifications of a candidate for a professional position.
5. Shall not assist a noneducator in the unauthorized practice of teaching.
6. Shall not disclose information about colleagues obtained in the course of professional service unless disclosure serves a compelling professional purpose or is required by law.
7. Shall not knowingly make false or malicious statements about a colleague.
8. Shall not accept any gratuity, gift, or favor that might impair or appear to influence professional decisions or action.

*Adopted by the NEA 1975 Representative Assembly.
Reprinted with the permission of the National Education Association.

FIGURE 2.2 *Continued*

Not all portfolios contain the same information. What goes into a portfolio reflects its intended purpose. For example, a *developmental portfolio* focuses on the goal of gathering evidence that will show improved proficiency in a specific category of information over time. If one of the concerns at the beginning had to do with numbers of learners participating in class discussion, then information about this issue would be included in the portfolio, with the hope that over time the teacher's instruction would prompt a higher percentage of students to become active participants in discussions.

On the other hand, an *employment portfolio* seeks to present information about a teacher that would be of interest to a potential employer. Often employers want to know how well prospective teachers can plan lessons, assess learners, and maintain classroom control. As a result, evidence pertaining to these issues receives considerable attention in employment portfolios.

Though purposes of portfolios help shape their emphases, many typically include these basic categories of information:

- teacher-prepared material,
- contributions of observers, and
- learners' work.

Teacher-Prepared Material

If you were putting together a portfolio, you would use the teacher-prepared section to state your own views about "good teaching." You would probably describe the learners with whom you work and some contextual constraints that affect your performance (e.g., local and state regulations, kinds of materials available, and problems associated with facilities). This part of the portfolio often refers to course objectives.

You might also choose to mention your preferred instructional and evaluation methodologies. This part of the portfolio is an appropriate place to display examples of instructional units, tests, and lesson plans. You might also include examples of below-average, average, and above-average work that has been graded. This showcases your ability to differentiate among learners whose performances reflect varying achievement levels. In addition, you might explain specific actions you have taken to deal with exceptional students and with others with special learning characteristics and needs. Finally, you might include in this section some reflections about the adequacy of your instructional performance.

Contributions of Observers

In some schools, principals or other administrators regularly evaluate teachers. Sometimes, too, there are peer-evaluation systems where teachers observe and evaluate lessons taught by other teachers. If you are in a building where other professionals have observed your instruction, results of these evaluations typically would go into your portfolio. Opinions and other reactions from learners and comments from parents, if available, represent other categories of information that you might wish to include.

Learners' Work

Records of learner scores on quizzes and examinations often are featured in this section. Examples of their work may include essays, models, completed projects, term papers, and other products that reflect what they have learned.

Organizing Portfolios

A variety of schemes for organizing portfolios have been adopted. An approach developed by James Green and Sheryl Smyser (1996) features five basic categories:

- *Personal background.* In this section, you provide details about your educational and professional experiences, with special reference to your current teaching responsibilities.
- *Context information.* In this section, you discuss the physical characteristics of the classroom, the specific nature of your learners, the adequacy of instructional materials, and other environmental factors that may affect how you can teach and how members of your class learn.
- *Instruction-related information.* In this section, you include information about your lesson plans and unit plans and provide examples of materials and instructional aids you have developed. This part of the portfolio gives you an opportunity to include comments and reflections about the adequacy of your instructional approaches, especially related to how they have influenced what people in your classes have learned.
- *Responses to special needs of individuals.* This section allows you an opportunity to describe actions taken to individualize instruction to meet specific student needs. Here you will include examples of differentiated assignments, varied learning materials, and alternative assessment procedures.
- *Contributions to the overall mission of the school.* This section allows you to display evidence that demonstrates how your actions have contributed to improving the teaching and learning environment of the entire school. In this section, you might include information such as professional-development objectives and plans for meeting them and committee work focusing on school-wide and community-wide educational reform issues.

Assessing Portfolios

Similar kinds of information do not appear in every portfolio. Hence, to some degree, assessment procedures need to be tailored to the specific portfolio that is being evaluated. One of the challenges in assessing portfolios concerns the issue of consistency or reliability. Guidelines need to be developed that allow different reviewers to apply a similar standard in assessing a given portfolio. For example, if reviewers are expected to assign portfolios a rating of "unsatisfactory," "satisfactory," or "outstanding," these terms need to be clearly defined so that different raters will apply them in the same way. This need is often accomplished through the development of a *scoring rubric.* The scoring rubric specifies in considerable detail how a portfolio would look that would be assigned one of the available rating points. See Figure 2.3 for an example.

Working with an appropriate scoring rubric, the portfolio reviewer looks for clues regarding the teacher's hopes and priorities. Then, he or she hopes to find portfolio examples that confirm behaviors are consistent with these priorities or that indicate the noted behaviors are at odds with them.

For example, a reviewer might look at what the teacher has described as key features of "good teaching" as a backdrop for considering evidence in the portfolio. Are materials presented in the portfolio consistent with the stated vision of good teaching? Does the provided information support the view that practices were consistent with stated priorities?

This *scoring rubric* was designed for use with teacher portfolios that focused on teachers' use of a specified set of "advanced technology competencies" that were mandated by action of a state legislature. Note how the scoring rubric helps define the three rating points, "Needs Work," "Satisfactory," and "Exemplary."

Needs Work: The portfolio fails to include data in support of each identified competency. Examples that are provided fail to make a compelling case that the associated competency has been mastered. Teacher reflections, where present, are written in vague, general terms that fail to address specific issues and problems associated with mastering the required competencies. The organizational scheme is not clear or, alternatively, it has not been consistently implemented throughout the portfolio.

Satisfactory: The portfolio exhibits examples that address all advanced technology competencies. These examples display evidence sufficient to support that mastery of essential features/components of each competency has occurred. A clear organizational scheme is evident, and it is executed consistently throughout the portfolio. Reflections focus clearly on complexities associated with mastering competencies, though some of them may reflect deeper, more reasoned consideration than others.

Exemplary: The portfolio exhibits strong and overwhelming evidence that each advanced technology competency has been mastered. A rich array of pertinent evidence is presented to support the mastery claim for each competency. Examples provided are multiple, varied, and appropriate. A clear organizational scheme is evident, and it is executed carefully throughout with no "thin" sections. Reflections respecting all competencies evidence a solid grasp of issues and careful, rational analyses of problems and, perhaps, unexpected "easy stretches" associated with the mastery of each.

FIGURE 2.3   An Example of a Scoring Rubric for Portfolio Assessment

Teacher evaluation that is based on portfolios has important advantages over traditional schemes that depend on data gathered from one or two classroom observations. Information in portfolios tends to be assembled over a considerable period of time and tends to be from multiple sources. The completed portfolio provides a comprehensive view of a teacher's behavior.

Potentially, at least, portfolio evaluation can provide a much more complete picture of what teachers do than data gathered from the traditional occasional classroom observation by a principal or other administrator. Today, portfolio assessment is gaining in popularity, and it is likely that more schools will adopt the process in the years ahead.

ROLES WITHIN PROFESSIONAL EDUCATION

Approximately one of every six Americans is a student in a public school. Great numbers of employees are required to serve the needs of these young people. These employees work in diverse environments, and they discharge varied functions. When we speak of the "education profession" today, we refer to the incredible range of roles that must be discharged as educators help people grow toward productive and personally satisfying lives.

A colleague looks over a portfolio prepared by a fellow teacher. Increasingly, teachers are using portfolios to document what they have done.

Classroom Teachers

Teachers are by far the largest single category of employees in the schools. In the United States today, slightly more than 3 million people are employed as teachers in the public schools. By the year 2008, this number is expected to grow to approximately 3.5 million (Gerald & Hussar, 1998). Because initial preparation programs for educators focus primarily on helping prospective newcomers get ready for roles in the classroom, you are probably well acquainted with the roles teachers play. In a sense, teachers function as keystones of the entire educational edifice. Their professional expertise leads them to unite important subject-area knowledge, planning and organizational skills, and abilities to motivate learners. They develop their capacity to respond to individual learner needs, and they develop their skill in articulating and defending their teaching practices to parents, interested community members, political leaders, and others.

Following the Web 2.2

Portfolios

If you put the term "teaching portfolio" into a Web search engine, you may get a list with more than 1,000 sites. The overwhelming majority focus on the use of portfolios by college and university faculty members. The sites listed here provide information about portfolio use in elementary, middle, and secondary schools.

 For hot links to these sites, visit the companion Web site, located at *http://www. prenhall.com/armstrong*. Select Chapter 2 from the front page of the Web site, then choose the Following the Web module on the navigation bar on the left side of the page.

Designing Teacher Portfolios

- *http://www2.ncsu.edu/unity/lockers/project/portfolios/portfoliointro.html*

    This site features excellent examples of portfolios developed by preservice teachers, by teachers in their first years of professional practice, and by teachers who have received National Board Certification.

Dr. Helen Barrett's Favorite Links on Alternative Assessment & Electronic Portfolios

- *http://transition.alaska.edu/www/portfolios/bookmarks.html*

    This site provides numerous links to other Web sites with good information about portfolios and other approaches to alternative assessment.

RESOURCES: Authentic Assessment and Portfolios

- *http://www.oise.utoronto.ca/~czmach/second~1.htm*

    This site provides several topics related to the development of portfolios designed for use in elementary, middle, and secondary schools.

Electronic Teaching Portfolios

- *http://transition.alaska.edu/www/portfolios/site98.html*

    This site provides particularly detailed guidelines for storing portfolio information electronically.

Bibliography of Assessment Alternatives: Portfolios

- *http://www.nwrel.org/eval/ea_bibs/folio.html*

    This site features an extensive listing of journal articles and other publications that have focused on school use of portfolios.

[Note: Web addresses change frequently. If you are unable to locate one of these sites using the listed URL, try putting the site name in a standard search engine.]

Grade-Level Leader or Department Chair

Many elementary schools have *grade-level chairs* with responsibilities for leading all teachers in the building who teach the same grade. In many middle schools and high schools, a person serving as the department chair plays a similar role. This person exercises leadership in a specific subject area (for example, English, social studies, mathematics, or science). Duties vary, but grade-level leaders often engage in such activities as ordering supplies, evaluating new faculty, coordinating staff-development opportunities, and disseminating information about school policies. In general, grade-level leaders and department chairs act as liaisons between school administrators and other teachers.

Typically, grade-level leaders and department chairs are selected from among the most experienced teachers. They have credibility both with their teaching colleagues and with school administrators. In some schools, grade-level leaders and department chairs teach a reduced load to allow them time to perform other assigned duties. They may receive extra salary, and they often work more days each year than regular classroom teachers.

Curriculum Leader

The position of *curriculum leader* may also be titled *curriculum director, curriculum supervisor,* and *curriculum coordinator.* By whatever title it is known, this position features leadership in such areas as curriculum planning, inservice planning, and instructional-support planning. In small school districts, a single curriculum leader may have responsibilities for several subject areas and grade levels and may even continue to teach part-time. In larger districts, curriculum leaders may be responsible for only a few grade levels or a single secondary-level subject area. In such districts, curriculum leaders often do not teach. In many districts, curriculum leaders have offices in the central administrative headquarters of the school district where they work.

Curriculum leaders are individuals with knowledge of up-to-date trends in the grade-level areas and/or subject areas for which they are responsible. They are in a position to influence the nature of the instructional program throughout the district in their areas of responsibility. Many curriculum leaders hold advanced degrees, work a longer school year than teachers, and receive higher salaries.

School Administrator

Most school administrators start their careers as classroom teachers. By taking advanced courses, often including completion of at least a master's degree and relevant administrative certification requirements, they qualify for administrative positions. These positions exist both at the school level and at the central district administrative level. Typical administrative positions at the school level are assistant principal and principal. Examples of positions often found at the central administrative headquarters of a school district include director of personnel, assistant superintendent, and superintendent.

Administrators must prepare budgets, develop schedules, prepare paperwork for state and federal authorities, and evaluate teachers and other staff members. They also function as official representatives of the schools to the community. Consequently, administrators must have good public relations skills. School administrators usually work a longer school year than teachers and are also paid higher salaries.

Critical Incident

Two Offers, One Problem

"Guess what, Letitia. I've got two—count 'em—*two* job offers, and my life is just the pits." One week following student teaching and graduation, Linda Norton was sharing a private moment with her long-time friend, Letitia Carlisle.

"Come at me again with that, Linda," said Letitia. "You've got *two* job offers, and that's a *problem?!* I'm tempted to say 'be still my heart' and 'send some of that agony my way.' So what's the deal? Where's the negative that's escaping my notice?"

Linda smiled briefly and said, "I know I should be excited, happy, all those good things. I mean, we've talked before about how great it would be to finally be out of school and actually doing the stuff we've been preparing for. The deal is, though, that these two job offers are quite different. And everybody's giving me different advice."

"Different how?" asked Letitia.

"Well, one of them is for a math opening in a middle school. That fits pretty well with my math background, and I did enjoy my student teaching with a group of sixth graders. The other one is from this electronics company. They want me to work in their training division helping newcomers who need to sharpen up their basic math skills. The thing is, this job pays $7,000 more a year to start than the teaching job."

"So, what's the problem? You could make some good car payments with that extra $7,000, couldn't you?" asked Letitia.

Linda nodded and replied, "That's true enough. But there are some other things to think about. For example, the teacher who worked with me during student teaching is really distressed that I may not end up working with kids in the school. He tells me that good math teachers are scarce and that I could be one of the best. He said I should consider all the kids whose lives I could help over the years if I stayed in the classroom."

"So you're feeling a bit guilty? Is that the situation?" asked Letitia.

"You've got it," acknowledged Linda. "The 'go to work as a teacher' argument is being counterbalanced by my mother's attitude. She says women have always been underpaid and un-

School Counselor

Some school counselors begin their careers as classroom teachers. There is debate within the professional community of counselors about whether school counselors should have had classroom teaching experience before becoming counselors. Those who support the idea argue that such experience gives the counselor a better understanding of what learners have experienced in their classrooms. Others argue that teaching is basically a controlling function and that counselors who have been teachers may not be able to change their roles from that of a controller to that of a listener and a facilitator.

Usually, school counselors must complete academic course work beyond the bachelor's degree to qualify for their positions. Many enroll in master's degree programs with a school-counseling emphasis. In addition to personal and academic counseling, many school counselors also are expected to perform a number of administrative tasks. Sometimes counselors are responsible for establishing the master teaching schedule for a school, and they are often in charge of all standardized testing. They must spend a great deal of time attending special meetings.

derappreciated. If an employer is out there who is willing to pay me more, I should go for it. Besides, she says, a private company that can pay a higher starting salary probably can pay me more money in the future than I'll ever earn as a teacher."

Letitia sat quietly thinking for a minute. Then, leaning closer to her friend, she counseled, "Okay, Linda, you've told me what a couple of other people think you should do. But, it's your life and your career. What do *you* want to do?"

"I'm trying to tell you that *that's* the problem," Linda replied, her face showing some strain. "I flat out don't know. I come to the point of making a decision and then I feel guilty about not making the other choice. Then, I convince myself to take the other job and feel guilty all over again. It would be nice if somewhere along the line somebody gave us a book titled *The Guide to Making Great Choices for Happy and Fulfilled Living.*"

"That would be terrific," agreed Letitia. "But, I suppose you can't defer your choice until some publisher brings out this much-needed volume. So, what are you going to do?"

. . .

What is Linda really worried about? She says she feels guilty. What is the source of this guilt? Has she considered the advantages and disadvantages associated with each choice? How accurate is the information she has received from the teacher and from her mother? Are there other people she should consult? Are there other sources of information she should consider? How would you respond to her dilemma?

To respond to this Critical Incident online, and to save or submit your response electronically, visit the companion Web site, located at *http://www.prenhall.com/armstrong.* Select Chapter 2 from the front page of the Web site, then choose the Critical Incidents module on the navigation bar on the left side of the page. Instructors and students may also wish to use these scenarios as discussion topics on the Message Board for the companion Web site.

Counselors usually work a longer school year than teachers, and they are paid more. Time available for working with individual students often is surprisingly limited.

State Education Agency Employee

All states have education departments or agencies largely staffed by professionals with backgrounds in education. State education agencies hire people with a variety of backgrounds and for diverse purposes. For example, subject-area specialists coordinate curriculum guidelines and inservice training throughout the state for teachers in specific subjects (for example, English, social studies, music, science, mathematics, vocational education, or physical education). Typically, state education agencies also have assessment specialists who coordinate statewide testing programs. In addition, they usually staff teacher-certification or licensure specialists who work with colleges and universities to ensure that teacher-preparation programs are consistent with state regulations.

Many state education agency employees have had considerable prior experience working in the schools. Large numbers have at least a master's degree, and many have doctoral degrees. Many state employees must travel frequently to meetings at various locations throughout the state they serve. Usually, state education agency employees are on the job 12 months of the year and are often paid salaries that are higher than those of classroom teachers.

Teacher Educator

Successful teachers sometimes seek opportunities to share their expertise with future teachers. One way for them to do this is to become a teacher educator. Most teacher educators are faculty members of colleges and universities, though a few are employed by large school districts. Almost always, teacher educators hold doctoral degrees.

The role of the teacher educator is varied and complex. Although exemplary teaching contributes to success as a faculty member in teacher education, still more is necessary. As university faculty members, teacher educators must demonstrate initiative in improving preparation programs, stay current on findings of researchers, conduct research, and write for publication. In addition, they must seek opportunities to make presentations at regional and national meetings, maintain good working relations with other departments and with the schools, serve on many committees, maintain good links with state education agencies, and counsel students. All of these obligations require processing of massive quantities of paperwork.

Teacher educators typically are employed for nine months a year. Many of them have opportunities to work during the summer months as well. Salaries are not particularly high; in fact, some beginning teacher educators are paid less than some experienced public school classroom teachers. Although beginning salaries of teacher educators tend to be modest, top salaries for experienced teacher educators are higher than those paid to classroom teachers.

Two Examples of Out-of-School Opportunities

For a variety of reasons, some teachers decide to leave the classroom after just a few years. Does this mean their preparation was wasted? Not at all. There are employment options outside of the public schools for individuals with backgrounds in teaching.

Publishers of textbooks and other instructional materials hire people with backgrounds in education to work both as editors and salespeople. The expertise they bring from their background in the classrooms helps firms ensure that materials they develop and market are appropriately designed. In addition, there is an important added element of credibility when the salesperson talking to a teacher who is a prospective buyer can say that he or she has been a classroom teacher.

Large firms, some of which have large training divisions, also employ people with backgrounds in education in their employee training programs. The term *human resource development,* often abbreviated HRD, is frequently used to describe the corporate training function. If you are interested in education and training in the private sector, go to your library and find a publication called *Training and Development.*

Not everyone who has been prepared as an educator works in a public school. For example, publishers of educational materials often hire people who have gone through teacher preparation programs.

It is the official journal of the American Society for Training and Development (ASTD), a professional organization for educators in private industries.

Key Ideas In Summary

- The phrase "preparing for teaching" does not suggest that the process of preparation has a definite ending point. Rather, it implies that "preparation" is a career-long process of professional growth and adaptation.
- The *pre-training* phase of professional development includes all experiences a person has before enrolling in a formal teacher-preparation program. These experiences leave people with certain attitudes that affect how they initially engage experiences in their preparation programs.
- The *formal preparation* phase of teachers' professional development divides into three parts. "Core studies" include academic content that educated adults are expected to know, regardless of their college or university major. The "teaching specialization(s)/academic major(s)" component embraces content of the academic major (in the case of prospective secondary teachers) or academic content of the several school subjects they will teach (in the case of prospective elementary teachers). The "professional education" component consists of preparation experiences related to instruction, evaluation, and management of school learners.

- The *induction years,* the first years of fully licensed classroom teaching, are among the most challenging in a teacher's career. During this period, teachers learn to adapt to the particular characteristics of their learners and to the special characteristics of their schools and communities.
- During the *continuing growth* phase of a teacher's career, there are many opportunities for continued professional development. Among them are (1) staff-development opportunities sponsored by local school districts and local, state, and national professional associations; (2) college and university courses; and (3) possibilities for involvement with local, state, and national units of major professional groups.
- Two large national organizations represent the general interests of the teaching profession. The largest of these is the National Education Association (NEA). Another important general organization for teachers is the American Federation of Teachers (AFT), a group that is affiliated with organized labor.
- Teachers are expected to reflect patterns of behavior characterized by high ethical standards. An important "Code of Ethics of the Education Profession" program has been adopted by the NEA. It obligates teachers to certain patterns of behavior with respect to their learners and with respect to the teaching profession.
- In recent years, there has been growing interest in the use of *teaching portfolios* to document teachers' accomplishments. Teaching portfolios attempt to gather evidence that attests to teachers' effectiveness and performance over time and in a variety of situations. Teaching portfolios often include examples of teacher-prepared materials, comments of people who have observed the teacher's work, and samples of work produced by the teacher's learners.
- There are many roles within the profession of education. People with initial preparation for classroom teaching may find themselves employed at some point in their careers in roles such as: (1) classroom teachers, (2) grade-level or department chairs, (3) curriculum leaders, (4) school administrators, (5) school counselors, (6) state education agency employees, (7) teacher educators, (8) textbook editors or salespersons, or (9) trainers in business or industry.

Chapter 2 Self Test

 To review terms and concepts in this chapter, take the Chapter 2 Self Test on the companion Web site, located at *http://www.prenhall.com/armstrong.* Select Chapter 2 from the front page of the Web site, then choose the Self Test module on the navigation bar on the left side of the page. Feedback for the Self Test is immediate. You can keep track of your Self Test scores yourself, or you can choose to submit your scores via e-mail to your instructor.

Reflections

 To respond to these questions online, and to save or submit your response electronically, visit the companion Web site, located at *http://www.prenhall.com/armstrong.* Select

Chapter 2 from the front page of the Web site, then choose the Reflections module on the navigation bar on the left side of the page. Instructors and students may also wish to use these questions as discussion topics on the Message Board for the companion Web site.

1. How would you explain the meaning of the phrase "preparing for teaching" to someone with little understanding of the teaching profession?
2. What are some phases in the professional development of teachers?
3. Why might the personal experiences you had as a student in the schools not give you useful insights about the challenges you will face as a new teacher?
4. How would you describe differences in the general orientations of the two largest teacher organizations, the National Education Association (NEA) and the American Federation of Teachers (AFT).
5. Some people argue that the NEA and AFT act to attract public attention to problems educators face and help to win public sympathy for education. Others argue that they appear to outsiders as organizations pushing the narrow interests of teachers and that they diminish the status of teachers in the eyes of many people. What are your views on this issue, and why do you take the position you have adopted?
6. Why do you think the teaching profession needs a code of ethics? How well does the one adopted by the NEA do what an ethics code should do?
7. Why do you think there is so much interest today in *teaching portfolios,* and what advantages or disadvantages do portfolios have over more traditional ways of gathering information about teachers' effectiveness?
8. Why has it become necessary to develop *scoring rubrics* for use in evaluating teaching portfolios?
9. What kinds of roles do grade-level leaders and department chairs play in our schools?
10. Describe three or four professional roles in education that do not involve traditional classroom teaching. What is your relative interest in each of these roles, and why?

Field Experiences, Projects, and Enrichment

1. Interview a teacher who has been in the profession for at least 15 years. Have this person describe his or her preparation for teaching and any inservice or other developmental activities he or she has experienced over the years. Make a report to your class on the topic: "The Professional Life Space of a Teacher: One Person's Experience."
2. Contact an administrator in the central office of a local school district with responsibilities for staff development. (Your course instructor may be able to suggest the name of an appropriate person.) Try to obtain information about (1) the kind of inservice development the school district expects of its teachers and (2) the kind of inservice opportunities the school district provides to its teachers. Report your findings to others in your class.
3. Go to the Web pages of the NEA and the AFT. Using information from the Web sites of the two organizations, prepare a chart that compares activities, benefits for members, and other characteristics of the two organizations.
4. Some people argue that teachers should have higher ethical standards than the population as a whole. Others suggest that this kind of a standard ensures that only atypical people will serve in the classrooms and that such individuals will be unrealistic models for young people. Organize a class debate on the issue, "Resolved that Teachers Must be More Ethical than Typical Citizens."
5. Many large corporations have large employee-education staffs. The American Society for Training and Development is a

professional organization to which many of them belong. Look at several issues of this group's journal, *Training and Development*. How would you compare and contrast articles from *Training and Development* with those appearing in journals that are directed at audiences of school teachers? (Your instructor may be able to suggest some journals you should review.) Present your findings in the form of a short paper.

References

Gerald, G. E., & Hussar, W. J. *Projections of education statistics to 2008.* Washington, DC: National Center for Education Statistics. [http://nces.ed.gov/pubsearch/;pubsinfor.asp?pubid=98016]

Green, J. E., & Smyser, S. O. (1996). *The teaching portfolio.* Lancaster, PA: Technomic.

Hom, A. *The power of teacher portfolios for professional development.* New York: National Teacher Policy Institute. [http://208.215.132.53/ntpi/finals/hom.htm]

3

Legal Issues Affecting Teachers

OBJECTIVES

This chapter will help you to

- identify sources of legal influences on teacher behaviors.
- state the legal purposes of certification.
- define the legal issues related to seeking employment.
- explain purposes of tenure laws.
- state the conditions under which teachers have the right to due process.
- describe the legal responsibilities of a teacher in reporting suspected cases of child abuse.
- define legal principles that need to be considered when teaching the curriculum.
- describe the influence of copyright law on the use of materials in the classroom.
- define teacher negligence.
- explain the rights and responsibilities of teachers in areas associated with their personal lives outside the classroom.

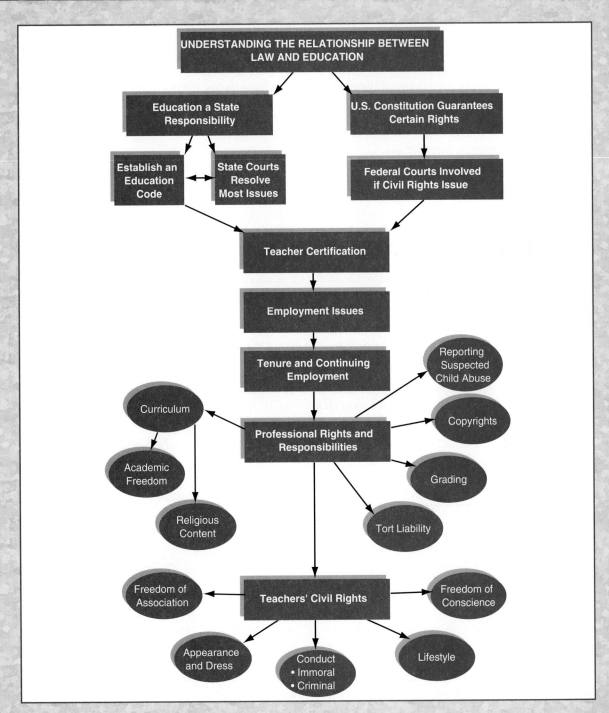

FIGURE 3.1 Legal Issues Affecting Teachers

INTRODUCTION

If you were enrolled in a teacher-preparation program 10 or 20 years ago, you may not have been told much about legal issues affecting teachers, for litigation involving teachers was rare. Today the situation is much different. If you begin your work in the profession unaware of important legal issues, you may get in trouble. If your behavior violates even laws you do not know exist, you may face unpleasant consequences. Ignorance is not an acceptable excuse. Your best protection is to develop a basic understanding of law-related issues that affect teachers so you can avoid potential legal pitfalls.

It is important to realize, however, that it is impossible to provide unerring guidance about how the law interprets particular issues. Since individual situations have their special characteristics, features unique to each case often influence decisions of the courts. However, some general patterns do tend to emerge over time. For example, a review of Supreme Court decisions and related case law often can help you identify basic legal principles associated with certain issues. An understanding of these principles can help you make more informed decisions when confronted with a decision that has legal implications. In this chapter, we will review some important court decisions about subjects that will concern you in your role as a teacher.

THE RELATIONSHIP BETWEEN LAW AND EDUCATION

As a beginning point, you need to understand something about the relationship between the law and education. This relationship often is described in terms of some answers to key questions such as:

- What are the rights and responsibilities of teachers?
- Who establishes the legal framework that guides educational practice?
- How does the system work?

Constitutional Provisions

Interestingly, the Constitution of the United States fails to mention education. This means that legal authority for education falls under the provisions of the Tenth Amendment. The 10th Amendment states that "powers not delegated to the United States by the Constitution, nor prohibited by it to the states are reserved to the States, respectively, or to the people." This means that the primary responsibility for education rests with the individual states. Each state establishes laws governing educational practices within its borders. Relevant laws, rules, and regulations for individual states typically are gathered together in the *Education Code*.

This does mean, however, that the federal government plays no role in adjudicating educational disputes. Remember that the federal government is charged with making sure that the rights guaranteed to the citizens under the Constitution are protected. Individual states cannot establish laws that are contrary to these rights. If a legal issue pertaining to education addresses a basic right or privilege claimed under the Constitution, then the federal legal system becomes involved. For many years, few challenges to public school policies and practices reached the federal courts. Those cases that were decided by the federal courts involved issues such as the funding of public schools and the setting aside of land for school use (Zirkel & Richardson, 1988).

In the past several decades, the range of cases considered by federal courts has increased tremendously. However, a much higher number of cases continue to be heard by state courts. The side-by-side existence of two court systems, one state and one federal, contributes to the confusion many people have about the legal principles that guide decision making. Each of these two legal systems has several layers of courts with different jurisdictions.

Federal courts include district courts and 13 circuit courts of appeal. Each circuit court has jurisdiction over a specific geographic region. A legal action is first taken to a district court. That decision can be appealed to the appropriate circuit court, and the decision of the circuit court can then be appealed to the Supreme Court. Only the decision of the Supreme Court has jurisdiction over the entire United States. When the Supreme Court rules on an important case, it is often called a "landmark case." These cases set out legal principles that are followed by all courts.

Not all cases are accepted for litigation by the Supreme Court. The Supreme Court chooses those cases that are believed to involve important constitutional questions. This means that a case dealing with the same issue may be decided in one way by a circuit court in one part of the country and another way by a circuit court in another part of the country. Each ruling will apply to the region over which the individual circuit court has jurisdiction.

Legal issues that are not related to basic constitutional questions are settled in the state court system. These decisions are based on the constitution of the individual state. State court systems also have different levels of authority beginning with local courts, moving to superior courts, then to appellate courts, and finally to a state supreme court. The decisions of the State supreme court apply to all jurisdictions within the state. This means that the rulings on a specific question can vary from state to state. For example, questions regarding issues such as financing of schools may be decided differently in Wisconsin than in Iowa.

Sources of Laws Relating to Education

What are the sources of legal directives for the schools? There are several, including written constitutions, statute law, administrative law, and court-decisional law.

Written Constitutions   Written constitutions represent the highest legal standard. A constitution is considered the voice of the people and expresses basic principles with which all court decisions are supposed to remain consistent. Judges spend considerable time grappling with the intent of written constitutional principles as they apply to a specific issue (Valente, 1994).

Constitutional authority supersedes all others. Since constitutions are intended to be documents that apply to changing circumstances, they are, by design, difficult to alter.

Statute Law   *Statute law* is comprised of enactments of elected legislatures. They are the second highest form of law. As long as statutes satisfy constitutional requirements, they are binding on all citizens within the jurisdiction of the body that passes them (Valente, 1994). For example, each state has enacted many laws that deal with education, and specific legislation varies from state to place. As a result, each state has a unique set of requirements that govern the operations of its schools. These requirements are often assembled into a collection of education-related legislation called the *education code.*

Administrative Law   The largest and most detailed mass of law is found in *administrative law.* Statutes passed by state legislatures tend to be quite broad. To be put into operation, their language must be interpreted and cast into language that suggests how provisions are to be implemented. The resultant administrative law specifies the particular rules, directives, procedures, and regulations that must be followed in the application of adopted statutes.

Disagreements about the legitimacy of administrative law are common. For example, some critics believe that rules and procedures developed to facilitate implementation of a law are inconsistent with what the legislature intended. When this happens, people who want to challenge the adopted administrative guidelines may challenge them by appealing to an appropriate authority. For example, if administrative law related to a statute is passed by a state legislature, the Attorney General of the state may be asked to rule on the legitimacy of the adopted administrative law guidelines. As long as administrative procedures are unchallenged or ruled to be consistent with the higher levels of law, they have the full force of law (Valente, 1994).

Court-Decisional Law   The courts provide the ultimate check on the actions of school officials. As they respond to legal challenges concerning educational issues, courts may fashion legal principles not covered in other sources of the law. The result is the creation of *court-decisional law.*

For example, cases often involve conflicts between two or more rights. As the courts seek to interpret and apply constitutional guidelines to specific cases, they often formulate legal principles that guide their decision. These principles are then applied to future cases concerning related issues (Valente, 1994). In addition, courts may overturn statutes or administrative law that they rule to be unconstitutional.

TEACHER CERTIFICATION

One set of legal regulations you will encounter as you prepare to enter the teaching profession concerns guidelines for obtaining a *teaching certificate.* A teaching certificate (sometimes referred to as a *teaching credential* or a *teaching license*) is a document that gives the holder a legal right to hold an appointment as a teacher in the schools of the state that issues it.

State law usually governs requirements related to teaching certificates. Hence, state legislators often play an important role in policy discussions related to certification.

Each state has the right to establish regulations concerning the qualifications of those who will be allowed to teach in its schools. Therefore, each state has its own teacher-certification requirements. There is no basic "right" to hold or obtain a credential other than by following standards established by state regulations. Once a teaching certificate is granted, the state maintains the right to change the requirements by passing new statutes relating to certification. For example, the state may pass a new regulation requiring teachers to take additional courses or to pass a competency test in order for their certificates to remain in force (Valente, 1994). Though teachers who already have a certificate are often exempted from new regulations that are passed after they have received a certificate, they have no legal right to be exempted from new requirements that are passed at a later date.

Although each state has its own certification requirements, this does not mean that a teacher who holds a teaching certificate from one state and then moves to another must start all over again. Most states have reciprocal agreements. This means that one state will grant a teaching certificate to someone with a valid certificate from another state. However, the new state may require the teacher to take some specific courses or meet some additional requirements within a given time period in order to maintain a valid teaching certificate.

A teaching certificate is essentially a license to practice; it confers specific benefits. Holders of a valid certificate are entitled to either the minimum salary mandated by the state or to this salary plus any supplements provided for on the locally adopted teachers' salary schedule. In addition, possession of a credential is "an assumption of competence." This means that charges of incompetence against the holder of a certificate must be backed up with evidence that is compelling enough to convince authorities of the error of the competence assumption.

Your teaching certificate will be issued by your state, not by the institution of higher education that you attend. Many states use a *program-approval approach* as a way of identifying individuals who have qualified for an initial teaching certificate. In a program-approval approach, state authorities examine elements of the teacher-preparation program, which are judged for their adequacy against a set of specific criteria. If the state approves the program as meeting state regulations, the state will grant a credential to those who successfully complete the program.

There are restrictions placed on colleges and universities with teacher-education programs that have been authorized by a program-approval approach. For example, a student may attempt to get a program requirement such as student teaching waived. The institution may not have the authority to grant this exception because it is a state requirement.

You must have a valid teaching certificate to accept employment as a public school teacher. In some places, you may find that private schools also require teachers to have teaching certificates. Individuals who do not possess valid certificates and sign contracts to teach have often been declared by the courts to be "volunteers" who have no rights to any monetary compensation.

This means that you need to make sure that you have completed all of the requirements for a credential and that a credential application to the state has been submitted before you sign a contract with a school district. Most school districts will not enter into a contract unless these two conditions are met:

1. The applicant presents them with the certificate, or
2. The applicant presents them with verification from a designated higher education official that all requirements have been met and that an application for the credential has been submitted to the appropriate state agency.

In addition, once you begin teaching, you need to make sure you meet all state and local requirements for renewal of your certificate. Often it is difficult to meet these requirements at the last minute. For example, if you are required to take a certain number of college or university courses by a certain date and you wait too long, it may be impossible to complete them in time.

GAINING EMPLOYMENT

Once you have your program that will lead to initial certification, you need to spend some time thinking about what is involved in getting hired as a teacher. You need to be aware of some key legal issues that relate to the employment process.

Pre-Employment Issues

One key issue concerns *fair employment* regulations that are designed to prevent discrimination in the employment process. Typically, they prohibit employers who hire more than a small number of individuals from discriminating against applicants or making pre-employment inquiries about applicants' age, gender, marital status, race, creed, national origin, color, or sensory, mental, or physical handicaps unless they can demonstrate that the presence or absence of these conditions bears a clear relevance to the position sought. In other words, during the hiring process, you must not be asked questions such as marital status, religious affiliation, family status, or the presence of a disability unless that factor would prevent you from accomplishing the tasks required by the job.

This area of the law is complex. For example, if a particular condition can be demonstrated to hinder the ability of the person to teach or interferes with the mission of the school, it may be legally included as a condition for employment. This means that a private school with a particular religious orientation or mission may legally inquire about or give preference to those individuals with a particular religious affiliation or philosophy.

The presence of fair employment practices does not ensure that employers always act in ways consistent with the rules. An older student recently reported that he had overhead the personnel director of a school district state that she would not hire anyone over the age of 40. This personnel director was either ignorant of the law or foolish. An important point for you to understand is that there is no agency routinely checking to ensure that personnel responsible for hiring are following fair employment guidelines. It is up to the individual who feels these guidelines have not been followed to seek counsel and file a formal legal complaint.

There are obligations placed on the applicant as well as the prospective employer. Your most important obligation is to be honest. When you complete an application for a position or actually sign a contract, you need to make sure that information you include is truthful and accurate. If the application asks you to list all of the colleges attended, you need to do so. Do not leave out the one where you may have had a less than successful experience. Many applications include a question regarding any felony convictions. Once again, if you have a conviction in your past, regardless of how long ago it might have occurred, you need to be truthful in your response.

If it is determined that you provided inaccurate information, consequences can be severe. You could be dismissed from your position, lose your teaching certificate, and face other legal consequences. If you have any concerns relating to the information you are asked to provide on official documents related to employment, you should seek some legal advice.

The Contract

The *teaching contract* is one of the most important documents you will encounter as a teacher. The contract defines the salary and the conditions of employment. When you are presented with a contract, read it carefully. It is a document that sets forth

This teacher is supervising learners who are boarding a school bus. Sometimes this kind of responsibility is included in a teacher's contract; sometimes it is not. If you have questions about non-teaching duties, you need to ask them before you sign your contract.

your responsibilities as well as those of the school district. You need to be sure that you agree with the stated provisions and are willing to fulfill the responsibilities you are asked to discharge.

You should also understand that, in some instances, nonteaching duties may be required that are not spelled out specifically in the contract. For example, you might be expected to serve as a sponsor of a school club. These nonteaching duties must bear a reasonable relationship to your teaching assignment, and you must clearly understand your obligations before accepting the contract.

As a general rule, when one party to a contract breaks it, the other party is entitled to a legal remedy that provides compensation for any damages caused. For example, if you have a contract with a district, you are entitled to expect the salary and the benefits provided by the contract. If the district does not honor the contract, you may seek a legal remedy to recover what you lost.

On the other hand, if you sign a contract with a school district and then decide not to honor the contract, the school district can also seek a legal remedy to recover what it has lost. For example, you could be required to reimburse the school district for the costs of finding your replacement. If the school district has to pay the replacement teacher a higher salary, that cost can be added (Fischer, Schimmel, & Kelly, 1999). You might also be liable to reimburse the school district for costs associated with advertisements, interview time, and substitute teacher pay.

What Do You Think?

The Unexpected Move

Lois Hansen was in the final phase of her teacher-preparation program. As a result of the good record she had established during her student-teaching experience, the local school district offered her a contract. She signed the contract and returned it to the personnel office of the school district. About two weeks later, her husband came home with some exciting news:

"The boss called me in today and told me how pleased he was with my work. He offered me a promotion in one of the branch offices. I know it will mean a move, but it will also be a raise in salary and will open some new opportunities."

After the initial excitement wore off, Lois was struck with a sobering thought. "I've signed a contract with the school district. What should I do?"

What Do You Think?

1. What could be the consequences if Lois decides not to honor the contract?
2. What should be her first step?
3. If her contract has been accepted by the school board, what course of action should she pursue?
4. What are the possible outcomes of this situation?

The issue of oral agreement or oral contracts is another topic of discussion. For example, a person applying for a teaching position may believe that a spoken offer from a personnel officer representing the school district constitutes a binding contract. It does not. The school board (sometimes known as the board of trustees or by some other title), the governing authority of the school district, is the only party that can legally bind the school district. Therefore, to be a legal contract, the school board must approve the contract. If in approving the contract they enter into the minutes of the meeting information about an oral or unwritten commitment, then the oral promise would be binding on the district.

This means that you need to receive a written contract, and you must scrutinize the contract to make sure that the written provisions are consistent with what was presented to you orally. For example, if you understood that you were to receive a stipend for extra duties such as sponsoring a club or coaching, this must be included in the written contract. Otherwise, the school district is under no legal obligation to pay the additional money.

TENURE AND CONTINUING EMPLOYMENT

Once you have signed a contract, your next concern is continuing your employment. Some people are attracted to teaching because they see it as providing a high degree of job security. This may or may not be true, depending on specific local conditions. Places that tend to offer more job security often have systems that feature some form

of *tenure.* A teacher with tenure has a right to re-employment provided certain stipulated conditions are met.

Typically, a person who is just beginning as a teacher is given a *yearly contract.* Either party can terminate a yearly contract at the end of the duration of the contract.
For example, if you are working under the terms of a yearly contract, at the end of
the academic year (usually by mid-April in many districts), the school district may
inform you that you will not be needed for the coming year. You may have had good
evaluations and recommendations, but these positive ratings do not matter. The district is not required to provide a reason for not offering you re-employment. The only
exception might be that if you believe the district's decision was based on a violation
of your constitutionally guaranteed rights. For example, you may have a case if you
can prove that the decision to not rehire was based on your actions as a member of
the teacher union or because of your religious affiliation.

In places that offer teachers tenure, there is typically a probationary period of
about three years where teachers are given yearly contracts as "nontenured" teachers. If you complete this probationary period and are then given a contract for the
coming year, you have tenure. The pattern varies somewhat from place to place.
In some states, tenure laws and probationary periods apply to all districts within
the state. In other states, individual school districts are allowed to choose if they
will offer tenure contracts to teachers. Once you achieve tenure, a new set of conditions apply.

Tenure gives you contract rights that cannot be easily altered by school officials.
In other words, tenure provides you with a right of expected employment for an in-
definite period of time and allows for dismissal only for reasons specified by law.

Tenure came about because of a belief in our society that an open exchange of
ideas and free discussion of issues are core values and are at the heart of a free,
democratic society. In other words, teachers who are afraid to openly discuss ideas
that may not be politically popular with selected political and school officials because of a fear of job loss cannot provide a learning environment that promotes a
free and open society. Tenure is designed to protect teachers from this political
pressure and to keep good teachers in a district by guaranteeing them long-term
employment.

In recent years, some state legislatures have discussed eliminating or modifying tenure laws. The argument made by opponents of tenure is that the system
guarantees lifetime employment to tenured teachers and acts to protect incompe-
tents. Some critics claim that this makes school reform difficult. They also argue
that this gives teachers more job security than individuals working in other occupational roles.

While there may be some merit in these concerns, the argument that tenure
guarantees lifetime employment is not true. Tenure laws generally spell out a number of circumstances under which a tenured teacher can be removed. However, because the burden of proof is with the school district that initiates the action, it is a
time-consuming process that requires systematic collection of data that support the
proposed dismissal decision. Some school districts lack the will to do this. In addition, if the data-gathering process is not done carefully and with legal safeguards, the

process can result in damaging countersuits by the teacher who is the target of the dismissal action. The process can also be expensive for school districts. In one California case, it took eight years and an expenditure of over $300,000 in legal fees to dismiss a tenured teacher (Richardson, 1995).

Many supporters of tenure argue that teaching is fundamentally different from other occupations. Teachers have the power to influence the future of the nation. Hence, they need protection that will allow them to teach politically unpopular content without fear of retribution. The past is littered with attempts to dismiss teachers for such offenses as involvement in political campaigns, active participation in union activities, having unpopular religious affiliations, and teaching about the civil war from different perspectives. This historical record suggests that it should not be easy to remove a teacher.

However, there *are* circumstances that justify the dismissal of a tenured teacher. To be successful, a dismissal action must be supported by complete and compelling evidence. Tenured teachers can be dismissed for reasons that include:

- *Incompetence:* The conditions that have been used to dismiss a teacher for incompetence include lack of knowledge, failure to adapt to new teaching methods, violation of school rules, lack of ability to impart knowledge, physical mistreatment of learners, and failure to maintain discipline. Failure to maintain discipline is one of the most common causes for dismissal actions filed against tenured teachers.
- *Incapacity:* This standard includes any physical or mental condition that keeps a teacher from performing his or her assigned duties.
- *Insubordination:* This is most commonly applied to teachers who stubbornly and willfully violate reasonable school rules and policies. Usually a series of insubordinate acts are required to support a dismissal on these grounds.
- *Conduct:* This is a broad standard that can embrace behaviors as varied as insulting other teachers, espousing political causes in the classroom, taking time off without permission, and even shoplifting. Some specific instances where school districts have successfully dismissed teachers for inappropriate conduct have involved drinking to excess, serving alcohol to learners in the home of the teacher, and telling wrestling team members to lie about their weights when registering for a tournament.
- *Immorality:* The courts have consistently ruled that moral fitness is a standard that teachers must meet. Dismissal actions related to this standard may include criminal activity, sexual misconduct, drug use, and dishonesty.
- *Other causes:* Many tenure laws provide for dismissal for a number of other reasons such as intemperance, neglect of duty, cruelty, and willful misconduct.

As this list illustrates, there are many reasons a teacher can be dismissed. A problem faced by the school district is gathering sufficient evidence to support dismissal actions in a court of law. While charges such as incompetence require careful documentation, charges such as involvement in criminal activity may be somewhat easier to support.

PROFESSIONAL RIGHTS AND RESPONSIBILITIES

There are numerous opportunities for you to encounter legal difficulty while performing your professional responsibilities as a teacher. Because you are in a position that exercises considerable influence over impressionable young people, questions have frequently been raised in courts relating to the appropriate balance between the rights of professional educators and the obligations of schools not to tread upon basic rights of learners and parents.

There is a considerable amount of misinformation concerning some of these areas, and basic knowledge of these legal issues can help you avoid problems as you work with your learners in the classroom.

Reporting Suspected Child Abuse

In recent years, there has been a great deal of public concern regarding child abuse. As a result, all 50 states and the District of Columbia have laws that require mandatory reporting of suspected instances of child abuse by certain professionals, including teachers and medical personnel. Because you are in prolonged contact with learners in the classroom, you are considered to be in a particularly good position to spot young people who have been abused.

Mandatory reporting laws place a legal obligation on you to advise authorities when you see instances of suspected child abuse. A failure to do so can result in both civil and criminal penalties. In one state, the penal code provides that the failure to report child abuse makes the person guilty of a misdemeanor that is punishable by six months in jail, a fine of $1,000, or both (California Teachers Association, 1992).

You do not need a high level of suspicion before reporting suspected child abuse. Terms often used in describing the grounds for suspected abuse include phrases such as "reasonable grounds," "cause to believe," or "reasonable cause to believe." You should not fear retribution as a consequence of your reporting. All states provide some form of protection from lawsuits against mandatory reporters who have reported their suspicions in good faith. On the other hand, if it can be demonstrated that a teacher filed a report for malicious reasons, he or she may face legal action.

Some states include a provision for the state to pay attorneys' fees for a suit filed as a result of a teacher's report of suspected child abuse. In addition, in most cases, the identity of the person reporting will not be known, as most statutes afford anonymity to mandatory reporters. These regulations also often stipulate that reporters may not be disciplined by their employers for reporting a suspected instance of child abuse (Underwood, 1994).

Curriculum and Instruction

What are your rights and responsibilities in assigning grades, using instructional materials, using specific instructional methods, and expressing personal and moral convictions in the classroom? All of these are questions that have come before the courts.

Academic Freedom   The concept of *academic freedom* refers to teachers' rights to speak freely about the subjects they teach, to experiment with new ideas, to select the materials they use in the classroom, and to decide on teaching methods. Courts have held that academic freedom is based on First Amendment rights and is fundamental to a democratic society. Academic freedom protects teachers' rights to evaluate and criticize existing practices in order to promote political, social, and scientific progress (Fischer et al., 1999). Since the school board does have an obligation to make sure that the adopted curriculum is taught, conflicts between your rights as a teacher and those of the school board may arise.

On the one hand, the courts have ruled in favor of teachers in attempts by school officials to prescribe how teachers will teach, and they have agreed that teachers have wide discretion in the selection of materials for the class. For example, in one case, an 11th-grade English teacher was told by school administrators to stop using a literary work they described as "literary garbage." The teacher felt the piece was a good selection of literature that was important for the students to read. She continued to use the work and was dismissed. The teacher felt this action violated her academic freedom, and the courts agreed. The judge ruled that the school district had to demonstrate that the use of the material would result in "material and substantial disruption of discipline" in order for it to be banned. In its decision, the court also pointed out that teachers have an obligation to defend selection of materials in light of educational objectives and the age and single maturity of the learners being taught (*Parducci v. Rutland,* 1970).

Courts generally have upheld the power of the school district to select and eliminate textbooks. In one case, books were removed from a high school reading list because of sexual content and vulgar language. When this decision was challenged, the court upheld the authority of the school district leaders to delete the title from the reading list, because their action was based on a legitimate educational concern (*Virgil v. School Board of Columbia County, Florida,* 1989).

In a similar case, teachers protested the omission of several books from an approved list passed by the school board. The court upheld the district's decision after its representatives demonstrated that the action was not arbitrary but based on concerns legitimately tied to education. However, as part of the same decision, the court stated that the district could not bar teachers from mentioning or even briefly discussing the books that were removed from the list (*Cary v. Board of Education, Adams-Arapahoe School District,* 1979).

Findings of courts in these cases are relevant for ongoing efforts of groups that continue to seek removal of certain books from schools and classrooms. These decisions require school districts to follow certain guidelines before rejecting or removing books. The decision to remove or reject books must be arrived at in a constitutional manner, and books cannot legally be removed because school authorities disagree with the ideas they present. In addition, books cannot be eliminated because they are inconsistent with a particular religious or political view, because authorities wish to prevent certain ideas from being discussed, or because they contain content that fails to adopt a particular position on an issue such as racial discrimination (Fischer et al., 1999).

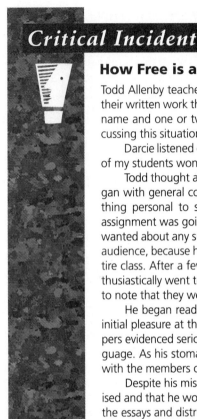

Critical Incident

How Free is a Teacher to Choose Teaching Methods?

Todd Allenby teaches 9th graders. Members of one of his classes are not motivated. He thinks their written work this semester has been abysmal. Often, all he gets is a page with the student's name and one or two barely coherent sentences. At the end of last week, he spent time discussing this situation with Darcie Schwarts, another English teacher.

Darcie listened carefully and asked, "Are you letting them write what they want? I find most of my students won't give me much unless they have a personal interest in the topic."

Todd thought about this idea over the weekend. On Monday, when his class filed in, he began with general comments about how people can become frustrated when they have something personal to say and nobody listens. He went on to point out that the next writing assignment was going to provide members of the class with an opportunity to write what they wanted about any subject. He concluded by promising that these thoughts would reach a broad audience, because he would see that every student's essay was copied and distributed to the entire class. After a few preliminary questions, members of the class for the first time all year enthusiastically went to work. Todd collected the papers at the end of the period and was pleased to note that they were considerably longer than those he usually received.

He began reading the papers that night at home. About halfway through the papers, his initial pleasure at the increased amount of writing turned to despair. Though several of the papers evidenced serious thinking, a number of them included a sprinkling of sexually explicit language. As his stomach began knotting, Tom reflected on his promise to share all of the essays with the members of the class.

Despite his misgivings about the content of some papers, Todd decided that he had promised and that he would have no credibility if he did not follow through. He made copies of all of the essays and distributed them to all students in the class. Two days later, he received a call to report to Duwayne Clark, the school principal. When he arrived at Mr. Clark's office, Todd noticed that several of the student essays were spread across the top of his desk.

"Todd," began Mr. Clark. "What in the world were you thinking about? It's bad enough these kids use this language to begin with, but to make copies and distribute them in class—

Court judgments related to censorship have not always gone in favor of teachers. Individual cases tend to be decided based on special circumstances involved. Examples of cases that have not been decided in favor of teachers include:

- one in which a teacher continued to teach sex-related content in a health class because he believed that the content was of greater interest to the learners than other health content,
- one in which an art teacher actively promoted her religious beliefs in class and encouraged students to attend religious meetings, and
- one in which a math teacher encouraged learners to protest the presence of military recruiters on campus.

Academic freedom does not give you the right to ignore the required course of study. The material that is introduced in the classroom must be relevant to the course

that's just too much. Can you imagine what some parents are going to say when they discover that a teacher has done this?"

"Look," replied Todd. "I'm not thrilled about some of the content of the papers. But, these kids *did* write something. For many of them, that's a first. The public is on our case about not teaching students how to write, so we need to figure out how to get students to do it. I did make a commitment to distribute their papers, and I felt I had to follow through in order to keep my credibility intact. I'm sorry about what happened, but I felt that something drastic was needed to get these student to learn."

"That's a commitment you had no right to make," Mr. Clark replied. "It put you in a position of agreeing to distribute anything, even obscene material. That's not professional. In fact, it is not behavior that we tolerate in this district. You need to know that this is a serious matter, and that I am going to initiate a formal complaint to the central office. You'll be apprised of what is happening. You need to know this situation could lead to an official dismissal hearing."

· · ·

What are the issues involved in this incident? Do you think Todd did the right thing by distributing copies? Do you think his approach was reasonable given the nature of the class and his past experience with them? How much professional freedom should a teacher have? Was Todd unprofessional in his actions? What might he have done differently to avoid the situation? What criteria should be applied to determining whether specific approaches are "unprofessional"? What would you do if you were Todd? We do not know if Todd is tenured or untenured. How might this make a difference? What do you think the likely outcome of this case will be?

ᏳᏯ To respond to this Critical Incident online, and to save or submit your response electronically, visit the companion Web site, located at *http://www.prenhall.com/armstrong*. Select Chapter 3 from the front page of the Web site, then choose the Critical Incidents module on the navigation bar on the left side of the page. Instructors and students may also wish to use these scenarios as discussion topics on the Message Board for the companion Web site.

and appropriate for the age and maturity of the learners. For example, dismissals of some teachers were upheld because they were distributing movie brochures with sexually explicit themes and drug use in classes in which such content bore no relationship to what the learners were studying. In another case, a teacher was dismissed for showing an R-rated film to 9th- through 11th-grade students on a nonacademic day (Fischer et al., 1999).

However, there are times when actions of teachers that are not related to the regular curriculum are legally protected. For example, in one case, high school students in a study hall asked a teacher her views about interracial dating, and she responded. The school district did not rehire the teacher because of the incident, claiming that her job was to teach math and that her comments were potentially disruptive. The judge in the case stated that the teacher's responsibility was to guide students in their studies during study hall; hence, her responses did not have to focus entirely on math. In addition, the judge noted that when students asked questions about an important social issue, the teacher need not remain silent. In fact, the judge suggested that the teacher had a right, and perhaps even a duty, to respond (*Scruggs v. Keen,* 1995).

Academic freedom also extends to the instructional methods chosen by a teacher. In one case, a social studies teacher used a simulation exercise that evoked strong student responses on racial issues. Acting on the complaints of several parents, the school board told the teacher to stop using the exercise. When she continued, the school board chose not to renew her contract. She took the issue to court. In its decision, the court ruled that the district had violated her First Amendment rights and ordered her reinstated (*Kingsville Independent School District v. Cooper,* 1980).

In another case, a high school psychology teacher was fired for using a masculinity survey from *Psychology Today* in class. The court upheld the teacher's contention that her firing violated her constitutional right to "engage in a teaching method of her choosing even though the subject matter may be controversial." The complaining school district failed to show that the use of this method caused substantial disruption and that there was a clear regulation prohibiting it (*Dean v. Timpson Independent School District,* 486 F. Supp. 302 (E.D. Tex. 1979).

In a similar case, a high school English teacher used an article from a magazine that included repeated use of a vulgar word. Parents protested, and the teacher was dismissed. The teacher challenged this action. In its decision, the court ruled that the article was of high quality and that the use of the vulgar term was important to the thesis of the author (*Keefe v. Geanakos,* 1969).

In another case, a teacher gave a class assignment to a group of poor readers. These learners were allowed to write about anything they chose, and the teacher shared the stories they wrote with the entire class. One paper included vulgar and sexually-explicit language. A copy of this paper found its way to the principal's mail box. The principal initiated action that resulted in dismissal of the teacher. The teacher challenged this action in court. In the end, the dismissal action was overturned by the state appeals court, ruling that the teacher had a good record and that the incident that prompted the school district to take action had not caused a disturbance in the classroom or contributed to a discipline problem. In testimony taken during this case, two experts explained that having students write about something that interests them is a sound educational approach (*Oakland Unified School District v. Olicker,* 25 Cal.3d 1098 (Ct. App. 1972).

In summary, while decisions related to academic freedom issues tend to be situation-specific, there are some general patterns. These decisions suggest that as a teacher, you have a right to deal with controversial issues that are relevant to the topic you are teaching. You also are free to choose methods and materials that are appropriate for the age and maturity of the learners you are teaching. However, the material or methods you select must not be banned by clear school district regulations and their use must not result in substantial disruption of the learning process or contribute to a breakdown of discipline.

Religious Content of the Curriculum

Few areas feature more legal confusion than those related to including religious content in the curriculum. The important point to remember is that it is permissible to deal with content related to religion so long as it is appropriately handled. For example, it is acceptable to deal with topics associated with religion in courses teaching comparative religion, the history of religion, art, music, or social studies (Fischer et al., 1999). Indeed, the study of civilization in social studies would be incomplete if the important role of religion in human affairs were omitted.

Religious contents that are prohibited include religious celebrations, exercises, or rituals. The principles that guide decisions about the inclusion of religious content were established in 1971 in the landmark *Lemon v. Kurtzman* case. In deciding this case, the Supreme Court established what has become known as the "Lemon test." In deciding on the appropriateness of religious content or activities, the following three questions need to be answered "yes":

1. Does the policy or practice have a secular purpose?
2. Is the primary effect of the policy or practice one that neither inhibits nor advances religion?
3. Does the policy or practice avoid excessive entanglement with religion?

Many school choirs include religious music in their repertoire. This is acceptable if the goal is a secular one of teaching the learners music. The study of art similarly includes many important pieces of art with religious themes. Again, this is acceptable if the purpose is teaching art concepts or the history of art.

On the other hand, including celebrations of religious holidays such as Christmas can be viewed as furthering a particular religious belief. While some schools have attempted to meet this challenge by balancing Christmas celebrations with Hanukkah celebrations, this only means that the school is violating the standard twice (Fischer et al., 1999). Today, the preponderance of common law stands in support of the view that religious celebrations are not to be included in the school program. Other practices that have been declared as advancing a particular religious belief include posting the Ten Commandments, conducting Bible readings, distributing Bibles on the school grounds, or displaying religious symbols.

Courts are likely to view as excessive entanglement between the school and religion such practices as sanctioning or supporting a religious activity, allowing a religious activity to take place in the school building, or approving a supervision of a religious activity by school personnel during the normal work day. For example, if a religious group were formed among the learners at a school, the school district or school employees must not sponsor the meetings and should attend meetings only as nonparticipants.

The issue of school prayer continues to engender controversy. The practice of officially sanctioned prayer conducted either by a teacher or delivered over an intercom system has been repeatedly defeated on the grounds that it serves a religious rather than a secular purpose. Prayer at other sanctioned events such as graduation and athletic events have often also been ruled as inappropriate by the courts.

These restrictions do not mean that prayer in schools is illegal. Remember that the schools cannot inhibit as well as not further a particular religious belief. If a learner chooses to pause for a moment of silent prayer, nothing improper has occurred, and this kind of personal action is permissible.

In general, courts have been more tolerant of schools that have adopted silent meditation periods rather than formal prayer sessions. In one case, the Eleventh Circuit Court of Appeals upheld a Georgia act that required each teacher to have a brief period of quiet reflection for not more than 60 seconds at the beginning of each school day (*Brown v. Gwinnett County School District,* 1997).

Another controversial aspect of religious content in the curriculum relates to the teaching of creationism. Those in favor of teaching creationism argue that it is a theory that deserves equal treatment with the theory of evolution normally taught in science classes. In a few places in the country, there are regulations requiring that creationism and evolution be given equal instructional time. The courts have not looked favorably on such rules, because they do not pass the Lemon test. In 1987, The Supreme Court ruled that creationism was primarily a religious as opposed to a scientific belief and that its purpose was to promote religion. Hence, rules mandating that creationism be taught alongside evolution were declared to be unconstitutional (*Edwards v. Aquillard,* 1987). The theory of creationism can be discussed in a social studies class as a theory believed by some religious groups.

Although there has been some indication that the Supreme Court might be reexamining the Lemon test (Fischer et al., 1999), it is still the standard that can be used to make decisions about the inclusion of religious content in the curriculum. Teaching about religion is acceptable, but any practices that further a particular religion is not.

Grading   Another curriculum issue that will be of immediate interest to you when you begin teaching has to do with your rights to award grades to your learners. In a litigious society such as ours, learners or their parents or guardians occasionally threaten legal action when they are dissatisfied with the grade a teacher has awarded. The courts have generally considered school officials to be uniquely qualified to judge the academic achievement of learners. As a result, they have been reluctant to overturn teachers' grading decisions unless there is overwhelming evidence that grades have been given for arbitrary, capricious, or bad-faith reasons. This means that you need to have clear grading standards, keep accurate records, and make sure that the grades are awarded for academic achievement and not as punishment for poor behavior.

A related issue deals with learner privacy. Humiliation may result if someone other than an authorized person becomes aware of a grade, particularly a low one, that has been awarded to an individual learner. For this reason, it is best not to publicly post the grades or read grades out loud in class. Making graded learner papers easily accessible to anyone and having other learners correct papers are also questionable practices.

Finally, school officials generally may prescribe guidelines for the administration of a grading system. However some courts have ruled that it is violation of teacher rights if these guidelines are overly prescriptive. In a Minnesota case, the court ruled as inappropriate a grading policy stating that the grades given by an individual teacher could not deviate by more than two percent from the grade distributions of other similar classes (*In re* Termination of James Johnson, 1990).

Observing Copyright Laws   Good teachers are constantly searching for interesting and relevant material to use in class. For example, as you seek material to make lessons more interesting, you may decide to use articles from magazines or journals, videotapes of interesting television programs, or copies of material from the Internet. Before you use these materials, you must make sure that you are not violating *copyright regulations.*

Copyright laws protect creative works of others. These works may include musical, dramatic, pictorial, as well as printed material. Copyright regulations stipulate that permission must be granted before copies can be made and distributed.

The doctrine of *fair use,* however, recognizes that it is sometimes in the public interest to allow for the reasonable use of copyrighted material without first securing the creator's permission. The federal copyright act identifies criteria that the courts can use in determining whether a particular instance of distribution of copyrighted material without permission of its creator constitutes a legitimate example of fair use (Fischer et al., 1999). The following four criteria are used:

1. the purpose of the use (this consideration focuses on whether the use was for commercial or for nonprofit use),
2. the nature of the copyrighted work,
3. the amount used in relationship to the copyrighted work as a whole, and
4. the effect of the use on the potential market or on the value of the work.

These criteria have been extended into more specific guidelines for educational use. Teachers are permitted to make single copies of the following for their own use in scholarly research or classroom preparation:

1. a chapter from a book;
2. an article from a periodical or newspaper;
3. a short story, essay or short poem; and
4. a chart, diagram, drawing, cartoon, or picture.

Multiple copies can be made of some copyrighted material for use in the classroom. However, the material copied for use in the classroom must not exceed one copy per learner and must meet the tests of *brevity, spontaneity,* and *cumulative effect.* "Brevity" refers to the amount of material copied. Specifically, a complete poem may be copied if it is less than 250 words in total length, and an excerpt from a longer poem not to exceed 250 words can be used. A complete article, story, or essay of less than 2,500 words can be copied as can an excerpt from a written work not to exceed 1,000 words or 10% of the total work. Finally, one chart, diagram, picture, or cartoon per book or periodical can be used.

"Spontaneity" refers to a situation where there is insufficient time to obtain permission if maximum instructional effectiveness of the material is to be achieved. For example, suppose you see an article in a magazine or a program on television with relevance for what you must teach within the next two weeks. It would not be reasonable to expect you to obtain permission in time to use the material in a timely manner.

"Cumulative effect" refers to the total use and impact of the copied material. This means that the material must be for only one course in the school. No more than one poem, article, or story from the same author may be copied, and no more than three from the same collective work or periodical. In addition, there should be no more than nine instances of multiple copying for any one class during a term.

Following the Web **3.1**

Censorship and the Internet

Educators and the general public have debated issues associated with restricting the kinds of information provided to school learners for many years. Traditional cases have focused on such concerns as contents of school newspapers, school libraries, and textbooks, and religious orientations reflected in certain curricular materials. Increasingly, schools have computers that make it possible for learners to access the Internet.

Much recent discussion about school censorship has centered on what regulations, if any, there should be regarding learners' use of the Internet. Many Web sites feature information relevant to this issue. Some examples that you might find interesting are provided here.

 For hot links to these sites, visit the companion Web site, located at *http://www.prenhall.com/armstrong*. Select Chapter 3 from the front page of the Web site, then choose the Following the Web module on the navigation bar on the left side of the page.

The Bill of Rights and Related Issues

- *http://www.fiu.edu/~khill/bor.htm*

  This site provides information about a large number of links to many issues associated with cases related to the Bill of Rights. It is an especially good place to find names and Web addresses of national organizations interested in defending particular categories of rights.

Censorship in America's Schools

- *http://www.eff.org/pub/Censorship/Academic_edu/school_censorship_aclu.article*

  The American Civil Liberties Union prepared this article. It provides an excellent summary of recent court cases that relate to the general issue of censorship in the public schools.

Electronic Frontier Foundation

- *http://www.eff.org/*

  This is the home page of the Electronic Frontier Foundation, a group dedicated to preserving liberty on the Internet. It features a useful search engine. If you put the

If the material you want to use meets standards associated with brevity, spontaneity, and cumulative effect, then you may make multiple copies for classroom use one time. If not, you will need to obtain permission.

Special standards apply to the use of videotaped material. Television programs broadcast for general use may be videotaped and used by a nonprofit educational institution. However, the tape may be kept for only 45 days. If permission has not been granted for the repeated use at the end of 45 days, the tape is to be erased or destroyed. You may use the tape for instructional purposes during the first 10 consecutive school days following the taping and may repeat it one time for purposes of reinforcing learning. After the 10-day period, you cannot use the material again unless you have been granted permission to do so.

words "school censorship" into the search engine, you will be directed to many links with information about school censorship, particularly as it relates to Internet information.

All About Sex: Censorship—When Is It Justified?

- *http://www.allaboutsex.org/censhorship.html*

  At this Web site, you will find an argument opposing censorship of Internet material even for avoiding censorship when such censorship claims to "protect" learners.

Internet Free Expression Alliance

- *http://www.ifea.net/*

  This is the home page of the Internet Free Expression Alliance, a group that opposes restrictions on access to the Internet as improper infringements on free speech. The group monitors legislative and court actions related to Internet access and provides summaries of this information on its Web site. You will find information here about efforts of schools to impose "filtration" systems to restrict learner access to certain Internet sites.

Internet Sex Note Hurts College Hunt

- *http://secure.eff.org/pub/Censorship/Academic_edu/school_censorship.article*

  In this report, you will learn of a case involving a high school senior who posted a message about his school on a Web site and, at the same time, directed people to a number of Web sites featuring sexually oriented material. In response, school officials withdrew their endorsement of the student as a National Merit finalist and took other actions.

[Note: Web addresses change frequently. If you are unable to locate one or more of these sites using the standard URL, try putting the site name in a standard search engine.]

Guidelines related to use of material copied from the Internet are not yet clear. This is an evolving area of the law, and it is one you need to pay attention to in the years ahead. There are guidelines related to other kinds of computer-related content. For example, it is illegal to make additional copies of copyrighted electronic content except of a single backup copy (Fischer et al., 1999).

TEACHERS' TORT LIABILITY

A *tort* is defined as civil as opposed to criminal wrongdoing. It results when one person suffers loss or harm as the result of improper conduct of another (Lamorte, 1996). Settlements of tort disputes often conclude with the award of some kind of

Video Viewpoint

Dangerous Hallways

WATCH: In this ABC News video segment, two 7th-grade girls named Christina and Jessica discuss the harassment they suffered at the hands of four older students. Although the victims' parents approached the assistant principal, the superintendent of schools, and finally the school board to report the death-threats and verbal and physical abuses their children experienced, the harassers were never punished. Jessica and Christina's parents were advised to home-school the two girls. The parents of the victims have brought a lawsuit against the district.

THINK: With your classmates or in your teaching journal, consider these questions:

1. What responsibilities does a teacher or administrator have to keep a student safe?
2. If you were a teacher or administrator involved in this situation, would you have done anything differently?
3. Do you think the teachers and administrators behaved negligently? Did their behavior constitute malpractice? Use the definitions of these terms in this chapter to make your case.

LINK: How are other students harmed when their peers suffer harassment?

compensatory monetary damages to the injured party. As it relates to education, a tort is the result of intentional wrongdoing or negligence in exercising the legal duties or the "duty of care" required of a teacher. Tort suits against teachers have been increasing in number. Today, many professional organizations offer group insurance designed to protect teachers from judgments that might be awarded to complainants in tort actions. Tort law differs from criminal law in that it is based on common law and the concept of fault or intent. In tort cases, as opposed to criminal cases, findings do not need to prove fault "beyond a reasonable doubt" (Valente, 1994).

As a teacher, you will have responsibility for the health and safety of the learners under your charge. If you are negligent in accepting or exercising this responsibility, you may face a tort action. Some of the questions relevant to injury-related suits against teachers include:

- Did the teacher have a duty of care under the law to avoid the injury?
- If so, was the duty breached?
- If a breach of legal duty occurred, was it the proximate cause of the injury?

The test applied to determine whether you have a "duty of care" is whether the probability of an injury could be foreseen and how a reasonable person with similar training would have acted (Valente, 1994). In other words, if you observe a learner climbing a tree to retrieve a ball, there is a probability that this person might fall and be injured. You have duty of care to stop the learner from engaging in this kind of activity. Additionally, your actions in response to a situation where injury could occur must be based on good professional judgment. Your action will be evaluated based on how other professional educators would respond to a similar situation. In addition, your breach of your duty of care must be directly related to the cause of the injury.

Teachers and administrators regularly check playground equipment to ensure its safety. Legal liability problems can result if learners suffer injuries because equipment has not been properly maintained.

For example, in one case, an 8th-grade teacher took a group of girls to an athletic field where some 8th-grade boys were playing ball. The teacher left the group unsupervised and returned to the school building. The boys started throwing pebbles at the girls, and one of the girls was hit in the eye and injured. The courts found that the teacher had failed to exercise reasonable care and was negligent and that her presence could have prevented the injury (*Sheehan v. St. Peter's Catholic School,* 1971). On the other hand, an injury that occurs because of a spontaneous act of another learner is not likely to result in a charge of negligence. For example, if you had walked by a group of learners, and shortly thereafter one of them unexpectedly picked up a rock, threw it, and injured someone, you would probably be judged to have exercised reasonable care.

Negligence

Negligence is the failure to use reasonable or due care to prevent harm. Since many cases involving tort liability involve negligence, it is important that you understand what it means. There are three different types of negligence: *misfeasance, nonfeasance* and *malfeasance.*

"Misfeasance" occurs when a teacher acts unwisely or without taking proper safeguards. The teacher may have had a worthy motive but acted in a manner that allowed harm to a learner. For example, a teacher of very young children might ask a child to carry a glass container from one location to another. If the child falls or drops the container and is cut by the broken glass, the teacher could be charged with misfeasance. The teacher was not intending harm to the child but acted unwisely in asking a young learner to perform this type of a task. A teacher who is knowledgeable about child growth and development should know that there is a high probability that a young child might drop a container. Therefore, allowing a child to carry a glass container is an unacceptable decision, given the probability of injury. This kind of decision amounts to the teacher having established conditions that acted to increase the likelihood of injury.

"Nonfeasance" occurs when the teacher fails to act when there was a duty to do so. For example, if a teacher were to watch a fight between two learners, making no attempt to halt the fight, and if one of the learners were injured, the teacher could face nonfeasance charges. Many cases involving nonfeasance concern injuries that occurred when the teacher was away from his or her assigned place of responsibility. Some examples include situations where injuries occurred when a teacher with assigned playground duty failed to supervise the learners or when an injury occurred to a learner during a regular classroom period when, for no acceptable reason, the teacher had left the room.

The determination of nonfeasance often focuses on the issue of whether proper supervision could have prevented the injury and on whether the absence of the teacher was justifiable. For example, if the reason the teacher was absent from the classroom was to extinguish a fire in the lavatory across the hall, the absence would probably be deemed justifiable. If a learner is injured in an accident that could not have been foreseen and no amount of supervision could have prevented it, then the teacher would probably not be charged with nonfeasance.

"Malfeasance" involves behavior that is undertaken deliberately and knowingly to harm someone else. For example, a teacher might impose a form of discipline that requires a learner to perform a task that involves risk, and the learner suffers an injury. The teacher's action deliberately placed the learner in jeopardy. As a result, the teacher could be charged with malfeasance. Other examples might involve a teacher who uses excessive force in discipline or who injures a learner while breaking up a fight.

Malpractice

As applied to education, *malpractice* refers to an action that is either unprofessional or that is inappropriate for the receiving individual and results in negative consequences for this person. Even though such suits are uncommon, you need to know that malpractice complaints are sometimes brought against teachers. Among the conditions that might lead to a malpractice suit against a teacher are (Valente, 1994):

- a failure to bring learner achievement up to satisfactory levels;
- an injury to the development of the learner because of a lack of professional practice in testing, evaluating, and placing the learner; and
- a failure to act protect a learner who finds himself/herself in a situation where personal harm may result.

Attempts to sue teachers for malpractice when academic achievement levels are not as high as complainants feel they should be have not been successful in courts.

Part of the difficulty involves clearly defining the limits of teacher responsibility for learning. The courts have recognized that many other variables other than the work of an individual teacher affect learners' achievement levels. These range from home backgrounds, motivational levels, the nature of the support materials provided by the school, and the support provided by members of learners' families. Most authorities do not look for much change in the reluctance of courts to support claims of malpractice. However, in the current climate where teachers are being held more accountable for learner achievement and where more frequent checks of achievement are performed, there is a possibility we will see more malpractice suits against teachers in the future.

Few successful malpractice suits against teachers have featured disputes over whether a learner was improperly evaluated and placed. In general, the courts have required complainants to have overwhelming documentation in support of their claims of teacher malpractice. Nevertheless, you need to know that the possibility exists for malpractice suits against teachers who are careless in evaluating and placing learners, and you need to document decisions carefully.

There are varying circumstances in which a teacher might be charged with failing to provide adequate protection for a learner. One example might be when a teacher fails to act when a learner complains of being threatened by another learner. If actual harm comes to the learner, the teacher might face charges.

The legal responsibilities of a teacher for action when learners share information with them are not clearly defined. For example, sometimes information relates to a potentially dangerous situation, such as an intent to commit suicide. If the teacher fails to act on this information and the learner follows through with these intentions, there may be grounds for a successful malpractice suit (Valente, 1994).

Slander and Libel

The type of harm that might trigger a tort action does not have to be physical harm. False statements or statements that expose another person to contempt, ridicule, or disgrace may also cause harm. When these statements are spoken, they are called *slander;* when they are written, they are called *libel* (Fischer et al., 1999).

You can run into difficulty in recording comments on permanent learner records. Since making derogatory comments about learners can lead to a defamation suit, any comments written about learners should describe relevant, observable behavior. You should not make written comments that are simply based on your personal judgments or opinions. For example, do not write something that makes a summary judgment, such as "This person is a thief." Instead, you should write a comment focusing on an observed behavior or action, such as "This student was reprimanded for removing school property." When care is taken to record these comments in a professional manner, the courts have generally held that teachers are not liable for statements unless they are made with malicious intent (Fischer et al., 1999).

Sexual Harassment

In recent years, concerns about sexual harassment have risen dramatically. Because of increased litigation in this area, many teachers fear being falsely accused of sexual harassment by vindictive learners. In response to this situation, some school districts now caution teachers about touching learners and ask them to take particular care to use good judgment when working with learners independently in out-of-class settings.

The Supreme Court has ruled that learners who are victims of sexual harassment can sue for damages (*Franklin v. Gwinnett County Public Schools,* 1992). The Office of Civil Rights has issued guidelines clearly stating that a school will be held liable for sexual harassment of learners by its employees if the school has received notice that the harassment has been occurring (Fischer et al., 1999).

Schools must also be prepared to act in situations of learner-to-learner sexual harassment. One circuit court ruled that a school could be held liable if it fails to respond to a reported case of peer sexual harassment. In this case, a fifth-grade girl had been repeatedly harassed by another learner for over six months.

In response to concerns about sexual harassment, the United States Department of Education has issued guidelines defining sexual harassment as behavior (1) that is sufficiently severe or pervasive to interfere with the education of a learner or (2) that creates a hostile and abusive educational environment. Today, there is general agreement that school districts cannot ignore sexual-harassment complaints. They must take corrective action to remedy the situation (Fischer et al., 1999).

TEACHERS' CIVIL RIGHTS

Not too many years ago, few questioned the legitimacy of asking teachers to forego certain rights as a condition for employment. In some places, they were forbidden to smoke or consume alcohol, and many years ago, teachers were even forbidden to marry. Another historic requirement insisted that teachers regularly participate in religious services. As a teacher today, you will face relatively few restrictions that differ from those applying to the general population. Not everybody agrees that this should be the case.

Some people maintain that teachers are role models for impressionable youngsters. As such, they should be expected to behave in a more exemplary manner than a "typical" citizen. In cases that have been litigated, courts generally have ruled that teachers cannot be punished for exercising their constitutional rights. However, the United States Supreme Court has noted that the exercise of constitutional rights by public school teachers and administrators has to be balanced against the interests of the general public (Valente, 1994). In one case that supported this view, a court declared that certain professions such as teaching impose limitations on personal actions that are not imposed on people engaged in other occupations (*Board of Trustees of Compton Junior College District v. Stubblefield,* 1971).

You may recall from the discussion of tenure earlier in the chapter that immorality is one ground for firing a tenured teacher. Immoral behavior than can lead to dismissal is not restricted to actions occurring on school property. However, when the immorality argument has been made in a court of law to support dismissal of a teacher, school districts typically have had to present convincing evidence that the teacher's behavior interfered with his or her ability to function effectively in the classroom. In these cases, judges have paid particular attention to the impact of the "problem" behavior on the teacher's ability to play a credible leadership role with learners and to work positively with parents or guardians and other professionals.

Freedom of Association

There have been cases where teachers were dismissed for belonging to so-called radical organizations or even for being active in more conventional partisan politics. Other have been dismissed or threatened with dismissal because of a blood relationship to a school board member or because they married a board member or school district administrator.

In general, the courts have ruled that teachers cannot be dismissed simply because they belong to a controversial group unless there is evidence that they have supported illegal activities. In addition, courts have required that school districts prove that membership of teachers in these groups has been detrimental to the functioning of the school (Valente, 1994).

The courts have almost uniformly ruled that teachers cannot be dismissed because of their political support of candidates for school boards or other elected offices or for participating in partisan political activities (including wearing political buttons to school). The line has been drawn, however, when teachers attempt to indoctrinate learners. As with similar issues, the courts typically consider whether the teacher's activities have seriously disrupted or impaired the instructional process (Fischer et al., 1999).

Freedom of Conscience

You need to be aware of how courts have viewed issues related to separation of church and state. There are some important distinctions between the constitutional rights of teachers and learners. Compulsory attendance laws require learners to attend school. Teachers, on the other hand, are paid employees who have a choice of employment opportunities. Therefore, certain restrictions can be placed on teachers that are not placed on learners.

These restrictions affect freedom-of-conscience issues in different ways and raise interesting questions such as the following:

- What rights does a teacher have in refusing to teach some parts of the curriculum that conflict with religious beliefs?
- Does a teacher have to lead the pledge of allegiance to the flag if giving such a pledge violates a religious belief?
- Can teachers wear distinctive religious clothing?
- Can teachers be absent from school in order to observe religious holidays?
- What are the rights of teachers in voicing their religious views?

Consider a student teacher who insisted on sharing her religious beliefs with her learners. When she was questioned about this practice, she said her beliefs required that she share her convictions with others at every given opportunity. Numerous court cases affirm that such behavior is not appropriate. They have generally ruled that teachers have no right to impose their beliefs on what is essentially a captive audience.

In many places, teachers are required to begin the school day with ceremonies that involve a flag salute and the pledge of allegiance. Some teachers have objected to participating in these activities because of their personal religious convictions. In one case that went to court, the teacher, though refusing to participate personally, stood by respectfully while another teacher led the class in a flag salute. The court upheld the right of this teacher not to participate (*Russo v. Central School District No. 1,* 1972).

In another case, a teacher belonged to a religious group that opposed all references to patriotism and national symbols. She told her principal that she would not teach any curriculum content related to these topics nor would she acknowledge national holidays such as Washington's Birthday. The school district challenged the teacher's legal authority to take this position. The case ultimately ended up in a federal court that decided the First Amendment of the United States Constitution does not provide a license for a teacher to teach a curriculum that deviates from the one prescribed by the state. The court went on to point out that although the teacher had a right to her own religious beliefs, she had no right to require others to submit to her views. To do so would be to deprive learners of an expected part of the educational experience (*Palmer v. Board of Education of the City of Chicago,* 1980).

Another freedom-of-conscience issue that has been litigated concerns teacher dress. Cases generally have supported the position that a school district can establish a dress code for teachers that may prohibit their wearing distinctive religious clothing. Courts have reasoned that such clothing may give children the impression that the school supports a particular religion.

Courts generally have supported teachers' rights to take a leave for religious holidays, so long as the absence does not cause an undue hardship on the school district and the amount of time taken off is not excessive. However, the courts have also noted that school districts are under no obligation to pay for such leaves unless there are stipulations in teachers' contracts requiring such payment.

In summary, the religious beliefs of teachers are protected, and teachers cannot be terminated on the basis of their religious beliefs or required to sign an oath or take a pledge that violates their beliefs. However, the actions that teachers can take in a school setting in practicing their beliefs can be limited if those actions relate to a compelling state interest in the education of children.

Personal Appearance

Courts have considered numerous cases concerning the rights of school districts to impose dress and grooming standards on teachers. Decisions reflect a mixed pattern. One line of reasoning holds that teachers do not have a substantial constitutional right in this area; hence, schools have the right to establish dress and grooming standards for teachers. Another line of reasoning follows the principle that limits on teachers' behaviors must be tied to a school district's responsibility for ensuring an orderly educational environment. According to this view, any dress and grooming standards for teachers must be shown to be necessary to maintain an orderly educational environment (Valente, 1994). In recent years, most court decisions have favored the first line of reasoning. To date, dress and grooming standards for teachers have not been viewed as issues warranting action by the Supreme Court.

Lifestyle Issues

Courts have considered many cases that relate to teachers' lifestyles. Cases have focused on issues such as sexual orientation, unmarried cohabitation, adultery, use of vulgar language, and even breast-feeding infants in the school setting. Generally, the courts have maintained that teachers have a right to privacy and that school officials cannot take actions that infringe on this right. However, right-to-privacy decisions have varied depending on the particular circumstances for each case. For example, many courts have rejected dismissal actions against gay or lesbian teachers. In these decisions, the courts have ruled that districts failed to prove that the teacher's sexual orientation posed a significant danger to learners or other school employees or that it impaired the teacher's ability to discharge his or her professional role. However, teachers have not won all cases where sexual orientation was used as a rationale for dismissal. In particular, dismissals on the grounds of sexual orientation have been upheld in situations where teachers publicly flaunted unconventional sexual conduct (Valente, 1994).

A number of cases have considered the legitimacy of dismissal actions taken against a teacher charged with unmarried cohabitation. In one such case, a teacher moved in with her boyfriend. Two months later, the school administration told her she could either resign or be fired. Ten days after receiving this information, she married her boyfriend. Nevertheless, the school district fired her on the grounds of immorality. She challenged the decision in court, and the court upheld her position. In its decision, the court noted that prior to the dismissal action, most of the people in the community had been unaware of her living arrangements. Furthermore, there was insufficient evidence to sustain the contention that her behavior had interfered with her effectiveness in the classroom (*Thompson v. Southwest School District,* 1980).

On the other hand, the dismissal of another teacher was upheld because of cohabitation with a male friend in a small rural community where a large number of parents petitioned her dismissal because of her living arrangement. The court ruled that there was a need to balance the privacy rights of a teacher with the legitimate interests of the school district in promoting the education of learners (*Sullivan v. Meade Independent School District No. 101,* 1976).

Many other lifestyle issues have been litigated. Among them have been cases brought as a result of dismissal actions initiated against unwed but pregnant teachers, teachers who have used vulgar language, and teachers who have breast-fed their babies at school. In deciding these cases, courts typically have given strong weight to the impact of teachers' actions on their ability to teach and relate to learners and parents. However, the decisions are very situation-specific. In making rulings related to lifestyle issues, courts generally consider the size, sophistication, and the values of the community, the reactions of learners and parents, and the notoriety of the activity (Fischer et al., 1999).

Immoral Conduct

Frequently, cases concerning alleged immoral or unprofessional conduct of teachers come before the courts. Immorality and unprofessional conduct, as noted earlier in the chapter, are included in nearly all tenure laws as grounds for dismissal of a tenured teacher. When teachers have been found to have acted in immoral ways, the courts have usually supported dismissal decisions. The difficulty in these cases is in defining what constitutes immoral behavior. Courts increasingly are narrowing the scope of what can be considered "immoral."

In an important state case, the California Supreme Court ruled that a teacher cannot automatically be dismissed for behavior that some people might consider to be immoral (Morrision v. State Board of Education, 1969). In this case, a teacher admitted to having a same-sex relationship with another teacher. The court stated that it was dangerous to interpret unprofessional conduct too broadly. There was no evidence that the teachers had tried to establish gay relationships with learners or that their relationship had negatively affected their ability to get along with co-workers. In addition, the teachers' relationship did not have an adverse influence on their teaching. Accordingly, the court ruled in the teachers' favor. The principle established in this case was that any successful dismissal action related to a teacher's private life had to be supported by evidence establishing a tight connection between the private behavior of the teacher and his or her work as a professional. An Iowa court followed this rationale in holding that an admission of adultery did not automatically make a person unfit to teach (*Erb v. Iowa State Board of Instruction,* 1974).

This reasoning has supported dismissal actions in a number of cases. The dismissal of one teacher was upheld when the courts determined that she had had sexual relations with three men at a party, that this information was known to learners and families at the school where she taught, and that this behavior had undermined her credibility. In its decision, the court ruled that the teacher's conduct at a semipublic party reflected her total lack of concern for privacy or decorum and indicated a serious defect of moral character and common sense (*Pettit v. State Board of Education,* 1973).

In another California case involving an improper relationship between a college instructor and a learner, a dismissal action was upheld. The courts noted that people in certain professions have limitations not imposed on those in other callings (*Board of Trustees of Compton Junior College District v. Stubblefield,* 1971). In cases where teachers have had improper relationships with learners, even those who are not in their classes, the courts have almost always ruled against the teachers. For example, a 4th-grade teacher was fired for having sexual relations with a 15-year-old neighbor boy who baby-sat for her children.

Following the Web 3.2

Locating Information

Many Web sites feature information about legal issues and how they affect teachers. We have provided some examples that you may wish to visit.

For hot links to these sites, visit the companion Web site, located at *http://www. prenhall.com/armstrong.* Select Chapter 3 from the front page of the Web site, then choose the Following the Web module on the navigation bar on the left side of the page.

Find Law—Law Crawler

- *http://lawcrawler.findlaw.com*

  This site includes a highly useful search engine. You can use it to search for a variety of topics relating to legal issues. For example, by using the search engine, you can locate a number of Web sites with information on academic freedom and tenure.

EDLAW, Inc.

- *http://www.edlaw.net/edlawinc/edlawinc.htm*

  EDLAW, Inc. is a private company that specializes in producing newsletters, books, seminars, and databases that explain and interpret developments in education law. There are some free services available through this site. Others require payment of a fee.

Internet Law Library: Education and the Law

- *http://law.house.gov/99.htm*

  This site provides many links to sites with information related to education and the law in the United States and in many other countries. You will be able to locate education codes for the individual states, many examples of education legislation, summaries of court decisions, and many other kinds of information tied to legal issues and education. Some information here is quite specialized. For example, you will find links to information about what the constitution of Finland says about education, Estonian educational practices, and legal topics in Malaysian education.

Education Law: An Overview

- *http://www.law.cornell.edu:80/topics/education.html*

  Maintained by Cornell University, this site provides numerous links to federal and state materials related to education laws. You will also find information about court cases that have focused on education-related issues.

Supreme Court Collection

- *http://supct.law.cornell.edu/supct/topiclist.html*

  This well-organized site allows you to search for Supreme Court cases on numerous issues. For example, if you are interested in issues related to freedom of speech, it is possible to isolate just those decisions.

[Note: Web addresses change frequently. If you are unable to locate one or more of these sites using the standard URL, try putting the site name in a standard search engine.]

Criminal Conduct

Conviction or even indictment on a criminal charge can be the basis for dismissal of a teacher or revocation of his or her teaching certificate. In several states, prospective teachers must reveal whether they have been convicted of a felony when they apply for a certificate. Admission of such a conviction or failure to answer the question truthfully may be grounds for denial or revocation of a certificate to teach.

When cases involving dismissal or revocation of a teaching credential because of criminal conduct have been considered by the courts, the seriousness of the criminal conduct has heavily influenced courts' decisions. However, court decisions in this area have varied widely from place to place. For example, in a Pennsylvania case, the dismissal of a teacher who had been convicted of shoplifting was upheld (*Lesley v. Oxford Area School District,* 1980). On the other hand, in another case involving shoplifting, the court ruled that the conviction did not provide sufficient evidence that the individual was unfit to serve as a school counselor (*Golden v. Board of Education of the County of Harrison,* 1981).

Sometimes even teachers who have been convicted of misdemeanors can face dismissal charges. For example, a teacher in Alaska was fired after being convicted of illegally diverting electricity to his house. The courts upheld the dismissal, contending that the act was a form of theft and constituted moral turpitude (*Kenai Peninsula Borough of Education v. Brown,* 1984).

In summary, criminal activity will almost certainly lead to serious legal difficulties for a teacher. In addition, it is important to note that a failure of a court to convict does not mean that the worries of the teacher are over. An action leading to revocation of a certificate does not have to meet as strong a legal criterion as an action that can lead to a criminal conviction. In a criminal proceeding, the standard of evidence proving "beyond a reasonable doubt" must be met for a conviction. However in a dismissal case, only "a preponderance of evidence" is required.

Key Ideas In Summary

- Decisions from two different sets of courts, state and federal (with several layers in each system), establish a large and confusing body of common law. Identifying general guidelines for acceptable and unacceptable behavior requires careful analysis of volumes of information.
- Constitutions are considered the highest level of law. Statute and administrative law cannot establish principles that are contrary to constitutional provisions. Judges interpret constitutions and use these interpretations as a general legal framework for making their decisions. Their decisions may result in legal principles that are applied to future cases dealing with similar issues.
- Teacher certification is a function of state government. The certificate is essentially a license to practice. Individuals who accept a teaching position without the appropriate credentials may discover that they are ineligible to receive a salary.

- Contracts are legally binding documents that spell out the responsibilities for both parties. When one party breaks the contract, the other may be entitled to compensation.
- Free access to information not influenced by political leaders and those in power has been deemed critical to maintaining a free, democratic society. Tenure laws were established to protect teachers from arbitrary dismissal because they taught material that was politically unpopular. Tenure laws do not guarantee unconditional lifetime employment. However, they do indicate a narrow range of conditions under which a tenured teacher can be dismissed. They require that due process be followed and that the school district initiating the action provide substantial proof of its allegations.
- The courts have typically upheld teachers' rights to include course material or use teaching methods that are relevant to the content of the course of study. However, school districts do have the right to place some limits on the material that is used in class. School districts cannot use unconstitutional reasons for censoring material that is used in the classroom.
- Teachers and school officials are mandatory reporters of suspected child abuse. This means that they may be subject to criminal penalties that could include jail time and fines if they fail to report suspected abuse.
- A tort is a legal action that involves a suit by one individual against another for an injury that resulted because of a breach of legal duty. Torts in education often involve charges of teacher negligence or even malpractice.
- Because of their special relationship to impressionable youth, teachers' rights as individuals must be weighed against the right of the state to provide a proper education. This implies that in some instances, teachers can be held to higher standards of conduct than the public at large.
- Teachers' actions away from school may provide grounds for dismissal if these behaviors are found to impair the ability of the teachers to discharge their professional responsibilities or if they pose a threat to the welfare of others.
- Conviction or even indictment for a crime can lead to the revocation of a teaching certificate, dismissal, or both. Courts have not always assumed a criminal conviction automatically serves as an adequate reason for dismissal of a teacher. Cases have been decided in different ways because of circumstances unique to individual situations. In some jurisdictions, even convictions for misdemeanors have been upheld as adequate grounds for dismissal.

Chapter 3 Self Test

To review terms and concepts in this chapter, take the Chapter 3 Self Test on the companion Web site, located at *http://www.prenhall.com/armstrong*. Select Chapter 3 from the front page of the Web site, then choose the Self Test module on the navigation bar on the left side of the page. Feedback for the Self Test is immediate. You can keep track of your Self Test scores yourself, or you can choose to submit your scores via e-mail to your instructor.

Reflections

To respond to these questions online, and to save or submit your response electronically, visit the companion Web site, located at *http://www.prenhall.com/armstrong*. Select Chapter 3 from the front page of the Web site, then choose the Reflections module on the navigation bar on the left side of the page. Instructors and students may also wish to use these questions as discussion topics on the Message Board for the companion Web site.

1. What criteria would establish whether a case would be heard in a state court or a federal court?

2. The issue of certification is sometimes an issue that is debated. There are those who claim that certification requirements are an inappropriate barrier that deny the profession services of some people who would be good teachers. Do you agree? Why or why not?

3. Suppose you were to explain basic features of laws related to the use of copyrighted materials to a prospective teacher. What would you say? Do copyright laws provide unreasonable limitations on what you can and cannot use in the classroom?

4. How do you respond to the debate over tenure? Does tenure protect incompetent teachers, and should it be eliminated?

What would be some consequences of the elimination of tenure?

5. Suppose it is early in December. What must an elementary school teacher think about in deciding what, if anything, can be said about Christmas?

6. Identifying the limits of academic freedom can be difficult. What do you believe should be the limits, if any, to academic freedom in the classroom?

7. Some teachers and administrators are uncomfortable with their roles as mandatory reporters of suspected child abuse. They are fearful of being caught in a legal tangle that will bring down pressure from legal authorities and from parents or guardians. What is your feeling regarding accepting responsibility as a mandatory reporter of suspected child abuse?

8. What do you see as some of the key guidelines that you need to know in order to avoid litigation associated with negligence?

9. What are defining characteristics of *nonfeasance, misfeasance,* and *malfeasance?* Can you cite some examples of teacher behavior that might be consistent with each category?

10. Do you agree with the premise that teachers should be held accountable to higher standards of personal conduct than ordinary citizens? Why or why not?

Field Experiences, Projects, and Enrichment

1. Investigate the requirements for a teaching certificate in your state. Are different types available? How long is a certificate valid? What does a person have to do to maintain one? What is the process for obtaining a certificate?

2. Interview a local school administrator or local teachers' association representative

regarding teaching contracts and conditions of employment. How detailed is the contract? What are the provisions of the contract? What are the rights and responsibilities of teachers?

3. Look through recent issues of newspapers or educational journals for articles focusing on legal issues in education (*Phi Delta Kappan,* a

leading education journal, has a regular feature on legal issues). Identify the legal principles concerned and the implications for a teacher. Share your findings with a group and identify emerging issues and principles.

4. Organize a debate on the topic: "Resolved that tenure laws impede efforts to achieve meaningful reform of education."

5. Many state teachers' organizations produce information about the education code and legal concerns of teachers. Obtain a copy of this material, and compare the legal concerns in your state with those included in this chapter. What are some differences and similarities?

References

Board of Trustees of Compton Junior College District v. Stubblefield, 94 Cal. Rptr. 318, 321 (Cal. Ct. App. 1971).

Brown v. Gwinnett County School District, 112 F.3d 1464 (11th Cir. 1997) No. 95-9595, May 6, 1997.

California Teachers Association (1992). *Guide to school law.* Burlingame, CA.

Cary v. Board of Education, Adams-Arapahoe School District, 598 F.2d 535 (10th Cir. 1979).

Dean v. Timpson Independent School District, 486 F. Supp. 302 (E.D. Tex. 1979).

Edwards v. Aquillard, 482 U.S. 578 (1987).

Erb v. Iowa State Board of Instruction, 216 N.W.2d 339 (Iowa 1974).

Fischer, L., Schimmel, D., & Kelly, C. (1999). *Teachers and the law* (5th ed). New York: Longman.

Franklin v. Gwinnett County Public Schools, 503 U.S. 60, 112 S. Ct. 1028 (1992).

Golden v. Board of Education of the County of Harrison, 285 S.E.2d 665 (W.Va. 1981).

In re Termination of James Johnson, 451 N.W.2d 343 (Minn. Ct. App. 1990).

Keefe v. Geanakos, 418 F.2d 359 (1st Cir. 1969).

Kenai Peninsula Borough of Education v. Brown, 691 P.2d 1034 (Alaska 1984).

Kingsville Independent School District v. Cooper, 611 F.2d 1109 (5th Cir. 1980).

Lamorte, M. W. (1996). *School law: Cases and concepts.* Boston: Allyn and Bacon.

Lemon v. Kurtzman, 403 U.S. 602, 91 S. Ct. 2105, 291 L.Ed.2d 745 (1971).

Lesley v. Oxford Area School District, 420 A2d 764 (Pa. Commw. Ct. 1980).

Morrison v. State Board of Education, 461 P.2d 375 (Cal. 1969).

Oakland Unified School District v. Olicker, 25 Cal. 3d 1098 (Ct. App. 1972).

Palmer v. Board of Education of the City of Chicago, 603 F.2d 1271 (7th Cir. 1979), cert. denied, 444 U.S. 1026 (1980).

Parducci v. Rutland, 316 F. Supp. 352 (N.D. Ala. 1970).

Pettit v. State Board of Education, 513 P.2d 889 (Cal. 1973).

Richardson, J. (1995, March 1). Critics target state teacher-tenure laws. *Education Week,* pp. 1, 13.

Russo v. Central School District No. 1, 469 F.2d 623 (2d Cir. 1972), cert denied, 411 U.S. 932 (1973).

Scruggs v. Keen, 900 F. Supp. 821 (W.D. Va. 1995).

Sheehan v. St. Peter's Catholic School, 188 N.W.2d 868 (Minn. 1971).

Sullivan v. Meade Independent School District No. 101, 530 F.2d 779 (8th Cir. 1976).

Thompson v. Southwest School District, 483 F. Supp. 1170 (W.D. Mo. 1980).

Underwood, J. (1994). Child abuse. *The Schools and the Courts,* 20(1), 1027–1028.

Valente, W. (1994). *Law in the schools* (3rd ed.). New York: Macmillan.

Virgil v. School Board of Columbia County, Florida, 862 F.2d 1517 (11th Cir. 1989).

Zirkel, P., & Richardson, S. (1988). *A digest of Supreme Court decisions affecting education.* Bloomington, IN: Phi Delta Kappa Educational Foundation.

Learners and Their Diverse Needs

CHAPTERS

Multiculturalism

OBJECTIVES

This chapter will help you to

- identify a rationale for teachers to pay particular attention to school experiences of minority-group and female learners.

- recognize the changing demographic characteristics represented in the population of school learners and describe some implications of these differences for educational practice.

- point out some patterns of within-school segregation that have persisted despite attempts to eliminate them.

- describe how some school programs have used race, ethnicity, or gender as criteria for determining which educational experiences to provide to certain categories of learners.

- recognize the growing disparity between demographic characteristics of teachers and learners.

- identify some places where materials and programs can be obtained that seek to sensitize educators to multicultural and gender-equity issues.

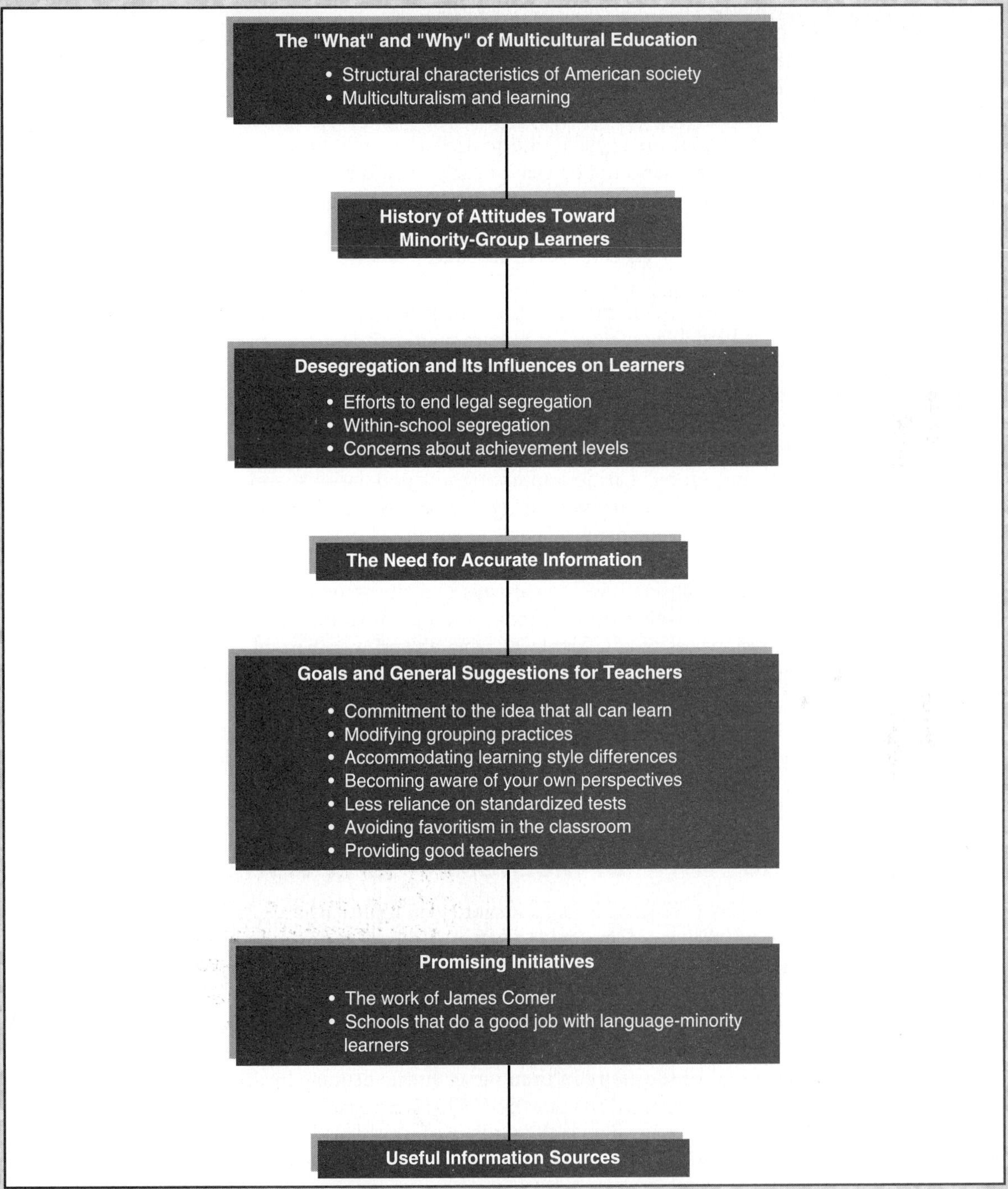

The "What" and "Why" of Multicultural Education
- Structural characteristics of American society
- Multiculturalism and learning

History of Attitudes Toward Minority-Group Learners

Desegregation and Its Influences on Learners
- Efforts to end legal segregation
- Within-school segregation
- Concerns about achievement levels

The Need for Accurate Information

Goals and General Suggestions for Teachers
- Commitment to the idea that all can learn
- Modifying grouping practices
- Accommodating learning style differences
- Becoming aware of your own perspectives
- Less reliance on standardized tests
- Avoiding favoritism in the classroom
- Providing good teachers

Promising Initiatives
- The work of James Comer
- Schools that do a good job with language-minority learners

Useful Information Sources

FIGURE 4.1 Multiculturalism

INTRODUCTION

When you start teaching, you will likely encounter many learners whose ethnic and cultural roots differ from your own. If you do not have personal familiarity with the groups from which many of your learners come, you will want to move quickly to learn about the special perspectives of these young people and their families.

It is important to have information that will allow you to provide instruction that is responsive to the particular backgrounds of your learners. The more you can accommodate the special perspectives of young people in your classes, the more successful they will be. Successful learners feel good about themselves and their experiences in schools. These positive attitudes, in turn, positively reinforce what you do as a teacher. They can lead to reduced discipline problems and help you grow in confidence as you see members of the class profiting from your instruction.

The laudable objective of maximizing each learner's potential has implications not only for how members of diverse ethnic and cultural groups are treated, but also for the issue of gender. Today's adult females are as likely to be employed as adult males. For this reason, "we . . . are no longer willing to accept the hypocritical inequities that this society has traditionally laid on our African-Americans and Native Americans, on our Latino and immigrant populations, and on all our poor and minority people, and our women" (Clinchy, 1993, p. 507). Women occupy important positions in government, the arts, medicine, law, and virtually every other area of modern life.

Female learners have not always had the same educational opportunities that have been available to males. Today's school programs recognize that human capital is a precious resource. Talents of females and members of ethnic and cultural minorities deserve to be fully developed. Society stands to benefit from their contributions when they leave school as confident, competent young adults, fully prepared to assume positions of responsibility and leadership. A commitment to providing an education that is multicultural in outlook will help you provide learning experiences that truly have the potential to serve needs of *all* learners who come to school.

THE "WHAT" AND "WHY" OF MULTICULTURAL EDUCATION

Geneva Gay (1994), a national authority on multicultural education, points out that "multicultural education means different things to different people." In her comprehensive survey of writing on the topic, she identified as many as 13 independent definitions of the term that appeared frequently in the professional writing she surveyed. Multicultural education specialists James A. Banks and Cherry A. McGee Banks (1995) proposed a definition that embraces many elements found in different descriptions of the term. In their view, multicultural education is designed to result in educational equity for all learners. This is accomplished by incorporating ". . . content, principles, theories, and paradigms from history, the social and behavioral sciences, and particularly from ethnic studies and women studies" (p. xii).

Forces that encourage multicultural perspectives in the schools include (1) structural characteristics of American society and (2) multiculturalism and learning.

What Do You Think?

Improving Girls' Achievement—Are Single-Gender Schools the Answer?

Researchers have found that girls sometimes do not perform as well as they should when they are enrolled with boys in typical coeducational classes. For example, there is some evidence that girls do not participate as frequently in classroom discussions as boys unless the class has a female majority as well as a female teacher.

In recent years, some parents have responded to this situation by seeking support for single-gender schools. In New York City, for example, many private girls' schools have been established in recent years (Lewin, 1999). In addition, there has been an especially high level of interest in enrolling female children in all-girl kindergartens.

What Do You Think?

1. How would your own school experiences have differed if you had gone to a single-gender school?
2. What advantages and disadvantages do you see for single-gender schools?
3. Will the effort to establish single-gender schools detract from efforts to assure that female learners are appropriately supported and challenged in coeducational schools? Why, or why not?

Structural Characteristics of American Society

The complex diversity of American society is evident in the nation's variety of religious, ethnic, economic, social, and racial groups. Even if you live in a small town, you probably recognize at least divisions based on the economic status of individuals and families.

You probably would be more accurate in describing our society as a "mosaic" rather than as a "melting pot." There has been little evidence that the special identities people have because of their membership in certain racial, ethnic, economic, social, or religious groups tends to melt away over time. Your own background helps define your identity as a human being. While you probably would acknowledge the wisdom of learning about others with different backgrounds and of welcoming these differences as a legitimate part of our diverse national family, you probably would resent any attempt directed at "melting away" your personal heritage.

Those who see the United States as a mosaic point out that a defining feature of our society is the ability of individual groups to retain their special identities while, at the same time, acknowledging the rights of other groups to preserve theirs. For the schools, this means striking a reasoned balance between two competing needs. First, school programs must allow individuals enough latitude to retain sustaining personal identities with their individual groups. At the same time, they must teach common, shared values that bring all citizens together as Americans.

Many individuals who support more attention to multicultural education suggest that schools have done a better job of promoting common American values than they have of acknowledging the legitimacy of perspectives of young people from minority racial, social, and cultural groups. The intent is to "provide opportunities for individuals from diverse backgrounds to learn, live, and work together" (Gay, 1994).

Multiculturalism and Learning

Since children reflect cultural values of their families, difficulties arise when actions and expectations of teachers are inconsistent with what young people have learned at home. For example, in some cultures, children are taught that it is impolite to look directly at adults when speaking to them. When children from these backgrounds encounter a typical classroom where the teacher encourages members of the class to "look at me when you're speaking," they become uncomfortable. Should the children believe parents and relatives at home or the teacher? This problem is becoming critical in this country; while the vast majority of teachers continue to be drawn from the White middle class, the learners in the nation's classrooms reflect more racial, ethnic, and linguistic diversity with each passing year.

Cultural inconsistencies pose significant problems for many learners from minority groups when they come to school, for their anxieties often interfere with their learning. For this reason, you must to do more than simply recognize the diverse nature of the young people you will be serving. To be effective, you will need to be familiar with the special world view each brings to the classroom. With this information, you will be able to modify your practices in ways that do not send inconsistent messages to these learners.

A BRIEF HISTORY OF ATTITUDES TOWARD MINORITY-GROUP LEARNERS

Educators have long been aware that large numbers of learners from minority groups have not done well in school. An early explanation for this phenomenon was the *genetic deficit* view (Armstrong & Savage, 1998). People who subscribed to this position believed that minority-group learners lacked the necessary intellectual tools to succeed in school. Individuals who accepted this premise were reluctant to divert school resources to improve instructional programs for children who were perceived as incapable of profiting from them.

By the 1960s, the genetic deficit position had given way to a *cultural deficit* view (Erickson, 1987). Those who subscribed to this argument contended that poor school performance could be blamed on the failure of minority-group children's parents to provide an intellectually stimulating home atmosphere that prepared the learners for the expectations of the school. The cultural deficit view seemed to allow schools a way out when confronted with statistics revealing high dropout rates and other evidence of mediocre levels of school performance on the part of minority-group learners. This position permitted that blame for these dismal statistics be placed on learners' homes rather than on the school.

A more recent explanation for the schools' failure to adequately serve needs of minority-group learners has been the *communication process* position (Erickson, 1987). According to this view, language patterns of minority-group learners are substantially different from those of their teachers and majority-group learners; hence, they are not capable of understanding much of classroom instruction. This communication failure accounts for their poor academic performance. This position, however, has been attacked for failing to explain why some minority-group learners do extremely well in school.

In recent years, professional educators have been downplaying explanations for difficulties of minority-group learners that seem to shift the blame away from the schools. Increasingly, it is argued that school programs have failed to plan seriously for the success of *all* learners (even though educators' rhetoric has espoused this intent for years). Because of this failure, many minority-group learners and their parents may not believe the schools' claims that they are truly interested in promoting the development of each child. To establish credibility, we need to avoid instructional practices that can undermine the self-confidence of our learners, and we must prepare lessons that help our young people appreciate the benefits of living in a culture where diversity is seen as a national asset (Armstrong & Savage, 1998).

Today, educators are generally unwilling to make excuses for poor academic performance. This position is promoted by a premise that "all students can learn" and provides a superstructure for many education reform programs (Henson, 2001). If the curriculum is centered in truth, it will be pluralistic, because human culture is the product of the struggles of all humanity, not the possession of a single racial or ethnic group (Hilliard, 1991/1992).

Even though our diverse society includes people with many different views on the issue of multicultural education, in general, people remain strongly committed to the idea of multiculturalism. This point was emphasized in a poll that revealed that three fourths of Americans think the schools should promote both a common cultural tradition and the diverse cultural traditions of the nation's different population groups (Elam, Rose, & Gallup, 1994). This finding is consistent with the view that multicultural education should seek a unity that is enriched by diversity (Banks, 1995).

DESEGREGATION AND ITS INFLUENCES ON LEARNERS

For many years, it was difficult to promote the development of intercultural and interracial sensitivities in the schools because many schools were racially segregated. Then and now, concerns about desegregating schools and promoting more communication between learners from different racial and cultural backgrounds fall into three distinct categories (Simon-McWilliams, 1989):

- concerns about ending legal segregation and following court-ordered plans to achieve integration,
- concerns about *within-school* segregation of minority-group learners and females, and
- concerns about achievement levels of minority-group learners and females.

Efforts to End Legal Segregation

The 1954 Supreme Court case *Brown v. Board of Education* established a legal guideline that led to the dismantling of segregated school systems. However, the effort to achieve a school system featuring a cross section of students from a wide variety of

Critical Incident

Defending a Comprehensive Multicultural Education Program

While carefully balancing her cup of coffee, Cheri Leblanc took a seat in the chair next to the desk of Victor Birdsong, Elmwood Senior High School's vice principal for curriculum. Victor hung up the phone as he finished his call and looked up at Cheri, the school's highly respected head of the English department.

"I need some advice, Vic."

Victor nodded, smiled, and said, "How may I help?"

"It's about the school-wide curriculum committee you've had me chair—the one planning a new, comprehensive multicultural program."

"Oh yes," Victor replied. "That's the one with representatives from each department, some students, some parents, and a few community members. I thought you'd finished your work and were about to make your recommendation."

"That's just the difficulty. We *are* finished with our work. We've been at it for over a year now, and most of us think we've come up with a great plan. Members voted to recommend the program by a vote of 16 to 4. While it would have been nice to have everybody on board, given the controversial nature of the subject, I thought a 4-to-1 margin was as close to consensus as we'd ever get."

Victor reacted with a puzzled frown. "Tell me more. You've come to a decision that just about everybody supports, and there's still a problem?"

"Yes, there is," Cheri continued. "The four who voted against it absolutely refuse to accept the results of the vote. They plan to go the school board meeting tonight to express their dismay with our decision. They think they can convince the board to intervene and block implementation of the plan."

Victor's shoulders slumped at this news. "That's all we need—a public fight pitting one group of committee members against another. As a start, help me understand the specifics of the new plan."

Cheri pulled notes from a folder. Briefly, she scanned them looking for a summary she had written. "All right, Vic, here it is in a nutshell. If you think of the overall plan as a pie, we have three major slices or pieces: the curriculum piece, the learner-success piece, and the social-action piece."

"Tell me a little about each," said Vic as he reached for a yellow note pad and a pen. "I'll take a few notes."

"Fine. Let me begin with the curriculum piece. This part of the program features changes in the subject-matter content we teach. These changes will ensure that we provide good information about the contributions of people from many different ethnic, cultural, and language groups."

"The second major slice of the pie," Cheri continued," is the individual learner piece. This commits us to working closely with students from all groups to ensure they are achieving academic success. In part, this will require us to see whether there are any differences associated with ethnic, cultural, or language backgrounds of students and how students are doing in specific subject areas. If we uncover problems, we want to develop instructional approaches that will eliminate them."

Victor wrote a few comments on his notepad, looked up, and asked, "And the third piece?"

"The third piece, Vic, focuses on what we call social action. We propose providing lessons to students to encourage them to examine both legal and informal practices that sometimes have disadvantaged certain categories of people. For example, we know that sometimes people living in particular neighborhoods have had difficulty getting housing loans. We're not trying to create revolutionaries here. Our purpose is just to sensitize students to the idea of 'fairness' and to encourage them to participate actively in the political process to support efforts to promote equity."

Victor wrote a few additional notes. He continued looking down at his notepad. Satisfied that he had captured the essential points Cheri had made, he said, "Let's move on to the concerns of the four people who plan to speak at the school board meeting. Is there a particular one of these three pieces they object to?"

Cheri shook her head. "Vic, at first I thought there was something specific that was bothering them. If that were the case, I thought we might win their support by fine tuning or even eliminating something. When we pressed them for details, it became evident that they oppose the whole idea of a multicultural curriculum."

Victor looked pensive. "Cheri, that surprises me, given the changes in the makeup of the student population in recent years. The professional journals also have had article after article on the need for school programs that are attuned to perspectives of different groups. What exactly is it that these four don't like?"

"In general, their argument is that multicultural programs are unpatriotic," responded Cheri. "They believe that school programs should work harder at bringing people together. Several of them pointed out in our meetings that anyone who walks through our cafeteria at noon will see clusters of African Americans, clusters of Latinos, and clusters of students from other groups. They say students identify too much with 'their own kind' and that our multicultural programs, by emphasizing these differences, will make the problem worse. I think all of them would be more comfortable with something we might call the 'Americanism curriculum' that would emphasize those things members of different groups have in common rather than those things that separate them."

. . .

What are some values implied by the multicultural curriculum proposed by Cheri Leblanc's committee? How have members perceived any problems that should be addressed? What specific remedies have they proposed? What values are suggested by the positions taken by the four people who refused to endorse the curriculum committee's proposal? What things are important to these four, and what would they have the school do to address their priorities? What advice do you think Victor Birdsong will give to Cheri Leblanc? How do you think the school board will react to the positions taken by the four teachers who want to speak against the new multicultural curriculum? What would you do next if you were Cheri Leblanc?

GW To respond to this Critical Incident online, and to save or submit your response electronically, visit the companion Web site, located at *http://www.prenhall.com/armstrong*. Select Chapter 4 from the front page of the Web site, then choose the Critical Incidents module on the navigation bar on the left side of the page. Instructors and students may also wish to use these scenarios as discussion topics on the Message Board for the companion Web site.

Perspectives of individuals from different ethnic and cultural backgrounds enrich understandings of all learners.

ethnic and racial backgrounds has been only moderately successful. A key 1974 Supreme Court decision in the case of *Milliken v. Bradley* held that courts lacked authority to order busing between districts for the purpose of achieving racial balance in the schools. This has meant that busing has been authorized as an option only within the boundaries of individual school districts.

In districts with homogeneous populations, the *Milliken v. Bradley* restriction has made it difficult for school authorities to organize schools that reflect a broad ethnic and racial diversity. For example, the nation's inner cities are becoming increasingly African American and Latino, while the suburbs remain predominantly White. As a result, a large number of inner-city schools are overwhelmingly African American, Latino, or a combination of both. Similarly, many suburban schools are overwhelmingly White. Despite efforts to achieve integrated schools, "there is evidence that the number of U.S. students attending racially isolated schools is now on the rise" (Bates, 1990, p. 9).

Today, many learners attend schools with others who are much like themselves. This pattern suggests that they have few opportunities to interact with young people from other cultural and ethnic backgrounds. This means that many young people go to schools with student populations that are not representative of the cultural and ethnic makeup of our pluralistic society (Vergon, 1989). Educators continue to be concerned about this situation.

Within-School Segregation

Even in school districts that have managed to create student bodies that embrace a mixture of learners from different cultural and ethic groups, segregation continues to be a concern. The issue in such places relates not to a legal, physical separation of learners along ethnic or racial lines, but instead a kind of segregation that may result from how learners from different groups are assigned to courses.

Within-school segregation of students along cultural, racial, and even gender lines is particularly serious at the secondary school level. College preparatory courses in many high schools enroll disproportionately high percentages of White students. Remedial courses, on the other hand, frequently have much higher percentages of minority-group students enrolled than these students' numbers within the total school population would warrant.

In addition, male students comprise high percentages of some high school classes. For example, 80% of students enrolled in high school physical science classes are male (Simon-McWilliams, 1989). Males are also overrepresented in many special education classes; they are 1.7 times as likely as females to be classified as mentally retarded, trainable mentally retarded, or seriously emotionally disturbed. Minority-group students are 1.6 times as likely as White students to be placed in special education classes (Simon-McWilliams, 1989).

There is a relationship between a student's race or ethnic group and his or her likelihood of being suspended from school. Minority-group students are suspended from school at nearly twice the rate of their White counterparts. African American students are particularly likely to be suspended; their rate of suspension is three times that of White students (Bates, 1990).

Professionals who are concerned about the issue of within-school segregation are not satisfied with a simple count of the number of learners from various ethnic and racial groups who are enrolled in a given school. They want evidence that there are efforts to serve *all* learners in ways that will maximize their individual development. Further, they argue that learners will not develop multicultural sensitivity and an acceptance for diversity if individual classes within the school resegregate the learner population.

Concerns About Achievement Levels

The issue of achievement levels ties closely to concerns about within-school segregation. If academic standards in classes to which certain groups of learners have been assigned are not high, it should be no surprise when these learners fare poorly on achievement tests. Many high school students who aspire to continue their education in a college or university take the Scholastic Achievement Test (SAT). African American and Latino students' scores on these tests have continually lagged behind White students' scores, and females have generally received lower scores than males on the quantitative portion of the SAT. These patterns suggest that the benefits of schooling are not equally accorded to students regardless of their race, ethnicity, or gender.

Generally, more benefits accrue to a learner the longer he or she stays in school. Ideally, there should be no difference in the dropout rates associated with race or ethnicity. This, however, is not the case. For example, in one recent year, percentages of

16- to 24-year-olds who were neither enrolled in high school nor had graduated from high school were 29.4% for Latinos, 13.0% for African Americans, and 7.3% for Whites (Pratt, 1998). Over time, dropout rates have improved for all racial and ethnic groups. For example, the dropout rate for African American children today is about half what it was in the 1970s.

Regrettably, the dropout rate of Latino learners, though improved over levels in previous levels, remains extremely high. Since Latinos are the nation's most rapidly growing minority group, these figures greatly concern educators. Unless we do a better job of preparing Latino learners, an ever larger percentage of our population is going to be ill-prepared to contribute to a society that increasingly requires an educated workforce.

As you think about these figures, you must not assume that learners' race and ethnicity alone explain these patterns. The reality is that African American and Latino learners tend to be overrepresented in other groups whose levels of school achievement falls below national averages. For example, investigators have found the following to be true of the general population of African American learners (Sable, 1998):

African American learners are more likely than White children

- to live in poverty,
- to live in single-parent households, and
- to live in urban areas.

There are similar patterns that help explain performance differences between Latino and White learners. Consider these points (Sable & Stennett, 1998):

- From the middle 1980s through the end of the 1990s, the likelihood a Latino child would be living in poverty with a single parent increased.
- Latino 3- and 4-year-olds are less likely to participate in preprimary education and in early literacy activities than are white 3- and 4-year-olds.

While it is true that performance levels of African American and Latino learners continue to lag behind those of White learners, you need to understand that there has been progress in addressing this concern. For example, we know that parents greatly influence what their children learn. The educational attainment of parents of African American children and their active involvement in their children's education have increased in recent years. Today, much higher percentages of African American high school students enroll in advanced courses than they did in the 1980s. Performance gaps between African American and White learners' scores in reading, mathematics, and science have narrowed over time (Sable, 1998).

In addition, Latino learners' parents' levels of education and tendency to become actively involved in their children's schools have increased in recent years. Latino children are taking more rigorous high school courses, particularly advanced placement courses, than they did in previous years. Latino high school graduates who go on to colleges and universities are more likely than White students to pursue degrees in computer and information sciences (Sable & Stennett, 1998).

We mentioned earlier the failure of females to score as high as males on the quantitative sections of the SAT. Although more women than men complete baccalaureate degree programs, relatively few elect to pursue advanced work in mathematics and the sciences. Inadequate mathematics background, which too often is a legacy of their experiences in the public schools, often explains the dearth of females in this group.

Some authorities have hinted that public education has not made a serious effort to develop female learners' abilities in mathematics because of a faulty assumption about their aptitude for the content (Chipman & Thomas, 1987). Some research has demonstrated very minor gender-related differences in males and females in terms of their abilities to deal with spatial abstractions. Chipman and Thomas (1987) argue that there has never been any established connection between the kinds of spatial abilities for which there are slight gender differences and the ability to master mathematics; however, a mythology has developed that females are not good at mathematics. Hence, at least in some schools, female students have not been held to the same achievement expectations in mathematics as have been males.

Unless this pattern is broken, females may be disadvantaged in their efforts to break into technical fields. Today, fewer females than males enroll in university programs in mathematics and the sciences. This is true despite the fact that females, as a group, attend colleges and universities in higher numbers than males (Pratt, 1998). A continuation of this under-enrollment in math and science courses may keep many females from well paid technical employment.

Today, educators strive to ensure that opportunities in all subject areas are available to male and female learners alike. As this photo shows, some subjects, such as woodworking, were in the past considered to be "male"; others, such as sewing and baking, were considered to be "female."

THE NEED FOR ACCURATE INFORMATION

To plan effective school programs, educators need accurate information about minority-group learners and the capabilities of male and female learners. Superficial understanding of these issues can lead to school practices that fail because they rest upon faulty assumptions. For example, as noted previously, researchers have found no basis for the widespread belief that females, as a group, are not good at mathematics. The companion piece of street wisdom about males is that they are not as good at reading and writing as are females. Research has also failed to support this myth.

Assumptions about learners from cultural and ethnic minorities also sometimes prompt irresponsible actions on the part of school officials. As a teacher, you need to recognize the important differences that exist *within* individual groups. For example, values and perspectives of African Americans in rural areas often have little in common with those of African Americans in the nation's inner cities. (Additionally, there is by no means a common world view that characterizes all urban African Americans or one that is common to all rural African Americans.)

The nation's Latino population is extremely diverse. Some critics charge that there has been a tendency for school authorities to view all Latinos as linguistically at risk and to treat them as "culturally deficient and linguistically deprived foreigners. This treatment helps to explain their high dropout rate, their underrepresentation in advanced courses, and their low rate of college attendance" (Grant, 1990, p. 27). Grant also points out that only a minority of Latino learners have a native language other than English. Clearly, school programs that presume the entire group to be nonnative speakers of English do them an injustice.

Developing school programs that reflect a genuine appreciation for issues associated with multicultural and gender equity requires you to be well-informed. The need you will face as a teacher to develop sensitivity to the special perspectives of groups from which your learners come will grow even more important as the nation's school population becomes more diverse.

GOALS AND GENERAL SUGGESTIONS FOR TEACHERS

Many individuals and professional groups seek to improve school programs in ways that will better serve the needs of ethnic and cultural minorities and females. There is a growing recognition that the nation can ill afford to do anything less than fully develop the talents of all of its young people. With each passing year, the number of jobs open to high school graduates decreases, and the number requiring at least a bachelor's degree goes up. Even though there has been some improvement in this situation, the high school dropout rate of minority-group learners raises serious concerns. If present trends continue, people with less than a high school education are going to find it difficult to secure employment.

Numerous recommendations have been made regarding what educators should do to respond to multicultural and equity needs (Banks with Clegg, Jr., 1988; Bates, 1990; Marshall, 1990; Armstrong & Savage, 1998). Several suggestions you might wish to consider are discussed under the topics that follow.

Commitment to the Idea That All Can Learn

Unless you sincerely believe that young people from ethnic and cultural groups can learn, there is little likelihood their learning performance will be impressive. Your assumptions about learners will influence your expectations regarding what they can do. If you do not expect much, you should not be surprised when few in your classes attain high levels of academic achievement. Learners who are not challenged achieve below their capacities and are not encouraged to stay in school. If you want the learners you teach to leave school ready for college, a university, or the workplace, you must have faith in the capacity of all of them to learn. If you do not, they will lack the confidence necessary for success.

Modifying Grouping Practices

Grouping practices in many schools have acted to the disadvantage of ethnic and cultural minority learners. Young people who are shunted into a low-ability group early in their school years tend to fall farther behind their peers with each passing year.

Grouping decisions occur at several levels. Sometimes, ability grouping results in the creation of entire classes of learners who are thought to be in a given category. For example, a high school may have a freshman English class specifically designated for low-ability students. This kind of grouping can undermine learners' confidence in their own abilities. In addition, the content to which they are exposed often is less rigorous than that introduced in so-called regular classes, thus impairing their preparation for more advanced work.

You need to be cautious about grouping practices that distribute learners into high-ability, intermediate-ability, and low-ability groups. Sometimes such approaches have resulted in assignment of disproportionate numbers of learners from cultural and ethnic minorities to so-called "low-ability" groups. If this happens in your own class, you may find yourself open to charges that your sorting mechanism was based not on a true measure of ability but rather on an assumption that learners from certain minority groups are less academically able than others in your class. In general, within-class groups function more positively when they are not organized with a view to standardizing ability levels of members within each group and when learners in each group constitute a representative racial, cultural, and gender sample of the entire class.

Accommodating Learning Style Differences

Individuals' learning styles vary. Researchers have found that learners' cultural backgrounds influence their preference for a given instructional style (Grant & Sleeter, 1994). This conclusion suggests that you need to plan lessons that allow individual learners to approach content in different ways. Some young people profit from opportunities to touch and manipulate objects. Others do just fine when they are asked to read new information. Still others respond well to opportunities to work with photographs, charts, or other graphic representations of data. The tendency for individuals to change their preferred learning styles as they mature complicates matters for teachers (Sternberg, 1994). This implies that you need to be "prepared to understand and meet the needs of students who come to school with varying learning styles, and with differing beliefs about themselves and what school means to them" (Darling-Hammond, 1993, p. 775).

Becoming Aware of Your Own Perspectives

Because majority-group perspectives are so pervasive, teachers who are White often fail to recognize the extent to which their own world views have been conditioned by their membership in the majority. The reality is that all ethnic and cultural groups, including the White majority, have certain established assumptions about "how the world is" and about what constitutes "proper" behavior.

If you have not taken time to think about your own assumptions about reality, you may make the mistake of assuming that everybody shares your basic views. This kind of thinking can create problems for you when you work with learners from ethnic and cultural backgrounds whose fundamental perspectives may be quite different from your own. For example, if you have not bothered to learn anything about the traditional culture of Thailand, you may be surprised at the negative reaction of a Thai child to a light touch on the head. Your intent may be to convey concern and friendship, but to a child raised in a Thai home, the gesture may be interpreted as an offensive invasion of privacy.

Less Reliance on Standardized Tests

In recent years, the producers of standardized tests have enjoyed prosperous times. Legislators throughout the nation clamor for information about the quality of public school programs, and standardized test results seem irresistibly attractive as a source of evidence people can use to identify good, mediocre, and poor schools. These tests summarize tremendous amounts of information in numerical form, and they allow for easy school-to-school comparisons. In addition, the public finds these numerical ratings easy to understand.

At best, standardized tests provide an extremely limited view of an individual learner's capabilities. Many tests probe only very low-level kinds of mental processes; few can assess higher level thinking skills. Because of the importance of test scores, in some places there are great pressures for teachers to "teach to the test." This has the potential to trivialize the kinds of content addressed in the classroom. For example, if you find yourself teaching in a school district that places an excessive emphasis on standardized-test results, you may be tempted to de-emphasize the importance of developing your learners' higher level thinking skills.

Standardized tests pose particular problems for young people from ethnic and cultural minorities. Critics contend that standardized tests serve to deny opportunities for minority-group learners to continue their education beyond the high school level. They also point out that a system that limits the continued academic development of the fastest growing component of the total school population makes little sense. Instead, they argue, assessment techniques are needed that foster the maximum development of minority-group learners' talents. Further, these assessment techniques should encourage the development of sophisticated thinking abilities, not simply reinforce the recall-level thinking called for on most of today's standardized tests.

Ideally, assessment procedures should take into account background characteristics that typify many minority-group learners. This means the vocabulary of assessment instruments needs to be responsive to the learners' environments. In addition, opportunities these learners have had outside of school should be considered. (For example, how many poor inner-city children have computers at home? How many have traveled extensively? How many of their families subscribe to a large number of periodicals?) In summary, teachers should use assessment techniques that look at these young people's potential for future development, not at what they have failed to learn because of conditions beyond their control.

Avoiding Favoritism in the Classroom

Teachers are human. When you begin teaching, you will find you have better relationships with some learners than with others. In the classroom, however, professionalism demands that you make an effort to encourage each learner's development. It is particularly important for your learners to believe that they will not be singled out in any kind of a negative way because of their ethnicity, race, or gender.

You need to strive for equity in your relationships with learners. Episodes of misbehavior must be treated similarly, regardless of who the offender is. Similarly, you need to provide encouragement to all who perform well. You must remember that all of your young people need to feel they will be treated fairly. Your credibility depends on this perception. When your learners believe you are not being fair, their motivation declines and academic performance deteriorates. As a result, you will likely find yourself dealing with more discipline problems.

Providing Good Teachers

In some instances, the concern of providing good teachers is related to the issue of grouping. The best teachers may be assigned to high-ability classes that often enroll few learners from ethnic and cultural minority groups. When this occurs, many learners who greatly need motivating and caring teachers do not get them. School leaders need to encourage outstanding teachers to work with minority-group learners. This step will require a clear break with present patterns where teachers in predominantly minority schools tend to be less experienced, more likely to be teaching out of their fields, and more likely to be holding emergency certificates than teachers in schools where White learners form a majority.

PROMISING INITIATIVES

Success in promoting positive attitudes about various cultures requires a willingness for you to go beyond just studying about these cultures. You also have to teach your learners about them. There is a growing recognition that multicultural perspectives

Following the Web **4.1**

Serving Learners from Minority Groups

Any good Web search engine will identify dozens of sites with information related to working with minority-group learners. Contents vary from scholarly treatments of research, to bibliographies, to general recommendations for teachers, to quite specific information about working with learners from particular minority groups. We provide some brief descriptions of sites you might like to visit.

For hot links to these sites, visit the companion Web site, located at *http://www.prenhall.com/armstrong*. Select Chapter 4 from the front page of the Web site, then choose the Following the Web module on the navigation bar on the left side of the page.

Guidelines for Addressing Student Sexist or Racist Interactions

- *http://equity.enc.org/equity/eqtyres/erg/111469/1469.htm*

    This site provides some excellent practical advice for responding to racist and sexist classroom behaviors. You will find some excellent practical answers to questions you might have about dealing with these situations.

Critical Issue: Educating Teachers for Diversity

- *http://www.ncrel.org/skrs/areas/issues/educatrs/presrvce/pe300.htm*

    If you are looking for an excellent overview of issues related to preparing teachers to respond to diversity in their classrooms, this is a site you should visit. In addition to general information about this important topic, you will find a lengthy list of organizations that you can contact for further assistance. Postal addresses, telephone numbers, and Web addresses are included.

Multicultural Mathematics: A More Inclusive Mathematics

- *http://inet.ed.gov/databases/ERIC_Digests/ed380295.html*

    Some learners from ethnic, cultural, and language minorities have not fared well in mathematics classes. The ERIC Clearinghouse for Science, Mathematics, and Environmental Education compiled this material. You will find some practical ideas for helping minority-group learners succeed in mathematics classes. This site also includes an excellent accompanying bibliography.

Resources for English Teachers

- *http://goldmine.cde.ca.gov/cilbranch/bien/bien.htm*

    Compiled by the California Department of Education, information at this site focuses on teaching learners with a home language other than English. You will find numerous links to other Web locations that feature information about working with bilingual and English-as-a-second-language learners.

Whose Side Are You On? Multicultural Education at the Close of the 20th Century

- *http://www.aacte.org/pubs/brf5498.html*

  This short article was prepared by the American Association of Colleges for Teacher Education. This national group links schools and colleges of education throughout the country. At this site, you will find an overview of issues related to multicultural education including (1) curricular reactions to racism, (2) status-quo multicultural education, and (3) multicultural, curriculum transformation.

A Synthesis of Scholarship in Multicultural Education

- *http://www.ncrel.org/sdrs/areas/issues/envrnmnt/go/leogay.htm*

  Geneva Gay, a leading scholar in the area of multicultural education, prepared the material for this site. Though it is somewhat lengthy, if you are looking for an excellent summary of recent scholarly work related to multiculturalism this is a "must-visit" site.

Fostering Intercultural Harmony in Schools: Research Findings

- *http://www.nwrel.org/scpd/sirs/8/topsyn7.html*

  The Northwest Regional Educational Laboratory, as part of ERIC's School Improvement Research Series, distributed this material, which was prepared by Kathleen Cotton. As the title suggests, you will find research-based information related to practices that have been found effective when the objective has been to promote racial harmony in schools.

National Equity Online Calendar

- *http://mdac2.educ.ksu.edu/calendar/3/m0.html*

  This is an example of a site with a narrow focus. You will find here a calendar that reports dates of events throughout the country that relate to equity issues. Visitors to the site are invited to add events of their own.

Welcome to the American Indian Science and Engineering Society—Multicultural Educational Reform Efforts

- *http://spot.colorado.edu/~aises/aises.html*

  This is an example of a site with a very specialized purpose, namely to promote the study of science and engineering among learners of Native American heritage. The site is maintained by the American Indian Science and Engineering Society (AISES), which has its headquarters in Colorado.

[Note: Web addresses change frequently. If you are unable to locate one of these sites using the listed URL, try putting the site name in a standard search engine.]

need to be developed across the entire curriculum. Minority-group learners are enrolled in every subject schools offer. It only makes sense for you to take their needs into account when you plan your instructional programs.

Increasing numbers of teacher-preparation programs now include content related to multiculturalism. In fact, the National Council for Accreditation of Teacher Education (NCATE), the national accrediting body for teacher-education programs, insists that such training be provided and that future teachers have opportunities for field experiences that bring them into contact with culturally diverse learners. Over time, these preparation programs may provide our schools with more teachers who have the knowledge base necessary to respond effectively to perspectives and needs of young people from varied ethnic and cultural backgrounds.

Problems associated with learners' race, ethnicity, and gender are serious, but there are school programs in operation that address them successfully. We will examine two such programs here.

The Work of James Comer

Beginning in the late 1960s, James Comer and several of his associates from the Yale Child Study Center developed a program that was adopted in two schools in New Haven, Connecticut. Learners in these schools had the lowest scores on standardized achievement tests and the poorest attendance records of all schools in the district. Populations of the two schools were 99% African American, and the vast majority of learners came from families whose incomes fell below the official poverty line. The Comer team installed a program based on well-researched principles of child development and participatory management. Fifteen years after the program began, although the racial and economic makeup of the schools' population was unchanged, standardized test scores of learners were above national averages. These scores were close to the top of all New Haven schools' scores, and attendance records of learners at the two minority schools were outstanding (Comer, 1988).

The plan initially instituted in the two New Haven schools, known now as the "Comer model," has been widely adopted. Perhaps its most important feature is *shared decision making.* Principals in Comer-model schools invite parents, teachers, and school support staff members (particularly those concerned with learners' mental health) to take part in the decision-making process. These individuals constitute a management team that sets school policies. The Comer model places an emphasis on developing solutions to problems rather than on assigning blame when young people fail to learn. These solutions have been supported by a bedrock assumption that all pupils and students in the schools *can* learn. The inclusive management structure and the flexibility to take quick action to respond to problems have been credited with much of the success of Comer-model schools.

James Comer has found shared decision making to be an important ingredient in schools that have successfully served large populations of minority-group students. These parents, teachers, administrators, and school support staff members are considering some changes in the school curriculum.

Schools That Do a Good Job with Language-Minority Learners

Millions of learners speak a language other than English as their first language. They need to know English to succeed in school and to be competitive in the job market. Congress recognized the special needs of these children when it passed the Bilingual Education Act in 1968. This act requires schools to provide initial instruction in a learner's first language until a level of English proficiency is reached that will allow for success in classrooms where only English is used.

The concern for educating these learners was underscored in the 1974 decision of *Lau v. Nichols,* which required local school districts to develop approaches that would ensure that learners with limited English proficiency were not denied a meaningful education. The court argued that simply providing these learners with the same curriculum and texts as native speakers of English would not suffice.

Many programs have been established to help nonnative speakers of English succeed. Some attempts have been undertaken to identify specific characteristics of schools that have served nonnative English speakers well. One study focused on secondary schools with huge majorities of students who had Spanish as their native language. Contrary to the national pattern, students in these schools scored high on standardized tests, tended not to drop out of school, and had much higher than average high school graduation rates. The researchers found special features in these schools that seemed to account for their success. Specifically, the team (Lucas, Henze, & Donato, 1990) identified the following characteristics:

- Value is placed on students' languages and cultures.
- High expectations of language-minority learners are made concrete.
- School leaders make the education of language-minority learners a priority.
- Staff development is explicitly designed to help teachers and other staff serve language-minority students more effectively.

Video Viewpoint

California Proposition 227

WATCH: In this ABC News video segment, Ron Unz, a co-author of Proposition 227, and Teresa Bustillos, an opponent of Proposition 227, discuss the bill that, if passed, would end the current system of bilingual education in California. Proponents of Proposition 227 argue that the current bilingual education program in California is a failure and that full immersion techniques for helping non-English speakers learn the language work most effectively. Critics of the bill say it is a one-size-fits-all solution that doesn't take into account different individuals' rates of language acquisition, the need for students to keep up in their other subjects, or local resources, and that it ignores bilingual education programs that work.

THINK: With your classmates, or in your teaching journal, consider these questions:

1. What are some effective classroom strategies for dealing with language-minority learners?
2. Do you agree with or oppose California's Proposition 227? Support your position.
3. Find out how California voters decided regarding Proposition 227, and discuss why the bilingual education issue is still making news several years after this election.

LINK: How might English-speaking students benefit from having students whose native language is not English in their classrooms?

- A variety of courses and programs for language-minority students is offered.
- A counseling program gives special attention to language-minority students.
- Parents of language-minority students are encouraged to become involved in their children's education.
- School staff members share a strong commitment to empower language-minority students through education.

Programs in these schools pay particular attention to developing learners' levels of proficiency in *both* English and Spanish. For example, some feature advanced literature classes that allow students to study the works of Cervantes and other luminaries of Latino literature in the original Spanish. The entire program builds learners' pride in their cultural heritage at the same time that it provides them with the tough intellectual tools needed to qualify for both university entrance and decent jobs in the workplace.

USEFUL INFORMATION SOURCES

In addition to the many places on the World Wide Web (see this chapter's "Following the Web" sections) where you can find information related to cultural, ethnic, and gender equity, much excellent print material is also available. Professional periodicals regularly publish articles with helpful ideas that you can use in the classroom. Some excellent books are also available. A particularly good one, which provides excellent lesson ideas for teachers, has been written by Carl A. Grant and Christine E. Sleeter; it is titled *Making Choices for Multicultural Education: Five Approaches to Race, Class, and Gender,* 3rd edition (New York: Maxwell Macmillan International, 1998). You might also enjoy reading *An Introduction to Multicultural Education,* 2nd edition, by James A. Banks (Boston: Allyn & Bacon, 1998).

Calendars with references to dates and events of interest to many different ethnic groups are available from these sources:

- National Conference
  71 5th Avenue
  New York, NY 10003
  (212) 206-0006
- Educational Extension Systems
  P.O. Box 259
  Clarks Summit, PA 18411
  (717) 586-6490

The following places are sources of other material that you can use to prepare lessons with a multicultural focus. Write them to ask for materials for classroom teachers and learners. In your letters, suggest grade levels of learners for whom you might be preparing lessons.

- The Balch Institute for Ethnic Studies
  18 South Seventh Street
  Philadelphia, PA 19106
  (215) 925-8090
  http://www.libertynet.org/balch/body_index.html
- Center for Migration Studies of New York, Inc.
  209 Flagg Place
  Staten Island, NY 10304-1199
  (718) 351-8800
  http://cmsny.org/
- Center for the Study of Ethnic Publications and Cultural Institutions
  Kent State University
  Kent, OH 44242
  (216) 672-2782
- Immigration History Research Center
  University of Minnesota
  826 Berry Street
  St. Paul, MN 55114
  (612) 627-4208
  http://www1.umn.edu/ihrc/index.htm#menu
- Institute of Texan Cultures
  801 South Bowie Street
  San Antonio, TX 78205
  (210) 458-2300
  http://www.texancultures.utsa.edu/

Following the Web 4.2

Gender Equity Information

Today, many Web sites provide information related to the issue of gender equity. Some of these sites focus on general educational issues, particularly those having to do with how female learners fare in the schools. Others contain material having a narrower focus, such as encouraging females to enter such traditionally male-dominated occupational areas as science and engineering. Consider visiting some of the sites listed below.

 For hot links to these sites, visit the companion Web site, located at *http://www.prenhall.com/armstrong*. Select Chapter 4 from the front page of the Web site, then choose the Following the Web module on the navigation bar on the left side of the page.

Gender-Equity Resources for K–12 Teachers

- *http://209.109.218.244/4000/gender.html*

  As the title suggests, you will find material here about gender-equity resources for teachers. This site, maintained by the American Association of University Women (AAUW), includes numerous links to useful information sources.

Equity Resources: Web Resources

- *http://equity.enc.org/equity/eqtyres/index3.htm*

  This site features 30 links to equity-related Web sites. Furthermore, there is a thumbnail description of kinds of information that each site provides. If you want to develop a quick "feel" for what kind of gender-equity materials are available, this site should be one of your first stops.

AAUW, Blacksburg Area Branch, Initiative for Educational Equity Committee: Listing of Gender-Equity Web Sites

- *http://www.mfrl.org/compages/aauw/gequity.html*

  This is another Web site that features a huge list of other sites with gender-equity information. Lists are subdivided into categories that include (1) AAUW K–12

There are also information sources for materials with a gender-equity focus. A good list of materials is available from the Upper Midwest Women's History Center for Teachers. The address is:

- Upper Midwest Women's History Center for Teachers
  Hamline University, 749 Simpson Street
  St. Paul, MN 55104
  (651) 644-1727
  http://www.hamline.edu/~umwhc/index.html

Other good sources for gender-equity information and materials include the following:

- Organization of the Equal Education of the Sexes
  P.O. Box 438
  Blue Hill, ME 04614
  http://www.parentsoup.com/library/organizations/bpd00424.html

Resources, (2) Gender-Equity Projects, (3) Science and Gender Equity, (4) Gender-Equity Education and Training, and (5) Other Gender-Equity Web sites.

AWSEM Gender Equity: Facts in Brief

- *http://www.awsem.com/gender.html*

  This page includes material distributed by Advocates for Women in Science, Engineering, and Mathematics. It features some fascinating statistical information. You will learn, for example, that over a third of high school girls reported a faculty member advised them not to take senior math and that females leave careers in science and engineering at twice the rate of males.

The WEEA Digest on Line

- *http://www.edc.org/WomensEquity/pubs/digests/index.html*

  The Women's Equity Education Act (WEEA) Equity Resource Center periodically prints its *Digest*. Each issue focuses on a timely issue related to theory, research, and policies with relevance for the education of females. For example, there have been issues focusing on esteem problems of female teenagers, sexual harassment, equity in sports leadership, and gender identity of middle school learners. You can look at individual issues or order multiple copies of the *Digest* at this Web site.

WEEA Resources for Black History Month

- *http://www.edc.org/WomensEquity/black.html*

  February is Black History Month. This site provides an interesting collection of materials related to African American females that might be included in lessons during this part of the school year. You will find nice synopses of each listed title.

[Note: Web addresses change frequently. If you are unable to locate one of these sites using the listed URL, try putting the site name in a standard search engine.]

- Population Reference Bureau, Inc.
  1875 Connecticut Avenue NW, Suite 520
  Washington, DC 20009-5728
  (202) 483-1100
  http://www.prb.org/prb/
- The National Women's History Project
  7738 Bell Road
  Windsor, CA 95492
  (707) 838-6000
  http://www.nwhp.org
- United Nations Development Fund for Women (UNIFEM)
  304 East 45th Street, 6th Floor
  New York, NY 10017
  (212) 906-6400
  http://www.unifem.undp.org

Key Ideas In Summary

- The learner population is becoming increasingly diverse in terms of its cultural and ethnic makeup. This reality challenges teachers to provide instruction that appropriately fits the background of each child in the classroom. The more lessons respect and respond to these differences, the higher the probability learners will achieve success at school. Academic success breeds self-confidence, and it also leads to positive attitudes toward schooling and teachers.

- Multicultural education seeks to result in educational equity for all learners. It does this by drawing on insights from history, the social and behavioral sciences, and especially from ethnic studies and women's studies.

- In the early and middle years of the twentieth century, many learners from ethnic and cultural minorities were viewed as having a genetic deficit that accounted for their low levels of academic achievement. Later, this explanation gave way to a cultural deficit view that attributed poor school performance to a failure of the learner's home environment to support school learning. The genetic deficit and cultural deficit positions are now generally rejected. It is recognized that the failure of many minority-group children to learn is due to the failure of schools to provide programs responsive to their needs.

- The case of *Brown v. Board of Education* (1954) led to the dismantling of segregated school systems. A subsequent decision, *Milliken v. Bradley* (1974), held that courts did not have a right to order busing *across* district lines for the purpose of integrating schools. As a result, schools in many places continue to enroll disproportionately large numbers of learners from certain cultural and ethnic groups because the groups are very heavily represented within the boundaries of their given school district. Many inner-city school districts, for example, have populations that are largely African American or Latino. There are not enough White learners in these districts to supply a high percentage of such learners to any school, even when the district tries to achieve a racial balance.

- There are many concerns today about within-school segregation. Many college-preparatory programs in high schools enroll higher percentages of White students than are represented in the overall student body, while learners from ethnic and cultural minorities are overrepresented in special education classes. Segregation by gender has also been observed; for example, the overwhelming majority of learners in high school physical science classes are male.

- Standardized achievement scores of African American and Latino learners have continually lagged behind those of White students. Dropout rates are also higher for African Americans and Latinos than for Whites. In recent years, the dropout rate for African American learners has improved; however, the rate for Latinos remains far too high.

- In responding to needs of minority-group learners and females, educators must take care to operate on the basis of accurate information. It is particularly important that they do not make incorrect generalizations on the basis of inaccurate or incomplete information. For example, the idea that female learners are less capable of mastering mathematics than males persists in many places despite contrary evidence. Generalizations regarding Latinos sometimes hint at their probable difficulty with English because it is not their native language, whereas, in fact, English *is* the first language for a majority of Latino learners. Similarly, not all African Americans lives in the inner city or are economically deprived.

- Recommendations for improving the quality of educational services for ethnic and cultural minority learners include (1) a commitment to the idea that everyone can learn, (2) modification of grouping practices, (3) making certain that teachers are aware of their own perspectives, (4) relying less on standardized tests, (5) ensuring that teachers avoid favoritism in the classroom, and (6) assigning good teachers to work with minority-group learners.
- James Comer and his associates have developed a model for organizing schools to promote greater achievement levels among minority-group learners. Achievement gains by learners in these schools have been impressive. The Comer-model schools feature shared decision making, whereby principals are but part of a management team that also includes parents, teachers, and school support members.
- This nation has a strong commitment to bilingual education, which involves teaching learners in their native language until they become proficient in English. This commitment was evidenced by the passage of the Bilingual Education Act in 1968 and was buttressed by a famous 1974 court case, *Lau v. Nichols,* which, in effect, required schools to provide meaningful programs for learners with first languages other than English.

Chapter 4 Self Test

To review terms and concepts in this chapter, take the Chapter 4 Self Test on the companion Web site, located at *http://www.prenhall.com/armstrong*. Select Chapter 4 from the front page of the Web site, then choose the Self Test module on the navigation bar on the left side of the page. Feedback for the Self Test is immediate. You can keep track of your Self Test scores yourself, or you can choose to submit your scores via e-mail to your instructor.

Reflections

To respond to these questions online, and to save or submit your response electronically, visit the companion Web site, located at *http://www.prenhall.com/armstrong*. Select Chapter 4 from the front page of the Web site, then choose the Reflections module on the navigation bar on the left side of the page. Instructors and students may also wish to use these questions as discussion topics on the Message Board for the Companion Web site.

1. How do schools differ in terms of their racial, ethnic, and linguistic characteristics?
2. How would you assess the adequacy of the genetic deficit and the cultural deficit positions as explanations for the failure of many minority-group learners to do well in school?
3. What are some reasons that certain schools, despite national progress toward desegregation, still enroll learners who

overwhelmingly are members of a single ethnic group?

4. Give some examples that illustrate within-school segregation.

5. What are some characteristics of schools that have high percentages of minority-group learners who score well on tests of academic achievement?

6. What does research say about females' abilities to learn mathematics?

7. What are some problems that have resulted when people have made careless generalizations about *all* members of a particular minority group?

8. Why have people who are concerned about the education of minority-group learners often criticized the schools for relying too much on information from standardized tests?

9. In the case of *Milliken v. Bradley* (1974), the Supreme Court held that courts could not order buses to cross school district lines for the purpose of achieving racial balance in a number of school districts in a given area. What were some consequences of this decision?

10. What are some features of Comer-model schools?

Field Experiences, Projects, and Enrichment

1. If possible, arrange to visit some classes that include a mix of learners from different ethnic and cultural backgrounds. Observe participation patterns. How frequently did learners from minority groups volunteer to answer questions? How often were they called upon? (You may wish to identify other questions that will help you to pinpoint the degree to which minority-group learners were actively involved in lessons.) Share your findings with others in your class, and respond to these questions as a group:
   • Were minority-group learners as involved in lessons as were majority-group learners?
   • What specific patterns did you note?
   • What might account for these patterns?

2. Some school districts have helped to provide special training for White teachers to sensitize them to perspectives of learners from ethnic, cultural, and language minorities. Interview local school administrators about programs that may have been implemented in their schools. Alternatively, consult professional journals for descriptions of such programs. Prepare a short paper for your course instructor in which you describe either one or two local

programs or several programs that have been outlined in journal articles.

3. Organize a panel discussion focusing on this question: "Do school programs today do a good job of serving female learners?" Find relevant materials from Web sites, journal articles, and other relevant sources. Allow time for other class members to ask questions and make comments.

4. Read about the Comer model and other successful attempts to improve the achievement levels of minority-group learners. Get together with four or five other classmates who have been working on the same task. Organize a symposium to present to your class on the topic "Hope for Learners from Ethnic and Cultural Minorities: Practical Examples from Real Schools."

5. Some have argued that schools, particularly in urban areas and their surrounding suburbs, would benefit if the courts supported busing learners across district lines for the purpose of achieving better racial balance in every school. Others disagree with this approach. Organize a debate on the issue "Resolved: Cross-District Busing to Improve Racial Balance in Schools Acts to Improve Education."

References

Armstrong, D. G., & Savage, T. V. (1998). *Teaching in the secondary school* (4th ed.). Upper Saddle River, NJ: Merrill/Prentice Hall.

Banks, J. A. (1995). Multicultural education: Development, dimensions, and challenges. In J. Noll (Ed.), *Taking sides: Clashing views on controversial educational issues* (8th ed., pp. 94–98). Guilford, CT: Dushkin.

Banks, J. A. (1998). *An introduction to multicultural education* (2nd ed.). Boston: Allyn & Bacon.

Banks, J. A., & Banks, C. A. McGee (Eds.). (1995). *Handbook of research on multicultural education.* New York: Macmillan Publishing Company.

Banks, J. A., with Clegg, A., Jr. (1988). *Multiethnic education: Theory and practice* (2nd ed.). Boston: Allyn and Bacon.

Bates, P. (1990). Desegregation: Can we get there from here? *Phi Delta Kappan, 72*(1), 8–17.

Brown v. Board of Education, 347 U.S. 483 (1954).

Chipman, S. F., & Thomas, V. G. (1987). The participation of women and minorities in mathematical, scientific, and technical fields. In E. Z. Rothkopf (Ed.), *Review of educational research* (Vol. 14, pp. 387–430). Washington, DC: American Educational Research Association.

Clinchy, E. (1993). Needed: A Clinton crusade for quality and equality. *Educational Leadership, 74*(8), 605–612.

Comer, J. P. (1988). Educating poor minority children. *Scientific American, 259*(5), 42–48.

Darling-Hammond, L. (1993). Reforming the school reform agenda. *Phi Delta Kappan, 74,* 756–761.

Elam, S. M., Rose, L. C., & Gallup, G. M. (1994). The 26th annual Phi Delta Kappa/Gallup poll of the public's attitudes toward the public schools. *Phi Delta Kappan, 76*(1), 41–56.

Erickson, F. (1987). Transformation and school success: The politics and culture of educational achievement. *Anthropology and Education Quarterly, 18*(4), 335–356.

Gay, G. (1994). *A synthesis of scholarship in multicultural education.* [http://www.ncrel.org/sdrs/areas/issues/envrnmnt/go/leogay.htm]

Grant, C. A. (1990). Desegregation, racial attitudes, and intergroup contact: A discussion of change. *Phi Delta Kappan, 72*(1), 25–32.

Grant, C. A., & Sleeter, C. E. (1994). *Making choices for multicultural education: Five approaches to race, class, and gender.* New York: Maxwell Macmillan International.

Henson, K. T. (2001). *Curriculum development for education reform,* 2nd ed. New York: McGraw-Hill.

Hilliard, J. (1991/1992). Why must we pluralize the curriculum? *Educational Leadership, 49*(4), 12–13.

Lau v. Nichols, 414 U.S. 563 (1974).

Lewin, T. (1999, April 11). Amid concerns about equity, parents are turning to girls' schools. *New York Times.* [http://www.nytimes.com/library/national/regional/041199ny-girls-schools.html]

Lucas, T., Henze, R., & Donato, R. (1990). Promoting the success of Latino language-minority students: An exploratory study of six high schools. *Harvard Educational Review, 60*(3), 315–340.

Marshall, R. C. (Chair). (1990). *Education that works: An action plan for the education of minorities.* Cambridge, MA: Quality Education for Minorities Project, Massachusetts Institute of Technology.

Milliken v. Bradley, 418 U.S. 717 (1974).

Pratt, R. (Ed.). (1998a). Indicator 22: Educational attainment. *The Condition of Education, 1998.* [http://nces.ed.gov/pubs98/condition98/c9822a01.html]

Pratt, R. (Ed.) (1998b). High school dropouts and completions by race/ethnicity and recency of migration. *The Condition of Education, 1998.* [http://nces.ed.gov/pubs98/condition98/c9824a01.html]

Sable, S. (1998). Issue in focus: The educational progress of Black students. In Pratt, R. (Ed.), *The condition of education, 1998.* Washington, DC: National Center for Education Statistics. [http://nces.ed.gov/pubs98/condition98/c98003.html]

Sable, S. & Stennett, J. (1998). Issue in focus: The educational progress of Latino students. In Pratt, R. (Ed.), *The condition of education, 1998.* Washington, DC: National Center for Education Statistics. [http://nces.ed.gov/pubs98/condition98/c98004.html]

Simon-McWilliams, E. (Ed.). (1989). *Resegregation of public schools: The third generation.* Portland, OR: Network of Regional Desegregation Assistance Centers and Northwest Regional Educational Laboratory.

Sternberg, R. J. (1994). Allowing for thinking styles. *Educational Leadership, 52*(3), 36–40.

Vergon, C. B. (1989). *School desegregation: The evolution and implementation of a national policy.* Paper presented at the annual meeting of the American Educational Research Association, San Francisco.

5

Exceptional Learners

OBJECTIVES

This chapter will help you to

- recognize that the category of "exceptional learners" includes different kinds of learners, including those with disabilities and those who are gifted.

- identify different kinds of disabilities.

- describe some concerns that contributed to passage of federal laws designed to encourage schools to better serve needs of learners with disabilities.

- point out some provisions of federal legislation that focus on helping learners with disabilities.

- describe appropriate teacher responses to different disabilities of learners.

- differentiate between the terms "mainstreaming" and "inclusion."

- describe characteristics of gifted learners.

- explain some productive teacher approaches to working with gifted learners.

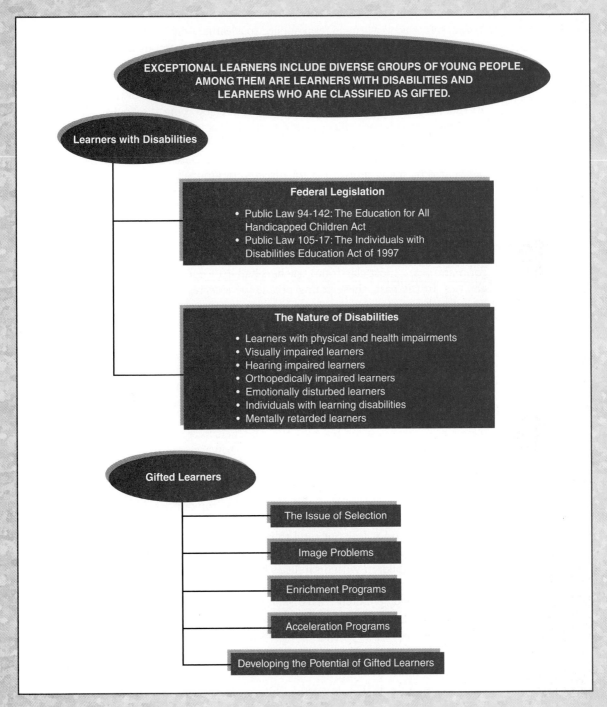

FIGURE 5.1 Exceptional Learners

INTRODUCTION

Exceptional learner is a general term applied to a learner who has special or unusual characteristics. Learners with disabilities and gifted learners are among the exceptional learners you will be teaching, and they share many of the characteristics of other young people who go to school. Some of them are tall, and some of them are short. Some of them are extremely bright, and some of them find learning difficult. Some of them have positive attitudes about school, and some of them do not enjoy being at school at all. There is as much diversity among exceptional learners as there is among the total school population.

In addition to appreciating important learner-to-learner differences when working with these young people, you also need to appreciate some common characteristics shared by many individuals within certain groups of exceptional learners. This chapter introduces some of these differences and describes approaches for working with learners who have certain disabilities and learners who are gifted.

LEARNERS WITH DISABILITIES

For many years, most classroom teachers had little contact with learners having disabilities. In the past, these young people were segregated from other learners and were taught in special classrooms. Teachers who worked with these students took preparation programs leading to certification as teachers of children with disabilities and generally worked only with groups of such learners.

The isolation of learners with disabilities ceased in 1975 with the enactment of Public Law 94-142, the Education for All Handicapped Children Act. The name of this legislation was changed in 1990 to the Individuals with Disabilities Education Act. Public Law 105-117, the Individuals with Disabilities Education Act of 1997, provided additional guidelines for working with learners with disabilities. Together these laws place a heavy emphasis on teaching these learners in regular school classrooms.

Collectively, federal legislation directed toward improvement of educational services provided to disabled learners has attempted to redress such problems as the following (IDEA '97: General Information, 1997):

- Twice as many children with disabilities drop out of school as children without disabilities.
- Children who drop out tend to not return to school, to have difficulty finding jobs, and to often end up in the criminal-justice system.
- Female children with disabilities become unwed mothers at a much higher rate than their nondisabled peers.
- Since many children with disabilities are excluded from the curriculum provided to their nondisabled classmates, they are denied opportunities to master material needed to meet high levels of academic performance.

Federal Legislation

The Education for All Handicapped Children Act of 1975, the Individuals with Disabilities Education Act of 1990, and the Individuals with Disabilities Education Act of 1997 are three key pieces of legislation that relate to providing better services to exceptional learners in the schools. In addition, the 1992 Americans with Disabilities Act, patterned after earlier legislation (Section 504 of the Vocational Rehabilitation Act), extends the civil rights of individuals with disabilities to private-sector employers, all public services, transportation, and telecommunications. The now nearly universal access ramps found in businesses, on city street corners, and in schools and universities are one clear result of this legislation.

Federal legislation directed to improve the futures of young people with exceptionalities has come about because of a concern that many learners with disabilities traditionally have not been well served by educational programs. During hearings related to this legislation held during the 1970s, members of Congress learned that over half of the approximately eight million children with disabilities in the country had no access to appropriate educational services. Testimony revealed the problem to be a lack of money to serve their needs properly. Some provisions of existing legislation deserve special mention.

Public Law 94-142: The Education for All Handicapped Children Act
Passage of the Education for All Handicapped Children Act in 1975 was a seminal event in the history of American education. It fundamentally changed assumptions about how educational services should be delivered to handicapped learners. Prior to its passage, the prevailing practice was to isolate these young people from the general school population. Subsequent to its enactment, the operating assumption has been that these young people are best served when they sit in regular classrooms alongside their nondisabled peers. Looked at in another way, "special education" used to be conceived of as a separate place. Today, "special education" is seen as a cluster of services that are delivered to youngsters with special needs who spend their days as members of regular classrooms. This view has been strengthened by follow-up legislation to Public Law 94-142, including the Individuals with Disabilities Education Act of 1990 and the Individuals with Disabilities Education Act of 1997.

Because Public Law 94-142 is so foundational to much that has happened since its passage, you might be interested in some of its provisions.

Funding.   Public Law 94-142 established a formula for providing federal aid to the states to support educational services for children with disabilities between the ages of 3 and 21. A formula based on the percentage of the average amount spent on each child's education in the United States and on the number of children with disabilities to be served was developed as a way of determining the amount of money to be spent. Educating a child with special needs costs a school district almost twice as much as educating a nondisabled learner, and in some cases, costs are even higher. The federal government initially promised to provide the states with funding to cover 40% of the cost of educating such learners but generally has not been able to pay nearly this high a percentage of the total bill. Thus, the states and local communities have had to make up the difference.

Individualized Education Programs (IEPs).   The law called for an Individualized Education Program (IEP) to be established for each child with disabilities. It must be developed and agreed to at a meeting that includes a representative of the

These school professionals are meeting with a parent to discuss preparation of an Individualized Educational Program for a learner with disabilities.

school district, the learner, and a parent or guardian of the learner. The IEP must include specific information about:

- the learner's present educational attainment level,
- goals and short-term objectives,
- specific services to be provided to the learner and the time required for each,
- the starting date and an estimate of the expected duration of services, and
- evaluation criteria to be used in determining whether the objectives have been achieved.

Least Restrictive Environment. Public Law 94-142 required states to ensure that, to the maximum extent possible, learners with disabilities are educated in the "least restrictive environment." This means that every effort must be extended to allow them to be taught in regular classes, alongside nondisabled learners. The assignment of learners with disabilities to special classes, special schools, or other alternatives to the regular classroom must be undertaken only when the severity of the disability is so great that education in regular classrooms with the use of supplementary materials and aids cannot be achieved satisfactorily.

The term *mainstreaming* is used to describe the practice of placing learners with disabilities in regular classrooms alongside nondisabled learners. Mainstreaming

Video Viewpoint

Disabled Student Dispute

WATCH: In this ABC News video segment, we meet 16-year-old Garrett Frye, whose family is suing the Cedar Rapids, Iowa School District. Paralyzed by a motorcycle accident when he was four years old, Garrett currently requires medical services that cost the school district approximately $40,000 a year. At the heart of this court case is the Individuals with Disabilities Education Act (IDEA), a federal statute intended to protect the rights of individuals with disabilities.

THINK: With your classmates or in your teaching journal, consider these questions:

1. Is it fair for a school district to pay this amount of money to support one child's education, when the district has a fixed amount of money to support its approximately 18,000 other students?
2. Consider the IDEA legislation, and its mandate for inclusion. What are the benefits and challenges—other than the cost to the district for medical services—associated with inclusion?
3. As a teacher, how will you feel about having students with disabilities like Garrett in your regular education classroom?

LINK: How do non-disabled students benefit from having students with disabilities in their classes?

seeks to infuse learners with disabilities into the main arteries of the educational system in as many ways as possible in order to prepare them for the adult world as much as nondisabled learners are prepared.

Public Law 105-17: The Individuals with Disabilities Education Act of 1997 The Individuals with Disabilities Education Act of 1997 extended the principle of involving learners with disabilities in regular school classrooms. To understand the direction taken by this legislation, you need to understand what is meant by *inclusion.*

In recent years, the term inclusion has been displacing the term mainstreaming. The two terms are closely related, but there are subtle and important differences. An operating principle behind mainstreaming is that regular classrooms have an obligation to take and serve exceptional learners. Inclusion proceeds from the assumption that traditional classrooms should not take special learners simply because federal law obligates them to do so. Rather, inclusion presumes that all learners, regardless of their individual characteristics, are *wanted* as members of regular classrooms. Supporters of inclusion argue that if some learners need unique kinds of help (special teachers, equipment, or programs, for example), then it is the obligation of the schools to deliver that help to these learners in the regular classrooms where they are regularly enrolled. In schools committed to the idea of *full inclusion,* there are virtually no special classes for exceptional learners. All modifications to their programs take place within the regular classrooms.

Following the Web 5.1

Inclusion

"Inclusion" is an idea that continues to prompt much discussion among educators today. There are spirited debates among those who are committed to "full inclusion" and others who think school practices that fall somewhat short of that objective better serve both learners with disabilities and their nondisabled peers. You will find many Web sites with information relating to inclusion. We have selected some here that you might wish to visit.

For hot links to these sites, visit the companion Web site, located at *http://www.prenhall.com/armstrong*. Select Chapter 5 from the front page of the Web site, then choose the Following the Web module on the navigation bar on the left of the page.

Inclusion

- *http://cisl.ospi.wednet.edu/CISL/Services/Teach/Inclusion/SE_INCLUSION.html*

  This site provides a listing of a number of journal articles that focus on inclusion. A number of them address issues associated with preparing teachers to work in full-inclusion settings. Synopses for individual articles are provided.

Assistive Technology

- *http://circleofinclusion.org/links/assistivetech.html*

  If you are interested in how technology can be used to assist learners with various learning disabilities, this is a site worth visiting. You will find numerous links to information about how technology, particularly computer-based technology, can assist these young people.

ERIC Clearinghouse on Disabilities and Gifted Education

- *http://ericec.org/*

  This site includes links to a wide array of information related to many topics associated with both learners with disabilities and gifted learners. Many of these links include information related to inclusion.

Proponents of full inclusion argue that this approach benefits both exceptional learners and so-called normal learners. Young people will grow to maturity in a diverse world, and experiences they get in full-inclusion schools help them appreciate that people with widely ranging characteristics can be interesting, contributing human beings. Researchers have found that learners in full-inclusion classrooms have some of the following characteristics (National Association for the Education of Young Children, 1997):

- They demonstrate increased acceptance and appreciation of diversity.
- They develop better communication and social skills.
- They show greater development in moral and ethical principles.

Inclusive Practices

- *http://www.cec.sped.org/bk/catalog/inclus.htm*

  If you are interested in locating titles of books that focus on how to provide instructional services in inclusive classrooms, this is an important Web site to visit. You will find excellent synopses of the contents of each title as well as ordering information.

The Council for Exceptional Children

- *http://www.cec.sped.org/*

  This is the home page for The Council for Exceptional Children, which is the leading professional organization for educators with particular interest in the education of learners with special needs. You will find links to a variety of topics associated with the education of exceptional children, including many that deal with various aspects of inclusion.

Federation for Children with Special Needs

- *http://www.fcsn.org/resource.htm*

  This is the home page of The Federation for Children with Special Needs. You will find an outstanding collection of links to additional sources of information about inclusion and other topics related to exceptional learners. These links include sites maintained by federal and state agencies and organizations.

Inclusion Press Home Page

- *http://www.inclusion.com/*

  This is the home page of a publishing company that specializes in producing books and other educational materials related to inclusion. You will find information about book titles and videos here. In addition, there are links to other inclusion-related Web sites.

[Note: Web addresses change frequently. If you are unable to locate one of these sites using the listed URL, try putting the site name in a standard search engine.]

- They create warm and caring friendships.
- They demonstrate increased self-esteem.

The Individuals with Disabilities Education Act puts some important legislative clout behind the idea that learners with disabilities are to be treated, as much as possible, as part of the regular population of learners to whom the schools have an obligation to educate. You might be interested in some key provisions.

Regular Teachers Must Participate in IEP Planning. To encourage the idea that learners with disabilities are part of the regular classroom, this legislation requires that the regular classroom teacher be a part of the team that puts together the IEP for each learner with disabilities. Though many states already had similar regulations, there was nothing in federal law that made it mandatory for the regular classroom teacher to be involved in preparation of the IEP. Today, such participation is obligatory.

Rights of Parents and Guardians.   In some states, implementation guidelines for the original 1975 Education for All Handicapped Children Act gave parents and guardians only the right to be included in IEP meetings. The 1997 legislation gives them an absolute right to be involved in *all* decisions concerning the eligibility of their children for particular programs and the placement of their children in these programs. Earlier legislation did not require schools to provide parents or guardians of learners with disabilities with regular reports on what progress their children were making in achieving goals set forth in the adopted IEP. The 1997 legislation requires that progress reports be provided to them.

Public Reporting of Achievement Data.   It has sometimes been the practice for individual school districts to excuse learners with disabilities from taking standardized tests or to not report scores of these learners when they have taken these assessments. Supporters of full inclusion who played an important role in passing the Individuals with Disabilities Education Act pointed out that forcing schools to administer and report test scores of learners with disabilities was important. In their view, this requirement would provide a strong incentive for schools to expose these young people to the same curriculum as their nondisabled peers. As adopted, the legislation requires that information about the achievement of learners with disabilities be included in regular public reports on test scores.

Working with Learners with Disabilities: General Guidelines

The inclusion principle places an obligation on teachers to not only welcome these young people as regular members of their classes but to provide them with the help they will require to succeed. This means that, as a teacher, you must know how to assist young people to learn who will be challenged by physical and other personal conditions that differ from those of many other learners. Part of your personal professional development program needs to be directed at preparing yourself to work with these special learners. Some teachers in the schools today feel ill-prepared to fulfill the needs of these young people. In response, the curricula of today's teacher-education programs are being adjusted to produce educators who are committed to welcoming exceptional learners as regular members of their classrooms.

One of your challenges will be to make these special learners truly feel that they belong in your classroom. Learners with disabilities often report great differences in the degree to which their presence is welcomed (Williams, 1998). When they feel they are an integral part of the class, their levels of motivation and potential for academic success increase (Gallager, 1996).

Perhaps the best thing you can do to make all class members feel they belong is to promote the idea that learners with disabilities are no different than other learners

What Do You Think?

Preparing Other Learners to Accept Those with Disabilities

You are a seventh-grade teacher. Your principal has told you that, starting about the third week of school, you will have two new learners in your classroom. One requires the use of a wheelchair; the other walks with crutches and braces. Consider what you might do to prepare members of your class to welcome these newcomers.

What Do *You* Think?

1. What initial reactions do you expect from other members of the class?
2. Specifically, what will you do to welcome these newcomers?
3. What ideas do you have for encouraging present class members to make these new learners feel like a part of the group?

(Janney & Snell, 1996). Interestingly, when teachers take this approach, young people without disabilities quickly ignore their classmates' disabilities (Williams, 1998).

The Nature of Disabilities

There is some danger in preparing a simple list of disabilities. The general characteristics of individuals who have these conditions are just that—*general*. Great diversity exists among learners in each category. Further, there is a tendency to overlook the point that many school learners fall into several categories simultaneously. The information presented regarding each category should be approached with an appreciation of within-category diversity and multiple-category membership of many individual learners.

Learners with General Physical and Health Impairments Challenges faced by learners in this broad category are diverse. These young people confront some physical or medically related limitations that can affect their performance in the classroom. Because this category embraces such a wide range of conditions, your first step in working with these young people is to gather as much specific information as you can about individual learners. Parents or guardians and school counselors are among the people you should consult. Information they provide can help you make instructional modifications to meet the special needs of these young people.

Kinds of modifications required will vary from learner to learner. For example, in a laboratory situation, some of these learners may find it difficult to move quickly from place to place. You may need to change the physical layout of the room to accommodate this situation, and you may need to allow these learners more time to complete assigned tasks. If you take time to diagnose these learners' individual circumstances and make appropriate adjustments, you will find that many of them will cope well with your instructional program.

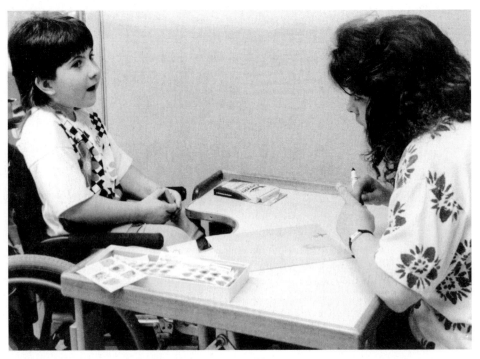

Teachers today serve learners with physical limitations of various kinds in their regular classrooms.

Visually Impaired Learners   Individuals who are visually impaired or blind can compete well with other learners in regular classrooms provided that their communications skills are well developed. As a teacher, you also need to modify your instructional program appropriately. For example, when making assignments, you need to provide information orally to your visually impaired learners. Sometimes you will want to make audio recordings of both assignments and of important lesson-related information.

Many blind learners use personal computers to communicate in writing with their teachers. Additionally, blind learners often produce braille (using machines called braillewriters) as well as read it. For example, you may find blind learners in your class using this equipment to take notes for later reference.

While young people in this category may have mobility problems, many of them develop good mental pictures of areas they visit frequently. You should provide them with opportunities to walk around your classroom at times when other learners are absent. This will give them opportunities to learn how the room is arranged. You also need to keep physical changes to a minimum and alert visually impaired learners when changes have occurred. They will require time to master the new arrangements and develop a good level of comfort in moving from place to place.

Hearing-Impaired Learners   Hearing-impaired learners' most marked differences from nonimpaired learners include their difficulties in producing speech and in acquiring language skills. They fall into two basic categories. *Deaf* learners have a hearing loss so serious that their ability to acquire normal use of language is greatly impaired. *Hard-of-hearing* learners have significant hearing loss, but they are still able to acquire normal speech patterns.

Because some learners who are hearing impaired have learned to read lips, you need to face the class when addressing groups that include learners with severe hearing problems. Avoid exaggerating your speech patterns, as lip readers learn to read lips that produce speech in a normal way.

When you introduce a lesson that requires presentation of much oral information, consider giving hearing-impaired learners a printed outline of your comments. Include major topics and subtopics. You may also wish to provide these learners with lists of important terms you will be using.

You need to supplement oral information with visual information. For example, you might write assignments on the board, work with an overhead projector, or use computer-based presentation software. Some teachers write a brief outline of their remarks on a roll of acetate mounted on an overhead projector and refer to this outline as they talk to the class.

Some learners with hearing impairments use hearing aids. You need to know how these work, and it is especially important for you to become acquainted with how batteries are replaced. You may want to keep a supply of batteries in your desk. If you have these items on hand, you will be able to replace a battery immediately and avoid the possibility that a learner will lose the benefit of a whole day's instruction.

Orthopedically Impaired Learners   It is difficult to generalize about learners who are orthopedically impaired. These learners may suffer from one or more of a number of conditions that limit their physical abilities. You need to learn the nature of the disability and its implications for the instructional process before you can pinpoint the specific needs of the individual learner.

Special equipment may be required in the classroom. Wheelchairs, special typewriters, and standing tables are examples of items that might be needed. You have to think carefully about potential threats to safety of orthopedically impaired learners that are posed by the general physical environment of the classroom. For example, highly polished floors can be dangerous for individuals who must use crutches. Care must be taken to ensure against accidentally tipping over a wheelchair. Because orthopedically impaired learners who use special equipment usually cannot move as fast as other learners, you may ask them to leave classes early so they can avoid congested hallways and arrive at their next class on time.

Special aids to learning and retention may help orthopedically impaired young people to succeed on assigned tasks. Those who have difficulty with handwriting sometimes do much better with computers. Small, hand-carried tape recorders can serve as notetakers for these individuals. Other aids are also available, depending on a given learner's particular needs.

Emotionally Disturbed Learners   Emotionally disturbed learners deviate from the kinds of behaviors expected for learners in their age group. Their behavior patterns interfere with their development as individuals and their ability to establish and maintain harmonious relationships with others.

What Do You Think?

Providing Academic Benefits to All Learners

You are a sixth-grade teacher in a middle school, and find yourself dealing with two well-organized groups of parents and guardians. One group has a high interest in school programs that are heavily weighted toward traditional academics and are designed to prepare learners who will go to high school and, for the most part, on to colleges and universities.

A second group of parents and guardians includes people with children who suffer from a variety of disabilities. They want evidence that you are spending enough time with their children. Many of them feel that their sons and daughters have been shortchanged in the past and that teachers have not given these children the kind of help they need to succeed.

What Do You Think?

1. What incompatibilities exist in the views of the two groups?
2. Is it possible to satisfy both groups of parents?
3. Given this situation, what would you do?

Many of these young people find it almost impossible to make independent decisions, and their peers heavily influence them. Even though they tend to look to peers for guidance, often their peers do not particularly like them. Many of these young people sense themselves to be isolated from others of their own age, and often they have low self-esteem. Many do not do well in school.

In working with emotionally disturbed learners, you should keep in mind four key principles (Armstrong & Savage, 1998):

- Your activities must be success oriented. Learners must sense they have a reasonable chance to succeed.
- Your behavior expectations must be communicated with exceptional clarity, and you must enforce them consistently.
- You must minimize distractions to reduce the likelihood learners will lose their focus on tasks that have been assigned to them.
- You must help these learners understand that a clear and definite connection exists between their behaviors and the consequences that result from these behaviors.

Many of these learners do not function well when they are exposed to too many stimuli at one time. There are several courses of action you can follow when confronted with this problem. For example, you can assign them to do seat work in carrels or partially enclosed booths where extraneous visual stimuli are minimized.

Individuals with Learning Disabilities   People with learning disabilities have difficulty using the mental processes required to understand written or oral language. They may experience difficulties in listening, writing, reading, spelling, or in handling basic mathematical operations. Such labels as *perceptual handicap, dyslexia,* or *minimal brain dysfunction* sometimes are used to refer to learning disabilities.

You will find that people with learning disabilities in your classes often will find it hard to follow your directions. Sometimes they just cannot seem to get started on an assignment, and often they have a low tolerance for frustration. In response, you need to work hard to help develop these learners' organizational skills. You will find they need help in separating important from unimportant information. Actions you take to highlight key ideas and to suggest ways they can organize information into meaningful patterns will assist people with learning disabilities.

A specific type of disability that represents an especially serious form of learning disability is *attention deficit disorder (ADD)*. Learners diagnosed with this condition are eligible for special services under the provisions of the 1990 reauthorization of the Education for All Handicapped Children Act. In addition to having problems with organization and attending to assigned tasks, many youngsters with this condition appear to be hyperactive. In your classroom, you may find them hurtling from idea to idea and turning in hastily done, sloppy work—a result of a compulsion to finish assignments quickly.

You need to provide well-organized, highly structured lessons for ADD learners. Adding color, shape, and texture to your lessons can help maintain the attention of these young people. In addition, you will find that they do better in small classes and with content that features short blocks of direct instruction.

Mentally Retarded Learners   There are many reasons for mental retardation, and there are many levels of retardation. There are three general categories that have been used to describe learners who are mentally retarded: *educable, trainable,* and *profoundly retarded.* Most learners who spend all or part of their school day in regular classrooms are in the *educable* category. This group includes learners who are mentally retarded who deviate the least from the so-called normal range of mental functioning. You will find that many of these young people respond well to many widely used instructional techniques.

Educable learners often have language and speech deficiencies. Because they often have short attention spans, you need to prepare lessons for them that are brief, direct, and to the point. Concrete examples of what is to be done in their lessons help them to understand what you expect. Directions provided orally as well as in written form are also helpful. You may find they benefit when you ask another member of your class to work with them, particularly for the purpose of helping them understand what they are to do.

You might keep some of the following principles in mind (Armstrong & Savage, 1998):

- Your lessons should be short, direct, and to the point.
- Your material should be introduced in short, sequential steps.
- You should reinforce content introduced in written form with visual and oral examples.
- You should consider assigning another member of your class to work as a tutor with an educable learner.
- Your directions should be clear and should be delivered in a vocabulary educable learners understand.
- Your lessons should not place educable learners in highly competitive situations.

- You should give educable learners more time to complete tasks.
- You should help educable learners build confidence by reducing the number of tasks they are to do and ensuring that they complete them successfully.

GIFTED LEARNERS

For three decades, the federal government has been interested in programs for gifted learners. As long ago as 1972, Congress established the Office of Gifted and Talented. Public Law 91-230 (*United States Statutes at Large,* 1971, p. 153) defined "gifted learners" as "children who have outstanding intellectual ability or creative talent, the development of which requires special activities or services not ordinarily provided by local education agencies." With the passage of Public Law 93-380 in 1974, more federal attention focused on gifted learners. This legislation allocated federal funds to local and state agencies for the purpose of improving gifted and talented programs. Additional federal support for these programs was authorized by the Jacob K. Javits Gifted and Talented Students Education Act of 1994. This legislation authorized the United States Department of Education to award grants, provide leadership, and sponsor a national research center focusing specifically on educational needs of gifted and talented learners.

The Issue of Selection

Selection of learners for special programs for the gifted has often prompted controversy. In years past, educators relied almost exclusively on standardized test scores to identify gifted learners. Recently, however, there has been a trend toward widening the definition of "giftedness." Today, selection criteria often also include special psychomotor abilities and creative talents. In addition, there has been an effort to ensure that selection procedures are not biased against learners from ethnic and cultural minorities.

Image Problems

Some educators have long worried about potential self-image problems of gifted learners. There has been a concern that these young people, because they are "different," may not be socially acceptable to their peers. Fortunately, most studies have suggested that gifted learners are well-accepted young people. One important study found that "extremely precocious adolescents" may experience more peer-relations problems than "modestly gifted adolescents" (Dauber & Benbow, 1990). This suggests that, as a teacher, you need to be aware of potential problems and resultant feelings of extremely gifted learners. These extraordinarily bright young people may face pressure from other students to "do less." When this happens, they may be among those in your class who urge you not to set expectations for the class as high as you would like.

Parents and guardians and, regrettably, some teachers pressure gifted learners to perform flawlessly. If these learners feel they must be perfect, they may develop unrealistic self-expectations and frustration. You need to understand what excessive pressure can do to gifted learners and work to help them focus on their strengths and

Critical Incident

Dealing with a Gifted Learner who has a Behavior Problem

Mario is an extremely bright fifth grader. He ranks in the 99th percentile in every category on the standardized tests used in his school district. He reads novels and other materials that rarely interest young people his age. He spends hours each evening at his computer cruising the World Wide Web. Though Mario's academic potential is high, his performance at school is not good.

He does assigned work when pressed, but he tends to rush through assignments. His answers are usually technically correct, but the work is sloppy and reflects little serious thought. Mario seems bent on hurrying through his own work to gain time to bother others while they are doing theirs.

His teacher, Lorena McPhee, has tried to deal with this situation by asking him to do a bit more than others in the class. He complains that this is not fair. He has gone so far as to publicly challenge the teacher about both the regular assignments and the proposed extra work. In his words, all of these things are "bogus." He seems to enjoy doing and saying things that appear deliberately intended to make Ms. McPhee look bad, even incompetent, to other members of the class.

. . .

What thoughts do you have about Mario's general pattern of behavior? What might be motivating him to act the way he does? How do you think Mario is viewed by other class members? How do you think Mario sees himself? What options are open to Ms. McPhee? What do you see as the relative strengths and weaknesses of each? If you were Ms. McPhee, what would you do next?

To respond to this Critical Incident online, and to save or submit your response electronically, visit the companion Web site, located at *http://www.prenhall.com/armstrong.* Select Chapter 5 from the front page of the Web site, then choose the Critical Incidents module on the navigation bar on the left side of the page. Instructors and students may also wish to use these scenarios as discussion topics on the Message Board for the companion Web site.

accomplishments, not their shortcomings. It is important for these bright young people to understand that everyone has strengths and weaknesses and that it is no sign of personal failure to be less than perfect in some areas.

Enrichment Programs

Enrichment programs seek to provide learning experiences for gifted young people that are in addition to or go beyond those provided to other learners. They are designed to challenge gifted learners to maximize their use of their considerable abilities. At the same time, enrichment programs seek to maintain continuous contact between gifted and nongifted learners by keeping them together in regular classes and by moving them through the K–12 instructional program at the same rate. This means, for example, that gifted learners will take United States history at the same time as their nongifted age mates. But it also means that the specific learning experiences provided

© 1998 Randy Glasbergen.   www.glasbergen.com

**"My generation will be running the world soon.
If we say 4+4=9 then that's the way it's going to be!"**

for them in the context of the United States history course will be different and more challenging than those to which nongifted learners are exposed.

If you are involved in an enrichment program, you will need to make a conscious attempt to ensure that what you ask gifted learners to do truly differs from what you require of other learners. It is not appropriate for you to simply introduce them earlier to material that they would ordinarily encounter further along in the school program. If you do this, problems will result in subsequent years for both gifted learners and their teachers. For example, if gifted learners are taught the regular grade-12 English material in grade 10, they may find themselves being retaught what they have already learned two years later, when they reach grade 12.

The guarantee that enrichment programs for gifted learners will truly be different is important for another reason as well. Because gifted learners are able to progress through traditional material at a more rapid rate than are nongifted learners, it may be tempting for you simply to ask them to do *more* of the same. For example, while nongifted learners might be asked to complete 10 mathematics problems, you might think about requiring your gifted learners to do 15. If you do this, you are sending a message that says giftedness is a burden rather than a blessing, and your gifted learners may conclude that you have decided to punish them for their special abilities.

In summary, the enrichment approach is the most popular one for responding to the needs of gifted learners. It enjoys wide support from parents, guardians, and administrators, and it is consistent with a view of the school as a place where all kinds of learners come together. It also conforms to a widely held feeling that there are benefits of keeping learners of approximately the same age together as they progress through the school program. Finally, enrichment programs are relatively easy for school leaders to implement.

For a discussion of some issues associated with enrichment, see the "Critical Incident" on page 141.

Acceleration Programs

Acceleration programs increase the pace at which gifted learners complete their schooling. For example, in an accelerated program, a gifted learner might complete the entire high school program in just two years. There is no attempt to keep gifted learners in classes with nongifted learners in the same age group. Supporters of acceleration programs reject the idea that there is something useful or inherently beneficial in keeping learners in a given grade for an entire academic year. They also see no particular need to keep them in classes with learners of approximately the same age. They believe that giftedness is best developed when bright learners are as intellectually challenged as possible. Often this means moving these learners into classes with older learners, where more advanced content is taught.

There are two types of acceleration programs: *subject-matter acceleration* and *grade-level acceleration*. Subject-matter acceleration allows gifted learners to take courses earlier than would be typical. For example, a sixth grader might be enrolled in a ninth-grade algebra class. Grade-level acceleration occurs when a learner is allowed to skip an entire grade and enroll as a regular member of a class of older learners. For example, a bright third grader might be accelerated to become a member of a fifth-grade class.

Some critics argue that accelerated programs may interfere with the social adjustment of gifted learners. For example, how is a bright 11-year-old who is accelerated to grade 10 going to deal with the male–female social relationships typical at the high school level? How is a 14-year-old college graduate going to fare in a work environment that may restrict hiring to people who are several years older?

The percentage of gifted learners who are in accelerated programs is small compared to the percentage enrolled in enrichment programs. It has been much easier to convince education policymakers of the benefits of enrichment programs. Enrichment is simply more consistent with traditional patterns and assumptions than is acceleration.

Developing the Potential of Gifted Learners

Robert J. Sternberg and Todd I. Lubart (1991), recognized authorities in education of the gifted, have identified several things you can do as a teacher to encourage creativity among your gifted learners. First of all, you can provide opportunities for these young people to engage in responsible risk taking, something that has been identified as an essential ingredient of mature thinking (Henson & Eller, 1999).

Some traditional classroom practices definitely do not encourage risk taking. For example, consider the results of a teacher's award of a low grade to a learner who turns in a drawing rather than an essay when asked to present reactions to a short story. A bright learner soon "learns" that risk taking, particularly creative risk taking, does not pay. The message for you as a teacher is that you must think about what kinds of signals you send learners. If the signals are negative when they engage in risk taking, they will soon learn that risk taking is a behavior to be avoided. On the other hand, if you send positive signals when learners come up with creative and unexpected responses, you create a safe, encouraging environment that tells them that risk taking has some value.

Following the Web 5.2

Gifted and Talented Learners

The high interest in education of the brightest school learners is reflected in the hundreds of Web sites that provide information related to helping these young people develop their talents. Large numbers of national, regional, and state-based support organizations regularly contribute material to these sites. We have selected some for mention here that represent a sample of the diverse information you will find on the Web related to teaching these learners.

For hot links to these sites, visit the companion Web site, located at *http://www.prenhall.com/armstrong.* Select Chapter 5 from the front page of the Web site, then choose the Following the Web module on the navigation bar on the left side of the page.

The National Research Center of the Gifted and Talented

- *http://www.gifted.uconn.edu/nrcgt.html*

  This is the home page of the National Research Center of the Gifted and Talented (NRCGT) directed by Dr. Joseph S. Renzulli of the University of Connecticut. NRCGT is a federally funded operation that involves a consortium of universities including the University of Connecticut; City University of New York, City College; Stanford University; the University of Virginia; and Yale University. You will find links to a variety of useful publications, articles, and organizations.

The National Association for Gifted Children

- *http://www.nagc.org/home.htm*

  The National Association for Gifted Children (NAGC) is an important national advocacy group for gifted and talented learners. You will find links here to many other sites with information about programs that serve this segment of the school population.

International/National Resources for Gifted Education

- *http://ericec.org/fact/gt-asso.htm*

  This site is maintained by the ERIC Clearinghouse on Disabilities and Gifted Education. (For the home page of this Clearinghouse, see "Following the Web 5.1" earlier in this chapter.) You will find here an extensive listing of organizations in the United States, Canada, Europe, and elsewhere in the world that are dedicated to serving the needs of gifted and talented learners. World Wide Web addresses are provided for many of them.

State Resources for Gifted Education

- *http://ericec.org/fact/stateres.htm*

  This is another site maintained by the ERIC Clearinghouse on Disabilities and Gifted Education. At this site, you will find a listing of groups and contact people in each state and in some United States territories with interest in promoting high-quality school programming for gifted learners.

Gifted Students with Disabilities

- *http://ericec.org/faq/gt-disab.htm*

   Many learners who have disabilities of certain kinds are also classified as "gifted." At this site, you will find a collection of articles in the ERIC system that focus on approaches to working with these learners in the school classroom.

How We Can Evaluate Gifted Programs

- *http://ericec.org/faq/gt-eval.htm*

   At this site, you will find an excellent collection of documents in the ERIC system that focus on approaches to evaluating programs for gifted learners. Short synopses are provided for each.

Underachievement Among Gifted Minority Students: Problems and Promises

- *http://www.cec.sped.org/digests/e544.htm*

   An issue that frequently comes up in discussions of gifted programs is whether they adequately serve gifted minority learners. This monograph by Donna Fort and Antoinette Thomas brings some key issues into focus.

Homeschooling Gifted Students: An Introductory Guide for Parents

- *http://www.cec.sped.org/digests/e543.htm*

   There are gifted learners among homeschooled youngsters as well as among those in public school classrooms. In this 1998 monograph, author Jacque Ensign provides some guidelines for people who are concerned about homeschooling gifted children.

Differentiating Instruction for Advanced Learners in the Mixed-Ability Middle School Classroom

- *http://www.cec.sped.org/digests/e536.htm*

   Suppose you are interested in providing differentiated instruction in your classroom. Part of your plan is to develop programming appropriate for gifted learners. What do you do? In this 1995 monograph, Carol Ann Tomlinson provides some practical ideas for helping gifted youngsters who are enrolled in a mixed-ability middle school classroom.

[Note: Web addresses change frequently. If you are unable to locate one of these sites using the listed URL, try putting the site name in a standard search engine.]

Gifted and talented students often are characterized by high degrees of creativity and sophisticated thinking.

It is also important to take special steps to help gifted learners understand how the knowledge they will be acquiring can be used. Gifted learners have a need to see that new information is important to them personally and to understand how it can be employed to help them perform innovative and creative tasks (Sternberg & Lubart, 1991).

Gifted learners need help in defining problems of their own. In addition, you need to assist them to consider ways in which assignments are relevant to their own interests and personal lives. This kind of personalization helps to stimulate the creative powers of gifted learners. When these bright young people play a role in identifying the problem or goal, they tend to develop a stronger sense of purpose. In turn, this commitment often will result in their generating responses that fully utilize their considerable intellectual and creative resources.

Key Ideas In Summary

- The term *exceptional learners* is applied to learners who have special or unusual characteristics. Learners with disabilities and learners who are gifted are among groups of exceptional learners in today's schools. Differences among exceptional learners are as great as those among the total learner population of the school.
- Before the passage of relevant federal legislation, teachers in traditional classrooms had little daily contact with exceptional learners. When the school served

these young people, they were assigned to special classrooms and taught by teachers who worked with them exclusively. Existing federal laws ask educators to regard learners with disabilities as just some of the youngsters who come to school and to provide services to them in regular classrooms where they sit alongside their nondisabled peers.

- Learners with general physical and health impairments confront some physical or medically related limitations that can affect their performance in the classroom. Individual situations vary enormously, and modifications to their instructional programs differ according to their particular personal circumstances.

- In general, visually impaired and blind learners can compete successfully with nonimpaired learners, but this depends on early attention to the development of their communications skills. Often, these students are provided with special equipment such as braillewriters, personal computers, and audiotape recorders that can help them take notes and prepare responses for the teacher.

- Hearing-impaired and deaf learners often have difficulty producing speech and acquiring language skills. Teachers need to understand how their hearing aids work and how to make minor repairs on them. Because some of these learners are lip readers, it is important for teachers to face these students directly when speaking. Supplementing oral directions with written versions is an additional helpful practice.

- There are many different kinds of problems faced by orthopedically impaired learners. Many of these young people require special equipment such as wheelchairs, and teachers must make provisions for such learners to use their equipment. Because some of these students move more slowly than non-impaired learners, teachers often make arrangements for them to leave class a few minutes early to allow them sufficient time to get to their next class.

- Emotionally disturbed learners deviate from the kinds of behaviors that are expected from learners in their age groups. These patterns often interfere with their personal development. Large numbers of these children find it difficult to establish and maintain harmonious relationships with others.

- Young people with learning disabilities have difficulty in using the mental processes that are required to understand written or oral language. Learners with these conditions may have problems listening, writing, reading, spelling, or handling important mathematical operations. Terms such as *perceptual handicap, dyslexia,* or *minimal brain dysfunction* are sometimes used to describe young people with learning disabilities.

- Three categories used to describe learners who are mentally retarded are *educable, trainable,* and *profoundly retarded.* Mentally retarded youngsters who are in the educable category are most likely to spend all or part of their school day in regular classrooms. Many learners in this category, though they may have somewhat limited attention spans and some language or speech deficiencies, respond well to many widely used instructional techniques.

- Gifted learners have outstanding intellectual or creative abilities that need to be nurtured by special school programs that go beyond those provided for nongifted young people. Learners are selected for special school programs by multiple criteria that often include test scores, special creative and psychomotor abilities, and recommendations of teachers and counselors. Some gifted learners experience self-image problems. One common difficulty results when, in response to parental and sometimes teacher pressures, they set impossibly high performance standards for themselves.

- Programs for gifted learners are of two basic types. *Enrichment programs* keep learners in their regular age-group classes and courses but provide special learning experiences designed to develop these learners' special capabilities. *Acceleration programs* are designed to speed gifted students' passage through the school program by allowing them to skip grades and enroll in courses with older learners. Enrichment is by far the more popular of the two approaches.

- It is important that programs for gifted learners do not inadvertently punish these young people by simply requiring them to do more of the same kind of work that nongifted learners are required to do. Rather, programs should be designed to encourage risk taking and creative endeavors. Further, they should help gifted learners to understand how the new knowledge being taught will be particularly useful to them as individuals. Finally, gifted learners should participate in identifying the problems they will solve and in redefining problems selected by the teachers in order to make their assignments more relevant to their own needs and interests.

Chapter 5 Self Test

 To review terms and concepts in this chapter, take the Chapter 5 Self Test on the companion Web site, located at *http://www.prenhall.com/armstrong*. Select Chapter 5 from the front page of the Web site, then choose the Self Test module on the navigation bar on the left side of the page. Feedback for the Self Test is immediate. You can keep track of your Self Test scores yourself, or you can choose to submit your scores via e-mail to your instructor.

Reflections

 To respond to these questions online, and to save or submit your response electronically, visit the companion Web site, located at *http://www.prenhall.com/armstrong*. Select Chapter 5 from the front page of the Web site, then choose the Reflections module on the navigation bar on the left side of the page. Instructors and students may also wish to use these questions as discussion topics on the Message Board for the companion Web site.

1. What are some kinds of learners that fall under the general heading "exceptional learners"?

2. What are some important provisions of the Education for All Handicapped Children Act and the Individuals with Disabilities Education Act of 1997?

3. What are some ways teachers can help learners who are blind or visually impaired?

4. What are some learning difficulties commonly faced by deaf and hearing-impaired learners?

5. Why do teachers sometimes allow orthopedically impaired learners to leave classes before the other students are dismissed?

6. What are some principles to observe in working with emotionally disturbed learners, and why might it sometimes be desirable to minimize the number of stimuli to which they are exposed?

7. How would you describe some difficulties faced by young people with learning disabilities? In particular, describe some characteristics of learners with attention deficit disorder, and suggest some things teachers can do to help these young people learn.

8. Why do teachers of gifted learners need to be especially sensitive to these learners' potential self-image problems?

9. Why have enrichment approaches generally been favored over acceleration approaches when programs to serve the needs of gifted learners have been established?

10. What might a teacher do to promote the development of creativity among gifted learners?

￼ Field Experiences, Projects, and Enrichment ￼

1. Invite to your class a director of special education or another official from a local school district who is responsible for overseeing programs for learners with disabilities. Ask this person to describe the kinds of federal and state regulations that must be observed, and request information regarding how decisions are made regarding learning experiences to be provided to each child who is served. If possible, ask to see a copy of a typical individualized education plan.

2. Interview two or more classroom teachers who teach a grade level you intend to teach. Ask them about special things they do to provide instruction for exceptional learners. What kind of special training or assistance do they get from the district to help them with these young people? How do they react to working with these learners? Share your findings with the class in the form of a brief oral report.

3. Prepare a collection of professional journal articles that focus on practical things teachers can do to meet the needs of learners with disabilities who are regular members of their classes. Organize a symposium with several others in your class on the topic "Practical Approaches to Developing a Successful Full-Inclusion Classroom." Draw content from your article collection.

4. Make arrangements to visit a class for gifted learners. (Your course instructor may be able to provide some assistance.) What kinds of instructional techniques did you see being used? Were learners asked to do things that were truly different from the activities of regular classes? Were you able to form impressions of how learners felt about being in the class? Share your findings with your instructor in the form of a brief reaction paper.

5. Some people argue that gifted learners are so bright that they will succeed regardless of what the school provides. Believing this to be true, these critics suggest that it makes little sense for schools to use scarce resources to assist gifted learners. This money, they contend, would be much more wisely spent on average and below-average learners, who need all the help they can get to profit from their school experiences. Organize a debate on this topic: "Resolved: It Is Unwise and Irresponsible to Spend Scarce Educational Dollars on Programs for Gifted Learners." Debate the issue in front of the class, and then organize a follow-up discussion.

References

Armstrong, D. G., & Savage, T. V. (1998). *Teaching in the secondary school: An introduction* (4th ed). Upper Saddle River, NJ: Merrill/Prentice Hall.

Dauber, S. L., & Benbow, C. P. (1990). Aspects of personality and peer relations of extremely talented adolescents. *Gifted Child Quarterly, 34*(1), 10–15.

Gallager, S. L. (1996). *Adolescents' perceived sense of belonging.* Unpublished master's thesis, Fort Hays State University, Kansas.

Henson, K. T., & Eller, B. F. (1999). *Educational Psychology for Effective Teaching.* Belmont, CA: Wadsworth.

IDEA '97: General Information (1997). [*http://www.ed.gov/offices/OSERS/IDEA/overview.html*]

Janney, R., & Snell, M. (1996). How teachers use peer interactions to include students with moderate and severe disabilities in elementary general education classes. *Journal of the Association for Persons with Severe Handicaps, 21,* 72–80.

National Association for the Education of Young Children (1997). *The benefits of an inclusive education: Making it work.* [http://ericps.ed.uiuc.edu/npin/respar/texts/special/inclu697.html]

Sternberg, R. J., & Lubart, T. I. (1991). Creating creative minds. *Phi Delta Kappan, 72*(8), 608–14.

United States Statutes at Large. 91st Congress, 1970–1971, Vol. 84, Part 1. Washington, DC: U.S. Government Printing Office, 1971.

Williams, L. J. (1998). *Membership in inclusive classrooms: Middle school students' perceptions.* Unpublished dissertation, University of Arizona, Tucson.

6

Learners' Rights and Responsibilities

OBJECTIVES

This chapter will help you to

- point out some responsibilities of learners in school.
- explain how application of the legal doctrine of *in loco parentis* has changed in recent years.
- describe *due process* and point out conditions under which it is applied.
- explain limitations of freedom of expression in school settings.
- describe some principles used in deciding cases involving challenges to curriculum content.
- explain some standards that are applied in search and seizure situations.
- state conditions where establishing grooming and dress codes might be constitutional.
- describe implications for teachers of the Family Rights and Privacy Act.

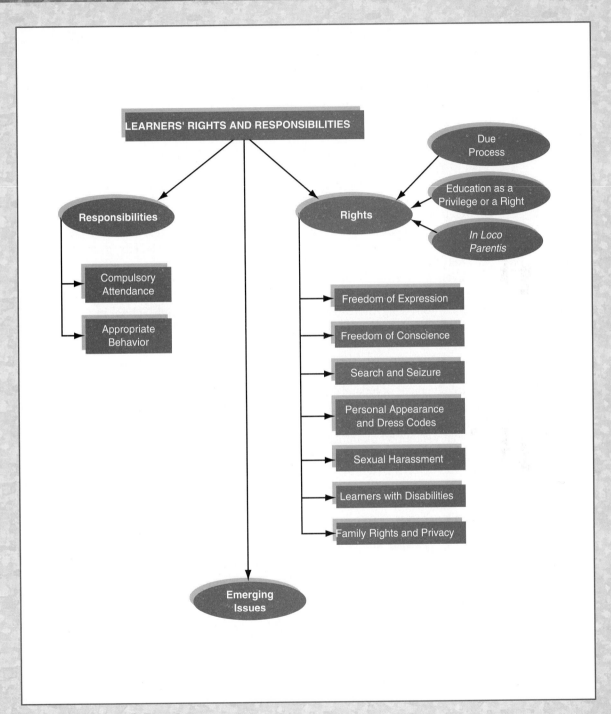

FIGURE 6.1 Learners' Rights and Responsibilities

INTRODUCTION

Years ago, professional educators had little need to concern themselves about rights of learners. Schooling was largely regarded as a privilege. In exchange for this privilege, learners were expected to conform unquestioningly to rules and guidelines established by school authorities. Young people who failed to abide by school regulations could be summarily dismissed.

Today this situation has changed. By and large, young people in the schools enjoy the same constitutional protection as adult citizens. When teaching today, you must be aware of the legal rights of learners to ensure that you do nothing that could lead to legal action.

Staying current on legal guidelines affecting young people in the schools is not easy. Over the past few decades, many courts have considered cases of learners' rights. In some instances, decisions have acted to clarify and expand learners' rights. In others, courts have chosen not to do so. In still other cases, decisions have been a confused mix of expanding learners' rights in certain narrowly defined circumstances and keeping them much as they have been traditionally viewed in others.

Even when learners' rights have been buttressed by court decisions, special circumstances sometimes lead school authorities and others to try to weaken them. For example, following the tragic shooting at Columbine High School in Colorado in 1999, nervous school officials in many parts of the country attempted to impose new, dubiously legal restrictions on learner speech and learner dress (Graves, 1999). These restrictions led to a number of court challenges by learners, parents, and guardians who argued they violated learners' civil rights.

Involvement of federal courts in learners' rights issues began to accelerate during the 1960s. Federal courts began to hear more school-related cases as part of a general trend for more concern about protecting citizens' civil rights and about ensuring the national welfare by guaranteeing access to education and training (Valente, 1994). From these beginnings, there has been a tremendous growth in the number of federal cases involving rights of learners in the schools.

LEARNERS' RESPONSIBILITIES

Over the past several decades, court decisions and statute law have generally been expanding rights of learners. This trend sometimes leads to a downplaying of the point that, in addition to their rights, learners in schools also have important responsibilities.

Attendance

The most fundamental responsibility of the learner is to attend school. It has been recognized that there are several compelling reasons why the state has an interest in the education of all citizens. First of all, democracies cannot survive without educated and informed citizens. Second, higher levels of education correlate with lower crime rates and higher average incomes. For example, the California Superintendent of Public Instruction recently stated that, while it costs approximately $3,000 a year for a preschool program, it costs the state $24,000 for every person jailed. These statistics suggest that dollars spent on education represent an especially good buy for Californians (Skelton, 1999). Third, an educated citizenry acts to attract new business and industry, thus improving society's economic base.

For these reasons, compulsory attendance has been the norm for decades and is an idea that has been copied by other nations (Fischer, Schimmel, & Kelly, 1999). However, there have been challenges to compulsory education statutes. Most of them have come about because of perceived conflicts between parents' rights to raise their children as they see fit and the needs of the state to produce educated citizens. In recent years, publicity focusing on problems with public schools has led large numbers of parents to seek alternatives to the public schools. As the new century begins, about 2% of the school-age population is being taught at home (Fischer et al., 1999). While this is a small percentage, it represents a sizable increase over previous years.

Compulsory education laws (whether provided in public schools, home schools, or other approved settings) have generally been upheld by the courts. Such laws have been found consistent with provisions of the United States Constitution and those of the various states. At the same time, however, the courts have recognized the rights of parents and guardians to direct the upbringing of their children.

The courts have held that the state cannot require all children to attend a *public* school. This means that compulsory education requirements can be met through either public or private schools. One issue related to mandatory school attendance has concerned the number of years learners must attend. In a case litigated in the state of Wisconsin, some Amish parents objected to the requirements of compulsory attendance to the age of 16. While supporting the need for basic literacy, they argued that secondary schools' emphases on competition, worldly success, and intellectual and scientific achievements were contrary to their basic religious beliefs and would destroy their close-knit community (*Wisconsin v. Yoder,* 1972). The courts decided in favor of the religious freedom of the Amish and ruled that the Amish way of life was an acceptable alternative to a formal secondary school. However, because of the unique circumstances and the reputation of the Amish, it is unlikely that this case will serve as a precedent in other circumstances (Fischer et al., 1999).

Another more recent question has surfaced regarding the definition of a private school. Are home schools private schools, and are they acceptable forms of mandatory education? Generally, courts have viewed home schools as acceptable alternatives to public schools so long as they operate in a manner consistent with the special requirements of their state.

The most common state requirement for alternative education is that the education provided must be "equivalent" in scope and quality to that provided in public schools. A typical state law requires that all branches of knowledge taught to children of the corresponding age in public schools must also be taught in any approved alternative schools. Some states require alternative schools to be approved by the local superintendent of schools or the local school board (Fischer et al., 1999).

Much litigation has focused on the issue of what constitutes equivalency. Some states have taken a strict interpretation of "equivalent" to apply not only to the curriculum but also to the teacher; in other words, certified or qualified teachers must teach the children. Other states are more lenient or even silent regarding this issue.

Many court cases have arisen in situations involving desires of parents or guardians to educate children at home. In an Illinois case, the state supreme court upheld the rights of parents to teach their daughter at home. The court ruled that, though state law required all children to be educated, it did not specify the place and particular manner of their education. The court also noted that the conditions of instruction in the home were consistent with the state's standards for private schools (*People v. Levisen,* 1950).

In a Maine case, a court ruled that the state had the right to impose reasonable standards on parents seeking to educate their children at home. When the parents in this case refused to submit their homeschooling plans for approval, their children were declared to be truant when they did not present themselves at the local public school (*State v. McDonough,* 1983). Similarly, a Kansas court found that homeschooling that was unplanned or unscheduled and taught by a parent who was not certified did not meet the legal requirements for an "equivalent education" (*In re Sawyer,* 1983). In general, the ability of private and home schools to meet compulsory attendance standards depends on a particular state's laws and on how the courts have chosen to interpret the equivalent-education requirement.

In a Massachusetts case, the courts upheld the right of the state to supervise homeschooling programs. The court ruled that local school officials could approve homeschooling programs based on the curriculum, the length of the program, the qualifications of the parent to instruct, the content of the instruction, and a process for evaluating progress of the children. In its decision, the court noted that, though no regulation required parents to have a teaching certificate, the state legitimately could evaluate the parents' competency to teach. In addition, standardized testing of homeschooled children was declared to be an acceptable approach to determining progress of these learners (Care and *Protection of Charles,* 1987).

The issue of school choice stimulated controversy in recent years. Proponents of school-choice approaches that would allow parents to direct public-education money to private schools suggest such policies increase competition between all schools (public and private). They contend this competition will force all schools to improve. However, the use of public money given to parents to allow them to enroll their children in the school of their choice raises legal issues. Among them are issues related to the separation of church and state when private schools have a religious affiliation.

Opponents of spending public money for private-school education contend that the practice is not in the best interests of society. For example, it may lead to increased economic, racial, and religious segregation (Fischer et al., 1999). In addition, some critics argue against the proposition that competition for funds will benefit all schools. They point out that private schools have the ability to select the learners they serve. Public schools, on the other hand, must accept all learners who live in the communities they serve. In addition, private schools in some cases do not have to comply with as many state regulations as do public schools concerning such issues as certification of teachers or providing special services for exceptional learners. The net result of these circumstances, it is argued, is that using public funds for both private and public schools will leave public schools with a disproportionate number of learners who are difficult and costly to educate.

Behavior

Learners have a responsibility to follow reasonable school rules. As a teacher, you have the right to establish reasonable rules and regulations in order to ensure a productive and safe educational environment. Learners have the responsibility to comply with these regulations and to submit to your authority in the classroom. This relationship is typically expressed in formal regulations regarding operations of the schools.

For example, the California School Code indicates that every teacher in the public school shall hold each learner accountable for his or her conduct on the way to and from school, on the playgrounds, and during recess. Any certified employee can exercise reasonable physical control over a learner in order to protect property or learner safety or to maintain conditions conducive to learning. Disrupting school and willfully defying valid authority are grounds for suspension and expulsion from school (California Teachers Association, 1992).

Refraining from the destruction of property is another responsibility of learners. Education regulations in many states hold learners liable for damages if they destroy or damage school property. Often there are provisions that allow grades, diplomas, or transcripts to be withheld if a learner or his or her parents or guardians have not paid for damages to school property.

This teacher is explaining playground rules to these children. Teachers can be held accountable for learners' conduct in this setting.

Video Viewpoint

Honor Students Controversy

WATCH: In this ABC News video segment, two unwed mothers who are honor students are suing their Kentucky high school, because despite their high grades, they were denied membership in the National Honor Society. School officials have taken the position that engaging in premarital sex is a mark against "character," one of the four criteria determining eligibility.

THINK: With your classmates or in your teaching journal, consider these questions:

1. Do you believe the two girls in the video, Chastity and Somer, should be inducted into the Grant County High School chapter of the National Honor Society? Why or why not?
2. ACLU attorney Sara Mandelbaum makes the point that boys in the same chapter of the National Honor Society may have engaged in premarital sex, as may have girls who have not gotten pregnant or who have had an abortion. How should those individuals be handled?

LINK: What messages do you think Chastity's pregnancy and her subsequent words and actions sent to other students at her school? What message do you think the school administration is sending to the rest of the students at Grant County High School?

Unsafe practices such as hazing and bringing weapons or controlled substances to school are also prohibited. Most states provide for immediate suspension and potential expulsion if a learner brings weapons or controlled substances to school. In addition, harming or threatening physical injury to another person is grounds for suspension and expulsion.

Learners are expected to behave in socially appropriate ways. In one high school, a student delivered a speech that was filled with sexual innuendo when nominating a friend for a school office. Though the student did not use explicit language, he was informed the next day that he was suspended for three days and that his name had been removed from the list of possible graduation speakers. The student filed suit, claiming that these actions violated First Amendment freedom-of-speech rights. The court ruled that rights of the student needed to be balanced against society's interest in teaching young people within the boundaries of socially appropriate behavior. Since the speech was plainly offensive, the actions of the school district were upheld (Zirkel & Richardson, 1988).

Behaving in a responsible manner is another responsibility of learners. They do not have the right to interfere with the establishment of a safe and effective school environment, and they must submit to the reasonable rules and regulations of school officials. However, the rules and regulations governing learner behavior must be clear, unambiguous, and not excessively broad. For example, courts have ruled against excessively vague regulations that require learners to "dress in good taste," or "avoid extremes in style" (Fischer et al., 1999). Similarly, rules such as one that would give the school principal the authority to make any rules "that are in the best interest of the school" have been declared to be excessively broad. Poorly defined rules fail to clearly inform learners of what constitutes acceptable behavior. Hence, courts have been concerned that these poorly drafted regulations may violate learners' constitutionally protected rights (Fischer et al., 1999).

LEARNERS' RIGHTS

In Loco Parentis

The traditional legal doctrine governing the relationship of the school and the learner was known as *in loco parentis.* According to this doctrine, the school acted "in place of the parent." This meant that the school and its designees (administrators and teachers) were free to treat young people much as they would have treated their own children. Common-law precedents relating to the parent-child relationship were extended to the school.

For example, children cannot take their parents to court and demand a hearing on the grounds of a disagreement over some parental directive. Parents are legally defined as having a custodial relationship with their children. Under *in loco parentis,* this same custodial relationship was vested in the school. Buttressed by this legal doctrine, school officials were given substantial authority in establishing rules and in disciplining learners.

The application of *in loco parentis* to school actions began to change in the early 1960s, when a number of human and civil rights issues captured public attention. Efforts to extend full constitutional privileges to all racial groups prompted people to become interested in whether constitutional guarantees really applied to everybody or only to some people. University groups were quick to speak out against institutional practices that seemed to deny learners the same constitutional protection they would enjoy if they were not enrolled in institutions of higher learning. Finally, an increasing public suspicion that the government was not being responsive to the general public will concerning the Vietnam War led to a closer scrutiny of all traditional sources of authority. In this context, it was only a matter of time before questions began to surface regarding the *in loco parentis* relationship between school officials and school learners.

Some critics of *in loco parentis* charged that the doctrine represented an outdated view of the relationship between schools and learners. Early schools were different from today's public schools. They often were small and were clearly institutions of the local community. The ability of local leaders to hire and fire teachers ensured a consistency between instructional practices and local values. Given the kind of person likely to be hired as a teacher, parents readily accepted the teacher as a surrogate parent for their children.

This situation has changed. Schools and teachers are more distant from parents. Many parents and guardians have only limited information about the teachers and school officials who work with their children. For the most part, they have no voice in the selection of their children's teachers. Consequently, parents and guardians often feel that they have little influence over what goes on in the schools, and they are often reluctant to accept all of the actions of school officials as consistent with what they would do.

What Do You Think?

Do Students Have Too Many Rights?

During earlier periods in the history of American education, schooling was considered to be a *privilege.* Accordingly, professional educators were free to impose rules and enforce sanctions, including expulsion, without much concern for legal rights of learners.

Over the past few decades, schooling has been redefined as a *right,* and full constitutional protection has been extended to school learners. This has placed limits on the kind of actions school authorities can take. Today, educators cannot infringe upon the constitutionally protected rights of the young people they serve.

Some have advocated this extension of rights as only reasonable. They note that education is an important activity that can influence the future direction of an individual's life. They point out that in the past, school officials have acted capriciously to remove students for arbitrary reasons that have no bearing on the safety and operation of a school. Such an important life task cannot be left to the whim of a school administrator who is mainly interested in promoting conformity and blind obedience. Individuals need to have some protection from those school officials who act unwisely. They contend that this focus has made schools better places, because school officials have had to act responsibly.

Incidents involving shootings in high schools around the nation have led others to the conclusion that learners have too many rights and that school officials need more authority in order to protect the safety of those attending the school. They contend that school officials should have the right to randomly search learners, limit the type of clothing they may wear, and act without fear of violating learners' constitutional rights. Others believe that the extension of full constitutional protection to learners has been a major cause of discipline problems in schools. In their view, teachers and administrators are no longer able to respond to problems in a forceful manner.

What Do You Think?

1. Should schooling be redefined as a privilege so that professional educators can more aggressively respond to problems without having to be so concerned about legal rights of learners?
2. Critics of the trend to extend more rights to learners contend that this has greatly contributed to violence and discipline problems in schools. How do you react to this assertion? Do you have evidence to support your view?
3. Do you think all of the different groups that collectively make up American society have similar views regarding the issue of extending full constitutional protection to learners? What are some groups that might include a large number of people favoring this trend? What are some others that might include a large number of people opposing it? How might you account for differences in these views?

As a result of the breakdown of the *in loco parentis* doctrine, you can no longer assume that parents and guardians will necessarily view your actions as being in the best interests of their children, and they may challenge some of your decisions. Further, you must operate with the understanding that learners today enjoy many of the same constitutional protections as adult citizens. This means that you need to consider your actions carefully so you will not leave yourself open to unwanted legal proceedings.

Education as a Privilege or a Right

Schooling was once regarded as a privilege to be enjoyed by those who could live by the rules, not a right that society felt was owed to all young people. Because schooling was not viewed as a right, learners were not considered to have any legal recourse when they were removed from school for violating a school rule or regulation. At that time, the absence of formal schooling or a school diploma was not seen as a serious limitation to a person's economic future.

The view of schooling as a privilege rather than a right started to unravel when critics began to point out that literacy had become necessary for economic survival in our society. Given the need for an educated population, it was argued that access to public schooling, an excellent vehicle for promoting literacy, should be considered "a substantial right" to which all citizens were entitled.

This important shift in the legal view of education as a right rather than a privilege carried with it important constitutional implications. The United States Constitution includes certain protections. One of these is the requirement that "due process of law" be observed in situations that could result in the loss of a right. In the days of *in loco parentis,* the due process clause did not apply to school learners. This was true because, legally, the full rights of citizens had not been extended to them. Important litigation changed their status.

One landmark case that helped to extend the rights of citizens to learners was the famous *Tinker v. Des Moines Independent Community School District* (1969). In this case, a group of learners in the Des Moines school district wore black arm bands to school to protest the United States' involvement in the Vietnam War. They refused to follow a school policy against wearing the armbands and were suspended. They challenged this action, and the case reached the Supreme Court of the United States. The Supreme Court indicated that once states establish public schools, learners have a property right to the educational services they provide. The Court further declared that neither learners nor teachers shed their constitutional rights at the schoolhouse door. This decision established that learners have a right to a public education and that they enjoy the constitutional protection of any citizen. These rights cannot be abridged unless specific *due process* procedures are followed.

Due Process

The Fourteenth Amendment to the United States Constitution outlines principles of due process. To be entitled to due process protection, a learner must show that he or she has potentially been deprived of either a *property right* or a *liberty right.* A "property right" is a right to specific property, whether tangible or intangible. For example, an actress might have a property right in her name and photograph and be able to sell these "properties" to others. The term "liberty right" refers to the right people enjoy to be free from all restraints except those imposed by law. In education, the loss of a free public education has been considered the loss of a property right, and the subsequent loss of reputation due to expulsion has been considered the loss of a liberty right.

The Fourteenth Amendment due process principle was extended by a court decision in the case of *Goss v. Lopez* (1975). This litigation involved several young people who were suspended from school for 10 days for acts of violence. Some of them claimed they were innocent bystanders and that they had not been granted a hearing. In its decision, the court ruled that suspension from school for 10 days was a serious punishment that could damage an individual's reputation and even interfere with later opportunities for employment. Therefore, it held that the schools had to respect the rights of learners to due process in disciplinary matters that might lead to suspension or expulsion.

Although many people understand that due process is designed to ensure that people receive fair treatment in an adversarial situation, the two specific components of due process are less well known. The first is the *substantive component,* which includes the basic set of principles on which due process is based. The second is the *procedural component,* which consists of the procedures that must be followed to ensure that due process rights have not been violated.

The Substantive Component
The substantive component of due process can be thought of as including the following principles:

- Individuals are not to be disciplined on the basis of unwritten rules.
- Rules are not to be vague.
- Individuals are entitled to a hearing before an impartial tribunal.
- The identity of witnesses must be revealed.
- Decisions are to be supported by substantial evidence.

In times past, educators sometimes overlooked one or more of these principles. For example, some administrators failed to specify rules out of a fear that written regulations would undermine their flexibility to respond to problem situations. Furthermore, many rules and regulations that were written were couched in such vague terms that people could not easily determine whether or not they were in compliance.

In the days when the courts were not insisting on due process guarantees for school children, there was a general reluctance to release witnesses' names to young people who were charged with violating school rules or regulations. There was a fear that such a disclosure might result in witnesses being intimidated and that, in future cases, people would hesitate to come forward with information.

It is undoubtedly true that the necessity to protect the due process rights of young people has increased the work of school administrators and has somewhat reduced their flexibility. On the other hand, given the amount of documentation that now must support charges, there probably has been a healthy reduction in the number of miscarriages of justice in cases involving young people and school authorities.

The Procedural Component
The procedural component is concerned with the procedures that must be followed to ensure that principles of due process will be observed. In general, the procedural component of due process includes the following:

- Rules governing learners' behavior must be distributed in writing to learners and their parents at the beginning of the school year.

- Whenever learners have been accused of a rules' infraction that might result in a due process procedure, the charges must be provided in writing to learners and their parents.
- Written notice of the hearing must be given such that there is sufficient time provided for learners and their representatives to prepare a defense. Usually, the hearing must be held within two weeks.
- A fair hearing must include:
  - the right of the accused to be represented by legal counsel,
  - the right of the accused to present a defense and introduce evidence,
  - the right of the accused to face his or her accusers, and
  - the right of the accused to cross-examine witnesses.
- The decision of the hearing board is to be based on the evidence presented and must be rendered within a reasonable period of time.
- The accused must be informed of his or her rights to appeal decisions.

There are a few circumstances where due process is not required. For example, due process procedures do not apply when the offense is a minor or trivial one that is not likely to result in suspension. For example, sending learners to the principal's office or putting them in brief detention does not require the implementation of due process. Secondly, if an emergency situation arises and the offense threatens the health or safety or people or property, school officials can act without first having a hearing. However, there is an expectation that due process procedures be instituted as soon as possible after the danger has passed (Fischer et al., 1999). In addition, only minimal due process is required for those who are suspended for less than 10 days. This less complex version requires that the learner be provided with:

- a presentation of oral or written notice of the charges,
- an explanation of the evidence if the learner denies the charges, and
- an opportunity for the learner to present his or her view of the situation (Zirkel & Richardson, 1988).

Freedom of Expression

One of the fundamental rights of United States citizens is freedom of expression. The famous *Tinker v. Des Moines Independent Community School District* (1969) case mentioned earlier laid down important freedom-of-expression guidelines for schools. You will recall that this case centered on concerns about learners who, contrary to policy, wore black armbands to school as a protest of the United States' involvement in Vietnam. In its ruling, the Court struck down the rule banning the arm bands, arguing that wearing the arm bands was a form of free speech—a right guaranteed to all citizens that could not be violated by school districts.

The ruling in this case, however, did not extend unrestricted free-speech rights to learners. Where this issue has been adjudicated, courts have consistently held that the rights of both parties must be considered. For example, school districts have a right to provide safe and orderly educational environments. Thus, in individual situations,

Following the Web 6.1

Due Process

Extension of due process rights to public school students represents one of the most dramatic changes in the legal status of learners over the past 40 years. As a teacher, you need to understand that learners in the classroom now generally enjoy the same legal protections as adult citizens. Guidelines regarding procedures school authorities must follow are particularly stringent when learners with disabilities are involved. The examples of Web sites introduced here will provide you with some good starting points should you wish to learn more about how due process is applied in school settings.

For hot links to these sites, visit the companion Web site, located at *http://www. prenhall.com/armstrong.* Select Chapter 6 from the front page of the Web site, then choose the Following the Web module on the navigation bar on the left side of the page.

Fourteenth Amendment: Due Process: Students

- *http://146.187.224.89/cehd/education/EDUC420/EDUC420DueProcessStu.html*

  At this Web site, you will find a succinct description of due process provisions of the Fourteenth Amendment to the United States Constitution. Implications for procedures to be followed in cases that may lead to suspension or expulsion are included. There is also a useful list of due process principles related to disciplining learners.

Summary of Due Process Procedures for School Suspensions

- *http://www.wcpss.net/Instructional/Dueprocess/policy.htm*

  You will find detailed information here about guidelines that are to be applied in cases that may result in (a) immediate removal from school, (b) short-term suspension, (c) long-term suspension/expulsion, (d) appeals of long-term suspension/expulsion, (e) administrative appeals, and (f) multidisciplinary reviews of exceptional children.

Supreme Court Cases

- *http://law.touro.edu/patch/CaseSummary.html*

  This site features succinct reviews of a large number of Supreme Court cases. Each case is described in terms of the relevant facts, the issue in dispute, and the opinion the Court rendered. One of the cases included is *Goss v. Lopez,* which resulted in a decision declaring that education is a property interest and that, hence, school students enjoy due process protections of the Fourteenth Amendment.

learners' free-speech rights must be balanced against the rights of the school district to maintain an orderly educational environment.

The decision in the Tinker case prompted considerable debate in educational circles. Some teachers were confused regarding exactly what authority they retained in the area of controlling learners. A few people saw the Tinker decision as interference in the school management process that could undermine the smooth functioning of the educational program. Others drew different conclusions, contending that the Supreme

Due Process Hearing Officer Manual

- *http://ericae.net/ericdb/ED417565.htm*

  At this site, you will find a description of contents of a manual prepared by the State of Arizona that details due process procedures. Special attention is devoted to information about due process procedures for learners with disabilities.

Due Process and FAPE

- *http://www.ed.gov/pubs/chartdisab/dueproc.html*

  At this site, you will find information about the relationship between the due process doctrine and the legal obligation schools have to provide a free appropriate public education (FAPE) for each learner. Results of a study are described that point out educators' obligations as they attempt to act in ways consistent with due process requirements.

Provisions of Special Interest to Parents

- *http://www.ed.gov/offices/OSERS/IDEA/Brief-12.html*

  This material focuses on the Individuals with Disabilities Education Act of 1997. As the title implies, there is useful information here for parents, much of which informs them about due process procedures mandated by this legislation.

National Coalition of Advocates for Students

- *http://www.ncas1.org/*

  This is the home page of the National Coalition of Advocates for Students. This group has special interests in promoting a quality education for especially vulnerable learners . . . the poor, children of color, recent immigrants, and learners with disabilities. Directed toward parents, there are links at this site to information about issues related to due process and other rights of school learners.

Resources on Educational Rights of Students with Disabilities

- *http://cleweb.org/catalog/disab.htm*

  This Web site, maintained by the Center for Law and Education, includes titles of a number of books that focus on due process and other rights of learners with disabilities. A brief synopsis is provided for each listed title.

[Note: Web addresses change frequently. If you are unable to locate one of these sites using the listed URL, try putting the site name in a standard search engine.]

Court had done little to undermine the real authority of school officials. They saw the case as focusing primarily on the legitimacy of processes followed by school officials in exercising their authority. According to educators who viewed the outcome of the Tinker case as a positive development, the decision provided educators with an opportunity to develop procedures that would enhance public confidence in the schools. Not only would these procedures be constitutional, but they would also blunt criticism from people who felt that many actions of school authorities were arbitrary and irresponsible.

The freedom-of-expression issue was also addressed in the *Hazelwood School District v. Kuhlmeier* (1988) decision. In this case, a school principal censored an article in the school paper that dealt with the topic of teenage pregnancy. The students claimed that this was a limitation of their freedom of expression. The Supreme Court ruled that such activities as student publications and theatrical presentations are part of the curriculum and carry the implicit endorsement of the school. Therefore, expression occurring in connection with these activities could be legitimately subjected to more control than is true when expression occurs in contexts outside of the control of the school. Furthermore, the court made a distinction between the kind of speech that was at issue in the Hazelwood case as compared to the Tinker Case. It noted that expression in the Tinker case was "political speech," whereas expression in the Hazelwood case was "educational speech." In the Court's view, school authorities could legitimately regulate speech in this latter category.

Learners' freedom-of-expression rights allow them to criticize school policies as long as they do it in a nondisruptive manner. However, critical speech that incites violence, calls for a learner strike or a building takeover, or abuses school officials with vulgar and profane language is not protected.

Freedom of Conscience

Controversies in this area have centered on several key issues, including concerns related to the teaching of certain content, objections to requirements for learner participation in ceremonies involving saluting the flag, and disputes relating to the issue of free exercise of religion.

Objections to the Curriculum   In general, the courts have agreed that learners can be excused from certain parts of the academic program if they have religious or moral objections to what is being studied. Two issues have often been considered in deciding cases of this kind. The first relates to whether the subject being objected to is deemed essential for citizenship and, therefore, is of vital interest to the state. The second issue concerns the degree to which the schools have a right to make and enforce regulations to ensure the efficient and effective operation of schools. Court decisions have tended to focus heavily on the specifics of the situation being litigated.

The most common objections to the curriculum focus on the issue of sex education. While these courses are voluntary in many schools, in some instances they are not. Proponents of sex education argue that there is a compelling state interest in providing such a course. They argue that the threat of AIDS and the social costs of teenage pregnancy are sufficiently serious to warrant their inclusion in the curriculum. Some learners and their parents or guardians object to the courses as a violation of their religious beliefs. A California court ruled that sex education courses do not violate freedom of religion, especially if the course is voluntary. In New Jersey, the Commissioner of Education ruled that required courses on family living, which included some sex education, were not a violation of freedom of religion (Fischer et al., 1999).

Other challenges to the curriculum have focused on objections to dancing in physical education classes, playing with cards, and watching movies. It is hard to argue that dancing in physical education classes is essential to citizenship and is of vital interest to the state. Hence, the courts have long upheld objections of learners who wished to avoid dancing because of their religious convictions. The issue of watching films as a part of the educational program is more complex. It could be argued that a film presents material in a way the learning of important content in ways that are hard to duplicate and there are no easily available alternatives. In addition, if granting exceptions to certain parts of the program such as a film results in serious disruptions of the educational process, then the exceptions may not be allowed.

In recent years, a number of challenges have focused on the objections to the use of certain books. Many of the objections have focused on the charges that certain texts and library books advance secular humanism and promote Satanism and witchcraft. The courts have generally upheld the inclusion of these books. They have stated that the books are not advancing some poorly defined religion and that the works of fiction and fantasy by well known authors promote legitimate education objectives and, hence, are acceptable (Fischer et al., 1999).

People who object to the teaching of evolution have initiated legal challenges to school programs. In Arkansas, the state legislature at one time passed a law forbidding schools in that state to include the teaching of evolution in the prescribed curriculum. The Supreme Court ruled this law to be unconstitutional on the grounds that it violated the First Amendment clause relating to the establishment of religion (*Epperson v. State of Arkansas,* 1968).

In some places, there have been attempts to force the schools to teach "creationism" or "scientific creationism" along with evolution. These efforts have generally been found to be unconstitutional on the grounds that creationism is a religious belief and that requiring it to be taught would violate the First Amendment's establishment-of-religion clause. On the other hand, at least one court has implied that creationism could be introduced in a social studies class provided it was described simply as a belief held by some people (*McLean v. Arkansas Board of Education,* 1982).

Saluting the Flag　　In general, the courts have agreed that learners can refuse to salute the flag because of religious or moral convictions. The courts have decided that a refusal to salute the flag does not constitute a serious threat to the welfare of the state; hence, the state has no compelling interest in ensuring that every learner engages in this activity. In the absence of this compelling interest, the courts have given precedence to the individual moral and religious principles of learners. The courts have also ruled that a learner cannot be required to stand or leave the room while others participate in the flag-salute ceremony (*Lipp v. Morris,* 1978).

Search and Seizure

The Fourth Amendment to the United States Constitution protects individuals against unreasonable search and seizure. Recent concern about drug abuse and crime in the schools has brought forth numerous challenges to the rights of school officials to conduct searches. When the doctrine of *in loco parentis* was still in force, school officials were free to search learners much as parents were free to search their own children.

Federal court decisions have decreed that students cannot be forced to participate in flag-saluting ceremonies.

With the weakening of the *in loco parentis* doctrine in recent years, teachers and administrators more and more have come to be seen as agents of the state rather than as surrogate parents. Hence, they have been obligated to consider the rights of learners in any situation that might lead to a search of a learner and his or her property.

Two general principles govern the right to search: *probable cause* and *reasonable suspicion*. Probable cause means that evidence of wrongdoing is sufficiently convincing to strongly support the view that a party is guilty of illegal behavior. The strict standard of probable cause often requires the testimony of a reliable witness and normally is required before authorities will issue a search warrant.

Reasonable suspicion is a much less stringent standard, requiring only that there be some reasonable suspicion that someone is guilty of an offense. Typically, this is the standard applied when school authorities decide that a search is warranted. More specifically, two other guidelines are applied: (1) the expectation of privacy and (2) the potential intrusiveness of the search. A search to be conducted in an area in which the individual has little expectation of privacy does not need as much justification as a search in an area in which an individual has a great expectation of privacy. For example, little expectation of privacy is associated with a school desk, which is public property. On the other hand, a purse is a personal possession and, logically, a person might have a higher expectation of privacy regarding its contents.

In general, the issue of intrusiveness has to do with the degree to which a search might come into close contact with a person's body. The closer the search comes to the body, the more intrusive it is. The most intrusive search of all is a strip search. Some states prohibit strip searches in schools. In California, for example, no school employee is allowed to conduct a search that involves the removal or rearranging of clothing (California Teachers Association, 1992).

When considering whether any kind of search is appropriate, school officials often apply four basic tests. The first concerns the target of the search. The greater the potential danger to the health or safety of learners in the school, the greater the justification for the search. A gun or a bomb poses an immediate and serious danger; on the other hand, a stolen CD player may offer little immediate threat. Hence, school officials might need a great deal of evidence to establish the likelihood that the object would be found before they would authorize a search.

A second test relates to the quality of the information that has led to consideration of a possible search. The reliability of the people reporting the information must be assessed. Several reliable individuals who divulge similar information provide a more defensible ground for a search than a tip from an anonymous caller.

The third test concerns the nature of the place to be searched. If this is an area where there is a high traditional expectation of privacy, school officials will want very solid information before authorizing a search. However, they might be willing to authorize a search based on less convincing information if the search is to be conducted in an area such as a school locker, where there is little traditional expectation of privacy.

The fourth test focuses on the nature of the proposed search itself. If searches of individuals are to be conducted, authorities will want substantial evidence before giving their approval. The age and sex of the person to be searched is also often a consideration.

The landmark case of *New Jersey v. T.L.O.* (1985) focused on several of the issues involved in searching learners in school settings. In this case, a teacher entered a girls' restroom and found T.L.O. (the initials of a learner) and another girl holding lighted cigarettes. Since smoking was against the school rules, both girls were taken to the office. When T.L.O. was asked to open her purse, she did so. Her open purse revealed additional cigarettes, drug paraphernalia, and other evidence that suggested she was engaged in selling drugs. T.L.O. claimed that the evidence could not be used against her because her purse was searched illegally. The Supreme Court ruled in favor of the school, rejecting the argument that probable cause was required in school searches. They indicated that schools have met the standard of reasonable suspicion for a search of this nature if the student has violated or is violating either the laws or school rules. Since T.L.O. was observed smoking, that provided sufficient grounds for reasonable suspicion. The fact that cigarettes were easily observable in her purse provided additional justification for the search of her purse.

Other questions have arisen when searches involve school lockers, school desks, and student cars. Although the Supreme Court has not ruled on any of these specific situations, lower courts have consistently applied the principle of reasonable suspicion established in the T.L.O. case to such searches. The exceptions seem to be if the search invades areas where the learner has a reasonable expectation of privacy or if the search was conducted because of a suspicion that some school rule might have been violated. For example, a girl in one case was observed in the parking lot when she should have been in class. When she was found to be in possession of some readmission slips that she should not have had, the administrator ordered a search of the student for drugs. The courts ruled against the school and stated that the violation of a school rule does not constitute reasonable suspicion that a specific law has been violated and that a search would produce evidence of that violation.

This dog is sniffing for drugs.

In another case, the courts ruled against a school official who searched the locker of a student when he observed the student giving a cigarette to another student. The principal took away the pack of cigarettes and then searched the locker. He found some marijuana in the coat pocket of the student. The court stated that once the pack of cigarettes had been seized, there was no reasonable suspicion to conduct a further search and that the coat pocket was a place where the student had a reasonable expectation of privacy.

As a general rule, the courts have upheld the searches of school lockers by school officials. They point out that after assigning lockers to individual learners, school officials still maintain a right of access to them. In fact, school officials may have a duty to search lockers if they have a reasonable suspicion that something illegal is being stored in these facilities.

In general, searching learners' clothing or engaging in body searches entail an invasion of privacy. Therefore the higher standard of probable cause is needed in order to justify such a search. In these cases, a consideration of what is to be seized is also a factor. For example, in an Alabama case (*Jenkins by Hall v. Talladega City Board of Education,* 1996), the court discussed a continuum with drugs and weapons at one extreme and less valuable items of nondangerous contraband at the other. They stated that strip searches would never be justified for those items found on the nondangerous contraband end of the continuum.

Critical Incident

To Search or Not to Search?

Ms. Shin, a first-year teacher at Upper Madrona Middle School, parked her car in the teachers' lot and began walking toward the office. She noticed a small group of students clustered at the end of one of the hallways. She recognized several of the boys as seventh graders who were in an English class taught by Madeline O'Toole, one of her friends. She had heard Madeline describe the boys as "discipline problems."

As Ms. Shin watched, she observed one of the boys take something out of his backpack and give it to the others in exchange for money. She thought she might be witnessing a drug transaction. She headed quickly toward the boy with the backpack. 'What should I do?' she wondered. 'Should I make him open the backpack? Can I legally do that? What are my rights here? What if this kid refuses to cooperate? Do I go ahead and look anyway?'

As Ms. Shin approached, the boy noticed her coming and quickly zipped his bag. He started to move away.

"Wait a minute," Ms. Shin called out. "What are you boys doing?"

"Not a thing," one of them replied. "Just talking."

"Come on, you'll have to do better than that," said Ms. Shin. "I saw some stuff come out of that bag and some money change hands."

"Oh, well, we were just swapping some trading cards." The speaker was the boy who had zipped up his bag.

"Could I see them?" asked Ms. Shin.

"Naw, they wouldn't interest you," the boy replied.

. . .

What does Ms. Shin suspect might be going on when she sees this group gathered together in the hall? Are her views based on solid evidence that relates to what is happening, or does the information she believes she has about these particular individuals color her perceptions?

How do the boys perceive Ms. Shin's line of questioning? Are their perceptions accurate? What prior experiences may have led to the kinds of feelings they may have about this situation?

What should Ms. Shin do next? Does she have a right to demand that the boys allow her to search their belongings? If they refuse, does she have the right to conduct a search? Do you think the courts would consider her actions justified in the event the boy or his parents challenged the legality of her actions? Should she just go on and report the behavior to the principal? Should she simply accept their explanation about swapping trading cards and ignore what she saw? What would be the possible consequences if she decided to forget about the incident and it later turned out that these boys had been dealing drugs?

To respond to this Critical Incident online, and to save or submit your response electronically, visit the companion Web site, located at *http://www.prenhall.com/armstrong*. Select Chapter 6 from the front page of the Web site, then choose the Critical Incidents module on the navigation bar on the left side of the page. Instructors and students may also wish to use these scenarios as discussion topics on the Message Board for the companion Web site.

In summary, case law in the area of search and seizure does not provide absolutely clear guidelines to educators. Because of this uncertainty, as a teacher, you should not attempt searches on our own initiative. Responsibility for authorizing searches should be left in the hands of those school administrators who are in a position to check their legal position with the school district's legal counsel.

Personal Appearance and Dress Codes

Issues associated with learner appearance and dress codes have received considerable attention in recent years. Interest has escalated, in part, as gang violence in schools has become a matter of broad concern. Members of many gangs wear identifying colors, insignias, jackets, or caps. In addition, some clothing styles such as loose-fitting clothes have become associated with gang activity because they make it easier for gang members to hide weapons. In response to concerns about gangs, many school officials have tried to limit kinds of clothing that learners can wear to school.

Some people have wanted to go so far as to require all learners to wear uniforms to school. They claim that this would eliminate any sort of gang identification, would help decrease discipline problems, and would lead to a healthier school environment where the emphasis was on learning. Some parents and guardians have agreed and supported efforts to establish dress codes. Others have seen such proposals as an unreasonable interference with their children's right to choose what they wear to school.

School dress regulations that seek to preserve health, safety, and school discipline have been found to be constitutional (Valente, 1994). This means that if school officials can demonstrate that wearing certain objects or attire results in violence or disrupts the educational environment, they have the authority to ban these items. Similarly, school officials have authority to make regulations related to wearing unsanitary clothing or clothing that is vulgar or offensive.

Guidelines are not so clear on some other personal-appearance issues. These include attempts to regulate hair length of males or prohibit the wearing of jeans by females. Challenges to appearance and dress codes generally focus on two issues: (1) whether choice of dress or appearance is a type of symbolic free expression protected by the First Amendment and (2) whether choice of dress involves constitutional "liberty rights."

Generally, the courts have considered restrictions on hairstyles as more of an invasion of privacy than learner choice of clothing. They note that hair length is quite fundamental to personal appearance, and restrictions on hair styles have an important impact on individuals. Similarly, it has been difficult to prove that hair length is related to issues of morality or to disturbances of the educational environment (Fischer et al., 1999). Further, courts have noted that there is a quality of permanence attached to restrictions on hair length that differs from restrictions on clothing. Learners can change their clothes after school; they cannot instantly change the length of their hair. In one case, the court stated that there was no compelling logic behind the view that decency, decorum, or good conduct required short hair for males (*Richards v. Thurston,* 1970).

In another case, a principal argued that hair length of male students needed to be regulated for reasons of health and safety. The court rejected this argument, noting that no similar argument had been made to explain why a similar requirement should not also restrict the length of girls' hair (*Crews v. Cloncs,* 1970). The Supreme Court has not chosen to consider a hair-grooming case, as the justices have not felt that the issue of grooming standards involves nationally important constitutional questions (Fischer et al., 1999).

Different circuit courts have ruled in different ways in individual grooming cases. For example, federal appeals courts in the First Circuit, Fourth Circuit, Seventh Circuit, and Eighth Circuit have all declared that an individual's right to establish personal grooming standards is constitutionally protected. On the other hand, courts in the Fifth Circuit, Ninth Circuit, Tenth Circuit, and Eleventh Circuit have declared that no such constitutional protection exists and, thus, courts should not interfere with school officials' attempts to establish grooming standards for learners.

Prohibitions on the wearing of jeans or pants by females have been upheld in Kentucky but overturned in Idaho and New Hampshire. In Idaho the court ruled that a prohibition of females wearing pants was unreasonable, capricious, and unrelated to the educational process (*Johnson v. Joint School District No. 60 Bingham County,* 1973). However, other states have held that the matter was not of significant enough importance to overturn school rules and have declared that these are matters best left in the hands of school authorities.

In recent years, the issue of wearing jewelry to school has arisen. In some cases, the wearing of earrings or jewelry has become a symbol of gang membership. Since the legitimate reason for the rule is to protect the safety of the learners and to prohibit the disruption of the educational environment, the prohibition of jewelry or earrings in these cases has usually been upheld. However, if compelling evidence of gang activity has been lacking, then this kind of prohibition has been difficult to defend.

These conflicting decisions suggest that no absolutely clear and consistent standards exist for judging the general appropriateness of dress and appearance codes. Individual decisions have often turned on the particular circumstances associated with individual cases. In general, school districts have found that their regulations will most likely withstand legal challenges when they have been able to demonstrate a clear connection between prohibited behavior and educators' obligation to provide learners with a safe and educationally sound learning environment.

Sexual Harassment

Courts will not tolerate sexual harassment of learners by teachers or administrators. In general, decisions have severely punished teachers or administrators who have been found guilty of sexual conduct with learners. One area that remains unclear concerns the extent of teacher and school responsibility for learner-to-learner, or peer, sexual harassment. In recent years, this issue has been the focus of several lawsuits. Although there is still a lack of consensus regarding school responsibilities in this area, some general principles are beginning to emerge.

In 1997, the United States Department of Education issued guidelines on peer sexual harassment. These guidelines define *sexual harassment* as behavior that is sufficiently severe, persistent, or pervasive to adversely affects a learner's education or that creates a hostile environment (Fischer et al., 1999). This definition establishes a fairly strict standard and implies that there must be evidence of severe and persistent patterns of inappropriate behavior for a charge of sexual harassment to be upheld.

You may have thought that the issue of learner-to-learner sexual harassment was something about which you did not need to worry much. Recent court cases have made it clear that this is not a valid assumption. Some courts have imposed a relatively high standard that must be met by complainants who are concerned about learner-to-learner sexual harassment. In their decisions, they have tended to support school authorities unless there is convincing evidence that the school intended to create a hostile environment that allowed for peer sexual harassment. Other courts have imposed a less rigorous standard. They have ruled that the schools and teachers can be held liable if they know or should have known of sexual harassment and failed to take appropriate action. More and more court decisions are reflecting this position. What this means is that if you become aware that learners in your classroom are being sexually harassed by others, you cannot simply dismiss this behavior as none of your business. You must act to assure that learners for whom you are responsible are protected from such unwanted behavior.

Rights of Learners with Disabilities

Before the middle 1970s, many learners with disabilities were excluded from school or were placed in special classrooms. A series of federal and state laws changed this situation. Today, to the extent possible, these learners receive school services in regular classrooms. In addition, they must be provided with services necessary for them to derive benefit from the educational experience.

As a teacher, you need to be particularly aware of the implications of regulations related to disciplining learners with disabilities. Strict due process rights protect learners with disabilities. These learners can be disciplined in the same ways as nondisabled learners only if their behavior is not a result of their disability and if mandated procedures are followed. Suspension or expulsion of learners with disabilities is considered a change of educational placement and can be done only by following the steps required by law. This generally means that a meeting must be held to revise the Individualized Education Plan (IEP) for the learner and that an alternative placement must be provided.

Family Rights and Privacy

In recent years, concern over potential misuses of many kinds of records, including school records, has been growing. For example, some people have worried that a learner who had difficulty with a teacher in the early elementary grades might be stigmatized throughout his or her entire school career by records suggesting that the learner was a troublemaker. Worries about possible misuses of records helped win passage for the Family Educational Rights and Privacy Act in 1974.

This act requires schools to provide parents and guardians free access to their children's school records. Furthermore, learners over age 18 and those in post-secondary schools have the right to view these records themselves. The act also restricts how schools can distribute these records. Before the act was passed, it was customary for many schools to release these records on request to government agencies, law enforcement agencies, and others. Since passage of the Family Educational Rights and Privacy Act, schools have been allowed to release records only after strict guidelines have been followed.

An implication for you as a teacher is that you need to choose your words carefully when entering information on learner records. Unsubstantiated or derogatory comments that label a learner unfairly can lead to legal action. You must support comments that reflect negatively on the learner with facts.

The Family Educational Rights and Privacy Act also has implications for you when you are seeking a teaching position. Usually when you prepare your teacher placement papers with your campus career center, you will be asked whether you prefer to have an open or a closed file. If you choose to have an open file, the Family Educational Rights and Privacy Act allows you to retain the right to read everything that goes into it. If you choose to have a closed file, this same federal legislation recognizes that you have waived the right to see what is placed inside.

People who write recommendations usually are notified by the placement center whether a candidate has opted for an open file or a closed file. Some professors and others who write recommendations hesitate to provide them to undergraduates who have opted for an open file. Furthermore, some school district personnel people tend to look differently at placement files that are open and those that are closed. Rightly or wrongly, some of them feel they get a more honest appraisal of a candidate's strengths and weaknesses in a closed file.

To summarize, learners are individuals with rights guaranteed to any citizen. You need to recognize this reality and make sure no actions you take are likely to be viewed as interfering with learners' legal rights. On the other hand, your learners need to realize that their rights are balanced by the need for you and others in the school to establish an orderly and safe educational environment. You do have the right to establish reasonable regulations and rules, and your learners have the responsibility to follow them.

EMERGING ISSUES

As society changes, the rights and responsibilities of individuals also change. For example, today there are new issues emerging that relate to the growing use of computers in school and access to the Internet. Some people have raised serious concerns about the ability of learners to access pornographic and inappropriate

Following the Web 6.2

Learners' Civil Rights

The topic of learners' civil rights includes a wide variety of issues. Much litigation in this area has focused on rights guaranteed to citizens by the first 10 amendments to the United States Constitution. If you are interested in these issues as they pertain to schools and school learners, consider visiting some of these Web sites.

 For hot links to these sites, visit the companion Web site, located at *http://www. prenhall.com/armstrong*. Select Chapter 6 from the front page of the Web site, then choose the Following the Web module on the navigation bar on the left side of the page.

First Amendment Law Materials (Speech, Press, Religion, Assembly)

* *http://www.law.cornell.edu/topics/first_amendment.html*

  This Web site includes a good overview of First Amendment protections related to speech, press, religion, and assembly. In addition, there are useful links to other materials related to the United States Constitution. Information is available related to recent United States Court of Appeals decisions that relate to religion, press, and speech.

Education Law

* *http://law.house.gov/99.htm*

  At this Web site, you will find the Internet Law Library's education section. This is a marvelous site that features links to a wide array of information focusing on education law as it relates to learners' rights and many other issues. You will be able to find material related to education law in individual states as well as to federal legislative and court decisional law.

Students' Rights

* *http://www.aclu.org:80/issues/student/hmes.html*

  This Web site is maintained by the American Civil Liberties Union, a group dedicated to defending civil rights of all citizens. You will find a useful overview of

commercial material on the Internet. These worries raise the following important new questions:

* Can the schools limit access to the Internet without violating the free-speech rights of learners to unpopular ideas?
* To what extent is the school responsible to make sure that learners do not access vulgar, obscene, or age-inappropriate materials?

Possible answers to these questions are widely debated today. It is probable that new regulations will be written and new court cases will be heard as our society grapples with these issues.

the students' rights issue as well as additional links to other Web sites containing information about learners' rights.

Supreme Court Collection: Education

- *http://www4.law.cornell.edu/cgi-bin/fx?DB=SupctSyllabi&TOPDOC=0&P=education*

  The Legal Information Institute has developed this Web site at Cornell University. It features links to individual Supreme Court cases that have dealt with issues related to education. By pursuing these links, you can access a tremendous volume of information about these important cases.

Internet Legal Resources on Special Education and Disabilities

- *http://aace.virginia.edu/go/specialed/resources/legal.html*

  As noted earlier in this chapter, rights of learners with disabilities enjoy strong legal protections. This Web site, which is maintained The Curry School of Education at the University of Virginia, includes links to sites containing laws and regulations relating to the rights of these learners.

Manual on School Uniforms

- *http://www.ed.gov/updates/uniforms.html*

  At this Web site, you will find a fascinating compendium of information related to legal and other issues associated with school uniforms. You can also find specific information about school uniform policies that are presently in force in selected school districts.

[Note: Web addresses change frequently. If you are unable to locate one or more of these sites using the standard URL, try putting the site name in a standard search engine.]

Another emerging issue that is of interest to educators relates to compulsory community service. In recent years, a number of states and local school districts have begun requiring high school students to perform a certain minimum number of hours of community service. Some individuals object to this kind of a requirement, arguing that it constitutes a form of involuntary servitude. Others argue that it interferes with the rights of parents and guardians to decide what their children should do outside of regular school hours. Since these experiences take place off school grounds and without constant supervision of school officials, liability issues also may be a concern. The few existing court cases that have focused on the community-service issue have tended to support the authority of school districts to make such service a requirement for all learners (Fischer et al., 1999). However, this pattern may change as more cases are brought in response to more widespread implementation of community-service requirements.

▬▬▬▬   ## Key Ideas In Summary   ▬▬▬▬▬▬▬▬▬▬▬▬▬▬▬▬▬

- Learners have responsibilities as well as rights. The most fundamental responsibility is that of attending school. Other responsibilities include respecting school authorities, following reasonable school rules and regulations, and behaving in socially appropriate ways. The courts try to balance the rights of a learner with those of the school to establish an orderly and safe educational environment. In short, learners cannot interfere with rights of school officials to operate the school or the rights of other young people to learn.

- Traditionally, the legal doctrine governing relationships between school authorities and learners was *in loco parentis.* This doctrine implied that the legal relationship between school and learner was much like that existing between parent and child. One implication of this doctrine was that learners did not enjoy the full rights of citizens and could not take school authorities to court to protest decisions. This doctrine began to break down in the 1960s, and today most rights enjoyed by citizens in the general public are extended to school learners.

- Today, due process guarantees apply to learners in the schools. Due process is designed to ensure that people are treated fairly in adversarial situations. The *substantive component* of due process references the basic principles on which due process is based; the *procedural component* outlines procedures to be followed to ensure that due process rights have not been violated.

- A number of First Amendment guarantees have been extended to school learners. A key case in extending Bill of Rights guarantees to learners was *Tinker v. Des Moines Independent Community School District* (1969). In this case, the Supreme Court acted to establish the principle that free-speech guarantees should be extended to learners in the schools. However, the issue of free speech in school does not allow learners total freedom. Expression that is considered a part of the curriculum can be controlled.

- A number of issues related to freedom of conscience have come before the courts. Among topics litigated are concerns related to the teaching of certain content, objections to learner participation in flag-saluting ceremonies, and disputes concerning the issue of free exercise of religion. In arriving at decisions, the courts have tended to weigh heavily unique dimensions of the specific situation under consideration.

- In considering the appropriateness of searches of learners and their property in schools, the courts have tended to consider the expectation of privacy and the intrusiveness of the search. In general, the less the expectation of privacy and the more distant the search is from the body of a learner, the more willing courts have been to support the search authority of school officials.

- Dress and grooming regulations that relate to preservation of health, safety, and discipline are constitutional. Of more questionable constitutionality are dress and grooming codes that are not reasonably connected to school needs. Challenges to appearance standards are usually based on the theory that dress and appearance is a form of symbolic speech or it involves a constitutional "liberty right." To date, the Supreme Court has not rendered a definitive decision on a case involving school dress and appearance codes. Different federal circuit courts have ruled in different ways on appearance standards.

- It is becoming clear that teachers and administrators have important responsibilities in the area of learner-to-learner, or peer, sexual harassment. The United States Department of Education has issued some guidelines to help school officials identify what constitutes this behavior.
- Learners with disabilities have a right to a free appropriate education in the least restrictive environment. In addition, they have a right to receive services that will help them benefit from education. Teachers who wish to discipline young people with disabilities must do so with care. They must be sure that they are not disciplining the learner because of a condition related to the disability, and they must realize that suspension or expulsion constitutes a change in placement and requires the strict following of the procedures required by law.
- School records are open to inspection by parents or guardians as well as by learners over the age of 18. They cannot be released to others without the permission of the parents or guardians. Teachers need to take care to ensure that comments entered on permanent records are done so in a professional manner and do not slander a learner.

Chapter 6 Self Test

To review terms and concepts in this chapter, take the Chapter 6 Self Test on the companion Web site, located at *http://www.prenhall.com/armstrong*. Select Chapter 6 from the front page of the Web site, then choose the Self Test module on the navigation bar on the left side of the page. Feedback for the Self Test is immediate. You can keep track of your Self Test scores yourself, or you can choose to submit your scores via e-mail to your instructor.

Reflections

To respond to these questions online, and to save or submit your response electronically, visit the companion Web site, located at *http://www.prenhall.com/armstrong*. Select Chapter 6 from the front page of the Web site, then choose the Reflections module on the navigation bar on the left side of the page. Instructors and students may also wish to use these questions as discussion topics on the Message Board for the companion Web site.

1. What is your response to the kinds of responsibilities of learners mentioned in the chapter? Do you agree with those who claim that learners have too many rights and too few responsibilities?

2. Do you think that recent court decisions extending rights to learners have resulted in more instances of learners defying teachers and administrators?

3. In what ways do you think the issues discussed in this chapter will influence your role as a teacher?

4. What are implications of the substantive and the procedural components of due process for teachers?

5. Do you believe that the full force of *in loco parentis* should be restored to teachers? Why or why not?

6. Some people have argued that it makes sense for older learners, particularly those in senior high schools, to be granted full rights of citizenship, but that these privileges should not extend to younger learners in elementary schools. The argument for this position is that these younger children lack the kind of maturity and insights people should have before full rights of citizenship, logically, should be extended to them. What are your views on this issue?

7. Parent protests and calls for censorship of certain curriculum content have become increasingly common. What is your view of the proper role of the school in responding to censorship and complaints about the curriculum?

8. What are some arguments that individuals are making about requiring organized prayer in schools? What is your position?

9. Different federal circuit courts have made different rulings on a number of issues related to rights of school learners. How do you explain these differences?

10. How do you feel about requiring all learners attending a school to wear uniforms? In particular, would this approach lead to less gang violence? Do you think the courts would find school regulations requiring learners to wear an official school uniform to be constitutional?

Field Experiences, Projects, and Enrichment

1. Review copies of professional education journals such as *Phi Delta Kappan* or *Educational Leadership*. Look for articles and sections dealing with legal issues in education. Identify the legal principles that are being discussed and applied to learners' rights and responsibilities. Share your findings in an oral report to your class.

2. Invite a local school administrator to speak to your class. Ask this person to describe the legal issues relating to the rights and responsibilities of learners that are particularly important for newcomers to the profession to understand. You might also ask this person to provide examples of difficulties some teachers may have encountered over the years because of a failure to understand the nature of rights learners enjoy today.

3. Organize a debate on one of the topics discussed in this chapter. For example, you might debate an area such as requiring uniforms for all learners in a school or protecting learners by censoring certain kinds of curricular content.

4. Obtain a copy or a summary of the education code for your state. Identify state rules in areas such as corporal punishment, expulsion, suspension, and mandatory attendance.

5. Review articles in the news for the past several months that focus on legal issues relating to the rights and responsibilities of learners. Identify any recent trends in the types of cases that are being brought forward or in the direction of court decisions. Write a brief paper that summarizes your findings.

References

California Teachers Association. (1992). *Guide to school law.* Burlingame, CA: Author.

Care and Protection of Charles, 504 N.E.2d 592 (Mass. 1987).

Crews v. Cloncs, 432 F.2d 1259 (7th Cir. 1970).

Epperson v. State of Arkansas, 393 U.S. 97 (1968).

Fischer, L., Schimmel, D., & Kelly, C. (1999). *Teachers and the law* (5th ed.). New York: Longman.

Goss v. Lopez, 419 U.S. 565 (1975).

Graves, A. B. (1999, May 10). Littleton ignited witch hunt, ACLU says. *The Charlotte Observer,* p. 3A.

Hazelwood School District v. Kuhlmeier, 484 U.S. 260 (1988).

In re Sawyer, 672 P.2d 1093 (Kan. 1983).

Jenkins by Hall v. Talladega City Board of Education, 95 F.3d 1036 (11th Cir. 1996).

Johnson v. Joint School District No. 60 Bingham County, 508 P.2d 547 (Idaho, 1973).

Lipp v. Morris, 579 F.2d 834 (3d Cir. 1978).

McLean v. Arkansas Board of Education, 529 F. Supp. 1255 (E.D. Ark. 1982).

New Jersey v. T.L.O. 105 S. Ct. 733 (1985).

People v. Levisen, 90 N.E.2d 213 (Ill. 1950).

Richards v. Thurston, 424 F.2d 1281 (1st Cir. 1970).

Skelton, G. (1999, March 22). Offering preschool to all wouldn't be child's play, *Los Angeles Times,* p. A3.

State v. McDonough, 468 A.2d 977 (Me. 1983).

Tinker v. Des Moines Independent Community School District, 393 U.S. 503 (1969).

Valente, W. (1994). *Law in the schools* (3rd ed.). New York: Macmillan.

Wisconsin v. Yoder, 406 U.S. 205 (1972).

Zirkel, P., & Richardson, S. (1988). *A digest of Supreme Court decisions affecting education.* Bloomington, IN: Phi Delta Kappa Educational Foundation.

Part Three

Teaching in Today's Classrooms

CHAPTERS

7

Effective Instruction

OBJECTIVES

This chapter will help you to

- identify the role of research in teaching.
- define the basic features of active teaching.
- explain the importance of teacher clarity.
- identify different time decisions teachers make, and explain how each relates to learner achievement.
- describe how teachers' expectations influence learners' levels of achievement.
- recognize elements of effective teacher-questioning techniques.
- describe some procedures that can be used to gather and record data about what goes on in a classroom during an observation session.

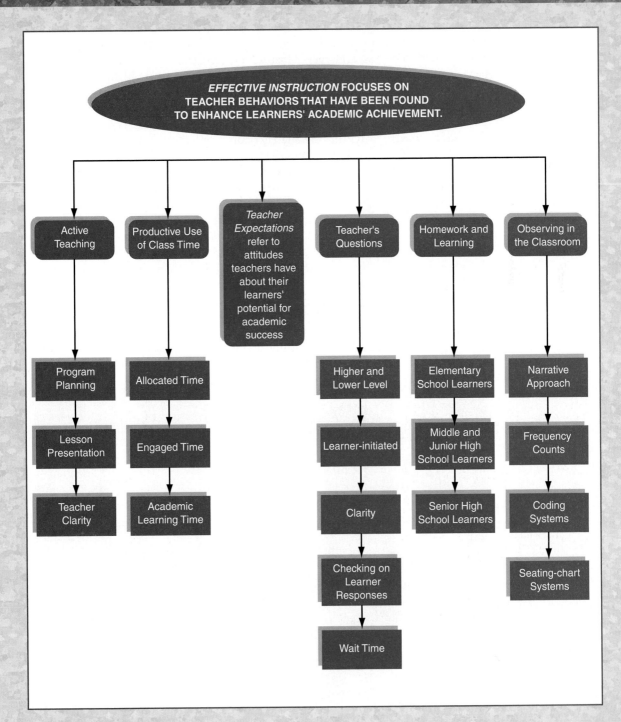

FIGURE 7.1 Effective Instruction

INTRODUCTION

As a teacher, you will manage classrooms, take care of administrative responsibilities, and accomplish other tasks. However, instruction more than any other activity will define your role. Of all the things you do, your obligation to instruct will most clearly differentiate your work as a teacher from that performed by members of other professions.

Teachers have long been judged on their instructional effectiveness. Debates over this issue have sometimes centered on the question of whether a body of research-validated knowledge exists that adequately defines "effective" teaching. Some people argue that there is such a body of knowledge and that prospective teachers should be trained to use it. Others scoff at this idea and believe that future teachers need no specialized training. They argue that good instruction will automatically result if prospective teachers have a good understanding of the subjects they teach. Critics of formal teacher preparation today argue their case against a body of evidence that increasingly counters their position. A growing body of research is pinpointing categories of teacher behaviors that have been found to be associated with promoting learning.

Most research on effective teaching has focused on teacher behaviors that relate to increasing learners' academic attainment. Instruction certainly also has other purposes. For example, as a teacher, you also have an interest in your learners' psychomotor development, social adjustment, and personal growth. You must attend to learners' affective needs because these simply cannot be separated from their cognitive needs (Henson & Eller, 1999). Ideally, you will create a classroom learning community where you and your learners will enjoy helping each other create knowledge,

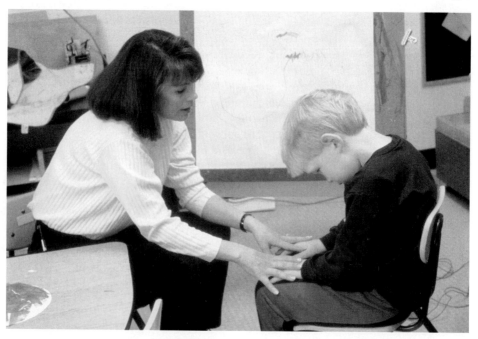

Researchers have found that learners' emotional needs cannot be separated from needs associated with content learning.

recognize that mistakes are accepted as an essential part of solving problems, and where each day you transmit a sense that joy and excitement are the proper companions of learning. Every day will not have all of these characteristics, but this kind of inviting learning community represents goals for which to strive.

Research on teacher effectiveness differs from research in such areas as the physical sciences. It focuses on people who may have different personal backgrounds, motivations, and experiences. Findings of teacher effectiveness research do not categorically assert that a specific procedure will work in a predictable way with every learner. Rather, this body of research seeks to identify principles that can guide you in making appropriate instructional decisions.

Teaching is a decision-making process. Familiarity with research findings related to teaching effectiveness can help you diagnose instructional problems and consider alternative courses of action. Results of teacher effectiveness research presented here are organized under the major headings of:

- active teaching,
- productive use of class time,
- teacher expectations, and
- teachers' questions.

ACTIVE TEACHING

A growing body of research suggests that active teaching is associated with enhanced learner achievement (Good & Brophy, 2000). The term *active teaching* refers to situations when, as a teacher, you will directly lead the class and play such roles as:

- presenter of new information,
- monitor of learner progress,
- planner of opportunities for learners to apply content, and
- re-teacher of content (to learners who fail to learn the content when it is initially presented).

The active-teaching role contrasts with the view of the teacher as a general manager or facilitator of instruction who does not get directly involved in leading the class and personally overseeing learning activities. Several important dimensions of active teaching are introduced in subsections that follow.

Program Planning

The Problem of Match   Active teachers play a leadership role in determining their learners' instructional programs (Good & Brophy, 2000). One problem you will face in the classroom is determining how to match your instructional programs to the special characteristics of your learners. To accomplish this task, you must make two kinds of decisions.

First, you must consider the difficulty level of the new material in light of your understanding of your learners' capabilities. If selected materials are too difficult,

What Do You Think?

Is Adapting Instruction to the Learner a Good Idea?

A teacher recently made these comments to a colleague:

> "I've just come back from yet another inservice presentation. Once again, we've been told to 'match instruction to the child.' After thinking about it, I've decided that this might not be a good idea at all.
>
> If I simply 'adapt instruction to the learner,' I'm really giving up on changing the child. This approach places the entire obligation on me. *I* have to change, but the learner does not. This just doesn't make sense. Shouldn't the people I teach feel some obligation to adapt to my instruction? Will 'matching instruction' to young people really help them grow? I don't think so."

What Do You Think?

1. Which parts of this teacher's arguments do you find to be the strongest?
2. Which parts do you find the weakest?
3. What kind of prior experiences might have led this teacher to adopt this position?
4. If you were to write a rebuttal to this teacher's arguments, what are some of the things you would say?

frustration is certain to occur, and little learning will take place. If the materials are too easy, boredom and motivation problems may result.

Second, you need to match the program materials to learners' interests. This is not to suggest that you should introduce no content in which learners do not initially display a high level of interest. Rather, your task is to identify interest levels, and when they are found to be low, think about creative ways to generate greater learner interest and enthusiasm. Ideally, you will develop plans for lessons that will stimulate learners to want to acquire the new information. Successful planning of this kind requires you to know your learners well. Your strategy for each lesson should be right for the content selected for that lesson (Acheson & Gall, 1992), right for the learners, and right for you (Walker & Chance, 1994/1995).

Task Analysis   As you make judgments about content for a given group of learners, you need to engage in task-analysis activities. These require you to look at a proposed body of content that your learners are to master with a view to breaking it into several smaller components or subtasks. To determine whether learners have the needed prerequisite information, you identify what each subtask presumes learners know before they begin work on it. Figure 7.2 provides a step-by-step breakdown of task analysis.

Specifying Learning Intentions   After you determine which content is appropriate, you next specify learning intentions. These identify what learners should be able to do after they have mastered the new content. Often, separate learning in-

Task analysis consists of two basic parts: (1) identifying the specific information learners will need in order to master some specific content and (2) determining a logical beginning point for instruction.

Suppose you were planning to teach a two- to three-week unit in a subject and at a grade level of your choice. Make a list of specific knowledge and skills your learners will need in order to master this content.

Needed knowledge: _____

_____

Needed skills: _____

_____

Now, prepare a brief description of how you would begin instruction. To make this determination, you first need to find out how much of the needed knowledge and skills your learners already possess. Then you can identify the appropriate starting point.

FIGURE 7.2 Components of Task Analysis

tentions are written for each of the subtasks identified during the task-analysis phase. Attainment of these learning intentions provides evidence you can use to judge whether members of your class have mastered the new material.

Lesson Presentation

When you function as an active teacher, you need to play a leadership role during all phases of instructional planning and implementation. This is particularly evident when you are actually presenting your lessons.

Stimulating and Maintaining Interest   You need to pay particular heed to what motivates learners during the process of identifying and selecting content. This does not constrain you to selecting only material in which all learners have a high initial interest. You have to think about your own abilities to select elements of content and introduce them in ways that grab learners attention and interest. As Rinne (1998) notes, this obligates you to think about a variety of approaches.

Not all learners will find the same information and presentation methodology equally interesting or equally dull. Your challenge is to devise approaches that will motivate the largest possible number of people to learn. Your motivational activities need to be embedded within your lessons. When this happens, motivation becomes an integral part of what you do when your learners become actively engaged in new material. During the presentation-of-instruction phase, three distinct periods of motivation that need to be considered are:

- motivation at the beginning of the learning sequence,
- motivation during the learning sequence, and
- motivation at the conclusion of the learning sequence.

The purpose of *initial motivation* is to engage learners' interest and to encourage them to want to learn the material. At this stage, you try to build on learners' general curiosity. Introducing something novel, unusual, or puzzling often works well. Learners need to understand how the new material connects to their own lives. What will mastering the content help them to do or understand? Why should they commit themselves to mastering it? You need to be prepared to answer these kinds of questions during the first phase of motivation.

You use *motivation during the lesson* to introduce novel or unusual material to help sustain interest levels. Learners are motivated by success. When they accomplish parts of a larger instructional task, you need to praise them for what they have done. This kind of support helps keep interest levels high. In general, motivation is facilitated when you maintain a positive classroom atmosphere that is free from threats and fear. Learners need to know that they have your solid support as they struggle with new content.

Motivation at the conclusion of an instructional sequence is important. At this phase of a lesson, you should take particular care to point out to learners how much they have accomplished. A sense of achievement functions as an important motivator. Achievement during one instructional sequence makes it easier for learners to be motivated as they begin the next one.

Sequencing   Over the years, many schemes have been proposed regarding sequencing of instruction. Centuries ago, the ancient Spartans developed a four-part sequence that required the teacher to follow these steps in presenting new material to learners (Posner, 1987):

- Introduce material to be learned.
- Ask learners to think about the material.
- Repeat the material again, and work with learners individually until they have it memorized.
- Listen to learners as they recite the material from memory.

In the nineteenth century, the famous learning theorist Johann Herbart suggested a lesson cycle featuring the steps of (Meyer, 1975):

- preparation for learning,
- presentation of new information,
- association (tying new information to old),
- generalization, and
- application.

In recent years, many school districts have recommended that teachers follow an instructional sequence suggested by Madeline Hunter and Douglas Russell (1977). The Hunter-Russell scheme includes these steps (Hunter & Russell, 1977):

- *anticipatory set* (focusing learners' attention on the instruction that is about to begin)
- *objective and purpose* (helping learners understand what they will be able to do as a result of their exposure to the instruction)

- *instructional input* (conveying information to learners)
- *modeling* (providing learners with examples or demonstrations of competencies associated with the lesson)
- *checking for understanding* (evaluating whether learners have the information needed to master the objective)
- *guided practice* (monitoring learners as they work on tasks calling on them to apply the new information)
- *independent practice* (assigning learners to work with new content under conditions where they will not have direct teacher assistance available)

Other sequencing models have also been developed (e.g., Denton, Armstrong, & Savage, 1980; Posner, 1987) that share many common features. Nearly all of them emphasize the importance of giving learners opportunities to apply new knowledge. Researchers have consistently found improved learning to be associated with instruction that allows learners to engage in application activities (Good & Brophy, 2000).

Lesson Pacing   Good active teaching features a presentation of lessons that moves at a brisk pace and provides for high levels of learner success. You need to maintain a smooth, continuous developmental flow, trying to avoid spending too much time on certain points or matters that are not directly related to the central content. As the lesson develops, you need to ask questions and take other actions to ensure that members of your class are learning the material.

Within-Lesson Questioning   Active teaching demands the skillful use of questions. Research reveals that questions should be asked at regular intervals and addressed to a large number of class members (Good & Brophy, 2000). Questioning of this type serves two basic purposes. First, it allows you to check on levels of learner understanding. Second, when learners know that you will be asking many people in the class to respond to questions about what they are learning, they stay alert. They realize that they need to pay attention, because they know you might call on them at any time.

Monitoring   Monitoring, a key ingredient of active teaching, occurs continuously throughout a lesson. It is particularly important after you assign members of your class to practice what they have learned by working on assignments that require them to use the new information. Effective monitoring cannot occur if you remain seated at your desk. You need to move about the classroom and check on learners' progress.

It is important to provide feedback both to learners who are performing the task correctly and to those who are experiencing difficulties. Successful performers need to know they are on the right track (Goodlad, 1984) and need to hear supportive comments from the teacher. Those learners who are having problems or who are not doing the work properly also need to be helped. You need to give them specific details regarding (1) what they are doing wrong and (2) how they can change what they are doing so they will experience success.

Effective monitoring helps learners to master new material.

When, as a result of careful monitoring, you discover that many learners are not performing at an acceptable level, you need to halt the independent practice activity. At this point, you engage in reteaching to clear up misunderstandings. Successful reteaching is tightly focused, dealing with only those points that seem to be causing problems for learners.

Teacher Clarity

Research reveals that *clarity* is a defining characteristic of effective teachers. It includes several variables, including:

- the teacher's verbal and nonverbal style,
- the teacher's lesson-presentation structure, and
- the teacher's proficiency in providing cogent explanation.

Verbal and Nonverbal Style   Several issues play a part in defining a given presentation style. One of these involves *paralanguage*. Paralanguage includes those things that help shape what is conveyed by words that are spoken but that are not the words themselves. Elements of paralanguage include voice intonation, precision of articulation of words, and rate of speaking. Paralanguage, which also includes many of our nonverbal behaviors, has a great influence on how listeners hear and interpret what we say.

You acquire paralanguage as a natural overlay of language as you grow to maturity within your family, friendship groups, and community. There are important regional and cultural differences. When the paralanguage patterns of a speaker and listener differ, the listener may have difficulty understanding all that is being said.

For example, if you were brought up in a part of the country where speech rates and vowel sounds differ dramatically from those in the area where you are now teaching, you may find that the learners sometimes have difficulty grasping what you say. You have to understand that communication problems sometimes result not from the level of difficulty of the words or message, but from the patterns of speech you use to deliver them.

Nonverbal behaviors sometimes also get in the way of clear communication. This can happen when you send a nonverbal message that is not consistent with your spoken words. For example, suppose you scowled and shook a fist at the class while saying, "I'm really proud of the good work you're doing." Signals here are mixed; the nonverbal behaviors are hostile and threatening, but the verbal behavior is warm and supportive. The resulting message is confusing.

It is not unusual for people to be unaware of many of their nonverbal behaviors. Because these behaviors are important, you need to develop some awareness of your nonverbal patterns. Class observers sometimes can help by providing you with feedback about what you are doing nonverbally to support your verbal instruction.

Lesson-Presentation Structure   Learners profit from an understanding of the general subject matter of new lessons and of how the content is to be organized. One way you can help learners grasp the framework of new lessons is through the use of *advance organizers.* An advance organizer is a label that describes a large and important category of content to be covered. It helps learners to sort out fragmented pieces of information and organize them under certain specified category labels. This simplifies their learning task.

Consider the following example. Suppose you wanted a group of your high school students to study advertising. One purpose might be to help class members understand that some advertisers make claims that go beyond the evidence available to support them. You might begin with these instructions: "Look through any five magazines of your choice. By Wednesday, bring me three or four ads that you believe make untrue or unfair claims."

This assignment will bring students into contact with a huge volume of information. The task, as assigned, provides few guidelines for them to follow in deciding which ads might be better than others as examples of misleading advertising. The students' task would have been greatly simplified had you provided them with one or two advance organizers.

For example, you might have begun the class with an explanation and a discussion of the term *glittering generality.* You could have outlined the task by saying something such as, "Look through any five magazines of your choice. By Wednesday, bring me three or four ads that contain glittering generalities." This assignment provides students with a good sense of direction by clearly communicating to them what they need to do to complete the task to your satisfaction.

A widely used type of advance organizer is the *learning intention,* sometimes called a "lesson objective." To assist learners in understanding what the lesson will emphasize, a well-constructed learning intention indicates what they should know or be able to do when they have completed the lesson. These need not be complex. For example, you might say something as simple as, "When we've finished this lesson, you should be able to identify at least four main parts of a short story."

As lessons are being taught, you need to maintain connected discourse. This means you try to achieve a smooth, point-by-point development of the content that is being introduced. Once started, the lesson is pursued and carried along to its logical conclusion. There are few digressions that take away from its main flow. The effort is to avoid mid-lesson stoppages that could result in confusion and, ultimately, diminished levels of learner achievement.

It is also important for you to take time to provide *internal summaries* as you teach your lessons. These are pause points that allow you and your learners to stop, take stock, and reflect upon what has been learned so far. Internal summaries allow you to clarify any misconceptions. When internal summaries are a regular feature of your teaching, learners tend to pay attention. This is true because they realize you may stop from time to time to ask someone in the class to summarize what has been learned.

Clarity is also enhanced when you use *marker expressions.* These are statements that underline or highlight something that has been said. Marker expressions are employed to communicate the importance of certain kinds of information. Examples include statements such as:

- Write this down.
- Pay close attention to this.
- Listen carefully to this explanation.

The importance of specific content can also be "marked" through changes in vocal intonation or volume.

A final aspect of lesson structuring is the summary provided at the end of a lesson presentation. The summary includes a recapitulation of major ideas that have been covered, drawing together what has been learned in a way that facilitates retention.

Providing Explanations   At various times during a lesson, you may be called on to explain something. Several things can be done to enhance the clarity of your explanations. For example, you need to take particular care in defining potentially confusing terms clearly. Newcomers to teaching sometimes assume that learners know more than they really do.

Consider as an example a high school teacher who developed a marvelous presentation to a class on the topic "Recent Political Trends." At the end of the teacher's lecture, a student cautiously raised a hand to ask, "What is a trend?" The teacher had not considered the possibility that the word *trend* would not be in the working vocabularies of all of the students.

Your explanations communicate best when they are free from ambiguous, vague, and imprecise terms. Some examples of phrasing you need to avoid include terms of approximation such as *kind of, sort of,* and *about.* Ambiguous designations such as

Following the Web **7.1**

Direct Instruction

The term "direct instruction" is sometimes used as a synonym for "active teaching." You will find many Web sites with information organized under this heading. We have selected some examples that you might wish to review to extend your understanding of this general approach to instruction.

For hot links to these sites, visit the companion Web site, located at *http://www.prenhall.com/armstrong.* Select Chapter 7 from the front page of the Web site, then choose the Following the Web module on the navigation bar on the left side of the page.

Direct Instruction

- *http://www.circleofinclusion.org/guidelines/curriculums/directinstruction.html*

  At this site, you will find information about the theoretical underpinnings of direct instruction. The site also includes details about general principles to keep in mind when implementing direct-instruction lessons. Finally, titles of books and links to other Web sites are provided that feature information about this approach to teaching.

Direct Instruction (DI)

- *http://www.aft.org/edissues/whatworks/six/di/index.htm*

  This site is maintained by the American Federation of Teachers, a leading national organization for teachers. You will find a succinct description of direct instruction that categorizes information under the headings of (a) grades covered, (b) curriculum materials, (c) instructional support/professional development, (d) school reform/restructuring assistance, (e) role of paraprofessionals, (f) cost of implementation, and (g) results/effect size.

Direct-Instruction Site List

- *http://www.aft.org/edissues/whatworks/six/di/page4.htm*

  At this site, you will find a list of names and addresses of organizations that are committed to use of the direct-instruction approach. One you might be particularly interested in is the Association for Direct Instruction. A large number of schools are associated with this group, and you can use a provided link to identify their names and locations.

"Using Direct Instruction to Integrate Reading and Writing for Students with Disabilities"

- *http://lsi.fsu.edu/cpt/TREE/gleas95.html*

  Many sites on the Web include examples of how direct instruction is applied to particular subjects or with specific categories of learners. This one features an article by M. M. Gleason that discusses application of the approach in integrating reading and writing for young people with learning disabilities.

[Note: Web addresses change frequently. If you are unable to locate one of these sites using the listed URL, try putting the site name in a standard search engine.]

somehow, somewhere, and *someone* also often fail the clarity test. Additionally, probability statements such as *frequently, generally,* and *often* do not mean the same thing to all learners.

PRODUCTIVE USE OF CLASS TIME

Researchers have found that learners in classes with teachers who maximize the amount of class time used for instruction perform better than those in classes where less time is spent on instruction (Good & Brophy, 2000). In some classrooms, as much as 50% of available time is devoted to nonacademic tasks. This situation deprives learners of much time needed for working on academic tasks. It can have a strong, negative, long-term influence on achievement.

As a teacher, you will make three basic types of time decisions related to allocated time, engaged time, and academic learning time.

Allocated Time

Allocated time decisions concern how much time is to be devoted to learning specific subjects or materials. While some of these decisions are made in light of state or local regulations, many of them fall to individual teachers. Researchers have found that teachers vary greatly in terms of how much time they allocate to given subjects or skills (Berliner, 1984).

Your decisions about how to allocate time will be influenced by several variables. One is the difficulty of the material you want to teach and the level of your own interest in it. Researchers have found that teachers allocate more time to difficult topics and topics in which they have high levels of interest. These findings suggest a need to provide sufficient time for learners to master content that may not be particularly interesting or exciting to you personally. Your time allocation decisions need to be based on your learners' needs not your own preferences.

The amount of allocated time varies from one school to another. These differences are explained by variations in administrative philosophy, developmental levels of learners, preferences of individual teachers, and other factors. Sometimes school-to-school differences are dramatic. Reinstein (1998) reported that one school where he taught provided 300 minutes of classroom instruction a week, while another school where he had taught provided only 200 minutes of classroom instruction per week.

Engaged Time

Allocated time is the total amount of time set aside for instruction related to a given subject or topic. *Engaged time* is that part of allocated time when instructional activities related to the subject or topic are occurring; other activities such as distributing materials, responding to learner questions of various kinds, and dealing with classroom management issues detract from the total amount of engaged time. Research reveals that teachers whose classrooms are characterized by high percentages of engaged time produce learners who achieve better than teachers whose classrooms are characterized by lower percentages of engaged time. Maintaining a high percentage of engaged time appears to be a particularly important variable in promoting the academic development of low-ability learners.

Engaged time is time spent on work that clearly relates to the lesson objective. There is no facilitating effect when learners are kept busy on activities that are unrelated to lesson content. However, when assignments are relevant and learners participate actively, they learn more (Finn, 1993).

Academic Learning Time

Academic learning time is that portion of total engaged time when the learner is experiencing a high degree of academic success while working on the assigned task (Berliner, 1984). This definition goes beyond a concern for learners' working on content-related tasks to a concern for their success rates while they are so engaged. Higher rates of academic learning time are associated with increased levels of achievement (Berliner, 1984).

Teachers whose classes are characterized by high percentages of academic learning time monitor learners carefully to ensure that the learners understand the lesson. These teachers frequently ask learners what they are doing and circulate through their classrooms as learners work on assigned tasks, providing corrective feedback to those students who are experiencing difficulties.

TEACHERS' EXPECTATIONS

Teacher expectations refer to their attitudes about learners' potentials for academic success. These attitudes predispose individual teachers to look for varying levels of achievement from different people in their classes. These expectations are rarely verbalized; however, they do exert subtle influences on how they interact with different learners. Learners themselves are often affected by their comprehension of their teachers' expectations.

Suppose a learner for whom you have low academic expectations volunteers to answer a question and is recognized. If this learner stumbles at the beginning of the response, you may conclude that his or her difficulty results from a lack of knowledge. In response, you may give this person part of the answer, call on someone else, or even praise him or her just for being willing to volunteer. Such responses communicate your lack of confidence in the learner's ability to respond correctly.

Your actions may be quite different when you believe the volunteering learner is someone who is academically talented. If such a learner initially experiences difficulty, you may provide cues and continue to work with the person until the correct response, which you believe the learner really knew all the time, is elicited. When you act in this way, you communicate to bright learners that you will hold them to a high standard of performance and work with them until they meet it.

Video Viewpoint

A Lesson They'll Never Forget

WATCH: In this ABC News video segment, we meet an extraordinary teacher, Dennis Frederick. When he was diagnosed with terminal cancer, instead of leaving his teaching job at Pleasantview Elementary, he decided to turn his own battle to live into a learning experience for his third-grade students.

THINK: With your classmates or in your teaching journal, consider these questions:

1. What do you think makes an effective teacher? Think back to the teachers you have had throughout your schooling. What teachers stand out in your mind? What qualities made those individuals effective or ineffective educators?
2. What do you think makes Dennis Frederick an effective teacher? Do you think he made the right choice in turning his battle with cancer into a "teachable moment"? Would you have done anything differently?

LINK: What do you think Mr. Frederick's students have learned from him?

Good and Brophy (2000) point out a number of findings from research studies focusing on teacher expectations. Some of these include the following:

- Teachers have certain behavioral expectations of learners in their classes.
- Teachers' behaviors toward individual learners vary according to their expectations regarding what the individual learners can do.
- Differences in how they are viewed by teachers result in different learner self-concepts, levels of motivation, and aspirations.
- Teachers who are conscious of the impact of their expectations can monitor and adjust them in ways that can result in enhanced learner performance.

TEACHERS' QUESTIONS

The view that to teach well is to question well has long had historic standing (De-Garmo, 1903). A large body of research supports the idea that effective teachers ask more questions than less effective teachers. In one study, effective junior high school mathematics teachers were found to ask an average of 24 questions during a class period, whereas their less effective counterparts asked an average of only 8.6 questions (Rosenshine & Stevens, 1986).

Interest in questioning encompasses more than the issue of how many questions teachers ask. For example, many researchers have looked into the character and quality of the questions themselves, and schemes have been developed to categorize types of questions. One very simple approach divides questions into two general groups: (1) *lower-level questions* and (2) *higher-level questions.* Lower-level questions call on learners to recall specific items of previously introduced information and do not demand sophisticated thinking. Higher-level questions, on the other hand, require learners to apply, analyze, integrate, create, or synthesize and use relatively complex thinking processes.

Critical Incident

Does Thinking at School Spell Trouble at Home?

Naomi Belton is in her sixth year of teaching 4th-graders at Lomax Elementary School. During the summers and at night, she has been working on a master's degree in education. At this stage of her career, she is especially interested in improving her classroom instruction. This interest has prompted her to read the teacher effectiveness literature in great depth, and she has also taken several courses on instructional improvement. From her study, she has decided to use more higher level questions in her discussions. She understands that, under some conditions, this might prompt people in her class to think more seriously. She has been quite pleased with the results of this change in her questioning patterns. Her pupils are doing a better job of analyzing sophisticated issues, and they have started to ask more penetrating questions on their own.

This success has come at a price. For the first time, she has had parents complaining to her principal. Only three parents have been involved, but Naomi has never had a parent complain about her instruction, so this development has been something of a shock.

Although specific concerns that individual parents have raised have not been exactly the same, all the complaints have centered around her efforts to turn her learners into more able thinkers. Pupils, it seems, are taking their newfound thinking powers home and are beginning to challenge statements their parents are making. The principal told Naomi that one parent said, "I'm tired of having a 9-year-old question my judgments. These kids are too young for this sort of thing. I want my child to listen to what I say and do what I tell her to do. Lately, it's just argue, argue, argue."

. . .

What does Naomi see as the purpose of her new questioning technique? Is it her intention to make members of her class more difficult for parents to handle? How might some members of her class be perceiving her changed instructional style? What might they believe the purpose of this kind of teaching to be? In what ways might their views differ from Naomi's?

How legitimate are the concerns of the parents who have complained? Specifically, what are they worried about? What do they believe Naomi's instructional priorities should be? How would Naomi react to their views about the purposes of "good" teaching?

To what extent should Naomi be concerned about the reactions of these parents? Should this situation be viewed as particularly troublesome by the principal? What might the principal recommend? What does this situation tell us about some differences between the values of Naomi and those parents who have complained? What do you think Naomi should do? What do your recommendations tell you about your own values and priorities?

To respond to this Critical Incident online, and to save or submit your response electronically, visit the companion Web site, located at *http://www.prenhall.com/armstrong*. Select Chapter 7 from the front page of the Web site, then choose the Critical Incidents module on the navigation bar on the left side of the page. Instructors and students may also wish to use these scenarios as discussion topics on the Message Board for the companion Web site.

When to Use Lower Level and Higher Level Questions

Lower Level Questions   Lower level questions are appropriate when your purpose is to check learners' understanding of basic information. A productive pattern for this kind of questioning involves a three-part sequence:

1. You ask the question.
2. The learner responds to it.
3. You react to the learner's response.

Research suggests that these questions should be delivered at a brisk pace and that learners should be expected to respond quickly (Good & Brophy, 2000). This allows for a large number of recall questions to be asked in a short period of time. It also provides opportunities for many learners in a class to respond. A fairly fast-paced pattern of questioning keeps learners alert and gives teachers opportunities to diagnose and respond to any misunderstandings revealed in answers from a wide cross section of class members.

Higher Level Questions   If your aim is to stimulate more sophisticated learner thinking, then higher level questions sometimes are preferred (Ramsey, Gabbard, Clawson, Lee, & Henson, 1990). Redfield and Rousseau's review of research related to questioning (Redfield & Rousseau, 1981) revealed that teachers' use of higher level questions is associated with better learner achievement. However, more recent summaries of research reveal inconsistent results regarding the effects of higher level questions on learner achievement (Good & Brophy, 2000).

For example, research has now established that asking higher level questions, by itself, does not ensure academic success. Learners must have the knowledge base necessary to engage in complex thinking tasks. For a well-prepared high school class, a higher level question such as, "How would you compare and contrast the late nineteenth-century foreign policies of France and the United Kingdom?" might produce some insightful responses from learners. On the other hand, if students who were asked this question lacked basic information about the nineteenth-century foreign policies of the two countries, responses probably would reflect more wild guessing than sophisticated thought.

Whether higher level or lower level questions are "best" seems to be determined by variables associated with the particular goals established for a specific lesson and with variables related to the individual instructional context (Good & Brophy, 2000). The impact of questions of various kinds on learners continues to be an area of interest to educational researchers.

Learner-Initiated Questions

Discussions about the effect of questions sometimes overlook the important category of learner-initiated questions. The questions your learners ask often reveal a great deal about the effectiveness of what you have taught. Learners' questions can also be an important information source for identifying some misconceptions they may have. Insights you gain from learner questions can be an invaluable aid as you plan lessons that are responsive to their instructional needs (Heckman, Confer, & Hakim, 1994).

Clarity of Questions

When you teach, you need to word your questions so that learners clearly understand what you are asking. Many questions that appear deceptively simple on the surface can, upon closer examination, be responded to in many ways. For example, a learner could logically answer the question, "Who was the first President of the United States?" with any of the following responses:

- a man,
- a Virginian,
- a general, or
- a person named George Washington.

To avoid this situation, questions should be posed in ways that make it unnecessary for learners to make guesses about what you are really asking.

Some research points out that it is unwise to begin a discussion with a series of questions. Cazden (1986) argues that it is better for teachers to provide some general background information before beginning to ask questions. This establishes a context for the questions to follow and results in better learner answers.

One practice that greatly interferes with clarity is asking a large question that contains two, three, or even more questions within it. Learners find this confusing, and they are often puzzled as to where to start their answers. Some of them deal with this dilemma by refusing to answer the question at all. It is better for questions to be asked one at a time, and shorter questions are preferred (Good & Brophy, 2000). Additionally, the vocabulary used in questions should be within the range of learners' understanding.

Checking on Learner Responses

Good lessons that feature questioning require more than well-designed questions. You also must be prepared to attend carefully to what learners say and to respond appropriately. At one level, this amounts to nothing more than listening to responses to ensure that learners have a basic understanding of the content. If they do not, you may need to provide them with additional information and to follow this with some lower level questions that will provide evidence that they now understand the material.

Teacher responses to questions should vary based on what is happening in the classroom. For example, you will want to use probing questions to challenge learners' judgments when they jump to premature conclusions about complex issues. When a discussion featuring many questions has endured for some time, you should pause to summarize what has been said. When learners are using vague terminology, you should stop them and ask for clarification. In summary, your reactions should convey to learners that their answers are being listened to carefully.

This lets them know that their responses are important and should be made thoughtfully.

Wait Time

The interval between the time a teacher asks a question and a learner responds is called *wait time*. Teachers have been found to wait an astonishingly short period before either answering their own questions, rephrasing their questions, or calling on different learners to respond. Rowe (1986) reported that, on average, teachers wait less than one second for learners to respond.

Abundant research exists that supports a connection between the length of time teachers wait for responses after asking questions and learner achievement. Achievement levels on tests demanding higher level thinking have been found to be higher for learners in classes where teachers wait at least three seconds for responses to questions (Tobin, 1987).

Efforts to increase teacher wait time have produced interesting results. When average wait time increases, teachers tend to ask a smaller number of total questions but to increase the number of higher level questions. When they wait longer, teachers also seem to make greater use of learners' answers in class discussions. Finally, when wait time increases, there often is a change in teachers' general attitudes about the capabilities of learners in their classes (Rowe, 1986). This attitude change appears to stem from the fact that when average wait times are longer, some learners who have not previously answered questions become more active participants in discussions, and these increased levels of involvement result in teachers' raising their estimations of these learners' abilities.

HOMEWORK AND LEARNING

Performance on homework is one source of information about what learners have derived from a lesson or series of lessons. Sometimes teachers assign homework out of a belief that it facilitates achievement. Sometimes it does, and sometimes it does not.

Herman Cooper (1989) reviewed many research studies focusing on the relationship between homework and learner achievement. He found that, although homework had a positive influence on achievement, the magnitude of this effect varies greatly depending on learners' ages. Homework has the most impact on the achievement of high school students. Homework's benefit for middle school and junior high school students' achievement is only about half as great as that for senior high school students. Homework only marginally affects the achievement levels of elementary learners.

For junior high school and senior high school students, length of homework assignments appears to have an impact. Academic achievement for junior high school students tends to go up with length of homework assignments until a limit somewhere between one and two hours a night is reached. Longer homework assignments do not have a facilitating effect on the learning of these students. Senior high school

"I don't like to give a lot of homework over the weekend, so just read every other word."

students profit more from somewhat longer homework assignments than do junior high school students.

OBSERVING IN THE CLASSROOM

You may want to know whether your patterns of classroom behavior are consistent with those researchers have found to be effective. Some basic tools you can use to gather this kind of information include *event sampling* and *time sampling.*

Event sampling requires the presence of an observer who records information about specific classroom events that might interest you. For example, an observer might be interested in noting what you do to motivate learners. In such a case, the observer would simply write down everything you did that relates to motivation during a lesson.

In time sampling, the observer records what is happening in the classroom at selected time intervals. For example, an observer could decide to take a sample once every 15 seconds. If you were lecturing at the end of the first 15-second interval, the observer would simply note "1—lecturing." If the lecture were still going on at the end of the next 15-second interval, the observer would write "2—lecturing." If you were asking a question at the end of the third 15-second interval, the observer would write "3—teacher question." This scheme generates information that provides a general profile of activity during a lesson. It tends to capture the flow of a lesson and can provide you with useful information for analysis.

Following the Web 7.2

Questioning

Questioning is one of the oldest techniques known to educators. There is evidence that teachers in ancient times valued this technique at least as much as educators today. The continued interest in questioning as an instructional tool is reflected in the large number of Web sites containing information about the approach. We have selected some sites related to questioning that you might wish to visit.

For hot links to these sites, visit the companion Web site, located at *http://www. prenhall.com/armstrong.* Select Chapter 7 from the front page of the Web site, then choose the Following the Web module on the navigation bar on the left side of the page.

Effective Techniques of Questioning

- *http://picce.uno.edu/SS/TeachDevel/Questions/EffectQuest.html*

    This site is typical of a number of Web sites that provide specific guidelines for teachers who wish to incorporate questioning within their lessons. There are references to adapting questions to needs of particular learners, wait time, and things you can do to encourage learners to respond.

Effective Classroom Questioning

- *http://www.oir.uiuc.edu/did/booklets/question/question.html*

    This site provides a comprehensive introduction to questioning. Among topics covered are those related to (a) planning questions, (b) levels and types of questions, and (c) methods for assessing questioning skills.

Teaching Questioning Skills: Franklin Elementary School

- *http://www.nwrel.org/scpd/sirs/4/snap13.html*

    This site is maintained by the Northwest Regional Educational Laboratory and features a discussion of research-based criteria for good questioning. These criteria are illustrated in the contexts of a case study focusing on a teacher in a state of Washington elementary school who uses questions as part of the instructional process.

Methods for Assessing Questioning Skills

- *http://www.oir.uiuc.edu/did/booklets/question/quest4.html*

    This site includes extensive information for helping you to assess your own proficiency in using questions in the classroom. You will find a discussion of such topics as (a) videotape self-review, (b) peer review, (c) using a survey, (d) learner evaluation of questioning skills, and (e) interpreting data collecting about your questioning techniques.

[Note: Web addresses change frequently. If you are unable to locate one of these sites using the listed URL, try putting the site name in a standard search engine.]

This classroom observer is using an observational tool to gather information that will be shared later with the teacher. The teacher will use the information to make decisions about changes in procedures.

Many different kinds of observational tools can be developed that are based on event sampling, time sampling, or a combination of the two. Some examples are introduced in the following subsections.

Narrative Approach

Observers using a narrative approach, sometimes referred to as *scripting,* try to capture information about what is happening in the classroom by rapidly writing down everything that is observed. Since much of what happens in a classroom is verbal, narrative approaches focus heavily on what teachers and learners say.

A basic problem with an unstructured narrative approach is that much happens in a classroom so quickly that it is impossible for everything to be recorded. What is recorded may reveal just a partial picture of what happened. To avoid this limitation, some observers prefer to use a more narrowly focused version, called *selective verbatim.*

When using a selective verbatim approach, the observer identifies a particular dimension of classroom verbal interaction as a focus. Then the observer records everything said that falls into this targeted category. Targeted categories might include such areas as "teacher questions," "motivational statements," "classroom control statements," and "praise statements." Only the creativity and interests of the observer limit the focus for a selective verbatim approach.

Suppose an observer is interested in the types of praise statements you make during a lesson. To gather information, the observer would write down everything you say when you are praising a learner. (Sometimes observers make an audio recording of the lesson so they can recheck the accuracy of what they wrote during the live observation.)

Focus: **Teacher Praise Statements**

Kind of lesson: **Arithmetic—Grade 5**

Time	Teacher Statements
9:02	Thank you for sitting down.
9:03	I appreciate that.
9:05	You have really been doing a good job on this unit.
9:09	Good answer.
9:10	Okay, good.
9:13	Good, I like that.
9:13	Right!
9:15	Good.
9:18	Juan, you used a good method for finding the answer.
9:20	I'm glad you all started to work so promptly.

FIGURE 7.3   Example of a Selective Verbatim Record

Results of a selective verbatim observation are organized into a *selective verbatim record,* which can provide data for a useful analysis. A series of questions is developed that can be answered by reference to this information. For example, if the focus of the observation were on praise behavior, the observer may develop questions such as:

- Did the teacher use a variety of praise statements?
- How adequate was the quantity of praise statements?
- Were praise statements tied more to academic performance or to other kinds of learner behavior?
- Were more praise statements directed toward individuals or to the class as a whole?

An example of a selective verbatim record is provided in Figure 7.3.

Frequency Counts

Frequency counts focus on the number of occurrences of behaviors of interest. The observer identifies behavior categories before the observation begins. Frequency count observations might focus on such categories as:

- the number of teacher praise statements,
- the number of high-level teacher questions (demanding sophisticated thinking),
- the number of low-level teacher questions (demanding only simple recall of basic information),
- the number of classroom disruptions,
- the number of times individual learners visit learning centers, or
- the number of times learners made correct (or incorrect) responses to teacher questions.

Focus: **Teacher Statements and their Relationship to Learner Participation in a Discussion**

Directions: Tally each teacher behavior that has a positive impact on getting learners involved in the discussion. (These are found under the heading "Teacher Facilitating Moves.") Also tally each teacher behavior that has a negative impact on getting learners involved in the discussion. (These are found under the heading "Teacher Inhibiting Moves.") Tally learner responses that are correct and those that are incorrect. Also provide a tally for each time the teacher asks a question and there is no learner response at all. Finally, tally each time a learner initiates a question or a comment. (These are to be made under the heading "Learner Responses.")

Teacher Facilitating Moves

- Asks clear question
- Asks for learner response (waits more than three seconds)
- Praises learner comment
- Uses learner comment in lesson
- Provides positive nonverbal reinforcement

Teacher Inhibiting Moves

- Asks ambiguous question
- Asks multiple questions
- Does not wait for learner response
- Criticizes learner response
- Sends negative nonverbal signals

Learner Responses

- Number of correct learner responses
- Number of incorrect learner responses
- Absence of any learner responses to question

FIGURE 7.4   Example of a Frequency-Count System

Frequency count systems are easy to use. A simple record is maintained of the number of times each selected focus behavior occurs. Tally marks are often used to indicate each occurrence.

Look at the example of a frequency count system provided in Figure 7.4. Because frequency count systems do not require much writing, it is possible for tallies to be made that relate to numerous behaviors. This example yields information that might help an observer to identify some teacher behaviors that prompted learner involvement in the lesson.

Coding Systems

Coding systems require the use of codes or symbols that represent behaviors of interest to the observer. Symbols may vary in their complexity, from a simple system of checks, minuses, and pluses to a complex scheme that assigns numbers to a wide array of individual behaviors. Usually, a record using the codes is made after a preestablished interval of time has passed. For example, the observer might use codes to record behaviors once every 20 seconds.

It is not always necessary for an observer to have the entire coding scheme completely developed before a classroom observation begins. Sometimes new codes can be

Focus: **Motivational Strategies**

Directions: During each five-minute time segment of the lesson, record the letters indicating the motivational strategies used by the teacher. Record letters in the sequence of their occurrence. If new motivational strategies are used that are not on the list, add them and give them a letter.

Motivational Strategy

Record

5 min.

a.   Uses novelty   _____

b.   Appeals to curiosity   _____

c.   Provides concrete reinforcer   _____

d.   Provides dramatic buildup   _____

e.   Indicates importance of task   _____

5 min.

f.   Relates to learner needs, interests   _____

g.   Provides encouragement   _____

h.   Predicts success or enjoyment   _____

i.   Warns about testing, grades   _____

j.   Threatens punishment for noncompletion   _____

5 min.

k.   _____   _____

l.   _____   _____

   _____   _____

   _____   _____

   _____   _____

5 min.

   _____   _____

   _____   _____

   _____   _____

   _____   _____

   _____   _____

FIGURE 7.5   Example of a Coding-System Observation Scheme

added during the observation itself as interesting behaviors occur that had not been included in the initial scheme. This ability to add new codes even during the observation gives a great deal of flexibility to observation systems using coding schemes.

For example, suppose an observer began an observation with a very simple coding scheme in mind. It might feature only the two codes:

　　1. indicates a learner who is working on the assigned task and
　　2. indicates a learner who is not working on the assigned task.

During the actual observation, the observer might note that some learners were out of their seat, talking, or working on school work other than the assigned task. The observer may decide to add specific codes to indicate these behaviors. (One way to do this would be to designate code *2a* for "out of seat," code *2b* for "talking," and code *2c* for "other school work." Code *2* would be reserved for all additional examples of learners' not working on assigned tasks.) An example of an observation system using coding is provided in Figure 7.5.

Seating-Chart Systems

Observation systems involving the use of seating charts often are appropriate when the focus is on learner behaviors. For example, you might want to know which learners are contributing to a discussion or which ones are staying on task when you assign seat work. A system might be devised that would record information about which learners you worked with during a given class period. Seating-chart schemes also work well when you are curious about your location in the classroom during different parts of an instructional period.

In developing a seating-chart system, the observer begins by making a sketch of the classroom that includes the locations of individual learner seats. Once this basic chart has been completed and learners have entered the classroom, the observer may want to record whether males or females occupy individual seats. This can be done by writing a small *m* for male or a small *f* for female on each seat represented in the chart.

Next, the observer develops a set of symbols to represent the various aspects of instruction that are to be emphasized. For example, a simple arrow pointing to a seat might indicate a teacher question to a particular learner, and a simple arrow pointing away from the seat might indicate a communication directed from a particular learner to the teacher. Numerals or letters can be designated to represent different kinds of things individual learners are observed doing at selected time intervals during the lesson. The location of the teacher at specific places in the room at different times could be indicated by a sequence of circled numbers (*1* indicating the first location, *2* indicating the second, and so forth). Any symbols that work for the observer are acceptable.

Look at the sample information provided in the chart featured in Figure 7.6. Many interesting questions can be answered by examining data gathered from a completed chart of this kind. For example, using the information in Figure 7.6, an observer might be able to answer questions such as:

- How many learners were involved in the discussion?
- Were more males or females called on?
- Did the teacher have a tendency to call more frequently on learners seated on one side of the room? seated in the front as opposed to the back of the room?
- How many learners who volunteered were not recognized by the teacher? What might be the long-term impact on willingness to volunteer if a learner were rarely recognized?

Observation focus: Identifying discussion participants

Lesson topic: Review for a test

Directions: Each space in the chart below represents a learner seat. Sex of learners should be indicated by an *m* for males and an *f* for females. The following symbols are drawn in the box denoting the learner's seat and are used to indicate the first time the particular behavior is noted:

- A learner raises a hand to volunteer (indicated by a vertical line).

- A learner is recognized and makes a contribution (indicated by an arrow pointed away from the learner).

- The teacher calls on a learner (indicated by a down-pointing arrow).

- A learner is called but fails to respond (indicated by a zero drawn immediately below the down-pointing arrow indicating a teacher question).

- Repetitions by the same behavior are indicated by horizontal marks across the vertical ones. Note examples below:

This learner volunteered four times but was not called on.	This learner was called on and made a contribution twice.	This learner was called on three times.

Seating Chart with Sample Data

m 1	m 2	f 3	m 4	f 5
m 6	f 7	m 8	f 9	m 10
f 11	m 12	f 13	m 14	f 15
f 16	m 17	m 18	f 19	m 20
m 21	f 22	f 23	f 24	m 25
f 26	f 27	m 28	f 29	f 30

FIGURE 7.6   Example of a Seating-Chart Observation Scheme (with sample data)

These observational techniques have relevance for you as a prospective teacher. When you use them to make carefully planned observations, you can gain important information about actions you take in the classroom that both help and hinder your attempts to guide learners.

SOME FINAL THOUGHTS

As you begin your role as an instructional leader, we want to pass along some encouragement and advice. Initially, you will not have all the skills necessary to be as effective as you can be. Good teachers improve over time and progress through a series of developmental stages, from novice to expert (Steffy & Wolfe, 1997). Do not be excessively self-critical, and give yourself time to grow.

Initially, you may feel alone in the process of becoming an expert teacher, but you are not. Teachers who are more experienced and skilled will surround you and can play an invaluable role in your development. Halford (1998) says, "As instructional leaders and master teachers, mentors can be a professional lifeline for their colleagues (35)."

Systematic growth will require your own efforts, and these will include, above all, a commitment to inquire into your own methodology. Continuing assessments of your instructional practices can provide information you can use to adapt your instruction to learners' needs. We wish for you the joy that comes from knowing that you can become more effective with each year in the profession.

Key Ideas In Summary

- Arguments have long raged about the existence of a body of research that can adequately define what is meant by "effective" teaching. Increasingly, though, evidence is indicating that at least some variables associated with effective teaching have been discovered.
- Most research on effective teaching has focused on teacher behaviors associated with increases in learners' levels of achievement. This emphasis has been supported in recent years by public concerns about the issue of subject-matter learning in the schools.
- In active teaching, teachers play a central role and lead the class in the role of a (1) presenter of new information, (2) monitor of learner progress, (3) planner of opportunities for learners to apply what they have learned, and (4) reteacher of content to learners who are confused.
- Active teachers are greatly concerned about the issue of matching their instruction to needs of individual learners. In achieving an appropriate match, they consider such things as the difficulty of the material relative to the individual learner's ability and the learner's level of interest in the content to be taught.
- Active teachers are very concerned about the issue of good lesson presentation. This involves actions designed to (1) stimulate and maintain learner interest, (2) present material systematically, (3) model expected behaviors and expected products of learning, (4) maintain an appropriate lesson pace, (5) ask questions

skillfully, (6) provide opportunities for learners to practice what they have learned, and (7) monitor learners' progress.

- Research has established the importance of clarity as a teacher variable associated with learner achievement. Among dimensions of clarity are the teacher's verbal and nonverbal styles, lesson presentation style, and proficiency in providing cogent explanations.

- Effective teachers use class time productively. They make decisions related to allocated time, engaged time, and academic learning time.

- Teachers' expectations have an influence on how individual learners perform. Researchers have found that (1) teachers have certain behavioral expectations of learners, (2) teachers' behaviors toward learners vary in terms of what they believe that individual learners can do, (3) learners' self-concepts are affected by how they perceive themselves to be viewed by their teachers, and (4) teachers who are conscious of the impact of their expectations can monitor and adjust them in ways that can improve learners' performance.

- Teachers' questioning patterns often influence learning. Teachers tend to ask questions of two basic types: lower level questions and higher level questions. Lower level questions call on learners to recall specific items of previously introduced information. Higher level questions require learners to use more complex thinking processes.

- Many observation systems are available that can provide specific information to teachers about what happens in their classrooms. Some of these approaches use time sampling, others use event sampling, and still others employ a combination of the two.

Chapter 7 Self Test

To review terms and concepts in this chapter, take the Chapter 7 Self Test on the companion Web site, located at *http://www.prenhall.com/armstrong*. Select Chapter 7 from the front page of the Web site, then choose the Self Test module on the navigation bar on the left side of the page. Feedback for the Self Test is immediate. You can keep track of your Self Test scores yourself, or you can choose to submit your scores via e-mail to your instructor.

Reflections

 To respond to these questions online, and to save or submit your response electronically, visit the companion Web site, located at *http://www.prenhall.com/armstrong*. Select Chapter 7 from the front page of the Web site, then choose the Reflections module on the navigation bar on the left side of the page. Instructors and students may also wish to use these questions as discussion topics on the Message Board for the companion Web site.

1. Is there research-based knowledge available today that pinpoints behaviors associated with effective teaching?
2. What criteria should be used in determining a teacher's relative effectiveness?

3. What are some general characteristics of active teaching?

4. What goes on during the task-analysis phase of instructional planning?

5. What are some differences between motivation that occurs (a) before a learning sequence begins, (b) during a learning sequence, and (c) at the end of a learning sequence?

6. What are the steps in the Hunter-Russell model?

7. Why is the issue of clarity so important, and what are some dimensions of teacher clarity?

8. Which is likely to produce the greater increase in scores on an academic achievement test: (a) a decision to increase *allocated time* related to the tested topic or (b) a decision to increase *academic learning time* related to the tested topic?

9. Research on the effect of asking higher level and lower level questions on learners' academic achievement has found mixed results. How might you explain these inconsistent findings?

10. What are some features of observation instruments based on (a) narrative approaches, (b) frequency counts, (c) coding systems, and (d) seating-chart systems?

Field Experiences, Projects, and Enrichment

1. Review ideas for gathering observational data. Select one category associated with teacher effectiveness that was introduced in this chapter. Visit a classroom and gather data related to this category using an observation system of your own design. You may wish to consider a scheme based on a narrative approach, frequency counts, a coding system, or a seating chart.

2. A thread that runs through much recent teacher effectiveness research is the idea that effective behaviors are contextual. This means that a pattern that is effective with certain kinds of learners and for teaching certain levels of understanding or skills may not necessarily work well with other learners and for teaching other levels of understanding. With your instructor's guidance, review some research literature associated with the topic of direct instruction. Under what circumstances does this approach seem to work well? Under what circumstances has it been found to be less appropriate? Present your conclusions in the form of a brief oral report.

3. Some of the research on teacher effectiveness has produced results that have surprised some people, particularly when the discovered information has challenged some popularly held beliefs. With your instructor's guidance, look up some research findings associated with teacher praise. Is teacher praise always good? Report your conclusions in the form of a short paper.

4. Today, teachers are increasingly getting involved with research in their own classrooms. Much of this research is directed at improving their own instruction. Review some articles in education journals (look for titles in such sources as the *Education Index* and the *Association of Teacher Educators Handbook of Research on Teacher Education, 2nd ed.,* Ch. 4.) that focus on the topic of the teacher as researcher. Then share with the rest of the class what you find out about the approaches teachers are taking to gather research about their own instruction and some of the things this research is revealing.

5. Prepare a list of source materials related to research data about effective teaching. Ask your instructor for some ideas to get you started. Combine your list with those prepared by others in your class. Eliminate common entries, produce a single composite list, and prepare copies for the files of all class members.

References

Acheson, K. A., & Gall, M. (1992). *Techniques in the clinical supervision of teachers.* White Plains, NY: Longman.

Berliner, D. C. (1984). The half-full glass: A review of research on teaching. In P. L. Hosford (Ed.), *Using what we know about teaching* (pp. 51–77). Alexandria, VA: Association for Supervision and Curriculum Development.

Cazden, C. (1986). Classroom discourse. In M. Wittrock (Ed.), *Handbook of research on teaching* (3rd ed., pp. 432–463). New York: Macmillan.

Cooper, H. (1989). Synthesis of research on homework. *Educational Leadership, 47*(3), 85–91.

DeGarmo, C. (1903). *Interest in education: The doctrine of interest and its concrete applications.* New York: Macmillan.

Denton, J. J., Armstrong, D. G., & Savage, T. V. (1980). Matching events of instruction to objectives. *Theory into Practice, 19*(1), 10–14.

Finn, J. D. (1993). *School engagement and students at risk.* Washington, DC: National Center for Education Statistics, U.S. Department of Education.

Good, T. L., & Brophy, J. E. (2000). *Looking in classrooms* (8th ed.). New York: Longman.

Goodlad, J. A. (1984). *A place called school.* New York: McGraw-Hill.

Halford, J. M. (1998). Easing the way for new teachers. *Educational Leadership, 55*(5), 33–36.

Heckman, P. E., Confer, C. B., & Hakim, D. C. (1994). Planting seeds: Understanding through investigation. *Educational Leadership, 51*(5), 36–39.

Henson, K. T., & Eller, B. F. (1999). *Educational psychology for effective teaching.* Belmont, CA: Wadsworth.

Hunter, M., & Russell, D. (1977). How can I plan more effective lessons? *Instructor, 87*(2), 74–75, 88.

Meyer, A. E. (1975). *Grandmasters of educational thought.* New York: McGraw-Hill.

Posner, R. S. (1987). Pacing and sequencing. In M. J. Dunken (Ed.), *The international encyclopedia of teaching and teacher education* (pp. 266–272). Oxford, England: Pergamon Press.

Ramsey, I., Gabbard, C., Clawson, K., Lee, L., & Henson, K. T. (1990). Questioning: An effective teaching method. *The Clearing House, 63*(9), 420–422.

Redfield, D., & Rousseau, E. (1981). A meta-analysis of experimental research on teacher questioning behavior. *Review of Educational Research, 18*(2), 237–245.

Reinstein, D. (1998). Crossing the economic divide. *Educational Leadership, 55*(4), 28–29.

Rinne, C. H. (1998). Motivating students is a percentage game. *Phi Delta Kappan, 79*(8), 620–628.

Rosenshine, B., & Stevens, R. (1986). Teaching functions. In M. Wittrock (Ed.), *Handbook of research on teaching* (3rd ed., pp. 376–391). New York: Macmillan.

Rowe, M. B. (1986). Wait time: Slowing down may be a way of speeding up. *Journal of Teacher Education, 37*(1), 43–50.

Steffy, B. E., & Wolfe, M. P. (1997). *The life cycle of the career teacher: Maintaining excellence for a lifetime.* West Lafayette, IN: Kappa Delta Pi Publications.

Tobin, K. (1987). The role of wait time in higher cognitive learning. *Review of Educational Research, 24*(1), 69–95.

Walker, V. N., & Chance, E. W. (1994/1995). National award winning teachers' exemplary instructional techniques and activities. *National Forum of Teacher Education Journal, 5*(l), 11–24.

8

Classroom Management and Discipline

OBJECTIVES

This chapter will help you to

- point out the relationship between management and discipline.
- identify the importance of space management.
- describe time management.
- define what needs to be considered when establishing the context for effective discipline.
- describe what negotiation means in relation to discipline.
- identify basic principles that need to be followed when responding to inappropriate behavior.
- list a range of alternative responses that can be used when addressing discipline problems.

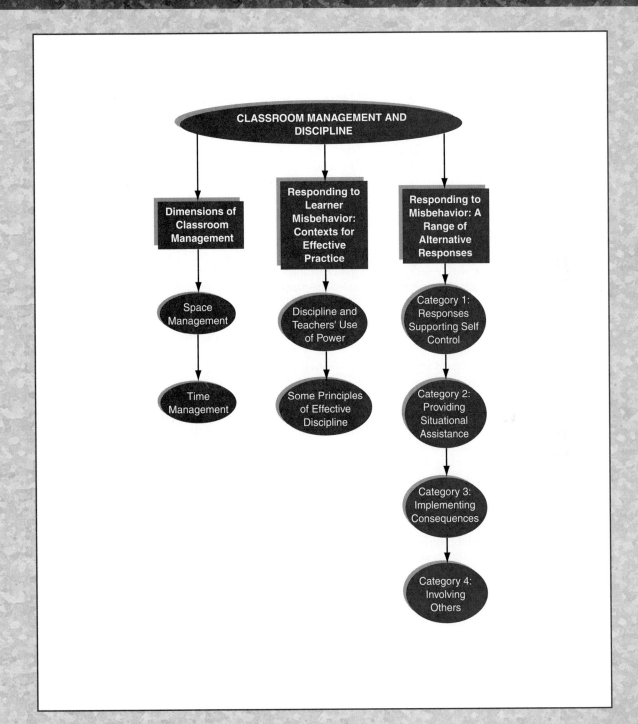

FIGURE 8.1 Classroom Management and Discipline

INTRODUCTION

To succeed in the classroom, you need to know how to manage learners and respond appropriately to their behavior. An inability to control the classroom is a major reason for teacher failure and dismissal. Well-meaning people who want to help beginners often willingly share a number of surefire prescriptions for success such as:

- Plan your lessons thoroughly.
- Love the students.
- Be enthusiastic.
- Do not smile until Christmas.
- Start off tough.
- Let them know you are the boss.

Although some of these statements may have an element of truth, they are inadequate for the complex task of managing the classroom, which clearly is one of the most challenging responsibilities teachers face (Williams, Alley, & Henson, 1999). It is true that you do need to plan carefully, but even teachers who devote lots of time to planning lessons occasionally encounter discipline problems. Certainly, too, members of our profession who like young people and who approach life enthusiastically often do exceptionally well in the classroom. But these characteristics alone are no guarantee that classroom control and management problems will not surface from time to time.

The hard truth is that all teachers occasionally must contend with problems associated with learner misbehavior. While there are no simple solutions to this challenge, there are some general principles that you can use to reduce the frequency of problem behavior. Part of your work as a teacher involves helping young people learn appropriate behavior patterns. Because a well-managed classroom is an essential part of the classroom climate required for academic learning, you have a responsibility both to establish sound management procedures and to teach academic content (Savage, 1999). The two roles complement one another; good teaching helps prevent management problems, and sound management provides a context within which good teaching can occur. There is evidence that suggests that as much as 80 percent of all discipline problems result from ineffective teaching (Brown, 1998).

Teacher-preparation programs often devote considerable time to acquainting prospective teachers with information related to good teaching. Classroom management, however, usually receives much less attention. This is because many instructors view management and discipline as dependent on personality traits and problem-solving skills that are difficult to teach. It is true that personality traits such as common sense and the ability to think quickly are important in managing a classroom. However, much can be done to prepare *all* individuals to better manage their classrooms.

This chapter addresses two basic aspects of classroom management. The first focuses on problem prevention through the use of good management, and the second introduces procedures that have been found useful as responses to inappropriate learner behaviors.

DIMENSIONS OF CLASSROOM MANAGEMENT

Many prospective teachers have questions about how to respond when problems occur. The most important aspect of classroom management and discipline, however, is the prevention of potential problems. For example, Kounin (1970) found that although successful and unsuccessful classroom managers responded to inappropriate learner behavior in similar ways, there were important differences in how they organized and managed their classrooms.

Successful classroom management requires you to understand the unique nature of the classroom and the role you play as the teacher. The classroom is a complex environment. Class members often vary greatly in their abilities, backgrounds, interests, maturity levels, and motivations, and they spend large blocks of time in close proximity. Events that take place in this type of an environment can be unpredictable.

Your responsibility is to take this mixture of individuals, provide them with appropriate materials, capture their interest, organize the space, and use the time so that learning occurs in ways that leave class members feeling positive about the instructional experience. Since what motivates varies greatly from person to person, you must seek ways to motivate all students. Indeed, some authorities have identified as many as 30 different categories of psychological motivators (Henson & Eller, 1999).

While you try to deal imaginatively with academic content, you also have to be prepared to respond to unanticipated and spontaneous events in a constructive manner. Fortunately, there are things that you can do to make instruction flow more smoothly and to reduce the number of potentially disruptive learner behaviors.

Researchers have suggested that smoothly functioning classrooms result when teachers take deliberate actions to plan a management strategy very early in the school year or even before school starts (Emmer, Evertson, & Anderson, 1980; Evertson, 1989). In making this connection, Carolyn Evertson (1989) commented, "Solving managerial and organizational problems at the beginning of the year is essential in laying the groundwork for quality learning opportunities for students" (p. 90). Teachers who follow this practice develop clear ideas about how they expect their classrooms to operate and then communicate those ideas to their learners.

Space Management

Classroom management begins with the organization and management of the classroom space. Architects and psychologists have long emphasized the impact of space on human behavior. In fact, they have coined the special term *behavioral setting* to explain this relationship. A behavioral setting is a space that influences the behavior of the individuals within that space. Consider a church, temple, or cathedral, for example. These environments seem to inspire awe in people and to communicate that quiet, respectful behaviors are required within them. When planning your own classroom environment, you need to consider what you can do to communicate your behavioral expectations to your learners.

In thinking about this issue, consider your reactions to different environments. How do you feel in crowded spaces where others invade your space? What is your reaction to clutter or unappealing places? What happens when you are in places that are hot or too cold? How are your motivation and learning affected by these variables? Individuals typically find that they are distracted, irritable, anxious, fatigued, and angry when confronted with these conditions. These are not the feelings that you want to engender in your learners.

In planning the classroom for instruction and the prevention of problems, you need to consider the attractiveness of the space, the degree of crowding, the comfort level of learners, the arrangement of materials and desks, and the location and availability of instructional materials. It makes sense to begin planning the physical layout of the classroom as early as possible, even several weeks prior to the beginning of the school year (Williams et al., 1999).

Wall Space   An important aspect of providing a stimulating and attractive environment is the use of wall space. Constructive use of wall space enhances the quality of the instructional environment. Parts of the walls can be devoted to motivational displays to stimulate interest in topics that are being studied. Particularly important in elementary and middle schools, spots can be reserved to display learners' work. Other areas can be used to display schedules, important announcements, and classroom rules. Adding a little color to the wall, occasionally changing the displays, and keeping the walls free of unnecessary clutter goes a long way in providing a pleasant classroom environment.

Floor Space   Developing a floor plan of the classroom is useful in addressing the issues of density and convenience. Seating must be arranged so that learners do not feel overcrowded, can observe and hear the teacher, and can see important educational centers such as chalkboards and overhead projector screens.

The nature of the instructional activities that are to be conducted in the space should have a major impact on decisions about the most appropriate organization of classroom floor space. Some types of activities feature whole-group instruction. Others require you to work with small groups of learners. Still others require learners to be scattered throughout the room at different learning or activity centers.

Whole-group instruction requires a physical arrangement that permits all learners to maintain good eye contact with the teacher; desks must be arranged to provide for this need. Occasionally, you will want to check on an individual learner's work or understanding during whole-group instruction. Desks need to be arranged to allow for aisles or spaces that permit you to move quickly to meet personally with learners who might be experiencing problems.

In planning floor arrangements for small-group discussion, learning spaces need to be arranged so you can continue to monitor the whole class while working with one small group. If possible, seating spaces for the small group you are working with should be placed some distance from other learners. This diminishes the temptation for small-group members to talk to others in the class. It also helps reduce the general noise level, something that makes it easier for all learners to stay at their assigned tasks.

Learning centers need to be placed in areas of the classroom that are easily accessible to all learners and yet are not distracting to those individuals who are not working at the centers. Because films, filmstrips, and other projected media can be very distracting to others, centers that feature them should be placed out of the direct sight lines of learners who are not working at the centers.

Traffic Patterns   In planning the physical organization of classrooms, traffic patterns must be considered. To begin, you need to identify those parts of the room that are heavily used. These would include such areas as doorways, places where learners' personal belongings and class materials are stored, book storage areas, and the vicinity of the teacher's desk. Spaces around these frequently visited parts of the classroom need to be kept obstruction-free. Desks should be arranged so that people going to and from these areas of the classroom can do so without disturbing other learners.

Teacher's Desk   Although many teachers do not give much thought to the placement of their desk, its location can have management consequences. In many classrooms, the teacher's desk is located at the front and center of the room. This setup is a custom dictated by tradition rather than sound management. A better choice is an unobtrusive place near the back of the room.

Locating the desk near the rear of the classroom has several advantages. One advantage is that it encourages you to stand up and move around the classroom, which often leads to more careful monitoring of learners' work. Teachers who circulate through the classroom and avoid sitting behind a desk are perceived by learners as "warmer" (Smith, 1987). A second advantage is that this placement does not allow you to get in the habit of teaching from behind the desk. Teaching while sitting at the teacher's desk does not convey to learners that you are interested in and enthusiastic about what you are doing. A third advantage is that it is normally easier to monitor learners' on-task behavior from the rear of the classroom. Members of the class will not know when you are observing them, and a feeling among learners that the teacher might be looking helps minimize problem behaviors. Finally, a desk at the rear of the classroom makes it easier to have individual learner conferences at the desk without attracting the attention of everyone in the room. This helps keep the maximum number of learners on task rather than observing the interaction between the teacher and learner.

Equipment Storage   Depending on the age of your learners and the subjects you teach, your lessons may require the use of a lot of specialized equipment. Many schools have items such as computers, projectors (e.g., 16 mm, slide, opaque, or overhead), video- and audiotape recorders, television monitors, and phonographs. Some of these items are kept in individual classrooms. Storage space for this equipment needs to be both secure and accessible. Although maintaining equipment in good operating order is a major headache for school officials, the possibilities for misuse or malicious damage decrease when equipment is stored in a way that permits access only by authorized people. When possible, it is wise to store equipment in cabinets or other areas that can be locked.

Placing your teacher's desk near the back of the classroom will encourage you to stand up and move around the classroom. In addition, locating the desk in the rear will make it easier to converse with individual learners without disturbing others.

Time Management

Time management is one of the most important and one of the most difficult of teachers' managerial tasks. When you teach, you have a limited amount of time to accomplish important educational goals. It is important that the time be used so that learners do not become bored because of wasted time or overwhelmed and frustrated because there is inadequate time. Researchers have found that in many classrooms, a high percentage of time is spent on noninstructional tasks (Smyth, 1987). Not surprisingly, they have also determined that learners in classes where teachers spend more time on instruction learn more (Berliner, 1984).

Time management involves handling routine tasks in a quick and efficient manner, taking action to ensure that members of the class get to work promptly, presenting necessary information in a clear and concise manner, and keeping learners engaged in learning throughout the lesson.

Transitions   Management of shifts from one part of a lesson to another is important. Many beginning teachers spend extensive periods of time planning lessons and give little thought to transitions between lessons. Transitions occur when there is a shift from one activity to another, and they offer the potential for much class time to be lost.

To avoid wasting time, careful plans need to be made for transition points. When materials are to be distributed or work returned during the transition points, it is useful to organize the material in advance. When this is done, things can be distributed to the learners quickly and efficiently. Sometimes transitions require learners to move from one part of an instructional area to another or from one room to another. Giving clear directions on how to make these changes and establishing a time frame within which the changes need to be made can save valuable time.

Beginning Class Some teachers take too much time getting their classes started. Lessons that begin promptly engage learners' attention, eliminate potential off-task behavior that can lead to problems, and maximize instructional time. This means that tasks such as taking attendance and other routine administrative duties need to be performed quickly.

It often is useful to establish a signal system that informs class members that it is time for learning. Some teachers move to a special place in the front of the class and look out over the learners. Others use a particular command such as "all eyes up here." At the beginning of the school year, you can explain to learners the specific signal system you want to use.

A lesson should not be started until all learners are paying attention. When you teach, you have to be careful not to strain your voice. This kind of strain can leave you hoarse and uncomfortable. It can make it difficult for you to sustain a volume level loud enough to be heard over learners' unauthorized side conversations. Also, when you insist on quiet before you begin, you signal to learners that what you say is important and worth hearing.

Lesson Pacing How you pace lessons has important behavior implications for learners. Lessons should move briskly, but not so fast as to be confusing. While a certain amount of repetition is necessary to highlight key points, excessive repetition leads to boredom. It is a natural human tendency to seek relief from boredom, which often results in inappropriate behavior in classrooms.

To determine an appropriate instructional pace, some teachers select a "reference group" in their class. Members of the reference group include four or five learners who represent a cross section of class members. You can watch members of the reference group to determine their reactions to what you are doing. Based on your observations of these class members, you can speed up, slow down, or maintain the present instructional pace.

Part of planning for pacing is in response to the point that some learners will finish assignments sooner than others. Follow-up activities need to be designed for early finishers so that they can immediately make the transition into another productive activity. The follow-up activities you choose should not be "more of the same." If this happens, bright learners may feel that they are being punished for finishing their work quickly. On the other hand, these follow-up experiences cannot be so enticing that learners race through the assigned task just to gain more time for working on them.

Providing Assistance   Often while learners are working on assignments, many of them will seek help from the teacher. A teacher with 25 to 30 learners can be frustrated when trying to help all of those looking for assistance. Frederic H. Jones (1979) has suggested some guidelines for responding to this problem. In his research, he found that the average teacher spends much more time working with individual learners than is necessary. To decrease the total time spent with each person and, hence, increase the opportunities to help more individuals seeking assistance, the following procedure is recommended for use with each learner:

- First, the teacher should build confidence by finding something the learner has done correctly and then praising the good work.
- Second, the teacher should provide a direct suggestion about what the learner should do next. (But the teacher should not do the work for the learner.)
- After completing the first two steps, the teacher should move on quickly to the next learner. The teacher may check back in a short while to make sure the learner is still on task. However, care needs to be taken that the teacher does not get trapped helping just one learner or creating a sense of dependency so that specific learners depend on the teacher to do most of the work and thinking for them.

Jones (1979) has pointed out that this process will enable the teacher to help a large number of learners in a relatively short time period. He has recommended that, on average, no more than 20 seconds at a time be spent with a single learner.

Establishing Routines and Procedures   A basic principle of classroom management is that routines and procedures need to be developed to handle recurring and predictable events. This helps simplify the demands on your time so you can devote your attention to the exceptions or the unplanned and unpredictable events. During a typical day, you will experience hundreds of personal contacts with learners. Unless systems for managing these contacts are developed, your emotional reserves will be drained, and the likelihood of making management mistakes will increase. Routines and procedures are often developed for such things as:

- what learners are to do as soon as they enter the classroom,
- what learners should do when they have a personal problem to discuss with the teacher,
- what procedures are to be used in passing out and collecting materials,
- when and where pencils are to be sharpened,
- how daily attendance is to be taken, and
- what learners are to do when they need to leave the room.

Once procedures and routines have been planned, those involving learner behaviors need to be explained to class members. With younger learners, this information sometimes is taught as a formal lesson. With more mature, secondary school students, a brief explanation of expectations and procedures may suffice. Figure 8.2 provides an opportunity for you to think about rules and procedures you would like to follow in your own classroom.

Researchers have found that effective teachers are especially good at establishing rules and procedures (Doyle, 1986). Effective teachers not only establish rules and procedures, they systematically teach them to learners. The rules and procedures need to be written in clear, explicit language so that learners know when they are in compliance. Furthermore, the rules and procedures need to be written and developed as they are needed. It is best to establish the rules with the class; however, there are a few that you may feel are absolutely necessary in your classroom. Take some time to reflect on the rules and procedures you believe you will need as a teacher. The chart supplied will help you in that task.

	Rules and procedures related to classroom conduct	**Rules and procedures related to academic work**
Rules and procedures that need to be communicated at the beginning of the school year		
Rules and procedures that may be established later		

FIGURE 8.2 Establishing Rules and Procedures

RESPONDING TO LEARNER MISBEHAVIOR: CONTEXTS FOR EFFECTIVE PRACTICE

Even in classrooms where lessons are exciting and teachers are good managers, learners occasionally misbehave. Dealing with inappropriate behavior involves more than a bag of tricks to be used in response to a specific incident. The effectiveness of a given response begins with the attitudes and the expectations of the teacher.

You might ask yourself the following questions:

- What do you expect of students? Do you believe they are interested in learning?
- How do you see your role as a teacher? Do you believe it is wise to "lay down the law"?
- How do you think teachers establish good discipline in the classroom?
- What is your image of the ideal classroom?
- What is your image of young people today?
- What is the appropriate relationship between teachers and learners?
- Are you comfortable sharing power with members of your class?

Answers to these questions can reveal your underlying attitude toward learners and your philosophy of teaching and learning. Your philosophy and attitude will have a strong influence on how you view classroom management and how you will respond when problems arise. Therefore, the images you have of what it takes to be a successful teacher and classroom manager need to be uncovered so that they can be investigated and dealt with in productive ways.

Following the Web 8.1

Planning for Effective Management

The issue of classroom management concerns educators everywhere. Accordingly, there are large numbers of sites on the World Wide Web that feature content related to this high-interest topic. We have listed a sampling of sites with information of particular interest to beginning teachers.

For hot links to these sites, visit the companion Web site, located at *http://www.prenhall.com/armstrong*. Select Chapter 8 from the front page of the Web site, then choose the Following the Web module on the navigation bar on the left side of the page.

Roles of the Teacher: Planning

- *http://titen.educ.utas.edu.au/HTML/roles/plan1.html*

  Information here has been provided by Australia's outstanding Teacher in Training Education Network (TITEN). It provides an excellent overview of a useful classroom-management planning process. Specific planning tasks are identified, and there are suggestions for implementing a management plan.

Roles of the Teacher: Motivating

- *http://titen.educ.utas.edu.au/HTML/roles/mot1.html*

  This is another site maintained by Australia's TITEN. As the title suggests, the emphasis is on motivating learners. There is a general discussion of differences between intrinsic and extrinsic motivation. Six useful strategies for motivating learners are introduced.

What Is Your Classroom Management Profile?

- *http://education.indiana.edu/cas/tt/v1i2/what.html*

  This site features a short self-test you can take to determine your own classroom-management profile. You will learn whether your individual management

Some people feel that the mere use of the term *management* suggests a metaphor that leads to the creation of an inappropriate classroom context (Bullough, 1994). Management is seen as reflecting top-down control with a primary focus on maintaining adult authority and learner obedience. The teacher sets the rules and establishes learning tasks independent of learner input or concerns. It is the role of the teacher to manage and control; it is the role of the learner to submit and obey.

Others recommend that the management metaphor be replaced with one of *negotiation* (McLaughlin, 1994). Negotiation implies a context in which the wants and needs of all interested parties are considered. This suggests that learners are to be treated with dignity and that they are given some power in deciding what happens in the classroom. The classroom is viewed as a community where cooperative learning, shared decision making, and group problem solving are the defining characteristics.

Learners are likely to understand rules they helped make much better than rules handed to them by the teacher (Latham, 1998), and it is never too soon to begin in-preference tends toward (a) an authoritarian style, (b) a laissez-faire style, or (c) an indifferent style. There are links that provide in-depth descriptions of characteristics associated with each of these style types.

Classroom-Management Plan

- *http://www.stratford.k12.wi.us/clmnplan.htm*

  This site features an example of a classroom-management plan prepared by one teacher. It features a general discipline plan with an accompanying set of "consequences" for learners who misbehave.

Classroom Management

- *http://www.quasar.ualberta.ca/ddc/incl/c10.htm*

  This Canadian Web site features general information about planning for classroom management. There are useful links to sites where individual teachers discuss their own experiences with classroom management.

Before School Starts

- *http://www.geocities.com/Athens/Delphi/4127/tutor.html*

  This Web page is provided by a school district in California to assist new teachers who have been employed to work in the district's schools. There are particularly good suggestions for establishing and following routines as a way to avoid classroom-control difficulties.

[Note: Web addresses change frequently. If you are unable to locate one of these sites using the listed URL, try putting the site name in a standard search engine.]

volving students in planning classroom behavior. Vars (1997), who believes teachers should begin involving students in goal setting the first day of class, stresses the need to be honest with students. If there are behavior expectations that are nonnegotiable, the teacher should be "up front" and say so from the beginning.

Negotiation as a metaphor is consistent with the *constructivist approach* to learning. This approach holds that learning occurs as individuals process information and construct their own meanings. Control forced on an individual from external sources such as the teacher does not provide conditions optimal for learning. You should strive for ways to help learners develop internal and personal commitments to desirable patterns of behavior. Some of the most important things young people take away from their years in school relate to experiences that have led to noncoercive self-discipline and self-control.

Negotiation does not mean that there is no control in the classroom and that all power is shifted to learners. Negotiation does not mean abdicating responsibility; it means taking the needs of others into account. As the teacher, you are still in charge of the classroom, and you deserve respect from learners in your role as leader. How you exercise this leadership is critical to the success of negotiation as a management technique. What constitutes appropriate leadership will vary depending on individual circumstances. There will be times, for example, when serious disruptions require you to exercise unilateral power.

The case for negotiation as a technique is buttressed by a major purpose of classroom discipline (and of education, in general): teaching learners how to exercise self-control and responsibility. Individuals with a wealth of knowledge but no self-control are unlikely to become productive individuals contributing to the good of humankind. Learning self-control and the acceptance of responsibility is enhanced when individuals are treated with dignity and are given responsibility. As they experience the consequences of their actions, they learn that "I cause my own outcomes. I have the power to choose alternative behaviors" (McLaughlin, 1994).

Several elements are involved in classrooms featuring negotiation. First, the degree to which individuals have self-control and a sense of responsibility is related to how they perceive reality. Those who believe that their environment is warm, trusting, and positive are more likely to exercise self-control than those who believe their environment is cold, indifferent, and negative. Opening many aspects of the classroom to negotiation and looking at the classroom as a place where the needs, concerns, and interests of the learners are taken into account goes a long way toward creating this type of a classroom climate.

Second, when you give young people opportunities to make choices, you help them to develop self-control and responsibility. Making decisions from among alternatives and living with the consequences are important aspects of maturing. Opportunities to choose provide learners with the feeling that they can exercise some personal control over their lives. People who have a sense that their personal actions and decisions count tend to act in more responsible, controlled ways than individuals who lack these feelings.

Third, learners with positive self-concepts are more likely to develop patterns of self-control and personal responsibility than those with negative self-concepts. Self-concepts derive from interactions with others. Since teachers exercise some control over classroom interactions, they are in a position to influence the nature of the self-concept developed by each learner. A success-oriented classroom in which every effort is made to help each person experience some feelings of achievement encourages the development of positive self-concepts among the learners.

Finally, learners who feel that they "belong" are likely to develop good self-control and a sense of personal responsibility. Pride in group membership is important to many young people. Providing learners with responsibility and being open to their concerns and interests can help them feel a sense of ownership and pride in being a part of the classroom.

In summary, creating a context within which good discipline can take place requires much more than just implementing a bag of tricks. It requires you to think carefully about what the "proper" role of the teacher is and about what it means to teach. In particular, you need to think about how teacher power is defined and used. The following section outlines several different types of power and how they might be used in the classroom.

Discipline and Teachers' Use of Power

When learners misbehave, you have to do something to remedy the situation. The nature of teacher power and how it is used can influence general patterns of classroom behavior. Several types of power you can use include (French & Raven, 1959):

- expert power,
- referent power,
- legitimate power,
- reward power, and
- coercive power.

Expert Power   Expert power is power that comes to a person as a result of possessing specialized knowledge. In general, people who are acknowledged experts in a given area exercise considerable influence over others. Their opinions are respected because they are thought to know a great deal about their specialties. This type of power is earned rather than demanded.

Referent Power   Referent power is power that results from a warm, positive relationship. Individuals are willing to give another some power when they perceive that the other person is trustworthy and is concerned about them. People accept advice they receive from those whom they like and respect. If you are to enjoy referent power as a teacher, you must be seen by learners as someone they respect and trust . . . someone who cares about them. As is the case with expert power, referent power cannot be demanded. It must be earned through actions that demonstrate trust, caring, and concern for others.

Legitimate Power   Legitimate power derives from the particular position a person holds. For example, city mayors can wield certain powers because of the office they hold. Teachers have some legitimate power because of the authority delegated by school administrators and the school board. For example, they have the power to make certain decisions about how to teach and how to deal with the behavior of class members.

Problems sometimes result because not all learners accept that teachers have legitimate power. This can cause difficulties for teachers who mistakenly assume that all learners accept their legitimate power. They do not. Teachers who think they can effectively manage classrooms simply by relying on their legitimate power are asking for trouble. On the other hand, teachers who build their authority in the classroom around expert and referent power—powers that have to be earned—will find that their legitimate authority is increased.

Reward Power   Reward power comes to individuals as a result of their ability to provide something that another person sees as desirable. As a teacher, you are in a position to provide benefits to learners in the form of praise, grades, and privileges; hence, you have some reward power. However, there are important limits to this kind of authority. You have a relatively small number of rewards available that can be dispensed to learners. Further, what you view as rewards are not always seen as desirable by all learners. Some of them may not care what grades they receive (and there are such people in the schools). These young people will not be influenced by teachers who offer good grades in exchange for good performance.

The power to give rewards comes with the position of being the teacher and is not a type of power that is earned. It is an effective type of power as long as there are rewards to give that learners value. This type of authority may vanish quickly when the rewards are exhausted or not desired. As with legitimate power, when a teacher establishes expert and referent power as a base, rewards such as grades and praise become more powerful.

Coercive Power   Coercive power is power that people wield because of their authority to administer punishment. Teachers who rely heavily on coercive power often do not have classroom environments that learners perceive as warm, caring, and positive. When coercive power is applied, many learners fail to see compelling reasons to adopt behavior patterns favored by their teachers. In an individual situation, when application of coercive power suppresses one undesirable behavior, another undesirable behavior often springs up to replace the first. Again, coercive authority is of little use when the ability to punish is removed or the prospect of being caught is perceived to be slight.

Expert power and referent power are the two types of power that are most important for you as you strive to develop positive working relationships with your learners. These two types of power are also most consistent with the metaphor of negotiation in classroom management. Young people are usually willing to accept leadership from teachers they perceive to be experts and ethical, warm individuals.

The desirability of being seen as an expert suggests the need for you to be well grounded in the subjects you teach. A solid grasp of content can give you the credibility needed to establish your expert power. At the same time, you need to establish positive classroom climates. When learners sense that you care about them personally and truly support them, you accrue valuable referent power. When expert and referent types of authority are present, classroom control problems are greatly diminished.

In summary, the way you attempt to establish and use authority and power in the classroom will have a significant impact on your success in controlling the classroom and disciplining learners. Negotiation as a metaphor encourages teachers to establish environments where learners' needs are addressed and where there is shared decision making. Expert and referent power are consistent with the concept of negotiation. They establish a context within which teachers' actions can be effective.

Critical Incident

Getting Tough

John Robbins is nearing the end of his first year of teaching seventh-grade history at Ride Middle School. The school is in a suburban area just outside a major midwestern city. John took the teaching job in this school because of the location. He was sure that the parents would be supportive of education and that the students would be motivated. He expected fewer discipline problems here than he might encounter in a more "difficult" setting. However, this has not turned out to be the case. In fact, he is wondering if he is up to returning in the fall.

John started his first year upbeat and optimistic. He knew he loved history and was sure that he could convey his enthusiasm to students by sharing the interesting anecdotes and insights he had obtained as a history major in college. He "just knew" he would relate well to students because he was much nearer their age than most teachers and could talk their language. He had had some difficulties in his student teaching, but he ascribed these problems to being in the classroom of another teacher and not having the freedom to do what he knew would be best.

John started the year by telling his students that he wanted to make things enjoyable for them. He was sure that if he made the class fun and was friendly and open to the students, they would be motivated to work and cooperate with him. After a month, however, he realized that the class was getting out of control. The students did not want to listen and were only interested in playing around. He became angry and decided that it was time to clamp down. Perhaps, he thought, a teacher really should not smile until Christmas.

In an effort to regain control, John decided to get tough. He laid down the law to his students and established strict rules and punishments. Although this seemed to stop some undesirable behaviors, it also resulted in students becoming increasingly negative. More and more of them seemed to take every opportunity to test the limits of his rules. He found that being engaged in a constant test of wills with his students was not much fun.

As the year draws to a close, John is feeling that he has accomplished very little. Many of his students now are openly expressing a dislike of history and are asking why it is important to learn something about a bunch of dead guys. John wonders if things are this bad in other schools. Maybe not. Perhaps he should try to get a job in a high school. Certainly other schools must have students with more mature attitudes who appreciate the value of learning something about history.

. . .

Do you think the problems would be easier at another grade? Do you think the problems are with John or with the students? Specifically, what does John perceive the problem to be? What do you think his students perceive the problem to be? What might have been the sources of the feelings of each?

What mistakes do you think John might have made? What suggestions would you give him? Do you worry about things like this happening to you? What do you think you could do about it? How do you respond to the suggestion of not smiling until Christmas and being tough from the first day of school? What are the alternatives?

To respond to this Critical Incident online, and to save or submit your response electronically, visit the companion Web site, located at *http://www.prenhall.com/armstrong*. Select Chapter 8 from the front page of the Web site, then choose the Critical Incidents module on the navigation bar on the left side of the page. Instructors and students may also wish to use these scenarios as discussion topics on the Message Board for the companion Web site.

Some Basic Principles of Effective Discipline

Regardless of the number of preventive actions you will take, you sometimes will have to deal with learner behavior problems. This is simply a part of being a teacher. Young people are human beings who lack experience, and they sometimes make wrong choices. There are some basic principles to keep in mind when responding to incidents of misbehavior. Understanding the following principles increases the possibility that your responses will be effective:

- Preserve the dignity of the learner.
- Private correction is preferable to public correction.
- The causes of misbehavior must be addressed, not simply the misbehavior itself.
- Distinctions must be made between minor and major misbehavior problems.
- Learners must be helped to understand that they have chosen to misbehave and, therefore, have chosen to experience the consequences.
- Responses to misbehavior must be consistent and fair.

Preserving Learners' Dignity   When correcting misbehavior, you need to be careful that your comments do not diminish learners' self-worth. Such responses have the potential to lead to more discipline problems (Jones & Jones, 1986). Teacher behaviors that assault learners' dignity often lead to power conflicts. Frustrated learners may feel that their only recourse is to respond with assaults on the dignity of the teacher. Older learners report that one of the reasons they misbehave is that they feel they have been "put down" by their teachers. Responsible teachers teach their students to be respectful. As Martin (1997) says, "Teaching respect begins by giving respect" (p. 7).

Private Correction versus Public Correction   One way you can diminish the likelihood that learners will feel that their self-worth has been attacked is to correct a misbehaving learner in a place where your comments cannot be heard by others. The verbal reprimand might take place outside of the classroom, for example. Private correction takes pressure off misbehaving young people. On the other hand, public reprimands may make them feel pressed to take action in order to "save face" in front of their peers. Private correction also promotes better, more personal contact between teachers and learners. Learners know that you are committing your full and undivided attention to the situation under discussion.

Addressing the Causes, Not Just the Behavior   Teachers who are good classroom disciplinarians take a long-term perspective on learners' behavior problems. Their responses are geared not simply to stopping misbehavior when it occurs, but rather they seek to change conditions so that problem behaviors will not recur. They seek underlying causes of improper behavior and try to remove conditions that reinforce unacceptable patterns (Brophy, 1983).

Serious and persistent misbehavior is often a learner's way of asking for help. It attracts your attention and prompts you to act. Given this sequence, learners occasionally will behave in ways they know are unacceptable simply to attract your attention to a serious problem. You need to recognize that some misbehaving young people are desperately seeking supportive, adult assistance.

Distinguishing Between Major and Minor Problems   Many incidents that happen in schools are a result of learners' immaturity rather than serious attempts to challenge authority. You need to be sensitive to the distinction between these minor behavioral lapses and those that represent more serious challenges to your ability to function as an instructional leader. This means you must avoid overreactions that can build learner resentment and lead to more serious misbehavior episodes.

Learners Choose to Misbehave and to Experience the Consequences   In teaching young people to be responsible, it is important to convey to them that unpleasant consequences of misbehavior result from their own irresponsible behavioral choices, not from arbitrary and vindictive actions that you, as their teacher, have decided to take. The objective is to help learners see the relationship between inappropriate behaviors and resultant consequences. To accomplish this, learners need to understand clearly what behaviors are unacceptable and what specific consequences will follow if they engage in these behaviors. The purpose is to help young people recognize that by choosing irresponsible behaviors, they are also choosing the consequences.

Consistent and Fair Responses   The principle of consistent and fair responses implies that there is a need to respond to all incidents of misbehavior. If you ignore some episodes, you signal to learners that there is nothing really wrong with this kind of behavior. When this happens, something that begins as a minor problem often escalates into a major one.

Consistency provides at least two key benefits. First, it communicates to learners that you are serious about discouraging a certain pattern of behavior. Second, it suggests to learners that you are fair. This perception is strengthened when you react similarly to a specified type of misbehavior regardless of which person in the class is involved.

RESPONDING TO MISBEHAVIOR: A RANGE OF ALTERNATIVES

Newcomers to teaching often are confused about how they should respond to misbehavior. One way of addressing this situation is by developing a plan that identifies a range of actions that might be taken in response to problems. This range of actions should begin with appropriately mild responses to minor problems that increase in severity when it is necessary to address more serious ones. This kind of planning allows you to consider alternatives in an unhurried way. Following the plan provides some assurance that you are maintaining consistent and fair patterns of responses when difficulties arise with different learners at different times.

Plans must be developed to fit individual circumstances. The subsections that follow list teacher responses in order of their severity. In this scheme, the teacher chooses options from the first several categories when minor problems arise and from categories farther down the list when more serious problems occur.

What Do You Think?

What if a Student Just Does Not Care?

Joe Silva, a 10th-grade English teacher, made these comments to Ceola Mathewson, chair of the English department.

> "Todd Morrison isn't a bad kid. In fact, he's really bright. But he's become just a pain in class. He just talks, talks, talks. He interrupts others. He doesn't spend time on his homework, and his grades are not good . . . not nearly what they could be.

> He works for his dad's software company. He lives and breathes computer code, and I understand he's already created some software that's bringing in some big money. He thinks time spent in school is just a painful interlude that he must endure before he can get back to his 'real life' at his dad's company. By the way, he thinks we teachers are a pretty sorry lot of folks. I think he believes we take low-paying teaching jobs because nobody else will have us. In any event, he just doesn't particularly care what we think of his behavior in class. He's a handful."

What Do You Think?

1. How do you react to Mr. Silva's assessment of Todd Morrison?
2. What general advice would you give to Mr. Silva that might enable him to work more effectively with this student?
3. As you reflect on your own personality, how might you approach a situation similar to the one described here?

Category 1: Responses Supporting Self-Control

One of the purposes of teaching is to help young people learn how to exert personal control over their behavior. When a teacher succeeds in communicating this kind of information, a learner may be able to replace an unacceptable behavior with an acceptable alternative. Teacher actions in this category are relatively unobtrusive. They are most appropriate for minor behavior problems.

Reinforcing Productive Behavior   One of the most important things you can do to help learners develop self-control is to reinforce desirable patterns of behavior. This can be done by rewarding individuals and members of an entire class when they have behaved well.

Rewards can take many forms. Verbal praise works well, and there may be special activities that class members particularly enjoy that function well as rewards. The specific rewards you use should vary with the interests of your learners. To be functional, a reward must be something that learners like. Simply because a reward appeals to you does not mean it will necessarily interest members of your class.

Using Nonverbal Signals to Indicate Disapproval   To the extent possible, minor episodes of misbehavior need to be handled so that the flow of the lesson is not interrupted. Nonverbal responses allow you to indicate to a learner that an inappropriate behavior has been noted. Such responses tell learners that they are being

Video Viewpoint

Survival Lessons: School-Based Mental Health Programs

WATCH: In this ABC News video segment, we learn about schools across the country that have set up full-time school-based mental health programs to identify and help troubled children.

THINK: With your classmates or in your teaching journal, consider these questions:
1. Do you think the types of mental-health programs mentioned in the video will help cut down on discipline problems or school violence of the type that occurred in 1999 at Columbine High School in Littleton, Colorado?
2. What are some other solutions for helping school-age children deal with some of the challenges of today's society, such as bullying, drugs, and violence?
3. If your school did not have a school-based mental-health program like those at Francis Scott Key Elementary and Middle School or Eastern High School and you noticed a child having some difficulties with schoolwork and peers, what would you do?

LINK: How are other students affected when their peers are troubled and don't receive guidance or positive messages from adults?

given time to correct their behavior and to avoid more serious consequences. Nonverbal signals include direct eye contact, hand signals, and facial expressions. These are useful tools in managing learner behavior in the classroom (Grubaugh, 1989).

Using Proximity Control   A minor behavior problem will often disappear when the teacher moves to the area of the classroom where it is occurring because many learners are less inclined to misbehave when the teacher is nearby. When a problem arises during a large-group lesson, frequently you can eliminate it simply by walking quietly to the part of the room where it is occurring. Often this can be done without interrupting the flow of the lesson.

Using a Learner's Name in the Context of a Lesson   Using a learner's name during a lesson informs the learner that his or her inappropriate behavior has been noted. It works something like this. If you notice that John's attention is drifting during a discussion of explorers, you might say, "Now, if John were a member of the crew sailing for the New World, he would have made his plans and . . . " The use of a learner's name will often result in a quick cessation of the inappropriate behavior.

Redirecting Learner Attention   Redirecting learner attention is especially useful for teachers who work with very young children, but also is sometimes effective with older learners. The idea is to watch class members carefully and take action to redirect misbehaving learners to a more productive pattern of behavior. A few brief words from the teacher designed to lead the learner back to the assigned task often are all that is required.

Encouraging Learners to Take Personal Action   Encouraging learners to take personal action when they are tempted to misbehave is implemented more

Proximity control; that is, moving close to individual learners, helps prevent discipline problems and also allows the teacher to monitor learner progress carefully.

frequently in elementary schools than in secondary schools. The children are taught to take some specific action when they feel compelled to act inappropriately. This approach is designed to give them time to reflect about what they are considering doing. It provides them with a chance to reestablish their self-control.

Sometimes young learners are taught to put their heads on the desk, clench their fists, or count to 10 when they sense themselves to be on the verge of misbehaving. These actions give the learners opportunities to relax and unwind before they do something that they might regret (Brophy, 1983).

In other classrooms, learners are urged to move to another part of the room and talk softly to themselves about the problem they are facing and possible responses they might make. This procedure works best when the teacher has taken time to teach learners the process of coping with problems by thinking about them aloud (Camp & Bash, 1981).

Category 2: Providing Situational Assistance

Responses in this category require more direct teacher intervention than those in category one. When teacher actions associated with category one have not been effective, then category two options should be considered. These actions are a little more direct and intrusive. In using them, you take assertive actions to help learners exercise self-control and responsibility. The focus is on preserving the dignity of the learners and in dealing with the problems in a relatively private manner.

Taking Time for a Quiet Word   To implement taking time out for a quiet word, the teacher moves toward the misbehaving learner. He or she quietly reminds this person of the kind of behavior that is expected. Once the teacher has delivered this message, there is a quick return to teaching the lesson.

Providing a Rule Reminder   Providing a rule reminder represents a slight escalation from taking time for a quiet word. When a behavior problem occurs, you can stop the lesson and speak to the misbehaving learner or learners in a voice loud enough for the whole class to hear. This is an example of a rule-reminder statement: "Bill's group, what does our list of class rules say about not talking when someone is asking a question?"

Removing the Learner from the Situation   To implement removal of a misbehaving learner, you arrange for the offending learner to move. You might require this person go to a different seat nearby or to another part of the room. Instructions related to this movement are brief, direct, and nonconfrontational: "Mary, take your material and go to the empty table. Continue working there." You might also remove the offender to a time-out area. When implemented, this strategy should be carried out quickly and quietly without a display of anger. Arguments can be avoided by simply stating, "Go to the time-out seat. We will talk later."

Responding with Clarity and Firmness   If some of the previous techniques have failed to squelch inappropriate behavior, more intrusive actions are required. Sometimes it is necessary to address a learner by name, using a clear, direct, authoritative, no-nonsense tone of voice. In implementing this approach, you make eye contact with the learner you are addressing, and your demeanor takes on an I-mean-business character as you specify the behavior that must stop and what must replace it.

Arranging Conferences with Misbehaving Learners   A next step often is an individual conference with the offending learner. During the conference, you explain exactly what must be done to correct the behavior problem. Threats are kept to a minimum. Typically, you identify the problem, share your feelings about it, and ask the learner what might be done to solve it.

Some conferences conclude with the preparation of a *behavior contract* that specifies what the learner will do. Behavior contracts often mention some good things that will result if the contract terms are met. Frequently there also are references to consequences that will follow if the unacceptable pattern of behavior continues.

Asking Parents or Guardians for Help   Beginning teachers sometimes are nervous about talking to parents or guardians. They should not be, for these concerned adults often are the best allies teachers have. Nearly all of them are concerned about the progress and behavior of their children, and they may be unaware that their children are misbehaving in school. Often a phone call to explain the unacceptable behavior will result in an excellent cooperative plan to solve the problem.

Involving parents or guardians does not always lead to the desired result, however. The success of involving them in situations related to misbehavior in school depends on many variables such as the age level of learner and the kind of relationship the learner has with his or her parents or guardians. The nature of your approach when contacting a parent or guardian is also important. In general, you should emphasize your interest in working together to solve the problem rather than assigning blame for inappropriate behaviors.

Category 3: Implementing Consequences

After responses in categories one and two have been tried with no success, or if the misbehavior is very serious, then learners need to experience the consequences of their actions. Consequences are most effective when they are used infrequently and are appropriate to the nature of the offense.

Losing a Privilege   Loss of a privilege functions as an effective punishment for some young people. The success of this approach rests on learners having some privileges available to them. Depending on age levels, these privileges might vary from a classroom job (such as taking care of erasers) to promises of seats in favored sections at athletic events to opportunities to go on out-of-town field trips. To be effective, learners must genuinely value the privilege that is taken away. If they do not, then your action is unlikely to influence their patterns of behavior.

Loss of a privilege works better if the privilege is not taken away permanently. The possibility that a valued privilege might be restored in exchange for a modification of behavior sometimes acts as a potent motivator for young people.

Providing for In-Class Isolation   In some elementary classrooms, teachers designate a certain part of the classroom as an area where misbehaving learners are sent. Often these areas are located in places where it is hard for offending learners to interact with others and observe what other class members are doing.

Sometimes people who have been sent to these isolated areas of the classroom are allowed to continue working on assignments. At other times, they are asked to reflect on the nature of their misbehavior and their ideas for change. Occasionally, learners are told to go to these areas and simply sit quietly. Many younger children find the resultant boredom to be an undesirable consequence.

Removing the Learner   If serious misbehavior persists, it may be necessary to remove a learner from the classroom. When this happens, the learner is often sent to the office of the principal or a counselor. Initially, the objective is not for the principal or counselor to work with the individual; rather, the idea is to send the learner to an area supervised by another professional. Learners are never sent to unsupervised areas such as hallways. If an accident occurred and a learner were injured in such an unsupervised area, as the responsible teacher, you might be liable for negligence.

Making Up Wasted Time   When you feel that a learner's misbehavior has resulted in class time not being used effectively, you can require the offending individual to make up the wasted time. Depending on the grade level, the learner may be kept in the room during recess or may spend extra time in class either before or after school. It is important that this punishment not be converted into a reward. For example, some learners enjoy chatting informally with teachers. If such activity occurs when wasted time is being made up, this approach to changing an inappropriate behavior pattern may fail.

It is not always possible to insist that misbehaving learners make up wasted time. In some schools, many learners ride buses to and from school. If they are kept after school, they have no way to get home. Teachers also are generally reluctant to keep high school students who have part-time jobs after school.

Category 4: Involving Others

Involving others is a category of last-resort options. When other measures have failed, you must arrange a conference to deal with the situation. Participants might include parents or guardians, other educational professionals including administrators and counselors, and personnel from agencies outside the school system.

Involving Parents or Guardians   There should be initial contact with parents or guardians to apprise them of the problem and seek their help in solving it before a formal conference is scheduled. If a conference proves necessary, you must prepare for it carefully. This often involves bringing evidence to the conference, including anecdotal records that document specific examples of problem behaviors and dates when they occurred. The best conferences feature a sharing of information and a communal effort to work out a proposed solution. You need to be particularly careful during this kind of a conference to avoid putting parents or guardians in a position of feeling that their own adequacy is being questioned.

Arranging Conferences with Other Professionals   Some teachers overlook one of the most valuable and easily accessible resources—their colleagues. According to Clark, Clark, and Irvin (1997, p. 55), collaborating with fellow teachers offers many advantages such as:

- improved teacher attitudes,
- improved communications,
- higher morale, and
- increased self-empowerment.

Sometimes it is wise to bring together a group of professionals to discuss a learner's unacceptable behavior patterns. Principals, counselors, psychologists, social workers, and others who might attend need to be introduced ahead of time to documentation regarding exactly what the learner has been doing. It is your responsibility as the teacher to prepare this material in advance of the meeting.

Meetings of this kind often result in the development of a specific action plan. For example, such a group might decide to place the learner in another class, temporarily suspend the learner from school, or assign the learner to a special counselor. The plan typically is put in place under the authority of the school principal. Usually, there are provisions requiring periodic reporting of results to either the school principal or someone whom he or she has designated to watch over the situation.

Building an action plan along the lines suggested in these four categories will help you deal with many of the behavior problems you will encounter in the classrooms. The vast majority of these problems can be corrected using actions chosen from categories one, two, and three. A carefully constructed plan consisting of systematically

A teacher meets with administrators, counselors, and other teachers to discuss possible ways of dealing with a learner who has become a severe discipline problem.

escalating responses will be of great value as you work to develop a positive and safe classroom environment for your learners.

Key Ideas In Summary

- Conveying information and managing learners are among the most important responsibilities of teachers. Teaching and managing are closely connected. Good teaching can prevent control problems, and good management establishes an environment for productive teaching.
- Classroom management is concerned with decisions teachers make regarding the organization of time, space, and materials. This organization is designed to facilitate smooth and efficient instruction. Good management produces an environment that reduces the likelihood of discipline problems. It is a product of careful teacher planning.
- Effective classroom teachers make good use of time. They strive to reduce periods when no productive learning activities are occurring. They develop plans for using their time efficiently when beginning each class period, helping learners to make a smooth transition from one activity to another, and working individually with learners who need special assistance.
- It is important for teachers to develop routines for handling recurring classroom events. Teachers who have mastered procedures for dealing with regular occur-

Following the Web 8.2

Responding to Management Challenges

Web sites referenced here are among those providing specific ideas for dealing with challenges associated with classroom management. You will be able to locate many other sites with this kind of content by simply inserting the term *classroom management* into any good Web search engine.

For hot links to these sites, visit the companion Web site, located at *http://www.prenhall.com/armstrong.* Select Chapter 8 from the front page of the Web site, then choose the Following the Web module on the navigation bar on the left side of the page.

Eleven Techniques for Better Classroom Discipline

- *http://members.aol.com/churchward/hls/techniques.html*

  As the title suggests, this site introduces 11 techniques for promoting good classroom discipline. These are (1) focusing, (2) direct instruction, (3) monitoring, (4) modeling, (5) nonverbal cueing, (6) environmental control, (7) low-profile intervention, (8) assertive discipline, (9) assertive I-messages, (10) humanistic I-messages, and (11) positive discipline.

Disciplinary Strategies for Teachers

- *http://www.ncrel.org/sdrs/areas/issues/envrnmnt/drugfree/sa2lk9.htm*

  This site features some general guidelines for dealing with control problems in the classroom. It also provides an extensive bibliography of books and journal articles dealing with topics related to disciplinary strategies for teachers.

The Discipline Problem—And Ways to Deal with It

- *http://www.cec.sped.org/bk/focus/1096.htm*

  This site is maintained by the Council for Exceptional Children. There is a good discussion of classroom management techniques that have proven to be effective with exceptional (special education) children.

Classroom Management

- *http://www.pacificnet.net/~mandel/ClassroomManagement.html*

  This site includes an outstanding selection of classroom-management techniques that have been developed for use in public schools. There are examples of techniques that have been used successfully in elementary, middle, and high schools. Descriptions are extraordinarily complete.

[Note: Web addresses change frequently. If you are unable to locate one of these sites using the listed URL, try putting the site name in a standard search engine.]

rences are better able to handle unexpected behavioral problems in ways that respond to problems and that are minimally disruptive to the instructional program.
- The goal of disciplinary procedures in the classroom is to teach learners responsibility and self-control. Methods used should be consistent with this aim.
- Effective classroom managers solve most discipline problems themselves. Only occasionally do they require assistance from principals and other school officials.

They seek long-term solutions to behavioral problems, and they look for remedies directed at the underlying causes of unacceptable patterns of behavior.

- Several principles are related to appropriate teacher responses to misbehavior in the classroom. Teachers need to respect learners, deal with problems quietly and unobtrusively, distinguish between minor and major problems, and help learners grasp the connection between unacceptable behaviors and unpleasant consequences that come their way as a result.

- Several basic types of teacher power and authority have been identified. These include expert power, referent power, legitimate power, reward power, and coercive power.

- Teacher responses to misbehaviors range across a number of alternatives. These vary from actions designed to allow the teachers to reassert their self-control to those requiring recommendations of groups of professionals with specialized skills.

Chapter 8 Self Test

 To review terms and concepts in this chapter, take the Chapter 8 Self Test on the companion Web site, located at *http://www.prenhall.com/armstrong*. Select Chapter 8 from the front page of the Web site, then choose the Self Test module on the navigation bar on the left side of the page. Feedback for the Self Test is immediate. You can keep track of your Self Test scores yourself, or you can choose to submit your scores via e-mail to your instructor.

Reflections

 To respond to these questions online, and to save or submit your response electronically, visit the companion Web site, located at *http://www.prenhall.com/armstrong*. Select Chapter 8 from the front page of the Web site, then choose the Reflections module on the navigation bar on the left side of the page. Instructors and students may also wish to use these questions as discussion topics on the Message Board for the companion Web site.

1. How serious is the problem of classroom management and discipline?
2. What is the relationship between good classroom management and effective teaching?
3. How does the organization of space influence your behavior?
4. What are some specific problems that are likely to arise as the result of poor time management?

5. What are some procedures and routines you would use for recurring and predictable events?
6. What did you learn about your attitude and philosophy of discipline as a result of reading the chapter?
7. What is your response to the idea of negotiation as a metaphor for dealing with discipline?
8. How do you think a teacher can establish the types of power and authority that are associated with what you would call a good classroom?
9. Which of the basic principles of effective discipline are especially important to you?
10. Which of the alternative responses are most comfortable for you? Why?

Field Experiences, Projects, and Enrichment

1. Observe in a classroom and pay special attention to how time is used in the classroom. How much time is spent on tasks other than instruction? What suggestions might you have about making the use of time more efficient?

2. Interview some teachers and ask them about the types of discipline problems that they encounter most frequently. Consider which of the alternative responses you might use in responding to the common problems identified by the teachers.

3. Interview a principal or school district official. Ask about common difficulties experienced by new teachers in the areas of classroom management and discipline.

4. Interview some school learners about their reactions to discipline problems in the schools. What do they see as the major causes of discipline problems? How can you use an understanding of those causes to plan for the classroom?

5. Begin to develop your plan for discipline by thinking about the rules you will need in the classroom, the ways you will organize the classroom, and the types of responses you will use when confronting misbehavior. Share your ideas with your course instructor and ask for comments.

References

Berliner, D. C. (1984). The half-full glass: A review of research on teaching. In P. L. Hosford (Ed.), *Using what we know about teaching* (pp. 51–77). Alexandria, VA: Association for Supervision and Curriculum Development.

Brophy, J. (1983). Classroom organization and management. *The Elementary School Journal, 83*(4), 265–285.

Brown, T. (1998, July 7). *Effective school research and student behavior.* Southeast/South Central Educational Cooperative Fourth Retreat: Making a difference in student behavior, Lexington, KY.

Bullough, R. J., Jr. (1994). Digging at the roots: Discipline, management, and metaphor. *Action in Teacher Education, 16*(1), 1–10.

Camp, B., & Bash, M. (1981). *Think aloud: Increasing social and cognitive skills: A problem solving program for children (small group program).* Champaign, IL: Research Press.

Clark, S. N., Clark, D. C., & Irvin, J. I. (1997). Collaborative decision making. *Middle School Journal, 28*(5), 54–56.

Doyle, W. (1986). Classroom organization and management. In M. C. Wittrock (Ed.), *Handbook of research on teaching* (3rd ed., pp. 392–431). New York: Macmillan.

Emmer, E. T., Evertson, C. M., & Anderson, L. (1980). Effective classroom management at the beginning of the school year. *Elementary School Journal, 80*(5), 219–231.

Evertson, C. M. (1989). Improving elementary classroom management: A school-based training program for beginning the year. *Journal of Educational Research, 83*(2), 82–90.

French, J. R. P., & Raven, B. H. (1959). The bases of social power. In D. Cartwright (Ed.), *Studies in social power* (pp. 118–149). Ann Arbor, MI: University of Michigan Press.

Grubaugh, S. (1989). Nonverbal language techniques for better classroom management and discipline. *High School Journal, 73*(1), 34–40.

Henson, K. T., & Eller, B. F. (1999). *Educational psychology for effective teaching.* Belmont, CA: Wadsworth.

Jones, F. H. (1979). The gentle art of classroom discipline. *National Elementary Principal, 58*(4), pp. 26–32.

Jones, V. F., & Jones, L. S. (1986). *Comprehensive classroom management: Creating positive learning environments* (2nd ed.). Boston: Allyn & Bacon.

Kounin, J. (1970). *Discipline and good management in the classroom.* New York: Holt, Rinehart and Winston.

Latham, A. S. (1998). Rules and learning. *Educational Leadership, 56*(1), 104–105.

Martin, M. K. (1997, March). Connecting instruction and management in a student-centered classroom. *Middle School Journal, 28*(5), 3–9.

McLaughlin, H. J. (1994). From negation to negotiation: Moving away from the management metaphor. *Action in Teacher Education, 16*(1), 75–84.

Savage, T. V. (1999). *Developing self-control through classroom management and discipline* (2nd ed.). Boston: Allyn & Bacon.

Smith, H. A. (1987). Nonverbal communication. In M. J. Dunkin (Ed.), *The international encyclopedia of teaching and teacher education* (pp. 466–476). New York: Pergamon Press.

Smyth, W. J. (1987). Time. In M. J. Dunkin (Ed.), *The international encyclopedia of teaching and teacher education* (pp. 372–380). New York: Pergamon Press.

Vars, G. F. (1997). Student concerns and standards, too. *Middle School Journal, 28*(4), 44–49.

Williams, P., Alley, R., and Henson, K. T. (1999). *Managing secondary classrooms: Principles and strategies for effective discipline and instruction.* Boston: Allyn & Bacon.

9

Assessing Learning

OBJECTIVES

This chapter will help you to

- explain the multiple roles of assessment in education.
- define commonly used assessment terms.
- describe the differences between formal and informal assessment.
- identify characteristics of a high-quality assessment and evaluation program.
- define the terms *placement, formative,* and *summative assessment.*
- explain the differences between authentic and traditional assessment.
- describe the strengths and weaknesses of authentic and traditional assessment.
- describe the role of the teacher in planning and implementing an assessment and evaluation plan.

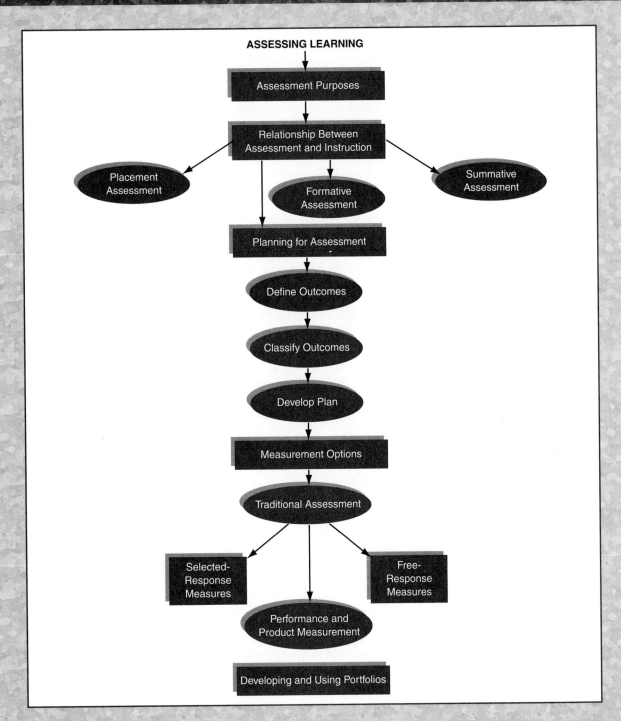

FIGURE 9.1 Assessing Learning

INTRODUCTION

Education is high on the list of important concerns for nearly everyone, for people see a quality school system as a key ingredient in a healthy and prosperous nation. We want our children and grandchildren to have a solid education that will provide the foundation for success in life. This interest has led to debates concerning the quality of the schools and the related question of whether tax money is being spent wisely.

There have been dozens of reports containing recommendations to improve the schools, and proposals to "fix" education have become a common feature of political platforms. Proposals for educational reform have come from both within and outside of the profession.

Much of the discussion about school quality features references to assessments of learner achievement and what they mean. Because they lack background in assessment processes, many people quite understandably become confused as they try to sort through conflicting claims and make decisions about important educational issues. Everyone needs some basic understanding of assessment in order to make informed decisions that will have important long-term consequences for education and the nation.

As a prospective teacher, you need to know even more about assessment. In the classroom, you will make daily decisions about the progress of your learners and about the effectiveness of your teaching. These decisions must be based on sound evidence. In addition, you will have a professional stake in assessment because findings today are often used to inform the public about the quality of individual schools and the relative excellence of those who teach in particular buildings. Therefore, your performance evaluations and possibly your right to keep your job may depend on assessment. These realities strongly underscore the importance you should attach to becoming a sophisticated planner, interpreter, and user of assessment data.

WHAT ARE THE PURPOSES OF ASSESSMENT?

Assessment is frequently viewed as an activity that takes place at the conclusion of instruction in order to determine grades. However, this is just part of the picture, for assessment also functions as an accountability tool for evaluating teacher and school effectiveness. In this context, the outcome of assessment may be used to generate a "report card" to the public that provides an indication of the relative quality of teachers and instruction in each evaluated school.

Because collected information focuses on learner performance, you need to know something about how assessment processes affect people in your classes. From the time learners first arrive at school, they desire indications of success. Data gathered from fair and appropriate assessment procedures can provide these affirmations. Evidence of success motivates them to continue working and creates an expectation of future success (Stiggins, 1997). If they are having difficulties, good assessment techniques can help them discover the causes of the difficulties and can lead to correction before the problems become major ones.

In addition, learners who are uncertain about their success may become uncertain about the value of their school experiences. Often these learners fail to see the value of what they do at school because they do not have a sense of accomplishment.

Video Viewpoint

What's Up at School? Test Anxiety

WATCH: In this ABC News video segment, we learn about test anxiety: what it is, why it happens, and how teachers, parents, and students can work to minimize it. With as many as 1 in 5 children suffering from test anxiety severe enough to interfere with their performance on tests, it's a growing problem.

THINK: With your classmates or in your teaching journal, consider these questions:

1. What are the benefits of testing? Why do you think national testing and grade-level proficiency testing initiatives are gaining in popularity?
2. Students take as many as 12 state-mandated tests a year in addition to the classroom quizzes, chapter tests, and midterm exams found in a regular curriculum. Are students being overtested?
3. Do you think students experience similar levels of anxiety when taking standardized tests and when participating in authentic assessment activities?

LINK: What are some things you can do as a teacher to help students deal with test anxiety?

Thus, you need to view assessment as an important and essential ingredient of the instructional process rather than as an intrusive "extra." Assessment that centers on helping young people learn can help you make intelligent and informed decisions about your teaching.

When you think about teaching a given lesson, a number of instructional approaches are available. Over time, attention to assessment data can help you decide which techniques proved to be more effective. You should reflect on specific approaches you used and then look at how well your learners mastered your instructional objectives. If they have done well, you can logically conclude that your instructional approaches have been effective. On the other hand, if large numbers of learners have not performed adequately, you will want to consider some alternative approaches to helping them master the content.

UNDERSTANDING ASSESSMENT TERMS

Several key assessment terms are used interchangeably, and a lack of understanding of these terms can contribute to confusion and misunderstanding. A solid grasp of these terms, on the other hand, can help you identify sources of error, clarify issues, and make informed choices.

Assessment

Assessment refers to the purposeful collection of data from a variety of sources (Gallagher, 1998). An *assessment plan* involves identification of various sources of data that are relevant to a specified set of learning outcomes. Useful information sources may include measurement tools such as tests, or they may draw on teacher observation of learners' in-class performance, ability to complete projects according to specified guidelines, and abilities to succeed on tasks associated with daily assignments. Under certain circumstances, such as during a test, learners know that they are being assessed. With less-obtrusive actions, such as teacher observation of the work of a group on an in-class project, learners may be less aware of the assessment.

When developing an assessment plan, you should decide whether what you propose to do is consistent with what you want learners to achieve. For example, if you are interested in promoting learner creativity, an assessment plan that places a heavy emphasis on the neat appearance of learners' work makes little sense. "Neatness" is not ordinarily considered a useful indicator of creativity. Instead, you should be looking for evidence suggesting that learners' work deviates markedly from the traditional or expected.

In addition to focusing on behaviors that make sense in light of what you want your young people to learn, your assessments need to be based on an adequate and fair sampling of behaviors that are of interest. How often was the behavior observed and under what conditions? Most coaches would not choose the starting lineup of a team based on one practice. Instead, they want numerous observations under various conditions in order to have a solid basis for making decisions.

Measurement

Measurement involves quantifying the presence or absence of a quality, trait, or attribute (Gallagher, 1998). For example, if you want to determine the height, width, or weight of an object, you measure it. Of course, the accuracy of this value depends on your using the right measurement tool. If you want to measure the length of something, you do not use an instrument designed to measure its weight. In addition, if you are interested in the size of a large object such as a football field, then you need a long, steel tape measure rather than a ruler. If precision is needed, you need a tool more exact than a ruler or yardstick.

Unfortunately, when you are faced with a need to choose the right measurement tool for use in school, the decision often is not as obvious as when you are choosing something used to measure size or weight. To illustrate this point, consider something everybody has encountered—the test. Particular types of tests are appropriate for measuring different traits and abilities. When you teach, you want to select one that will provide useful information about the kind of learning you are interested in assessing.

Sometimes nonspecialists are unaware that certain types of tests have special (and often limited) uses. For example, scores on the well-known Scholastic Achievement Test (SAT) required for admission to some colleges and universities often are cited in the media as a valid measure of learner achievement and school quality. This is a mistake. First of all, the SAT is a voluntary test that is taken by approximately one-half of the high school seniors in the nation. Thus, the scores reflect the characteristics only of students who choose to take the test rather than the characteristics of all high school seniors (Berliner & Biddle, 1995).

Secondly, the SAT samples only a limited range of content. As many of you know, the SAT is composed of two parts—a verbal section and a quantitative section. The verbal portion is designed to measure language usage and comprehension, and the

These students are taking a standardized test. Some uses of standardized test results have led to public controversy.

quantitative part focuses on mathematical knowledge and comprehension. Since the SAT does not assess learning in *all* subject areas taught in the schools, it makes little sense to use results as an indicator of the overall quality of a given school or the teachers who work there. Despite this logic and despite SAT's own admission that such use of total SAT scores is invalid, incomplete, and unfair, some people continue to use the scores as an indicator of overall school or teacher quality (Berliner & Biddle, 1995).

In addition to thinking about appropriate uses of standardized tests such as the SAT, you need to consider what you are measuring when you construct your own tests. Poorly constructed teacher-made tests may focus on too narrow a sample of what learners have been taught. Sometimes they feature numerous poorly worded or even "trick" questions. When this happens, learners' scores are not good indicators of what they know or have learned.

Evaluation

Up to this point, we have discussed gathering data. Evaluation is the next step. *Evaluation* refers to making a judgment about the worth or value of something. For example, a physician may measure the height and weight of a child. The importance of this information is realized only when the physician makes judgments about whether the child is developing satisfactorily.

Uninterpreted learner scores on a test reveal little. To answer the question of whether learner achievement is satisfactory, you must make an evaluative judgment. To make an appropriate evaluation, you need clear criteria. The two common ways to establish criteria are norm referencing and criterion referencing.

Norm-Referenced Evaluation   In *norm-referenced evaluation,* judgments are made based on how individual scores compare to others. The usual way of establishing these norms is by reference to a normal distribution or what is commonly referred to as the *bell-shaped curve.* This is a symmetrical curve derived from a mathematical formula. It is based on the assumption that any given trait or ability is found in the total population in a distribution that is similar to the bell curve. Most learners' scores will be grouped near the mean, or the average, and will decrease in frequency as one moves in each direction. In other words, there will be a few people on each end of the distribution with the numbers increasing toward the middle, or the mean.

Standardized tests are examples of norm-referenced tests. When they are prepared, developers administer the initial version to a sample of individuals. They plot these scores on a distribution and apply the mathematical formula to establish what are commonly called "norms" or derived scores. They attempt to include a sample of people who are representative of the total population of the United States so the norms or derived scores will approximate what one could expect if the test were actually given to the entire population of individuals.

When an individual takes a standardized test, the raw score is then compared with scores established during the standardizing process, and a derived score or a ranking is given. For example, if it is reported that a given learner's score places him or her at the 50th percentile, this means that 50% of the comparison population performed at or below the score of this individual on this test. If the learner's score were at the 90th percentile, 90% of the comparison population would have test results at or below this person's score. Usually when standardized tests are returned, both the raw score, which is the number the person actually got right, and the derived (standardized) score are given.

When you look at scores of members of your class on a standardized test, you need to ask several questions. How was the norm group selected? How should individuals' scores be interpreted? When were the norms established (Gronlund, 1998)? If you are to have confidence in the results, one of the things you need to determine is whether the norm group used to standardize the test has characteristics that are similar to your own learners. If curricula and learning conditions of the norming group vary markedly from those of the tested group, results will not be valid.

An example of this problem surfaced recently when the media focused much attention on the results of the Third International Mathematics and Science Study. Comparisons indicated that the averages for 12th-grade students in the United States were considerably lower than the averages of 12th-grade students in several other nations. This comparison ignored significant differences among educational systems and ages of students in the countries where tests were taken. Bracey (1998) points out that students taking the test in Iceland averaged 21.2 years of age, and the students tested in Germany, Norway, Italy, Austria, and Sweden were closer in age to college sophomores than to American high school seniors. In addition, in some nations, those students in the vocational tracks were not included in the sample (Bracey, 1998).

There can be problems even when norm-referenced tests are well designed, up to date, and properly administered to learners with characteristics similar to the norming group. Much of the difficulty has to do with misinterpretation of the results. This situation has been spoofed in the reference to the mythical town of Lake Wobegon

What Do You Think?

Scores of **Too Many Are Too Low**

An editorialist in a local newspaper recently made these comments:

> Despite additional money that has gone into the primary grades' reading program over the past five years, local pupils' scores continue to be unacceptably low. Fully 40% of our third graders scored below the national average. This simply is unacceptable. Community concern about reading was expressed to the School Board 5 years ago when the issue of increased funding to improve reading instruction was debated. As a result, thousands of additional dollars were committed to fix the problem. The dismal test results are a painful disappointment given the actions, it had been hoped, this new money would support.

What Do You Think?

1. Under what circumstances would it be appropriate to regard these tests results as "dismal"?
2. Under what circumstances would it be appropriate to consider these tests as being "good" or even "excellent"?
3. If you were to write a letter to the editor in response to these comments, what would you say?

on the National Public Radio show, "Prairie Home Companion" where all children are described as "above average." By definition, it is statistically impossible for all children to be "above average" or "above the norm." By definition, half of the population will be above the norm and half below the norm.

Criterion-referenced Evaluation

In *criterion-referenced evaluation,* judgments are made based on how well each individual compares to a standard or a set of criteria rather than on how well each person's scores compare to those of others. It focuses on identifying an individual's level of proficiency in terms of a preestablished standard of knowledge or skill (Gallagher, 1998). For example, if a company needs a worker who can carry 70-pound bags of fertilizer, the hiring officials are interested in whether the individuals they are considering can carry this mandatory load. They are not interested in how an individual applicant's load-carrying ability compares to a large group of people who were tested on their abilities to carry bags of different weights. It could be that the reference group consisted of people who could not lift more than 40-pound bags. If this were the case, an applicant who could lift a 50-pound bag would look superior in comparison to this norming group. However, he or she would not make sense as an employee for a position requiring sufficient strength to lift 70-pound bags.

Criterion-referenced evaluation often is especially useful in school settings, because it pinpoints specific performance of learners rather than providing an average or a ranking. This means you can use it to find out how well a member of your class compares to the average performance of a group.

Both norm-referenced and criterion-referenced evaluation can be applied to the same assessment (Gronlund, 1998). For example, many standardized testing companies report the norms as well as learner performance in skill areas. For example, a math test may include how many items the learner got right in the areas of addition, subtraction, multiplication, division, and word problems. In the classroom, this kind of information gives you the ability to realize that a particular learner, for example, did better than 90% of the learners in the class on the entire test (a norm-referenced conclusion) but failed to meet the minimum criterion for solving word problems (a criterion-referenced conclusion).

Two issues merit attention when you use criterion-referenced evaluation. First of all, you need to consider the appropriateness of what is being measured. It is sometimes tempting to focus only on what is easy to observe or measure. This is true because it is difficult to decide what to measure when the focus is on more complex content. For example, in geography it is much easier to construct tests focusing on use of latitude and longitude than on more complex geographic notions such as diffusion of innovations. Giving in to the temptation to use ease of measurement as a basis for constructing criterion-referenced tests can result in an inappropriate focus on less-important, even trivial, content.

Another issue relates to setting the criterion. What should be the level of acceptable performance? If your standard is set too low, people in your class who have not really mastered the material may be incorrectly judged to have done so. On the other hand, if you set too high a standard, those who have mastered a great deal of new content may be judged to have failed.

Setting the criterion level in the classroom is largely a matter of professional judgment. You will need to decide what is acceptable minimal performance, which will vary depending on the nature of the intended learning. Some tasks such as basic reading and mathematics skills are so important for the future success of learners that a high standard of expected performance makes good sense. However, other types of outcomes will be much less critical for future success. In these situations, you will be justified in setting a lower criterion level.

Grades

Grades are basically devices that communicate the results of evaluation. They are of interest to such parties as the learner, parents, employers, and higher education admissions officers. Because people other than those in your classes may have an interest in the grades you award, you must be prepared to explain features of your grading system to others.

A system commonly used in the United States awards letter grades. A grade of *A* is supposed to indicate excellence, a grade of *C* is supposed to indicate average, and a grade of *F* is supposed to indicate failing. The letter grading system often is used in conjunction with a norm-referenced system. The large group of learners clustered around the midpoint are given *C*s, a smaller number of learners are given *B*s or *D*s, and a few learners at each end of the distribution are awarded *A*s or *F*s.

Grades also can be awarded using a criterion-referenced system. When this is done, a different standard that a person must achieve is set for each grade. For example, you might indicate that all learners who accomplish 90% of the objectives of the course will get an *A,* those who master 80% will get a *B,* and so forth. Another criterion-referenced approach ties mastery of specific tasks to specific letter grades. In such an arrangement, tasks that are considered to be the minimum that a learner should know or do might be part of a list he or she must master to qualify for a grade of *C.* Additional tasks that go beyond the minimum might then be identified, and those who master them would get an *A* or a *B.* This scheme allows the learner to identify the level of mastery required for the grade toward which he or she will work. One interesting feature of criterion-referenced grading schemes is that they make it possible for all of the class to receive *any* grade; there is no mandatory distribution of *As, Bs, Cs, Ds,* and *Fs.*

In general, the worth of a letter grading system or any alternative needs to be judged on how well it communicates the results of evaluation to learners and to other interested parties. Critics of letter grades claim that they do not provide enough information and therefore are of limited value. For example, a letter grade may be an average or summary of several isolated performances and may mask the more typical strengths and weaknesses of a learner. A grade may be based on elements of behavior bearing only a tenuous connection to learning of academic content. For example, some teachers consider variables such as behavior, work habits, and effort. In such cases, a learner who does well on academic tasks may receive a lower grade because of discipline problems.

Some critics of letter grades suggest that they should be replaced by more extensive written comments prepared by the teacher. The claim is that written evaluations can communicate strengths and weaknesses of learners with more clarity than letter

This teacher is explaining grading criteria to members of the class.

Following the Web **9.1**

Grading Practices

Educators at all levels have a keen interest in grading practices. Issues associated with grading are featured at many World Wide Web sites. Those cited here will give you an idea of what is available.

     For hot links to these sites, visit the companion Web site, located at *http://www.prenhall.com/armstrong*. Select Chapter 9 from the front page of the Web site, then choose the Following the Web module on the navigation bar on the left side of the page.

Grading: Selected Resources for the Middle School Teacher

- *http://www.middleweb.com/Grading.html*

    As the title suggests, this site features information about grading that is of special interest to middle grade teachers. There are sections that deal with information for beginning teachers, grading policies, handling late assignments, settings standards, and grading software. You should visit this site for a good overview of issues and policies associated with grading.

Report Card Grading and Adaptations: A National Survey of Classroom Practices

- *http://www.valdosta.edu/~whuitt/psy702/files/grading.html*

    At this site, you will find an article that originally appeared in the journal *Exceptional Children*. It features an extensive review of grades K–12 grading practices across the country and includes particularly interesting materials on teachers' responses to the need to adapt grading to accommodate particular characteristics of special-needs children in their classes.

1st Class GradeBook

- *http://www.1st-class-software.com/*

    Much commercial software is now on the market that can help teachers compute and keep track of learners' grades. At this site, you will find an example of what

grades. In practical terms, important constraints limit the practicality of this approach. Good written evaluations require long commitments of teacher time, and opponents of this approach wonder whether this time might be better spent planning lessons and interacting with learners. In addition, the validity of a written evaluation, like a letter grade, depends on the quality of information that supports it. The worth of a written evaluation based on an inappropriate or excessively limited sample of learner behavior has no more value than a letter grade based on a similarly inadequate set of information.

you can now buy to help you deal with the challenge of grading. Interestingly, even a Chinese-language version of this software is now available.

K12ASSESS-L Listserve

- *http://www.ericae.net/k12assess/*

  Do you want to exchange information online with teachers who are concerned about various grading issues? If so, this is the site for you. It is a moderated discussion forum maintained by the ERIC Clearinghouse on Assessment and Evaluation.

Classroom Management

- *http://www.pacificnet.net/~mandel/ClassroomManagement.html*

  While the title of this site may lead you to suspect that it contains no information about grading, it is a bit of a misnomer. It is a general descriptor that has been used to label a content-rich site that includes many articles on topics of great interest to teachers. Two particularly good articles related to grading are "A Beginner's Guide to Figuring Your Grades" and "Thoughts About Grading: A Teacher's Influence."

Looking Beneath the Surface: Teacher Collaboration through the Lens of Grading Practices

- *http://www.middleweb.com/CollabGrding.html*

  How are grading practices influenced when teachers engage in collaborative curriculum planning and course delivery with other teachers? At this site, you will find results of a study that looked carefully at this interesting issue.

[Note: Web addresses change frequently. If you are unable to locate one of these sites using the listed URL, try putting the site name in a standard search engine.]

WHAT IS THE RELATIONSHIP BETWEEN ASSESSMENT AND THE INSTRUCTIONAL PROCESS?

Assessment plays multiple roles in the instructional process. These include (Gronlund, 1998):

- placement assessment,
- formative assessment, and
- summative assessment.

Placement Assessment

Placement assessment addresses the question "Where do I begin?" It occurs at the beginning of a new unit or course of study and often takes the form of a *pretest,* a test designed to provide information about what the learner may already know or think about content that is to be introduced.

Placement assessment information helps you know what members of your class already understand before you begin treating new content. This information provides a baseline you can use later as you seek to determine what value has been added to learners' store of understanding as a result of your teaching. Sometimes it also makes sense during placement assessment to gather some information about learners' attitudes toward new content you are about to introduce. This information can give you insight into the kinds of motivational challenges you may face as you begin teaching the new material.

The nature and depth of the placement assessment depends in part on the nature of the subject matter and the extent of your knowledge about your learners. For example, at the beginning of the school year, a high school math teacher will need considerable time to assess the prior knowledge of a group of students just beginning to take calculus. After the teacher has worked with these learners for weeks or even months, much less time will be required to gather placement assessment information in preparation for teaching new content.

Formative Assessment

Formative assessment takes place as an instructional sequence is occurring. Its purposes are to determine whether learners are making satisfactory progress and whether instructional approaches should be modified. Formative assessment may include short quizzes covering limited amounts of content that are given at frequent intervals during an instructional sequence. In addition to short tests or quizzes, daily or weekly work samples also provide good formative assessment information.

Formative assessment is undertaken to improve learning rather than to provide information for grading (Gronlund, 1998). It can be an invaluable aid as you seek to identify learning successes and failures and make appropriate changes in your instructional practices. For example, if your formative assessments show that your learners are experiencing a high rate of success, you can feel validated in terms of how you are organizing and pacing your instruction. On the other hand, if you find a high rate of failure, this can signal to you a need to alter your teaching approaches in ways that are well suited to the particular needs of your learners.

If persistent problems occur and reteaching a subject seems to have little impact, then you might want to consider a type of formative assessment called *diagnostic assessment* (Gronlund, 1998). The purpose of diagnostic assessment is to probe for specific causes of the failure. For example, if learners are making mistakes in responding to math problems, you might want to find out whether there is a consistent error pattern that reveals their lack of understanding of one of the basic computational procedures.

Summative Assessment

Summative assessment takes place at the conclusion of an instructional unit or sequence. The purpose is to determine which learners have accomplished the objectives and to provide an information source useful in communicating what the learner has learned. Information from this kind of assessment is used as a basis for assigning grades.

You need to plan your summative assessment procedures at the same time you plan your instructional units. Each learning outcome you identify needs to be accompanied by a planned scheme for assessing learner performance. When you do this kind of planning, your summative assessment will adequately sample what has been taught. Where there is not early attention to planning for summative evaluation, there is a danger that tests and other adopted procedures will not adequately represent the content of your lessons.

The consequences of poor learner performance on summative assessments are serious. They can mean failure of a course or even failure of an entire grade. The importance of summative evaluations places an obligation on you to design them well. In addition, the high-stakes nature of these assessments emphasizes the importance of developing good formative evaluation procedures. Formative evaluation results can provide an early alert to learning problems, and they occur when there is still time for you to salvage an instructional situation that is not going well. Corrective action in light of formative assessment information can lead to instructional modifications that will help your learners master the material.

PLANNING FOR ASSESSMENT

High-quality assessment requires considerable planning. A frequent problem is that teachers wait until the last minute to develop tests and other evaluation procedures. When this happens, there is a good possibility that poorly developed, inappropriate techniques will be selected.

Defining Educational Outcomes

Data gathered for use in assessment need to have clear ties to the desired outcomes of instruction. Hence, the first steps in planning for assessment involve (1) identifying important learning outcomes and (2) determining how they will be measured and evaluated. Ideally, assessment planning should take place at the same time that the learning outcomes are determined. This helps you ensure that all important outcomes are assessed and evaluated. When you review how learners performed, you will have confidence in the results as you think about the effectiveness of your lessons and the possible need to reteach some elements of content.

If you fail to spend the time needed to tie assessments clearly to the important learning outcomes you have identified, you may end up focusing on tasks that are easy to measure rather than ones that are important. If this happens, your learners may conclude that they need to concentrate on the trivial and unimportant dimensions of a learning task.

For example, suppose you were teaching a high school social studies class and had designed a unit on the Civil War featuring learning outcomes that asked learners to give serious thought to causes and effects of the conflict. If you develop a last-minute test that does nothing more than ask learners to name selected Civil War generals, you send a message inconsistent with your intended learning outcomes. Learners will quickly conclude that the large "cause-and-effect" issues are unimportant and that, despite what you might say in class, your *real* interest is having them memorize isolated facts.

Classifying Educational Outcomes

Educational outcomes vary in their complexity. Some outcomes require little more than recalling names, dates, or other facts. However, a sound instructional program also includes more complex outcomes such as those that call for interpretation, application, and creativity. Identifying the level of complexity of educational outcomes provides guidance in developing the assessment procedures. Some assessment procedures are useful when measuring less complex outcomes, and others are useful for measuring more complex outcomes.

Several *taxonomies,* or classification schemes, for educational outcomes have been developed that are very useful in focusing attention on the wide range of educational outcomes that should be considered when planning for instruction. These taxonomies have focused on three main domains of learning: the cognitive domain, the affective domain, and the psychomotor domain.

The *cognitive domain* includes a category of thinking associated with remembering and processing information. The *affective domain* includes affective attitudes, feelings, interests, and values. The *psychomotor domain* focuses on muscular coordination, manipulation, and motor skills.

The most popular cognitive taxonomy was developed by a team of researchers headed by Bloom (Bloom, Englehart, Furst, Hill, & Krathwohl, 1956). Though it is popularly known as "Bloom's Taxonomy," the full title is *Taxonomy of Educational Objectives: The Classification of Educational Goals.* An explanation of Bloom's classification scheme follows.

Handbook 1: The Cognitive Domain   This taxonomy is organized into six categories that are scaled according to their complexity. It begins with the relatively simple cognitive process of recall of factual information and moves to the more complex cognitive processes of applying, analyzing, synthesizing, and evaluating. The six levels are as follows:

1. *Knowledge.* This category refers to the recall of specific items of information such as recall of facts, procedures, methods, or even theories and principles. Many refer to this category as the "memory level" because it only demands the recall of information from stored memory.
2. *Comprehension.* This category requires a cognitive process that is a step beyond recall. It requires that learners not only recall specific items of information, but that they also reflect on their grasp of its meaning by interpreting, translating, or extrapolating. Many refer to this category when they say they want learners to "understand" the material.

3. *Application.* This category refers to the ability not only to understand material, but also to know how and when to apply information to solve problems. Thus, when confronted with a problem, the learner is able to identify the needed information or principles and apply that information without being told what to do.

4. *Analysis.* This category refers to the ability to break complex information down into parts and to understand how the parts are related or organized. This level involves having learners understand the structure of complex information. It involves cognitive processes such as comparing and contrasting.

5. *Synthesis.* This category refers to the cognitive processes that we usually associate with creativity. Synthesis is the reverse of analysis. It requires putting parts together in some new or unique way and might involve such tasks as writing a composition or designing a science experiment to test a theory.

6. *Evaluation.* This category refers to judging something against a set of criteria. This means that one is simply not making a value judgment about the worth of something. Evaluation requires that judgments be based upon specified criteria that might be provided by the teacher or, alternatively, developed by the learner.

In using Bloom's Taxonomy to plan your assessment procedures, you start by looking at your knowledge-level learning outcomes. Next, you choose measurement approaches that can provide information about learners' abilities to store and recall specific bits of information. For example, you might choose true-false or matching tests because they are useful in measuring this kind of thinking, and they are relatively easy to construct. For more sophisticated kinds of learning outcomes (for example, those at such levels as application, analysis, and synthesis), you would need to choose different kinds of measurement tools because true-false and matching tests are not capable of assessing learners' abilities at these higher cognitive levels. For these more sophisticated learning outcomes, you might choose essay tests, learner-developed projects, or other suitable procedures.

Cognitive learning is only one dimension of education. Schools also seek to engender positive attitudes and values. You probably would feel terribly disappointed if young people at the end of the year scored well on tests of reading proficiency but left the school vowing "never to pick up another book." Interests in promoting positive attitudes toward learning reflect educators' concern for the affective domain. Because this domain includes the more subjective area of attitudes and interests, the categories are not quite as precise as are those in the cognitive domain. However, they are helpful as guides for developing plans for instruction and assessment.

A team of researchers headed by Krathwohl (Krathwohl, Bloom, & Masia, 1964) developed the affective domain. The taxonomy they developed was published under the title: *Taxonomy of Educational Objectives: The Classification of Educational Goals. Handbook II: Affective Domain.* This taxonomy is organized into five categories on the basis of increased internalization of an attitude, interest, or value. The categories are as follows:

1. *Receiving.* The lowest level of internalization is that of showing an awareness of or being willing to receive other information or stimuli. This

category indicates that little of value can take place if an individual is unwilling to attend to information. For example, a learner is not likely to develop a more positive attitude toward reading if that person is unwilling to even engage in a reading activity.

2. *Responding.* The next level moves a step beyond the passive reception of information or stimuli and requires that the person make some sort of a response. It might be a willingness to ask questions, seek more information, or participate in an activity.

3. *Valuing.* At this level the individual has begun to internalize the attitude, value, or interest so that he or she expresses an interest in or commitment to activities or positions. A person at this level might demonstrate a commitment by choosing an activity when given a free choice. For example, the person might freely choose to read a book or pursue a topic. Another indicator would be a willingness to take a stand or publicly associate himself or herself with a belief or an activity.

4. *Organization.* At this level individuals start to integrate personal beliefs and attitudes and to establish a hierarchy. They begin to demonstrate priorities and use those priorities to make choices when confronted with decisions that involve conflicts between two or more of their values, beliefs, or commitments.

5. *Characterization.* At this level the attitudes, beliefs, and values have become so internalized that they become a way of life. Others can see the commitment of a person without being told because of the consistent choices and actions of the individual.

Assessments of behaviors in the affective domain cannot be performed with traditional tools such as paper-and-pencil tests. If you are interested in gathering information about affective behaviors of learners, you need to place them in situations where they have opportunities to receive new information and that give them opportunities to begin internalizing an attitude or value. Internalization is a long-term growth process that requires measurement over time.

The psychomotor domain has not been as clearly defined as the cognitive and affective domains. Several attempts have been made to develop psychomotor taxonomies, but none has become as well entrenched as the Bloom and Krathwohl taxonomies.

Criteria for Developing an Assessment Plan

There are some things that need to be considered either when designing an assessment plan or when evaluating an already existing assessment. The following questions suggest criteria or guidelines that will help you plan useful assessments.

- *Are the important outcomes assessed?* This question relates to the previous discussion. You need to make sure that what you assess is important and that all important learning outcomes are included. You do not want to make judgments about your learners or your instruction based on data that bear little or no relationship to what is important. You can avoid this problem when you take care to establish close links between your intended learning outcomes and your assessment procedures.

- *Are the assessment procedures appropriate for the nature of the outcomes?* This guideline focuses on the issue of validity. *Validity* is concerned with the degree to which a measurement tool measures what it is supposed to measure. For example, a ruler is not a valid measurement tool for determining weight. A valid measurement tool will elicit the type of performance or behavior specified by the learning outcome. It is unlikely that any one measurement tool, such as a single paper-and-pencil test, will be valid for measuring all learning outcomes. Good assessment plans include a variety of measurement tools.

- *Are there sufficient samples of behavior to allow for a fair judgment?* The major issue posed by this question concerns the inappropriate judgments that sometimes result when only a limited sample of learner behavior is considered. The remedy is to provide learners with several opportunities to demonstrate their level of mastery of individual learning outcomes.

- *Do the measurement tools meet adequate technical standards?* This guideline focuses attention on the need to establish assessment procedures that are clear and of a high quality. Tests should be free from trick questions, and test items should be appropriately formatted and error free.

- *Is the assessment appropriate for the developmental level of the learners?* Assessment devices that are appropriate for secondary-level students often are not appropriate for primary-level pupils. Some assessment procedures are not well suited for use with learners who have special needs. For example, a written examination that features complex instructions may cause severe problems for poor or slow readers. Their scores may be more a reflection of their inadequate reading skills than of their mastery of the content.

- *Are the assessment procedures free of bias?* Care needs to be taken to ensure that the assessment procedures do not conflict with cultural norms and beliefs. For example, timed tests may not be appropriate for those cultural groups that do not emphasize time or speed. When learner-produced projects are used as evidence that learning has occurred, young people from affluent homes with computers and other resources may be greatly advantaged compared to learners with fewer resources at their disposal.

- *How are the results of the assessment interpreted and used?* There should be clear criteria for evaluating the results of the assessment plan. You should be able to use results to pinpoint specific strengths and weaknesses of individual learners. A good assessment plan will allow you to make detailed analyses of the performances of everybody in your class. You want to be able to go beyond the ability to say, "Bobby is good in geography." If you have designed your assessment procedures well, you should be able to make statements such as, "Bobby can identify places on flat maps and globes using lines of latitude and longitude. He also has shown that he can identify names and locations of major ocean currents. He still needs to work on his ability to make analyses that require putting several kinds of information together at the same time. For example, he finds it difficult to predict what the climate at a given location on the globe might be when given its elevation, location on the continent, latitude, position relative to major bodies of water and mountain ranges, and situation with respect to prevailing winds."

MEASUREMENT OPTIONS

Numerous measurement tools are available that you can use to gather data about learners' performance. Individual tools should be selected based on the type of learning outcome being assessed and the purpose of the assessment.

Traditional Measurement Techniques

Traditional measurement options sort into the two broad categories of (1) standardized tests and (2) teacher-made assessment procedures of various kinds, including the traditional paper-and-pencil tests that have long been a feature of classroom life.

Standardized tests have the advantage of being written by test-construction experts. Thus, they usually are free from serious design flaws. Individual test items typically have been carefully field tested and, if needed, revised. These strengths, however, are counterbalanced by a serious problem. The content emphasized in a standardized test may not match well with what you have been teaching, which raises serious validity questions. It may be that learners scoring well on a standardized test have a good understanding of what you have been teaching, and it may be that learners scoring well on such a test have only a slight understanding of what you have been teaching. If there is not a tight connection between the content covered in the standardized tests and what you have been teaching, results simply are not a valid measure of what learners have taken away from *your* instructional program.

On the other hand, tests you prepare yourself can be tightly fitted to what you have emphasized. The possibility of establishing this congruence between what has been taught and what is tested is an advantage of teacher-made tests. The negative side concerns the fact that, to be valid measures of learner achievement, the tests must be well designed. Individual teacher tests do not get the kind of careful review to which new standardized tests are routinely subjected. This means that, as a teacher, you have to assume a lot of responsibility for designing test procedures carefully. When you do, you can get valid results that should allow you to draw confident conclusions both about performance levels of individual learners and about the effectiveness of the instructional approaches you have been using.

When you prepare traditional classroom tests, you can select from options that fall into one of the two basic categories of "selected-response measures" and "free-response measures."

Selected-Response Measures   *Selected-response measures* include those tests that require learners to choose answers from several provided choices. Test takers are not free to provide answers other than those represented among the options on the test. Examples of tests in this category include two-response (for example, true-

© 1998 Randy Glasbergen.

"Algebra class will be important to you later in life because there's going to be a test six weeks from now."

false), multiple-choice, and matching exams. Stiggins (1997) points out that the advantages of selected-response measurement tools include flexibility and efficiency. In addition, these types of measurement tools are efficient because they are objectively and easily scored.

Two-response Tests   Two-response tests include items that provide two possible answer choices, one of which is correct. The most common of this type is the true-false test. However, other choices might be yes-no, agree-disagree, supported-unsupported, cause-effect, or fact-opinion exams. Two-response tests can be used to measure cognitive as well as affective outcomes. For example, agree-disagree items are useful in measuring attitudes and opinions.

Two-response assessments are popular because they are easy to construct. However, this ease of construction can create problems. If you prepare a true-false test in a hurry, the result may be a poor set of questions that focus on trivial material with little connection to your priority learning outcomes. Creation of good two-response tests requires commitment of thought and time.

Because two-response items are easy to write and do not require a large response time, you can include a large number of items on a test. As a result, tests of this type permit you to sample a broad range of content. Generally speaking, more items and a broader sampling of content make for a more valid measurement.

One disadvantage of two-response items is that they emphasize absolutes. For example, true-false responses indicate that something is always true or always false. This makes it more difficult to construct good items, can confuse learners, and can result in some heated arguments concerning correct responses.

Well-written two-response items can be used to measure simple as well as complex outcomes. However, good two-response items that measure complex outcomes are difficult to construct. Many teachers prefer to use essays or other kinds of assessment approaches when seeking to evaluate learners' higher level thinking skills. In addition to their limitation in assessing higher level thinking, some critics dislike two-response items because they allow learners to guess at answers they do not know. Some attempts have been made to compensate for uneducated guessing by adding a correction space where learners must correct "false" items.

Multiple-choice Tests   Multiple-choice tests are the most widely used type of measurement tool (Gallagher, 1998). They require test takers to select an answer from among three or more alternatives. Individual test items include a "stem" that is often in the form of a question and three or more answer choices. One of the options is the correct or best choice, and the others are called "distractors."

Multiple-choice tests can be used to measure a variety of outcomes from simple to complex. They represent one of the few selected-response tests that is frequently used to assess learners' higher level thinking abilities, usually by asking individuals to do a series of tasks before making a selection from among available answer alternatives. For example, a learner might be required to work through a problem or apply a formula before choosing the correct option.

One of the attractions of multiple-choice items is that, like two-response items, they are easily scored. They also are less susceptible to guessing than two-response items because learners must select from among three or more answer choices.

An important key to preparing good items for multiple-choice tests is developing good distractors. When you write your items, your objective should be to provide distractors that are plausible choices that would be chosen by an individual who does not know the material. If this condition is not met, learners will easily eliminate the implausible distractors and select the correct answer, even if they really do not know the material.

As compared to two-response tests, multiple-choice tests can assess learners' abilities to deal with degrees of correctness or incorrectness. Learners can be instructed to choose the "best answer." This allows you to include a number of alternative answers, several of which might be partially correct, but only one of which will be the "best" response.

As is the case with two-response tests, multiple-choice tests can measure a broad range of content in a relatively short period of time. In addition, by developing distractors carefully and paying close attention to kinds of mistaken choices specific learners make, you can get good information about the nature of misconceptions held by individuals in your class.

There are some disadvantages to using multiple-choice tests. First of all, preparation of good items is difficult and time consuming. Time saved in scoring multiple-choice tests, however, may be more than counterbalanced by time required to construct good items.

Matching Items   The matching test is a variety of the multiple-choice test that has several special features. Individual items relate to a single topic. Further, all items in the set serve as distractors. For example, a matching item might ask the learner to match selections of literature with their authors. Thus, the distractors include all items in the long list of authors that is provided as part of the test. Matching tests usually consist of two lists. One list is the stimulus or the question; the second list includes possible responses.

Several formats of matching tests can be used. One features an arrangement whereby the numbers or letters for items in a list are placed next to the stimulus. Another option includes directions that direct learners to draw a line connecting each stimulus item with the correct response on the distractor list. This design often is used with young children who have not learned to form letters. Still another arrangement provides a blank space before each item on the stimulus list, where learners are asked to write in the correct response from the distractor list.

Similar to other selected-response tests, matching tests are easy to score, so each test can include quite a large number of items. To avoid making the test too easy, all items should relate to the same theme or class. If this is not done, you might end up with a test mixing together items focusing on such diverse topics as state capitals and mountain ranges. This arrangement makes it relatively simple for learners to eliminate some distractors (for example, all of the names of cities if the stimulus relates to mountains) and mark correct responses even though, in fact, they may not know the content well.

One of the main disadvantages of matching tests is that they tend to focus on relationships. This restricts the range of content they can assess. In addition, matching tests are not well suited to assessing learners' abilities to perform tasks requiring use of higher level thinking skills.

Free-Response Measures   *Free-response measures* require learners to generate responses of their own rather than to select responses from a list of provided alternatives. The most common types of free-response measures are essay, short-answer, or oral tests. Free-response tests provide learners with a stimulus that prompts them to produce an extended written or oral response. For example, you may ask them to provide an explanation or interpretation, solve a problem, defend a position, or compare and contrast events.

Free-response tests have the technical capability to assess a broad range of thinking. Selected-response tests can usually be corrected more quickly than free-response tests. Further, selected-response tests are well suited to measuring learners' abilities to perform tasks demanding lower levels of cognitive thinking such as knowledge and comprehension. For these reasons, free-response tests tend to be used most appropriately to measure more sophisticated learning that requires young people to perform at such levels as analysis, synthesis, and evaluation.

You can construct free-response items quickly, but good ones require serious thought. For example, questions need to be written in ways that enable learners to understand exactly what you are asking them to do, the approximate length of the response you are expecting, and general categories of information you hope to see in their answers. Poorly written items such as "explain the causes of the Civil War" are too broad and poorly defined. Entire volumes have been written on this topic, and historians have long debated some of the roots of the conflict. An improved version might read something like this:

> In a response not to exceed two pages in length, describe (a) at least two political causes, (b) at least two economic causes, and (c) at least two social causes of the Civil War.

In addition to writing free-response items with clarity and precision, you also need to pay attention to how the response will be evaluated. Your correction task will be easier if the question includes references to some specific categories of information you want to see included (such as in the previous example). To help you maintain a consistent correction pattern, consider preparing a model response or a checklist that includes information you hope to see in learners' answers (Gallagher, 1998). Even when you have prepared this kind of a correction guideline, you should be open to considering the appropriateness of alternative answers that, though varying a bit from your own expectations, represent reasonable responses to the question you have asked.

There are several disadvantages to free-response tests. One of the major disadvantages is in the scoring. Since each response needs to be read and analyzed, correction is time-consuming. Poor learner handwriting will also sometimes slow down the correction process. Because a range of possible answers may be appropriate for many free-response questions, you sometimes have to make difficult decisions about when and when not to award credit for a given item. The possibility of multiple "right" answers also inclines some learners to complain when you judge that a response they have made is not appropriate.

Another potential problem with scoring is that free-response items involve a number of different abilities such as writing, spelling, and handwriting. The tendency is to give more credit to those learners who have good writing or spelling skills. This is fine if the outcome to be measured includes these skills. However, if you are interested in the thinking or problem-solving ability of the learners, then the focus needs to remain on these abilities.

Because it is subjective, scoring can also be influenced by your mood or attitude when you score the responses, knowledge of the learner whose paper you are scoring and your expectations of that learner, and even the order in which the papers are read. Efforts need to be made to try and control these variables, which might require at least a second reading of all papers at a different time and in a different order.

Another disadvantage of free-response items is that they sample a limited amount of material, which can lead to errors in judgment. For example, you might ask a question on a free-response test that happens to be one of the few things that the learner knows. You may mistakenly assume that this person has a good grasp of the entire range of content you have been treating based on this person's successful answer to the one question included on the test. Similarly, a single item might focus on one of the few areas you have covered that the learner does not know.

The problem of placing too much emphasis on a learner answer to one free-response question can be helped if you broaden the content sampled by providing a number of short-answer items. The downside of this approach is that you take away the opportunity to probe the depth of understanding that you can get by asking learners to provide extensive answers to just one or two questions.

Performance and Product Measurement

Most traditional, paper-and-pencil types of measurements serve as surrogates or symbolic representations of learning. When you give a test, you do so based on a belief that the resulting score will tell you something about whether the learner has mastered the assessed content. This assumption may not always be true. For example, the test selected may not be based on an adequate sample of what the learner has learned. As a result, the score may be an invalid representation of mastery. In addition, successful learner performance on the test may not tell you very much about the ability a member of your class has to apply what has been learned outside of the artificial testing environment. In recent years, there has been a growing interest in assessing tasks in more realistic and relevant ways. This type of assessment has been called *authentic assessment, alternative assessment, direct assessment, performance assessment,* or *product assessment.*

Performance and product measurement can be used to measure tasks such as working with others, giving an oral presentation, participating in a discussion, playing a musical instrument, demonstrating a physical education skill, conducting an experiment, setting up equipment, and using the computer. It can also be used to assess collected learner work samples.

There are several factors that need to be considered when developing performance and product measurements. One of the first considerations is the purpose of the assessment. Are you intending to capture a learner's "typical" performance or a learner's "best" performance (Gallagher, 1998)? Different procedures are used depending on the purpose. Secondly, what are the outcomes that you are attempting to measure? This information will help you develop appropriate criteria for making valid judgments.

Developing the criteria for judging the task is an important step. Several terms such as *rubrics, scoring criteria,* or *performance dimensions* are often used to describe the criteria. One important aspect of clearly specifying the criteria is that this information makes public what is being judged and communicates your expectations to learners (Gallagher, 1998). If clear criteria are not developed, you risk the danger of compromising the validity of the measurement. Once you have developed the criteria, then you can select an appropriate measurement tool. You have a number of alternatives from which to choose.

Checklists Checklists are useful when only the presence or absence of a characteristic is required. Relevant behaviors are prepared on a list, and during an observation, you simply place a check mark by each behavior you see. Your main task in constructing a checklist is to make sure that all of the items on the checklist are observable.

To score a checklist, you simply count up how many listed behaviors were present and how many were absent. You will need to establish a cut-off score that indicates the minimum number of present behaviors for the performance to be "acceptable."

Rating Scales Rating scales are basically checklists that allow you to make finer distinctions than just noting the presence or absence of the criteria (Gallagher, 1998). Rating scales allow you to make judgments about the degree of appropriateness of

Critical Incident

The "Evils" of Portfolio Assessment

"I've had it. I've had it!" Garth Peterson, a second-year United States history teacher at Edison High School, grabs a stool and pulls it up to the desk where Estelle Garza, head of the social studies department, organizes a few papers. Just under the painting of George Washington overhead, the digital clock that just this year replaced the venerable Waltham reads 9:45 P.M. The open house has just ended, and the last parent is leaving the building.

Ms. Garza has been at Edison for 30 years. (Some students think Edison himself welcomed her to the opening of the building.) She tucks a final set of papers into a file folder, checks the desk top to assure everything is in order, and slowly looks over to Garth. "Another preconception out the window Garth? An unhappy parent? Someone with a lurking suspicion that you're spending 'all your time' with the kids who 'aren't motivated' while denying your talents to their 'eminently qualified, dedicated, and hardworking' sons or daughters who are 'really going to amount to something?' So, what's up? I doubt you'll shock me."

"A partial bingo for you, Estelle. It is about a parent, but the issue's not about my failure to give somebody a proper share of my time. It has to do with what I'm making the students do. To get to the point, Mrs. Hamlin, Stephanie's mom, is desperately anxious for Stephanie to get into an Ivy League school. She claims my evaluation procedures are insufficiently challenging and that I'm "killing" Stephanie's chances to get the high SAT scores she'll need to impress the Ivy League admissions people."

Estelle gives Garth her noncommittal I'm-listening-and-keep-talking nod and says, "What's the nature of this precipitous fall from the heights of evaluative excellence we've all aspired to here at Edison? Come clean. What kinds of terrible things have you been up to?"

"Come on, Estelle, you know nobody's as concerned as I am that our people leave here with a solid grounding in history. The last thing I would do is back away from high academic standards. It's just that, what I see as a scheme to push the kids harder, Mrs. Hamlin sees as something fluffy, soft, and nonchallenging. It's depressing."

"Garth, *do* get to the point. Exactly what have you done?" Estelle looks wearily at her watch.

"I'm in trouble because of the 'p' word . . . *portfolios.* I'm having people in my class put a huge amount of effort into preparing portfolios. Incidentally these *do* include their grades on all the usual traditional kinds of tests. My people, including Stephanie, have just done a great job putting materials together. They've written some sophisticated reflections on what they have been doing and what they've learned. I think I'm pushing these students much harder than I did when my only evaluations were multiple-choice and essay tests. I just don't understand where Mrs. Hamlin is coming from." Garth shakes his head in bewilderment.

"What exactly is her worry?" asks Estelle.

an observed behavior. Many rating scales feature three to five rating points. A midpoint often is defined as "acceptable," and lower and higher points are defined respectively as "unacceptable" and "above average" or "excellent."

Good rating scales identify what is meant by rating point descriptors such as "acceptable," "above average," and "excellent." Clear definitions allow different observers to reach similar conclusions when observing the same patterns of learner behavior.

"I've had a hard time figuring that out. But sorting through everything she said, I think there are two or three things bothering her. First of all, she believes that taking traditional true-false, multiple-choice, and essay tests will be the best preparation for the SAT because those are the kinds of items Stephanie will encounter when she takes it. Her logic is that time spent doing the portfolios diverts Stephanie away from the task of developing good test-taking skills."

"OK, that's one concern. What else?"

"Here's another one," Garth continues. "I think Mrs. Hamlin knows that there are lots of differences in the portfolios prepared by individual students. She thinks this makes fair grading impossible since contents aren't the same. Stephanie has had good grades. These grades have come from her ability to score well on traditional tests. I think Mrs. Hamlin sees portfolio evaluation as a threat to Stephanie's final history grade . . . something that could lower her overall average and reduce the probability of her being admitted to a top university."

Estelle nods. "Anything else?"

"One more thing. Mrs. Hamlin is dubious about the requirement for students to spend time writing reflections on their own learning and including them in the portfolios. She seems to believe that high school students are too immature to engage in this kind of analysis. Again, I believe it comes back to her concern for SAT test scores. I think she's afraid that time spent on reflective writing takes time away from learning the 'facts' Stephanie should be working to master."

"Well, Garth," Estelle comments, "you seem to have a pretty good idea of what's bothering Mrs. Hamlin. What are you going to do now?"

. . .

Garth's concerns stem from the concerns expressed by just one parent. Should he be worried about Mrs. Hamlin's comments? What do her concerns tell you about her values? What do we learn about those of Garth? Are differences in perspective between Garth and Mrs. Hamlin attributable to differences in their values? If you were faced with this situation, what would your next step be? Are there others who should be involved? If so, who are they, and what roles should they play?

C W To respond to this Critical Incident online, and to save or submit your response electronically, visit the companion Web site, located at *http://www.prenhall.com/armstrong.* Select Chapter 9 from the front page of the Web site, then choose the Critical Incidents module on the navigation bar on the left side of the page. Instructors and students may also wish to use these scenarios as discussion topics on the Message Board for the companion Web site.

PORTFOLIOS

In recent years, portfolio assessment has become a popular approach to evaluating learners' progress. A *portfolio* is a purposeful collection of products and performances that tells a story about a learner's effort, progress, or achievement. Typically learners play some role in selecting materials that are included. In using this approach, you need to develop guidelines that relate to such issues as categories of information to

Following the Web 9.2

General Information About Assessment

There are many sites on the World Wide Web with information dealing with assessment. Several examples follow that reflect the broad range of what is now available.

For hot links to these sites, visit the companion Web site, located at *http://www.prenhall.com/armstrong*. Select Chapter 9 from the front page of the Web site, then choose the Following the Web module on the navigation bar on the left side of the page.

ERIC Clearinghouse on Assessment and Evaluation

- *http://ericae.net/main.htm*

  The address above takes you to the home page of the ERIC Clearinghouse on Assessment and Evaluation. You will find links here to a huge volume of information dealing with all aspects of school- and learner-related evaluation.

FairTest—National Center for Fair and Open Testing

- *http://www.fairtest.org/*

  The fairness of school testing processes is a hot educational issue. This site is maintained by an advocacy group that is committed to ending certain abuses that sometimes have been associated with standardized testing. You will find additional links at this site to materials focusing on eliminating test biases that might negatively influence performance of test takers because of their gender, race, class, and cultural characteristics.

Assessment Resources

- *http://users.massed.net/~cgood/teachres.html*

  This site consists of an enormous list of links to other World Wide Web addresses containing information about various topics related to assessment. For example, you will find links to information about alternative assessment, performance assessment, open-response questioning strategies, development of rubrics, and assessing learning experiences based on World Wide Web content. There are also links to information about testing within specific subject areas.

Integrating Assessment with Instruction Readings

- *http://www.nwrel.org/eval/toolkit98/integratel.html*

  Maintained by the Northwest Regional Educational Laboratory, this site includes a number of short articles that suggest how assessment practices and information

be included, guidelines for selecting these items, criteria for judging the material, and guidance for learners related to providing them with opportunities for self-reflection (Stiggins, 1997). A portfolio may include results of learner performance on traditional selected-response and free-response tests as well as photos, sketches, visual displays, self-assessments, work samples, reflections on discussions, and other relevant materials. The goal is to provide as complete a picture or story as possible about the development of each learner.

can become an integral part of the instructional process. There are also a number of excellent references to assessment-related journal articles.

The Portfolio and Its Use: Developmentally Appropriate Assessment of Young Children

- *http://www.ed.gov/databases/ERIC_Digests/ed351150.html*

  Here you will find practical advice about preparing portfolios when working with very young learners. This material is disseminated under the auspices of the ERIC Clearinghouse on Elementary and Early Childhood Education.

Help Your Child Improve in Test Taking

- *http://www.ed.gov/pubs/parents/TestTaking/index.html*

  Parents and guardians want their children to do well in school. Information at this site features suggestions for parents who want to improve the test-taking skills of their children. The United States Department of Education's Office of Educational Research and Improvement developed the material.

The Mindful School: How to Assess Authentic Learning

- *http://www.business1.com/IRI_SKY/Assess/htaali.htm*

  In recent years, there has been a tremendous growth of interest in providing and assessing authentic learning. This article provides a thorough discussion of issues related to this topic and provides useful suggestions for teachers.

High Expectations for Students and Accountability for All

- *http://www.doe.mass.edu/doedocs/et396txt.html*

  Today, many states are interested in establishing common testing programs for learners in the school. Part of the agenda is to provide a common set of measures that can be used to see how well learners in different schools are performing. This site describes a statewide assessment program developed in Massachusetts.

[Note: Web addresses change frequently. If you are unable to locate one of these sites using the listed URL, try putting the site name in a standard search engine.]

You can use portfolios to document learning and growth of individuals over time. A sample of learner work products over a semester or a school year has the potential to provide much useful information to interested parties such as parents and guardians. Good portfolios yield a much more comprehensive picture of a youngster's development than a more traditional report focusing only on performance on traditional tests.

Because they can capture a rich array of material, portfolios can provide insight into areas that are normally overlooked such as learners' interests, abilities to persist when confronted with complex tasks, and self-concepts. In addition, portfolios involve learners directly in the information-collection process and provide an opportunity for them to take responsibility for gathering material and reflecting on their progress.

Portfolios are not panaceas; certainly they can be misused. It is a mistake to assume that use of portfolios in an assessment program automatically can be taken as evidence that a high-quality assessment program is operating (Stiggins, 1997). There are good portfolios, and there are bad portfolios. Portfolios that have been put together in the absence of well-planned criteria may look nice, but the information they contain may be trivial, and inferences made on their contents are suspect. Some guidelines that can help you prepare high-quality portfolios are as follows:

1. *Identify the purpose of the portfolio.* Remember that a portfolio is defined as a purposeful collection. It is not just a random storehouse. Keep in mind the outcomes of instruction. What is it that you are seeking to accomplish? Then consider the types of evidence you could use to reflect on the achievement of these important outcomes.

   Next consider whether you want the portfolio to be a working portfolio, a showcase portfolio, or a record-keeping portfolio (Gallagher, 1998). A *working portfolio* includes items that show the learner's growth over time and reveals strengths as well as weaknesses. A *showcase portfolio* features only exhibits that reflect a learner's most notable accomplishments. A *record-keeping portfolio* is used to keep material that might be passed on to other teachers to help them understand the progress of the learner and design instruction to better meet his or her needs. The type of portfolio selected will influence the types of entries that need to be made.

2. *Decide on the contents.* Since portfolios can contain a wide range of material, you need to exercise care to ensure that the contents of the portfolio are useful. If this is not done, the end result may be portfolios that include much material that is of little use in evaluating learners' attainment of important outcomes. All items included in the portfolio should have a clear relationship to important outcomes. Stiggins (1997) suggests that the content should tell a story. A useful way to conceptualize a portfolio is to define a story line that you want to be able to follow. Guidelines can then be given to learners to help them select representative material that best tells the story. It is important that enough items are included to enable you to make valid judgments.

3. *Prepare cover sheets describing categories of an individual item.* When learners choose items to include in the portfolio, they should be asked to assign the item to a particular category of information and to explain why they are including it. This helps evaluators and learners understand the importance and the meaning of the material. This is a useful step in making sure that learners reflect on their work and progress. If you provide learners with cover sheets identifying categories of content to be included, they will have an easier time deciding what kinds of information to include and how to categorize individual materials.

4. *Identify criteria to be used in scoring a portfolio.* Because so much material can be included in a portfolio and because items will vary from portfolio to

portfolio, evaluating the portfolio can be a challenge. To simplify this task and to avoid being influenced by extraneous variables such as attractiveness of presentation, you need to develop clear criteria you can use as you review each portfolio. These criteria should be specific enough so that a group of individuals viewing a given portfolio would score it in the same way.

As you consider criteria for scoring a portfolio, you should also consider how much weight you will give to specific entries. Not all items in a portfolio are of equal value in helping you decide whether or not a learner has accomplished worthwhile learning outcomes. Deciding on how to weigh individual categories of information ahead of time will save you considerable frustration when it comes to actually reviewing portfolios and making decisions about the performances of the individual learners.

In summary, portfolios can provide you with a rich array of information that will help you make sound judgments about individual learner performance. To be of use, they need to be carefully conceptualized and organized. If this is not the case, portfolios can become only a collection of items bearing little relationship to important learning outcomes.

This portfolio summarizes this learner's work. Increasingly, teachers are using portfolios as sources of evidence when they make judgments about the performances of individual learners.

Key Ideas In Summary

- Concern regarding the quality of the educational system has increased the importance of good understanding of assessment and assessment alternatives. A lack of understanding regarding quality assessment can lead to the collection of flawed data and inappropriate interpretations of the performance of learners and schools. This, in turn, may lead to proposals that do not address the critical issues.

- In addition to accountability purposes, assessment serves the important purpose of providing information for the teacher that can lead to increased success and motivation for learners and to improved teacher effectiveness. There are several relationships between assessment and instruction. One is in placing learners in instructional settings that are at the appropriate level of difficulty. Another is in providing formative information so the teacher can adjust the learning sequence to meet the needs of the learners. A third function is that of providing summative information at the end of an instructional sequence so that fair and accurate evaluations of progress can be made.

- Several key assessment terms need to be understood in order to avoid confusion. Assessment refers to the broad process of collecting data from a variety of sources about what individuals have learned. Measurement refers to the process of quantifying the presence or absence of an attribute or quality. Evaluation is the process of making a judgment about what the data gathered through the various measurement and assessment processes means. Grades are the methods of communicating the evaluation to other interested individuals.

- There are two basic methods for making evaluation decisions. One is called norm-referenced evaluation. This type of evaluation compares the scores of a learner against those of a group. It might be the other members of the classroom group or a broader national group. Criterion-referenced evaluation compares the scores of a learner against a standard or a set of criteria.

- The first major step that needs to be taken when planning for assessment is to define the outcomes of instruction. If this is not done, then trivial or unimportant knowledge may be measured, and inaccurate and unfair decisions may be made concerning which learners have attained the objectives and which have not. Understanding different learning outcomes and how to assess them is enhanced by understanding the taxonomies of educational objectives.

- When designing an assessment plan, it is important that there be an adequate sampling of learner behavior or performance, that the measurement tools are of an acceptable technical quality and are appropriate for the outcomes being assessed, and that the procedures used are fair and free of bias.

- Traditional measurement options include standardized and teacher-made tests and quizzes. These are used as an indicator that learning has taken place or that a learner can perform in a certain way. Some of the specific types of measurement options are two-choice selected-response items, multiple-choice selected-response items, matching items, and free-response essay and short-answer items.

- Performance and product assessments attempt to assess learner performance and learner products directly rather than through traditional assessment techniques. These include the use of checklists and rating scales or rubrics.

- Both traditional and performance assessment techniques can be purposefully gathered into a portfolio. These can provide a rich source of data that can then be used to make a judgment about what individuals have learned. In order for a portfolio to be useful, criteria must be developed to define what is to be included and specify how it is to be scored.

▮▮▮▮▮ Chapter 9 Self Test ▮▮▮▮▮▮▮▮▮▮▮▮▮▮

Cw To review terms and concepts in this chapter, take the Chapter 9 Self Test on the companion Web site, located at *http://www.prenhall.com/armstrong.* Select Chapter 9 from the front page of the Web site, then choose the Self Test module on the navigation bar on the left side of the page. Feedback for the Self Test is immediate. You can keep track of your Self Test scores yourself, or you can choose to submit your scores via e-mail to your instructor.

▮▮▮▮▮ Reflections ▮▮▮▮▮▮▮▮▮▮▮▮▮▮▮

Cw To respond to these questions online, and to save or submit your response electronically, visit the companion Web site, located at *http://www.prenhall.com/armstrong.* Select Chapter 9 from the front page of the Web site, then choose the Reflections module on the navigation bar on the left side of the page. Instructors and students may also wish to use these questions as discussion topics on the Message Board for the companion Web site.

1. How do you distinguish among the terms *assessment, measurement,* and *evaluation?*
2. What are some specific examples of how good assessment could help you improve as a teacher?
3. What do you see as the uses and advantages of norm-referenced and criterion-referenced evaluation?
4. Are there occasions when you see yourself using both norm-referenced and criterion-referenced tests? If so, describe these circumstances.

5. What are some issues you see associated with grading? How might your perspectives differ from those of parents or guardians, learners, principals, and others?
6. How would you explain the term *placement assessment* to a noneducator?
7. How might you use the categories in Bloom's taxonomy in planning your assessment program?
8. What are some strengths and weaknesses of two-response tests and multiple-choice tests?
9. Some authorities allege that rating scales allow teachers to engage in somewhat more sophisticated analyses of learners' performances than do checklists. What is the basis for this belief?
10. How would you describe strengths and weaknesses of learning portfolios as a way to assess learning of young people in the schools?

Field Experiences, Projects, and Enrichment

1. Collect articles out of the media relating to assessment of learner achievement. What types of measures are they citing? How valid are the measures? What is the validity of the conclusions that are drawn?

2. Visit a local school. Identify the standardized tests that are used to measure learner achievement in the district. Interview teachers that use the test, and ask them about the strengths and weaknesses of these assessments and about their reaction to the tests.

3. Identify some learning outcomes for a subject that is of interest to you. Identify what you think would be appropriate measurement tools for each of the outcomes.

4. Gather some tests that have either been used or are suggested for use in the classroom (they may even be tests you have taken). Take a look at the items included. Do they provide an adequate sample of the content? Which outcomes are measured? Are the items clearly written? How might the test be improved?

5. Enter the term *portfolio* into a well-known World Wide Web Search engine. Gather information about how portfolios for elementary, middle school, and senior high school learners are formatted. Prepare a report for your class in which you share some examples, paying particular attention to categories of information that are used and criteria that are employed to assess overall portfolio quality.

References

Berliner, D. C., & Biddle, B.J. (1995). *The manufactured crisis: Myth, fraud and the attack on America's public schools.* Reading, MA: Addison-Wesley.

Bloom, B. S., Englehart, M. D., Furst, E. J., Hill, W. H., & Krathwohl, D. R. (1956). *Taxonomy of educational objectives: Handbook 1, Cognitive domain.* New York: Mckay.

Bracey, G. W. (1998). TIMSS rhymes with 'dims,' as in 'witted. *Phi Delta Kappan, 79*(9), 686–688.

Gallagher, J. D. (1998). *Classroom assessment for teachers.* Columbus, OH: Merrill.

Gronlund, N. E. (1998). *Assessment of student achievement* (6th ed.). Boston: Allyn & Bacon.

Krathwohl, D. R., Bloom, B. S., & Masia, B. B. (1964). *Taxonomy of educational objectives: Handbook II: Affective domain.* New York: Mckay.

Stiggins, R. J. (1997). *Student-centered classroom assessment* (2nd ed.) Columbus, OH: Merrill.

Part Four

Influences on Teachers and Learners

CHAPTERS

10

Relationships Among Society, Schools, and Learners

OBJECTIVES

This chapter will help you to

- explain how values reflected in schools and school programs might not always "fit" all learners comfortably.

- describe functionalist, economic-class conflict, and status-group perspectives on schooling.

- point out roles schools are expected to play as institutions.

- explain potential conflicts between teachers' in-school and out-of-school roles.

- cite ways that groups to which individual learners belong can influence how they behave in school.

- point out possible sources of conflict for learners that can be caused by differences between expectations of teachers and school officials and expectations of their parents and guardians, their religious groups, and their friends.

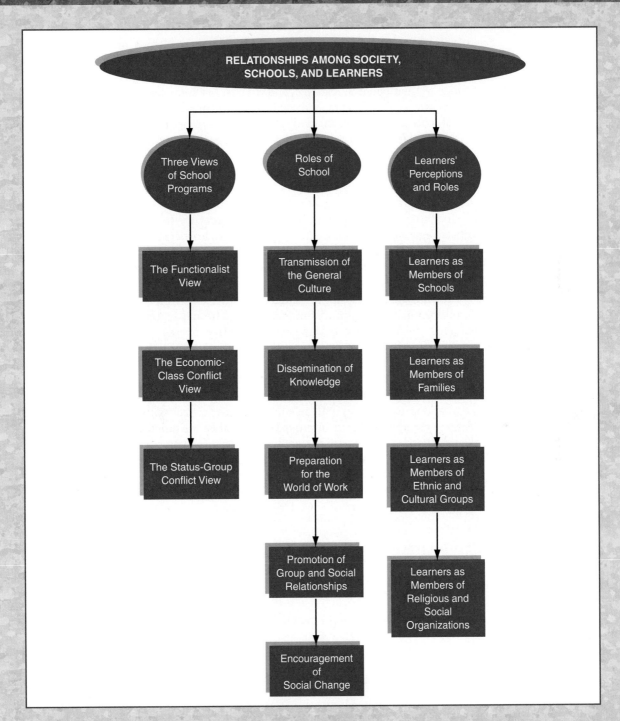

FIGURE 10.1 Relationships Among Society, Schools, and Learners

INTRODUCTION

Schools are not value-free places. What you teach, how you teach, and what you expect learners to do represent choices. The choices you make may not be troublesome to many of your learners, because much of what you do will be consistent with expectations of their parents, relatives, and friends. For some learners, however, what you try to accomplish as a teacher will be a sharp contrast to the world they know outside of school. This is a particularly common case for many children of immigrant parents whose families may know little about expected patterns of behavior for children in American schools. It is also often true for young people from ethnic, racial, and linguistic minorities who find themselves called upon to behave in unfamiliar ways when they come to school.

In the past, few people appreciated that groups to which learners belong can affect their adjustment to school. In the nineteenth century, for example, educators often took a negative and condescending view toward learners from minority cultures. Parents of Native American learners were widely criticized for allowing their children to "run wild." Many educators believed that these youngsters needed to experience the "benefits" of a highly controlled public school environment if there was to be any hope of turning them into model United States citizens (Coleman, 1993).

Similarly, nineteenth-century immigrants from Ireland and Eastern Europe initially encountered public schooling that was insensitive to their cultural perspectives (Scruggs, 1979). African American culture was so little prized in the nineteenth century that those few African Americans who were allowed to go to school endured the consequences of a dominant world view that openly dismissed their value as human beings. This was hardly a set of circumstances designed to help these young people emerge from their educational experiences with an enhanced sense of self-worth (Nieto, 1992).

Although conditions have improved greatly since the nineteenth century, young people from various groups still perceive prevailing school practices in different ways. Their views result from a combination of (1) reactions to the prescribed curriculum, (2) influences of the views of their families and friends, and (3) general perspectives of the particular cultural and ethnic groups to which they belong. These social factors suggest the importance of considering questions such as these:

- Whose interests do schools serve?
- What functions do schools fulfill?
- What roles do teachers play?
- How do families, ethnic groups, and other groups affect learners' reactions to school programs?

In this chapter, we introduce material that sheds light on some of these important issues.

THREE VIEWS OF SCHOOL PROGRAMS

Scholars who have studied how schools affect young people have worked from several perspectives. Among these are (1) the functionalist view, (2) the economic-class conflict view, and (3) the status-group conflict view.

Teachers must work sensitively with learners from many cultural and ethnic groups.

The Functionalist View

Functionalists see society as sharing a common set of values. Over time, these values have led to the development of institutions such as schools, families, governmental units, and religious bodies. Each of these institutions has a specialized responsibility or function, and performance of these functions helps keep our society going. Functionalists believe society is worth maintaining in its present form, because they believe that people in our society share more common values than values that might lead to conflict and discord. This harmonious social order deserves to be preserved and passed from generation to generation.

In our society, schools now discharge some responsibilities that once were taken care of by families. This is particularly true in the area of preparing our young people for the world of work. Today, most work is performed away from the home. Skills needed by employers have become so specialized that parents are no longer able to train their children for their future vocational roles. One result is that the role of families has increasingly become limited to providing for children's emotional and psychological needs. Preparation for economic life has largely been turned over to specialists in the schools.

Talcott Parsons (1959), a leading American functionalist, saw the school as the social agency that had the basic responsibility for providing our society with trained workers. Functionalists assume that all learners have the ability to profit from programs offered by the school. Those who get the best jobs are learners who, by virtue of their individual abilities and effort, take full advantage of what the schools have to offer. There is an assumption that economic rewards will be distributed on the basis of individual merit and that the school provides equal opportunities for all (Dougherty & Hammack, 1990).

The functionalist view is popular. It suggests that schools, by training people for occupations needed by our society as a whole, provide the necessary conditions for economic growth. This economic growth, in turn, is thought to yield benefits that will improve the lives of everyone. Functionalists believe that the potential of schools to stimulate economic growth establishes a rationale for spending tax dollars to expand educational services. This expansion is thought to benefit disadvantaged as well as advantaged groups.

Functionalists believe an important task of educators is to establish school programs that will provide learners with information they will need as adults. Once this is done, all learners will derive maximum benefits from their school experiences. Critics of this view argue that functionalists fail to adequately consider differences among groups of learners who attend our schools. They contend that school programs are not designed to serve interests of all learners equally well.

The Economic-Class Conflict View

Supporters of the *economic-class conflict* view reject functionalism's premise that there is broad agreement as to what the "common values" of our society are. They see our society as a battleground where contesting groups strive for supremacy. In their view, schools are places where contending interest groups compete for educational advantages. The "winners" succeed in having important educational resources dedicated to programs to serve their children. In general, it is believed that economically powerful groups win most competitions. Hence, young people from economically impoverished groups do not receive the educational advantages that are routinely provided to children from more affluent families. (See the "What Do You Think?" feature for an illustration of this point.)

The economic-class conflict position traces its origins to the work of Karl Marx and Friedrich Engels. Marx and Engels argued that the defining feature of a society was the conflict between a capitalist class that controlled the means of production and a working class that was forced to serve the capitalists.

As applied to education today, the economic-class conflict position has led to two somewhat different interpretations of what goes on in school. According to the *class-reproduction* view, school programs have expanded primarily because of capitalists' desires to serve the needs of their own class. People who believe this to be true cite efforts to infuse computer technology, advanced mathematics, and similar specialized content into the school programs as evidence of an intent to create school programs to meet the needs of future managers and owners. Similarly, they see attempts to upgrade vocational programs as efforts of the managerial and ownership class to ensure a steady supply of trained workers.

Another variant of the economic-class conflict position is the *class-conflict* view. Its supporters argue that educational change has not come about because of capitalists' desires to make school programs serve their own interests. Rather, changes have occurred because economically disadvantaged groups have expressed their unhappiness with existing school programs. Their actions, it is argued, have led to many

What Do You Think?

Who Benefits from an Advanced Calculus Course?

A reader recently made these points in a letter to the editor of a local newspaper.

> Our school board has done it again. Now we are to be "blessed" with a high school curriculum that features a spanking new *advanced* calculus course. We already have a regular calculus course that, according to my sources, serves a grand total of 10% of the school population. The new advanced course will be taken just by a select few who do well in the regular calculus course.
>
> Why are we committing scarce education money to a program that will benefit just a fraction of our students? I know the answer, and I don't like it. The high-income families who have a lot of political stroke want their kids to have an extra edge when they head off to study engineering at some prestigious private university. As for the rest of our kids—a vast majority, I might add—well, too bad. The district won't have money this year to take care of their needs.

What Do You Think?

1. What values are reflected in the statements of this writer?
2. What arguments might you make if you wanted to attack this position? What arguments might you make if you chose to support this viewpoint?

changes in what schools do. In particular, they have been successful in promoting the adoption of better learning opportunities for minorities and females.

Critics of the economic-class conflict position suggest that its supporters place too much emphasis on the economic standing of groups as an explanation for changes in school programs. They point out that many Americans have little personal sense of membership in a particular economic class. For example, some national elections have witnessed large numbers of people with modest incomes identifying with the same Republican candidates who have been strongly supported by large business interests. Further, there is evidence that many learners who come from working-class families manage to acquire the education necessary to move into managerial and executive positions. Even though access to schooling does not guarantee social mobility, movement of children into higher status, higher paid positions than their parents happens more often than might be predicted if schools were really controlled by wealthy and influential people who sought only to promote their own narrow economic-class interests.

The Status-Group Conflict View

The economic-class conflict position suggests that social status and power are a function of economics. The *status-group conflict* position, largely based on the philosophy of the German sociologist Max Weber, proposes that change results from conflicts among groups that compete for reasons that go beyond narrow economic interests.

According to this view, the economic condition of people alone is too narrow a basis for determining individual or group status. Status is awarded to influential leaders in social organizations, governmental units, religious bodies, and in other groups. Groups that award status to certain members serve the interests of people who work for or are affiliated with them. In doing this, they often come into conflict with other groups. It is conflict among these diverse status groups that is thought to explain why educational changes occur.

Supporters of the status-group conflict position suggest that today's school programs reflect efforts of specific groups to advance their own interests. For example, school knowledge typically is "packaged" into separate subject areas, and the school day is divided into time periods. Some people suggest that these patterns result from industrial managers' desires to familiarize learners with an industrial culture's working environment, which includes departmentalized functions and careful attention to time schedules (Khumar, 1989). Others believe that school physical education programs often draw support from military leaders who want schools to produce a supply of people in good physical condition ready for military service. Student government and other groups that require learners to work on committees to solve problems have been viewed as schemes to familiarize young people with the roles of government officials and to prepare some of them for future employment in government service.

Critics of the status-group conflict position contend that it overemphasizes conflict as a determinant of what goes on in schools. They acknowledge that there are differences between groups that frequently lead to disputes and accept that these conflicts sometimes influence school programs. However, these critics point to the continued existence of important shared national values that cut across individual groups. They argue that these shared values as well as between-group conflicts influence what goes on in our schools.

People committed to functionalism, economic-class conflict, and status-group conflict look at efforts to change school programs in quite different ways. Functionalists see disagreements about present school programs as arguments within a basically harmonious family whose members are trying to define a common ground. Changes adopted are believed to have potential for helping the entire society. Functionalists ask two basic questions: (1) Is this change consistent with broadly held values? and (2) Is it designed to benefit all?

People who are committed to either of the two conflict positions take a different view. They look for potential "winners" and "losers" when they evaluate proposals to change school programs. They do not see discussions of change as part of an effort to achieve a society-wide benefit. Instead, such proposals are considered to be part of a recurring pattern of conflict between groups—a pattern that almost always results in individual decisions that benefit some groups more than others. A major objective of conflict-position supporters is to reveal the probable consequences of a proposed school policy or program change for members of individual groups. They see debates about potential changes focusing on this question: Will this change benefit groups that deserve to benefit?

The functionalist position and the conflict positions often lead people to different conclusions about what schools are doing and what schools should do. For ex-

Following the Web 10.1

Sociology of Education

The views of school programs introduced in this section (functionalist view, economic-class conflict view, and status-group conflict view) represent some of the perspectives that have been identified by specialists in the sociology of education. The Web sites noted here contain information from the sociology of education that elaborates on what you have read in the chapter.

 For hot links to these sites, visit the companion Web site, located at *http://www.prenhall.com/armstrong*. Select Chapter 10 from the front page of the Web site, then choose the Following the Web module on the navigation bar on the left side of the page.

Politics of Education

* *http://www.gseis.ucla.edu/courses/ed191/transparencies/transparencies.html*

  This site features a number of "transparencies" that feature succinct explanations of various topics of interest to educational sociologists. You will find information contrasting functionalist and conflict-theory views of education. In addition, a good explanation of Talcott Parsons' contributions to functionalism is included.

Sociological Perspectives on Education

* *http://www.accessinn.com/socabs/html/noteus/5napr97.htm*

  This site provides links to many sources of information on groups and educational systems. For instance, you will find Web addresses for a large number of professional journals with content related to the sociology of education. In addition, a useful *Thesaurus* feature includes many terms related to this area of study.

Annotated Bibliography of Multicultural Issues in Mathematics Education

* *http://jwilson.coe.uga.edu/DEPT/Multicultural/MEBib94.html*

  Backgrounds of learners influence how they will react to the programs they encounter in the schools. Educators have attempted to focus on the nature of reactions of learners from different groups to specific elements of the school program. This site includes excellent materials focusing on how learners from different ethnic and cultural groups have dealt with the subject of mathematics. It contains an extensive listing of relevant materials.

[Note: Web addresses change frequently. If you are unable to locate one of these sites using the listed URL, try putting the site name in a standard search engine.]

ample, a functionalist might view a high school curriculum featuring many electives as a positive indicator of a program that is responsive to varying interests and needs of students. But someone committed to one of the conflict positions might see the same curriculum as a clever scheme of powerful interest groups to direct learners from noninfluential groups into courses that fail to prepare them for well-paid, high-status jobs.

ROLES OF SCHOOLS

As important social institutions, schools play many roles. Among them are responsibilities associated with:

- transmission of the general culture,
- dissemination of academic knowledge,
- preparation for the world of work,
- promotion of social and group relationships, and
- encouragement of social change.

Transmission of the General Culture

Schools transmit certain values, beliefs, and norms to learners. These perspectives have broad support in our society. But this does not mean that *all* individuals and groups subscribe to every value, belief, and norm that is explicitly or implicitly included in school programs. Disagreements about the extent of the school's responsibilities for shaping learners' attitudes sometimes lead to acrimonious debates about the proper limits of educators' socialization responsibilities.

Part of the difficulty results because the school is only one of several influences on learners' values. Families also greatly influence young people's patterns of behavior and thinking. This is especially true of younger children, but families continue to exercise some influence over older learners as well. Social organizations, churches, friends, and other groups also influence the perspectives of young people.

As an example of how cultural context influences people's beliefs, consider the findings of prominent Indian educational sociologist Krishna Khumar (1989), who compared representations of children in texts used in India and Canada. Khumar found that many more children were featured in the Canadian texts than in the Indian texts. Further, the children in the Canadian texts were portrayed as engaged in more creative and imaginative activities than those in the Indian texts.

Khumar attributed the infrequent use of children as characters and their relative passivity in the Indian texts as a reflection of the cultural context of India. He pointed out that because death rates among children are extremely high in India, not much "personhood" is attached to them. Consequently, relatively little thought is given to the special characteristics of children. On the other hand, in Canada, where survival rates of children are much higher, children are seen as people of consequence; hence, they play much more dominant and active parts in stories featured in Canadian school books.

As an educator today, you will find yourself tugged between two competing realities. On the one hand, you will recognize a need to respond in different ways to learners coming to you from different family and cultural backgrounds. At the same time, you will sense some obligation to transmit certain common perspectives to all the young people you serve. Seeking an appropriate balance between these two needs will be a professional challenge you will face throughout your career. From time to time, you and your colleagues may find yourselves at odds with some parents and community members who do not agree with some aspects of the school program.

Some perspectives provided to learners in the schools engender more controversy than others. One that has not typically led to disagreement is the idea that the schools have a special responsibility to prepare young people for the world of work (Goslin, 1990). Few families and other groups in our society have the needed expertise to discharge this responsibility.

The kinds of socialization programs that sometimes prompt hostile parental reactions are those that relate to personal behavior, such as sex education. Critics of instruction that deals with these kinds of personal issues often argue that this type of teaching should be left to family members or to religious bodies.

Dissemination of Knowledge

When you start teaching, you will be obligated to transmit specialized knowledge, particularly academic knowledge, to learners. The quantity and sophistication of information needed by young people today goes beyond what most parents know. Experts in the schools are expected to draw on their specialized information and pass it along to their learners.

Time for teaching is limited, and the quantity of available knowledge is vast. These two realities will make it impossible for you to "teach everything." In practice, the adopted curriculum functions as a screen or filter that identifies the specific information you will be expected to teach. Because the curriculum is a general repository of what is presented to youngsters in schools, certain groups sometimes attack its contents because of their concerns about the adequacy or appropriateness of the included information.

Some ways of selecting and organizing content have persisted for so many years that you may find it difficult to imagine alternative ways. For many years, the settlement and development of the United States has been described in terms of a wave of migration from the Atlantic Coast to the Pacific Coast. Some parents and educators who note that in just a few years Hispanics will become our most numerous minority group, wonder about this traditional east-to-west presentation of United States history. They point out that this organizational scheme has made it difficult for writers of history texts to include much information about Hispanic contributions to the development of our country. This is true because the Hispanic population, generally, has occupied the country from south-to-north rather than from east-to-west. Perhaps in the future more history curricula will present settlement of the United States from both an east-to-west and a south-to-north perspective.

Some learning materials deliver an unintended "lesson" that implies members of certain groups are less worthy than members of other groups. Krishna Khumar (1989) describes a widely used school story in India about a wealthy merchant who listens to the complaints of a poor worker who concludes his life is worthless. The wealthy merchant offers to buy one of the poor worker's eyes for a small price. The worker rejects the initial offer but continues to negotiate with the rich merchant, who gradually increases his offer to the princely sum of 100,000 rupees. At this point, the poor worker realizes that he does have value and thanks the merchant for providing him with this insight.

Several messages in this story may offend some people. For example, the narrative implies that wealth, wisdom, and virtue go together. It also suggests that the poor should follow the ideas of the rich. The subtext of the tale might be summarized as "Don't rock the boat, but appreciate what you have, even if you're poor."

Preparation for the World of Work

The economic existence of every society depends on its supply of qualified workers. The jobs that are required vary in terms of knowledge and skills needed. One function of the school is to prepare young people for these diverse job roles. In a sense, the school functions as a sorting agency for future employers. As learners progress through their educational programs, they develop varying levels of expertise that help them qualify for some positions and eliminate them as serious candidates for positions that require different kinds of abilities and talents.

Some occupational roles carry with them more prestige and, often, higher financial rewards than others. School programs that help our young people prepare for these valued occupational roles usually are academically rigorous. For example, learners who want to pursue careers in engineering often enroll in challenging mathematics courses. In theory, the difficulty of some of these courses ensures that competent people will enter engineering curricula. It also means that the number of potential engineers will not be too large and that many individuals who are attracted to engineering early in their school years will switch to other career paths.

Controversy may accompany decisions you will make as a teacher when you advise individual learners to pursue courses of study that seem related to preparation for particular careers. For example, there may be suspicions that you are directing certain kinds of learners (perhaps those from economically impoverished households or from certain cultural and ethnic groups) away from courses of study needed by people interested in entering high-prestige occupations. You need to be careful that recommendations you make about suggested courses or entire courses of study do not reflect unprofessional biases against certain categories of learners.

Promotion of Social and Group Relationships

Schools foster the development of learners' social and group skills. This occurs both by design and as a side effect of the special environment of the school setting. Recurring regularly-scheduled events such as pep assemblies and athletic contests encourage the development of a common group identity among all learners in a given school.

When young people identify strongly with their schools, they have more positive attitudes toward teachers, classmates, and the entire educational enterprise. This kind of group identity stands as a proxy for what many of the learners will be encouraged to do as adult employees of businesses and government agencies and as members of religious groups and other organizations.

Most schools, especially secondary schools, have official clubs and organizations. Young people who participate in these groups gain experience in working with others and, to some extent, in competing with people in other groups (for meeting space,

One function of the school is to help learners participate successfully as members of groups.

financial resources, and so forth). Other organizations that are not formally sponsored by the school sometimes arrange to use school facilities when classes are not in session. These include scouting groups, church youth groups, and junior branches of fraternal organizations. Many learners who are in these groups derive benefits from their membership in the same way that they and others profit from participation in school-sponsored organizations.

Schools are places where learners acquire socially appropriate patterns of interpersonal relations. School classes enroll learners from varied backgrounds and provide opportunities for learners to meet people who may be very different from themselves. Male and female relationships begin to flourish in schools as young people mature. Some school functions such as dances are specifically designed to support socially acceptable ways of developing these friendships. (See *What Did You Learn Outside of the Classroom* figure as you think about out-of-class experiences that influenced your own development.)

Encouragement of Social Change

Many people see the schools as social improvement agencies. This is particularly true at times when the public is concerned about serious social problems (Goslin, 1990).

Learners are taught many things in school that are not part of the official program of study. (For more information about this *hidden curriculum,* see Chapter 14.) Much of what young people take away from their school experiences comes from their involvement in clubs, organizations, and other out-of-class activities.

Identify at least six things you "learned in school" outside of the formal classroom that have proved useful later in your life.

1. _____

2. _____

3. _____

4. _____

5. _____

6. _____

FIGURE 10.2   What Did You Learn Outside the Classroom?

Faith in "better education" as a curative agent is widespread. Few politicians miss opportunities to make clear their intentions to reduce the crime rate, defeat alcoholism, diminish the use of illegal drugs, or combat promiscuity and unwed motherhood through the institution of "sound educational programs."

While the view that schools should function as powerful social reform agents appeals to some educators, others question this position. Critics point out that schools are part of the larger society that has produced the very problems they are charged with "fixing." For this reason, they doubt that changes in school programs will do much unless there are also changes in our society as a whole.

When policy makers ask educators to take on a task such as reducing illegal drug use, there is a good chance that the best-planned program will fail. Poverty, a lack of belief in a secure economic future, absence of strong families, a dearth of good role models outside the school, and many other variables may lead a given individual to turn to illegal drugs. The scope of the problem simply may be beyond what teachers and schools can address. This is not to say that professionals in the schools should not cooperate with other groups to work on the problem. However, to suggest that educators alone have the capacity to solve it is to ignore reality.

Despite concerns that have been raised about the appropriateness of asking schools to solve intractable social problems, the belief that education is a potent reform agent has wide support. There is some evidence that school programs that challenge learners to look seriously at problems that affect their own lives and actively connect with people trying to solve them increase their self-confidence (Boston, 1998). Such programs also may lead young people to see a more legitimate connection between what goes on in school and the "real world" where their parents and other adults live and work.

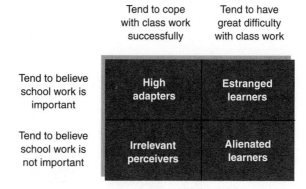

FIGURE 10.3   Four Categories of Learner Reactions to the School Program

LEARNERS' PERCEPTIONS AND ROLES

Even though the young people you will teach share many common school experiences, they do not all perceive them in the same way. Educational sociologists sometimes find it useful to develop classifications of learners based on their reactions to school programs (Bernstein, 1977). Four categories sometimes used are (see Figure 10.3):

- high adapters,
- estranged learners,
- irrelevant perceivers, and
- alienated learners.

High adapters are learners who believe that the content of the school program is important and who experience success in their classes. These learners see a good fit between the agenda of the school and their personal hopes and aspirations (and probably with those of their families, friends, and social, religious, and ethnic groups). In your classes, they will tend to support what you want to do and rarely challenge what goes on at school.

Estranged learners are also convinced of the importance of the school program. However, for intellectual, social, or other reasons, they do not do well in school. They often develop negative self-concepts and worry that their lack of success will permanently tag them as "losers." These young people often become increasingly disenchanted with school as the years go by, and many of them drop out before graduating from high school.

Irrelevant perceivers have the capacity to succeed in school. However, they do not consider school work to be important. Often they have personal priorities that they view as having little connection to what you may ask them to do in the classroom. One of the authors once had a young man in his class who was the son of a local wrecking-yard owner. By the time he began high school, this boy had been working for his father for years. He was already earning good money, and he was looking forward to working full time once he finished high school. In general, this young man thought that teachers were a sorry lot who had strange interests and who did not

"My teacher says Bill Gates is worth 80 billion dollars. I guess you need to buckle down and apply yourself if you're going to catch up, Dad."

make enough money to be taken seriously. He did just enough work in school to pass his courses and qualify for a diploma.

Alienated learners do not see the school program as personally important. They have not experienced success on those occasions when they have seriously tried to do the work. If you encounter some of these young people in your classes, they probably will have little good to say about what they have experienced in school. They frequently feel trapped in a situation that requires them to do things they do not believe are important under conditions that will not allow them to succeed. Many of these young people drop out of school before they graduate, and those who stay often experience problems. Their frustrations sometimes lead them to develop unacceptable patterns of behavior in the classroom.

In part, differences among learners who are high adapters, estranged, irrelevant perceivers, or alienated stem from social influences that have helped shape their view of the world. Young people must play many roles, and some of them conflict with others. Difficulties in school may arise when there are conflicts between roles learners must play as members of the school community and roles that are expected of them as members of families, specific cultural or ethnic groups, or religious and social organizations.

Learners as Members of Schools

Schools impose certain behavioral expectations on learners, many of which are unwritten. One of the most basic of these is the expectation that learners will accept direction from the teacher. Even though, as a teacher, you will encourage young people to raise questions as you present lessons, for the most part, you will assume they will accept the validity of the content you are providing.

In addition, you and other teachers expect learners to follow rules regarding such things as when and how they will move from place to place, where they will sit in classrooms, what they must do to complete assigned tasks, when they may eat, when they may leave the classroom, and when they may converse freely with oth-

Video Viewpoint

What Makes a Great School?: Parent Involvement

WATCH: In this ABC News video segment, education reporter Rebecca Chase focuses on Walton High School in Atlanta, a school where parents are actively involved. Then, after her report shows *how* parents can get involved, reporter Thomas Toch talks about *why* parents should be involved in their children's education, and what characteristics make a good school.

THINK: With your classmates or in your teaching journal, consider these questions:

1. How could you use technology to involve your students' families in classroom or school-wide activities?
2. What are some other ways you can involve families in their childrens' learning?
3. How can making parents active participants in the school help to prevent a "disconnect" between what goes on in school and what goes on at home?

LINK: How do students benefit when their families are actively involved with their classroom and their school?

ers while learners who adapt easily to the school environment cope easily with the many regulations that govern their behavior, others find this difficult.

Learners as Members of Families

Learners often adopt those views that are prevalent among members of their immediate families. For example, young people whose parents have strong commitments to organized labor often will espouse a commitment to labor unions. Such young people may find it hard to accept conclusions included in a textbook written by an author with a strong anti-union perspective. Although views of families are not always passed on intact to members of the younger generation, as a rule, this is quite common. As a result, when values or positions introduced at school conflict with those of learners' families, students may become less interested in what is introduced at school.

Sometimes parents actively intervene to push schools to serve agendas that are important to them (Fried, 1998). For example, well-educated parents may lobby school leaders for more gifted-and-talented classes. Some critics have pointed out that parents who are less educated and less affluent only infrequently make their voices heard when they seek a change in school practices (Kohn, 1998). Over time, this may mean more of a "disconnect" between what goes on in schools and the views espoused in homes of young people whose parents are neither well educated nor financially secure.

You must be careful when introducing value-laden content. You do need to teach such information, but you should take care to identify conclusions as consistent with a given point of view, not as unalloyed truth. When you take care to do this, learners understand that a variety of views, including those they hold personally, are acceptable.

Many young people acquire some of their values because of their association with special groups and organizations.

Learners as Members of Ethnic and Cultural Groups

Learners' ethnic and cultural groups influence their world views. These ethnic and cultural perspectives can affect their receptivity to what you do in the classroom. To illustrate the point, let's think about a young Native American girl who is taking a junior-level English course in high school. The teacher has asked the class to read some of Mark Twain's books. Recently, they have been reading *Roughing It,* a novel based on Twain's travels and experiences in the Far West. In this novel, Twain describes Native Americans as "prideless beggars" (Twain, 1872/1985, p. 167).

It is doubtful that this girl sees herself, her family, and other Native Americans as prideless beggars. If you were teaching this class and did not take care to instruct students that the phrase represents an isolated statement by one author (who, elsewhere, deals much more fairly with Native Americans) made at a specific time and in a particular historical context, the girl may conclude that whatever else is taught in the course is irrelevant. The conclusion that Native Americans are prideless beggars does not square with her view of reality. It would make sense, too, for you to introduce other materials that provide a more positive view of Native Americans and other groups of people who were not always treated sensitively by authors who wrote at a time when cultural diversity was less prized than it is today.

Learners as Members of Religious and Social Organizations

Many school learners are active in various religious and social organizations whose members often share strong commitments to particular viewpoints. Sometimes these perspectives conflict with what learners encounter in school. For example, school

Critical Incident

Is Dancing Devilish?

Gilberto Figueroa, a first-year 4th-grade teacher, slumped wearily into the faculty lounge couch. "This," he announced to the two or three colleagues who had gathered around the coffee pot, "has been *some* day."

"What's up, Gil?" The speaker was Latisha Carter, the school's long-time middle grades team leader.

"Sit down, Latisha. This is going to take a while."

Latisha took a seat on the couch, settled her coffee cup on the table, and looked up. "OK, Gil, let's have it."

"You remember when I told you about the folk dancing we did last summer in my physical education methods class? Well, it hit me a couple of nights ago that I could tie some folk dancing to some of the things we're doing in social studies. They're always after us to break down barriers between subjects, and this seemed a natural."

"Anyway," Gilberto continued, "I did some additional checking, found some music, and relearned the steps of four dances from four different countries. I took the kids to the gym this morning. I explained what we were going to do and taught them the steps. I thought everything was going splendidly until I noticed I was getting a lot of frowns from Louis."

"What was that all about?" Latisha asked.

"At first, I just didn't know," Gilberto replied. "I didn't let it bother me and kept on teaching. Then, I put some music on and let the kids try the steps. It was at *that* point things fell apart. Louis jumped up on a bench, started shaking his fist at everyone else, and began shouting, 'You're all going to hell!' Some of the other kids were really scared. In fact, Nellie and Joe spent some time with the counselor after lunch. And that's not the end of it."

"What else happened?" Latisha asked.

"About two o'clock I got a message from the office to call Louis's mother. He'd gone home for lunch and told her what he had done. I figured maybe she was calling to apologize for his behavior. Was I ever off base on that idea! I called her after school, and she proceeded to read me the riot act for subjecting her child to immoral activities. She lectured me for 20 minutes on the scriptural basis for the idea that dancing is the 'devil's work.' She's coming to see me tomorrow. I think I'm in for it. Got any ideas?"

. . .

What is Gilberto really worried about? Is it the impending confrontation with Louis's mother? Or, is he worried about where Louis's mother may go next? Or, is something else of greater concern? What alternatives might be open to Gilberto? Has he thought these through? What do we learn about Gilberto's values? How might these differ from those of Louis's mother? If there is a difference in these values, is Gilberto obligated to change his instructional program? Why or why not?

Cw To respond to this Critical Incident online, and to save or submit your response electronically, visit the companion Web site, located at *http://www.prenhall.com/armstrong*. Select Chapter 10 from the front page of the Web site, then choose the Critical Incidents module on the navigation bar on the left side of the page. Instructors and students may also wish to use these scenarios as discussion topics on the Message Board for the companion Web site.

Following the Web 10.2

Influences of Various "Memberships" on How Learners View Their Experiences in School

Learners' reactions to school often are influenced strongly by groups of which they are a member. The Web sites listed here include information that augments what you have learned in this chapter.

For hot links to these sites, visit the companion Web site, located at *http://www. prenhall.com/armstrong*. Select Chapter 10 from the front page of the Web site, then choose the Following the Web module on the navigation bar on the left side of the page.

Becoming at Risk of Failure in America's Schools

- *http://www.ed.gov/pubs/EdReformStudies/EdReforms/chap1a.html*

  This site provides an excellent brief summary of the long-term standing of "learner diversity" as a special characteristic of American schools. The kinds of diversity in today's schools, to some extent, were present in our schools even 100 years ago.

United States Department of Education Search Form

- *http://www.ed.gov/basisdb/publication/short/sf*

  This site allows users to identify topics they want to study in more depth. For example, if you were to type in the phrase, "learners and ethnic groups," you would get a long listing of articles and other information sources relevant to this topic, including one titled, "A Study of the Interaction Effects of School and Home Environments on Students of Varying Race/Ethnicity, Class, and Gender." Click on the title to get the full text of any article or information source of interest.

United States Department of Education

- *http://www.ed.gov/*

  This is the home page of the United States Department of Education. It provides access to a vast array of information, including material about students and what influences their reactions to schools.

counselors and teachers may encourage females to work hard to master mathematics because a good background in this subject is needed for many high-paying jobs. A few religious groups may object strongly to schools promoting the idea that women should prepare for employment outside of the home.

Learners who are members of groups that hold views differing from what is being taught at school may find themselves torn between a desire to please their teachers and a desire to please their religious leaders. These kinds of conflicts are common. Teachers must recognize that many young people are under pressure to do things that may be at odds with what professional educators believe to be in their long-term "best" interest.

Key Ideas In Summary

- What is done in schools is a reflection of a particular set of values. Whereas many learners come from homes that share the same values orientation as the school, this is not always the case. As a result, some learners find themselves in an unfamiliar social situation when they first come to school. Inconsistencies between the perspectives of the home and the school sometimes cause problems for learners who find themselves caught between conflicting sets of behavioral expectations.

- People who subscribe to the *functionalist* position believe that our society is strongly committed to a common set of values that should be reflected in school programs. Functionalists believe that when this is true, there is an excellent chance that all learners will commit to these values. It is assumed that school programs that are developed in response to common values will allow all learners in the school to take advantage of the benefits of schooling.

- Supporters of the *economic-class conflict* position disagree that our society features a large set of commonly held values. They argue that different kinds of people are committed to different values and that these differences lead to conflict. In particular, they see conflict between capitalists, who control most of the wealth and the means of production, and workers, who must do the bidding of the capitalists. According to the economic-class conflict position, school reforms result from one of two reasons. Some proponents of this view believe changes result from an interest in keeping our economic system going in a form that will maximize capitalist control and supply adequate numbers of workers to serve as employees. Others believe that school reforms come about because of challenges brought by working-class people who do not want school programs that promote the idea that present economic arrangements will go on forever.

- Individuals who are committed to the *status-group conflict* position also believe that there is more conflict than consensus in our society. They believe that conflict involves more groups than simply capitalists and workers. They draw much of their inspiration from the work of Max Weber, who pointed out that change often prompts conflict among many status groups. Status groups include social organizations, economic organizations, religious organizations, governmental organizations, ethnic and cultural organizations, and other groups. These groups try to maximize the benefits of their members. In doing so, they often come into conflict with members of other groups. Educational change comes about as a result of these conflicts. More specifically, changes are made in directions favored by conflict winners.

- As institutions, schools play many roles. Among them are their roles as (1) transmitters of the general culture, (2) disseminators of academic knowledge, (3) developers of learners for the world of work, (4) promoters of social and group relationships, and (5) encouragers of social change.

- Not all learners react in the same way to the school program. *High adapters* believe content of the school program to be important, and they generally experience success in their classes. *Estranged learners* believe content of the school program is important, but they often develop poor self-images because they experience little success in their classes. *Irrelevant perceivers* are learners who doubt the importance of the school program. They have the ability to succeed, but they commit only marginally to their studies, and often their performance levels fall short of their real abilities. *Alienated learners* neither believe in the importance of the school program nor do well in their classes. Many of them drop out of school before completing high school.

- Young people play many roles in addition to their roles as learners in school. For example, they are also family members, members of ethnic and cultural groups, and members of religious and social organizations. Perspectives of these groups may be at odds with some views to which learners are exposed at school. When this happens, learners may experience psychological pressures as they are torn between competing allegiances to people at home and in organizations and to teachers and the school.

Chapter 10 Self Test

To review terms and concepts in this chapter, take the Chapter 10 Self Test on the companion Web site, located at *http://www.prenhall.com/armstrong*. Select Chapter 10 from the front page of the Web site, then choose the Self Test module on the navigation bar on the left side of the page. Feedback for the Self Test is immediate. You can keep track of your Self Test scores yourself, or you can choose to submit your scores via e-mail to your instructor.

Reflections

To respond to these questions online, and to save or submit your response electronically, visit the companion Web site, located at *http://www.prenhall.com/armstrong*. Select Chapter 10 from the front page of the Web site, then choose the Reflections module on the navigation bar on the left side of the page. Instructors and students may also wish to use these questions as discussion topics on the Message Board for the companion Web site.

1. Why is it that some learners do not adapt as well as others to the expectations of teachers and the schools?
2. What are some characteristics of the functionalist position?
3. What are some similarities and differences between the economic-class conflict

position and the status-group conflict position?
4. In what ways do schools transmit the general culture and disseminate academic knowledge?
5. What are some things schools do to make learners more comfortable in group and social settings?
6. What kinds of roles do teachers play in schools?
7. What are some potential conflicts you might face as a teacher between your in-school professional role and your roles as a member of a family and as a member of out-of-school groups and organizations?
8. Why is it that many parents assume the worst when they get a call from the school

about their child, and what might you do to change this expectation of bad news?

9. How can learners' roles as family members, ethnic and cultural group members, and religious and social organization members place pressures on them at school?

10. What are some things you might do to help learners deal with potential conflicts between values reflected in their classes at school and values prized by out-of-school groups to which learners belong?

Field Experiences, Projects, and Enrichment

1. Invite a member of a local school district's central administrative staff to talk to your class about how the district responds to concerns that may be raised by parents or other school patrons about certain aspects of the curriculum. What kinds of concerns have been voiced? Have groups been satisfied with the district's responses? Are new teachers provided with guidelines for handling complaints from community groups?

2. Interview several teachers about the different roles they play both in and out of school. Ask about problems they face in managing their time. How do they resolve pressures they may face? Prepare a short report to share with others in your class.

3. Are our school programs designed to maximize the development of all learners, or are they designed to benefit a select few? Prepare a position paper in which you

support one of these two positions. Ask your instructor to comment on what you have written.

4. Ask five or six secondary students whether they have ever been told anything at school that conflicts with what they have been told at home. How did they feel when this happened? What did they do? What did their teacher do? Prepare a short written summary of your interview, and share it with others in your class.

5. Alienated learners often reject what schools have to offer, and they usually do not do well in their classes. Along with several other fellow class members, do some reading on the subject of learner alienation. What are some things the experts see as leading to this condition? What can teachers and other educators do to help these young people? Present your findings to your class in the form of a symposium.

References

Bernstein, B. B. (1977). *Class codes and control* (Vol. 3, 2nd ed.). London: Routledge and Kegan Paul.

Boston, B. O. (1998/1999). If the water is nasty, fix it. *Educational Technology, 56*(4), 66–69.

Coleman, M. (1993). *American Indian children at school, 1850–1930.* Jackson: University of Mississippi Press.

Dougherty, K. J., & Hammack, F. M. (1990). *Education and society: A reader.* San Diego, CA: Harcourt Brace Jovanovich.

Fried, R. L. (1998). Parent anxiety and school reform. *Phi Delta Kappan, 80*(4), 264–271.

Goslin, D. A. (1990). The functions of the school in modern society. In K. J. Dougherty & F. M. Hammack (Eds.), *Education and society: A reader* (pp. 29–38). San Diego, CA: Harcourt Brace Jovanovich.

Khumar, K. (1989). *Social character of learning.* New Delhi, India: Sage Publications India.

Kohn, A. (1998). Only for *my* kid: How privileged parents undermine school reform. *Phi Delta Kappan, 79*(8), 568–577.

Nieto, S. (1992). *Affirming diversity: The sociopolitical context of multicultural education.* New York: Longman.

Parsons, T. (1959). School class as a social system: Some of its functions in American society. *Harvard Educational Review, 49,* 297–318.

Scruggs, O. M. (1979). The education of the Afro-American: An historic view. In K. Hall & A. Young (Eds.), *Education and the Black experience* (pp. 9–24). Palo Alto, CA: R & E Research Associates.

Twain, M. (1985). *Roughing it.* New York: Penguin Books. (Original work published 1872)

11

Historical Roots of American Education

OBJECTIVES

This chapter will help you to

- point out that written history is influenced by the perspectives of the historian.

- describe criticisms that American education has not always developed in ways that served to advantage *all* learners.

- cite examples of some practices in today's schools derived from European precedents.

- identify patterns of American education as they developed in the colonial period and years of the early Republic.

- summarize key 19th-century developments that helped shape today's American education.

- identify basic principles that provided a rationale for the comprehensive high school.

- describe some contributions of Horace Mann and John Dewey to American education.

- cite some key issues in the development of twentieth-century American education.

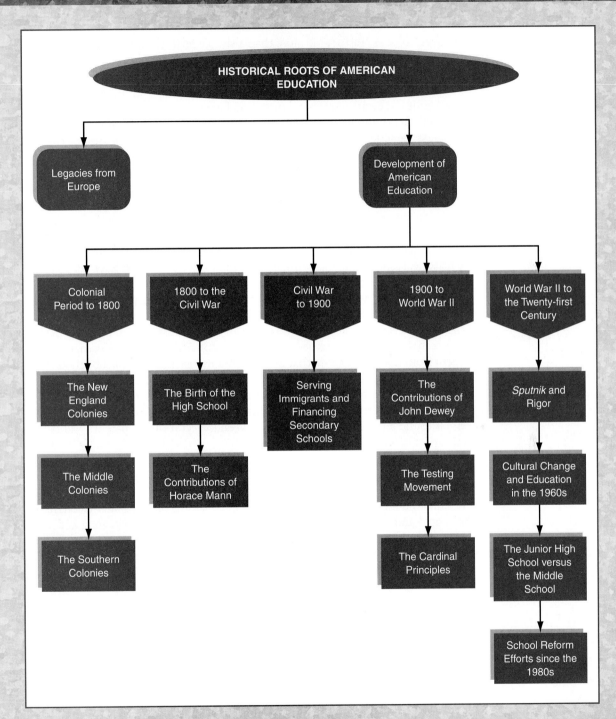

FIGURE 11.1 Historical Roots of American Education

INTRODUCTION

What is given to us as "history" is more than a simple recitation of past events. It is a presentation and analysis that is heavily influenced by the historian's beliefs, biases, and values. In the case of the history of American education, many writers have followed a tradition of presuming that today's educational system, although not perfect, is better than it has ever been. This assumption has supported historical writing that has "depicted past developments in education, especially public education, as continuous progress, beneficial to all" (Gordon & Szreter, 1989, p. 8). This kind of educational history reflects many of the biases of the majority of Americans who are White and of European descent. It acknowledges both the general "goodness" of the basic organization of education in this country and the legitimacy of the majority political power that has developed and maintained many long-standing school practices.

Few deny that the schools do reflect traditions that largely trace back to European practices; however, some educational historians today wonder whether our schools have always developed in ways that have well served *all* learners. Contemporary historical scholarship increasingly questions whether schools have adequately responded to special needs of young people from ethnic and cultural minorities.

Analysis of this issue is tricky. It is not that American educators for many years have failed to embrace the idea of serving all the children. Rather, it is a question of how their practices have actually affected young people from different groups. The key here seems to be the congruence between priorities and values learners bring with them from home and those that are reflected by teachers and in the school curriculum. Children from the majority White culture often have found the world of the school to be a simple extension of the values and priorities prized in their own families. Young people from ethnic and cultural minorities, on the other hand, have sometimes found a jarring discontinuity between expectations of parents and families and expectations of the school.

Even though schools today are much more sensitive to this problem than they were in the past, many learners from ethnic and cultural minorities do not do as well at school as their White majority age-mates. Increasingly, educators are coming to understand that "no child should have to go through the painful dilemma of choosing between family and school and of what inevitably becomes a choice between belonging and succeeding" (Nieto, 1992, p. xxv). For example, efforts are under way to examine curricular materials to eliminate negative stereotypes that can undermine the sense of self-worth for learners from certain groups. Think about how Native American youngsters must have felt not many years ago when the only textbook references to them mentioned "savages" who were introduced as obstacles to European development and progress.

Many educational historians today take pains to point out that this kind of sensitivity to ethnic and cultural differences is new. Throughout the nineteenth century and well into the twentieth century, individuals responsible for schools and school programs largely supported the idea that the majority White European-based culture was the "true" American culture; it was the task of all learners to conform to its perspectives. There was little tolerance or respect for minority culture. "Good" schools were not designed to respond to cultural differences. They were supposed to root them out and turn children from minority groups into "real" Americans (Coleman,

Video Viewpoint

The Fight Over Religion in Our Schools

WATCH: In this ABC News video segment, we examine the question of separation of church and state, and how state funding is applied to private, religious schools. Historically, the Supreme Court has upheld the separation between the two institutions. However, a recent Supreme Court decision allows public assistance to parochial schools, and some say the separation between church and state is beginning to crumble as a result.

THINK: With your classmates or in your teaching journal, consider these questions:

1. Why do you think the Supreme Court reversed its own 1985 action and ruled in favor of allowing the remedial education program to continue?
2. Do you agree with the Supreme Court's decision, and the criteria they used to judge the legality of using public funds to pay for the remedial education program in parochial schools? (The three criteria are: Does it result in government indoctrination, does it define its recipients by their religion, or does it create an excessive entanglement between government and religion?) Why or why not?
3. What do you think the implications of this court decision are for future school-based church-state jurisprudence?

LINK: How might this decision affect students across the nation in both public and private schools?

1993). As an example of this point of view, consider this statement from the 1888 annual report for a special residential school for Native Americans in which the school's superintendent lamented the negative influences on the school's children when, occasionally, they had to be allowed to leave to go home to visit their families: "Children leaving even the best training schools for their homes, like the swine, return to their wallowing filth and barbarism" (Annual Report of the Commissioner of Indian Affairs, 1888). Given such attitudes, it is not surprising that the idea that school programs should be responsive to ethnic and cultural differences was rarely discussed.

The point of this discussion is that some learners, particularly those from ethnic and cultural minorities, have not always been well served by our schools. In part, problems have stemmed from a lack of sensitivity to cultural differences. Schools *could* have modified some practices to accommodate cultural and ethnic differences years before this became a concern. There were existing educational models among Native American groups that could have been adapted in public schools that enrolled some Native American learners. There were also educational legacies from Africa, Asia, and the Hispanic world that might have been considered. It is not that such examples were not known, but rather that for many years, educational leaders considered them irrelevant.

American education developed under the assumption that "proper" and "correct" education derived from European practices. The following sections of this chapter are not intended to suggest that this was the only course that could have been taken or even that it was the most appropriate. But the reality is that the structure of today's educational enterprise is basically rooted in traditions from Europe. The

absence of information about educational models from other areas does not deni-
grate their importance. It simply reflects an educational history that for many years
failed to recognize the legitimacy of perspectives of non-European groups.

The continued growth of ethnic and cultural minorities in our schools and our increasing sensitivity to the need to develop the educational potential of each child are
encouraging more attention to the obligation to develop school programs that are responsive to the needs of all. These reforms are being inserted into an American school
system that historically did not hold responding to cultural diversity as a high priority. The difficulties that accompany these change efforts can be better understood in
the context of historical developments that have acted to shape the American system.

LEGACIES FROM EUROPE

Some things you encounter in life are so common that you may find it hard to imagine a world in which they were absent. For example, do you ever really think about
why a red light at an intersection conveys a warning to stop or why a green light
gives you permission to proceed? Why red, and why green? There is no reason that
blue and brown could not have been the colors used to control the flow of traffic.
Only long-standing tradition reinforces the nearly universal acceptance of red and
green as stop and go signals.

Commonplace assumptions about the realities that guide people's lives are
shaped by culture. Some of the things you do would appear strange to individuals
brought up in other traditions. People most frequently appreciate this point when
they find themselves cut off temporarily from their own cultural group and sur-
rounded by people who have different assumptions about how life should be lived.

Not many years ago, one of the authors found himself alone in a small community on the east coast of Korea. He witnessed women shopping in the village carefully examining live snakes in cages before purchasing one or two to take home to
prepare for the evening meal. Next to the live-snake store stood a shop selling deco-
rative lacquer-ware. In the center of the room, a large roast pig rested atop a table.
The pig's mouth was propped open to accommodate a large quantity of paper cur-
rency that had been stuffed between its teeth. To American eyes, housewives calmly
purchasing live snakes for supper and a knickknack shop featuring a roast pig with a
mouthful of money might seem unusual. To the residents of this small village, however, these events were just an unremarkable part of their everyday lives.

Lots of school practices are so familiar that many people can hardly imagine alternative ways of doing things. Many of your own assumptions about schools and
schooling probably reflect long-standing cultural choices. For example, chances are
that you have never worried excessively about any of the following ideas characteristic of American education:

- Content should be organized under major categories or headings.
- Knowledge should be divided among individual subjects.
- Teaching should occur in a setting that brings young people together in
  groups for instructional purposes.
- Schools should be organized into a sequence of grades.

What Do You Think?

Should Schools Attempt to Solve Social Problems?

The following editorial recently appeared in an educational journal:

Pick up any newspaper and somewhere you'll find at least one article on a difficult *problème du jour*. Some favorites are drug abuse, crime prevention, sexism, increasing incivility, alcohol abuse, gang violence, and sexually-transmitted diseases. After the usual hand-wringing about how much worse things are today than they used to be, the conclusion typically is that 'kids need to be taught more about _____ (insert your favorite intractable problem here).' There it is . . . the rosy assumption that a few good lessons in schools will 'solve' a problem that has defied the collective ministrations of our entire society.

This kind of expectation of the schools must stop. Education, after all, is as influenced by forces shaping undesirable behaviors as every other institution. The belief that schools can turn around major social problems is illusory. Further, by accepting responsibility for 'curing' major social ills, the schools excuse other agencies from an obligation to be part of the solution. Finally, making schools social reform agencies diverts them away from their primary and proper mission: the education of young people.

What Do You Think?

1. Why do people concerned about difficult social problems so often think schools can solve them?
2. Should schools be concerned about (a) no social problems, (b) some social problems, or (c) all social problems?
3. Suppose you were to write a letter to the editor of the journal that published this editorial. What would you say?

- As many people as possible should be educated.
- Individual differences should be considered by teachers in planning instruction.
- Schools should help learners develop rational thinking processes.
- Teachers should have some kind of specialized training.
- Schooling should be a preparation for responsible citizenship.
- Schooling should provide young people with some understandings and skills needed in the adult workplace.

Where did these ideas originate? For the most part, they evolved over the centuries from educational practices in Europe. The thinkers of ancient Greece, for example, developed the idea that knowledge could be organized into categories and that logical, rational thinking processes were important. The emphasis on education for citizenship likewise has roots in the concern of the ancient Athenians for producing adult citizens who could participate in democratic decision making.

The ancient Romans were very concerned that young people receive a practical education that would provide them with "useful" knowledge. This perspective is one that many present-day Americans share. The Romans, too, debated the question of whether harsh punishment for students was needed or whether gentler, more sensitive approaches made sense. Americans today also debate this issue.

Following the Web 11.1

International Roots

The Web provides a rich diversity of sites with information about development of educational practices in countries outside of the United States. Here are some examples that you might like to visit.

 For hot links to these sites, visit the companion Web site, located at *http://www. prenhall.com/armstrong*. Select Chapter 11 from the front page of the Web site, then choose the Following the Web module on the navigation bar on the left side of the page.

Bibliography of Childhood in Antiquity

- *http://faculty.biu.ac.il/~barilm/bibchild.html*

  This site provides an extensive listing of books and articles dealing with children in the ancient world, particularly Greece and Rome. Over 40 titles are represented, and they include works published in many different countries.

Children in the Past

- *http://www.schoolnet.ca/collections/huronia/KIDS/KIDS.htm*

  This site also deals with children in the past. However, the focus is on much more recent times . . . the early years of the twentieth century. There are interesting old photos of children and school buildings in Canada's Ontario province.

The Life of a Child in Elizabethan England

- *http://www.twingroves.district96.k12.il.us/Renaissance/Town/Children.html*

  This outstanding site features information about many aspects of children's lives in Elizabethan times. Among topics you will find treated are (1) clothing, (2) role at home, and (3) games. You can download a video that illustrates how children played with juggling sticks.

Important work on the development of knowledge into individual subject areas occurred during the Middle Ages. The tradition of churches taking responsibility for secular education also traces to this period. American parochial schools continue this legacy.

Today's concern for universal education is a continuation of a trend that became pronounced during the Reformation. Many church leaders during this period believed that the Bible was the repository of all wisdom; hence, it was desirable for as many people as possible to learn to read so they would have access to its truths. Somewhat later during the Renaissance, a growing emphasis on the worth and the importance of the individual evolved. It is from this perspective that our schools' concern for meeting individual differences developed.

In the seventeenth century, the work of Francis Bacon and others established the idea that truth could be challenged and modified through observation and careful weighing of evidence. This provided the foundation for the modern scientific method, something that continues to be enormously important in today's schools. Another great influence on the development of education in Europe and later in the

Basic Education in Africa

- *http://www.jica.go.jp/E-info/E-subsahara/MBp001.html*

  Materials on the history of education in Africa are scarce. At this site you will find good information organized under the three general time periods of (1) the pre-colonial period, (2) the colonial period, and (3) the period since independence.

A Comparison of Attitudes of the Philosophical Radicals and Socialists Toward Universal Education in Early Nineteenth-Century England

- *http://home.sprynet.com/sprynet/rlgreen/eps312r4.htm*

  Information at this site provides a good reminder that the idea of education for everyone once was highly controversial. You will find here some quite differing views by two groups that favored universal education in principle. However, one of these factions cautioned against allowing too many people to become "independent thinkers" out of a fear that large numbers of such individuals would threaten England's economic institutions.

The History of Education Site

- *http://www.socsci.kun.nl/ped/whp/histeduc/*

  This site is maintained by the University of Nijmegen in the Netherlands. It serves as an important archive for information about the history of education and the history of childhood. You will be able to use a special search feature that allows you to pursue topics of interest that are included within the extensive electronic holdings maintained here.

[Note: Web addresses change frequently. If you are unable to locate one of these sites using the listed URL, try putting the site name in a standard search engine.]

United States was John Amos Comenius. Among his many contributions was the idea of organizing learning into sequential, graded schools and of viewing education as something that should prepare people for happy lives.

The famous eighteenth-century educator Johann Heinrich Pestalozzi suggested that education could be an agent to improve society. While this was a revolutionary idea at the time, today it has become an article of faith among many Americans. No matter what intractable social problem is garnering headlines at a given moment, one predictable response by some to the problem is that more education is needed. Pestalozzi would have agreed. Pestalozzi also introduced the idea that teachers should be provided with special kinds of training.

The nineteenth century witnessed a wave of interest in education throughout Europe that resulted in widespread establishment of mandatory public school systems by the end of the century. The importance of educating young learners was recognized by Friedrich Froebel, who is regarded as the "father of the kindergarten." The idea of preparing systematic formal lesson plans was introduced by another nineteenth-century

Friedrich Froebel is remembered as the "father of the kindergarten." This early kindergarten is an example of many that were established as a result of his work.

educator, Johann Herbart. His scheme looks remarkably similar to many lesson planning formats used by teachers today. The nineteenth century also witnessed a tremendous growth of interest in the importance of the psychology of learning.

As you read material in the sections that follow, bear in mind that many assumptions that came to be reflected in American schools developed from practices that first appeared in Europe. European settlers of North America brought these perspectives with them. Because the population of today's schools is becoming more culturally diverse, the appropriateness of these European-based models is increasingly being debated. Should there be changes in our schools to better meet the needs of more diverse learners? Or can most existing practices be modified? These are questions you, as a future educator, will be asked to consider.

DEVELOPMENT OF AMERICAN EDUCATION

A study of the history of American education reveals that at different times, people have had vastly different expectations of what educators should emphasize. Varying expectations have led to quite different views regarding characteristics of a good school. Differing patterns of educational development over time have resulted in diverse answers to these key questions:

- What is the most important purpose of education?
- Who is to be educated?
- What are learners expected to take away from their educational experiences?
- How are learners to be educated?

As you read about the development of American education, think about how these questions might have been addressed at different periods in history. An understanding of changing perspectives on these issues will help you better understand positions in today's debates about educational policies and practices.

Colonial Period to 1800

The New England Colonies　Some familiarity with conditions in sixteenth- and seventeenth-century England will help you understand the nature of American education as it developed in New England during the colonial period. In England at that time, there was little room for open discussion of alternatives to the established Church of England. Because it was the official church of the English government, people who espoused religious views in opposition to those of the Church of England were considered by governmental officials to be disloyal not only to the church, but also to the state. In effect, the Church of England was seen as an extension of the legal authority of the government. Consequently, religious dissidents were dealt with harshly. The official view was that such people might represent a subversive threat to the power of the crown.

Views of the Puritans.　Political problems in England for groups such as the Puritans, who wanted to reform the policies of the Church of England, led them to develop an interest in emigrating to the New World. Equally important was their fear of remaining in England and exposing their children to what they considered to be the religious errors of the Church of England. The intransigent Puritans had definite ideas about what religious beliefs and practices should be and by no means were a tolerant people. (Witness, for example their persecution of the nonconforming Roger Williams. In the 1630s, Williams found it necessary to flee to the wilds of Rhode Island to escape the wrath of intolerant Massachusetts Puritans who objected to his open support for the idea that church and state should be separate.) Once they left England, those Puritans who settled in New England sought to establish a church and government different from those in England. Their belief that their own church and government were more consistent with the Bible's teachings had important educational implications.

The Puritans saw the Bible as the source of all wisdom. As a result, they placed a high priority on developing an educational system that would enable large numbers of people to read "God's Holy Word." The Bible, as the Puritans interpreted it, outlined a specific type of preferred government for both church and state. This contrasted importantly with practices in England, where authority in the Church of

Critical Incident

Why Study in High School?

"OK, OK. I grant you, we've tried hard to accommodate every group in the country. We've studied our history. Our intentions have been good. We've got this really complex system of elementary school, middle schools, junior high schools, senior high schools, community colleges, and four-year colleges and universities. We've had experts look at every imaginable educational question. But something is still screwed up. Some of our best kids just aren't responding in the right ways. It's really frustrating." Eric Blanton, having delivered himself of this pronouncement, slumped wearily into one of the old vinyl-covered chairs in the Ryerson High School faculty lounge.

From across the room, Suyanna Muyami, the head of the English department, looked up. "OK, Eric, what is it today—taxes, our corrupt politicians, or one of the kids?"

"Oh, I'll be all right, but I've been going round and round again with Roy Flynn. The kid is so bright, but he's just doing nothing, absolutely nothing. He gives things a nice once-over-lightly before the tests and manages to get grades just high enough to squeak by. He'll graduate, but just barely. What really gets to me is that he could be a contender for top academic honors if he would just care."

"If school doesn't turn him on, what does?" asked Suyanna. "Is it the usual love affair with a car?"

"That's exactly it," replied Eric. "He's working 20 and more hours a week to keep it in gasoline."

"And I suppose you've been trying to point out the error of his ways, the tragedy of wasting his God-given talent—all the usual arguments we trot out. Right?"

"Well, yes," responded Eric. "And it makes me mad that he's got all this talent and that he's just tossing it away. Just a few minutes ago I sat him down and tried to have a heart-to-heart with him about his future. The kid's sharp. He has an answer for every argument. What makes me mad is that we've set up a system in this country that encourages insightful kids like Eric to see high school as play time."

"What do you mean?" Suyanna asked.

"Well, I gave him the usual pitch about not preparing himself for college and that his grades are going to make it difficult for him to be admitted to many four-year colleges and uni-

England was highly centralized, and few decisions were left to the discretion of members of individual churches. The Puritans, however, believed that the Bible promoted a different organizational structure. In their view, power should be exercised by local church congregations, and the Puritans' churches in Massachusetts reflected this pattern. Such beliefs also helped establish the more general principle of local control over civil as well as religious affairs. It was out of this context that the tradition of local control of education evolved.

New England School Legislation.   Concern for education in Massachusetts was demonstrated in the Massachusetts School Law of 1642. This law charged local magistrates with the responsibility of ensuring that parents would not neglect the education of their children. Although the law itself did not provide for the establishment of schools, it did require that children attend schools. It represented the first attempt

versities. He had an answer for that one all figured out. He knows that any community college in the state will take him, no questions asked, once he finishes high school. He says he'll dig into the academics, get grades, and transfer to a good four-year school. And, you know, the system will allow him to do just that."

Suyanna followed Eric's thoughts with interest. "What do you conclude from all this?"

"I conclude," Eric replied, "that we have a system that sends bad signals to some of our brightest kids. They should be studying hard in high school. But why should they? The way things are now, it almost makes sense for these kids to see high school as goof-off time. I mean, we've arranged things so they can always get their academic act together later on."

"Fine, but what's the answer?" questioned Suyanna. "Should we get rid of our community colleges? Just a hint, Eric—that's not going to happen. So, what's your next move with Roy?"

. . .

What does Eric see as the problem? What alternatives does he see? What assumptions does he have about what high school students should value? How does he respond to this situation in light of these assumptions? Are there other responses that might have made sense? Which alternatives might you recommend, and why? How would your suggestions "connect" to what Roy Flynn believes is important in life?

Can you think of examples of incentives in our system that encourage learners to behave in ways you think are inappropriate? What historical situations might have led to the adoption of policies and practices that resulted in these incentives? Did these incentives come into being as a result of conscious acts, or were they unintended side effects of policies and procedures developed for other purposes?

To respond to this Critical Incident online, and to save or submit your response electronically, visit the companion Web site, located at *http://www.prenhall.com/armstrong*. Select Chapter 11 from the front page of the Web site, then choose the Critical Incidents module on the navigation bar on the left side of the page. Instructors and students may also wish to use these scenarios as discussion topics on the Message Board for the companion Web site.

in America to make school attendance compulsory. Reflecting the local-control tradition, this law placed responsibility for enforcement at the local rather than the state level.

The law of 1642 was extended by the famous "Old Deluder Satan Act" of 1647. The name was derived from wording in the act that promoted education as a buffer against Satan's wiles. The law required every town of 50 or more families to hire a teacher of reading or writing. The teacher was to be paid by either the community or parents of the learners. This act represented an early legislative attempt to establish the principle of public responsibility for education.

During the seventeenth century, concern for publicly supported education referred only to the very basic education of young children; few learners attended secondary schools. However, small numbers of secondary schools did come into being during the seventeenth century. One of the most famous of them was the

Boston Latin Grammar School, founded in 1635. This school had a specific purpose: preparation of boys for Harvard. The curriculum consisted of difficult academic subjects, including Latin, Greek, and theology.

The Middle Colonies   Most Puritan settlers of New England came from an area in eastern England known as East Anglia, where opposition to the Church of England was strongest. Many of these Puritan settlers came to the New World during the period of 1629–1641 (Fischer, 1989). People who settled the middle colonies of New York, New Jersey, Delaware, and Pennsylvania, however, came from different places than the Puritans and were also a more diverse group. Some of these settlers were descendants of the Dutch and Swedes who originally occupied parts of New York. Many English Quakers came to the New World during the 50 years between 1675 and 1725, and a majority of them settled in Pennsylvania. These immigrants came mostly from the northern Midlands of England and Wales, an area completely different from the East Anglican homeland of many of the Puritans. Western and frontier areas of the middle colonies were largely settled by people originally from the north of England, Scotland, and Ireland during a period extending approximately from 1717 to 1775 (Fischer, 1989).

Not surprisingly, given the mixed origins of the population, patterns of schooling in the middle colonies were varied. For example, merchants in New York sponsored private schools that emphasized commercial subjects thought necessary for young people who would play future roles in business and trade. In contrast, the Pennsylvania Quakers maintained schools that were open to all children. These Quaker schools were notable for their willingness to recognize the educational needs and rights of African Americans, Native Americans, and other groups that usually were not encouraged (and often not allowed) to attend school.

The Franklin Academy.   Benjamin Franklin was among the first to give American education a practical orientation. In his 1749 work, *Proposals Relating to the Youth of Pennsylvania,* Franklin proposed a new kind of school, oriented to the "real" world, that would be free of all religious ties. Two years later, he established the Franklin Academy, an institution that was nonsectarian and offered such practical subjects as mathematics, astronomy, navigation, and bookkeeping. By the end of the Revolutionary War, the Franklin Academy had replaced the Boston Latin Grammar School as the most important secondary school in America. Students at the Franklin Academy were able to make some choices about their course of study, thus setting the pattern of elective courses common in high schools today.

For all its strengths, relatively few learners attended the Franklin Academy. It was a private school, and tuition was beyond the means of most families. However, the establishment of the Franklin Academy directed a great deal of attention to the importance of secondary education. This interest was reflected in the subsequent establishment of many other private academies.

Contributions of the Academies.   Private academies popularized the idea that secondary education had something important to offer, and they laid the foundation for public support of secondary schools. Collectively, the academies helped establish the following important precedents for American education:

- American education would have a strong orientation toward the practical rather than the purely intellectual or theoretical.
- American education would be nonsectarian.
- American education would feature diverse course offerings.

The Southern Colonies   A revolution in England in the late 1640s resulted in victory for the side supporting Parliament and the Puritans against the king and the established Church of England. King Charles I was executed, and for a dozen years, England existed as a Puritan-controlled commonwealth governed for much of this time by Oliver Cromwell as Lord Protector. This was an especially dangerous period for large landowners, members of the nobility, and others who had supported King Charles I and wanted the monarchy restored (something that was finally achieved in 1660 when Charles II assumed the throne).

Because of dangers in England, many supporters of the king's cause migrated to the New World, often settling in the southern colonies of Maryland, Virginia, North Carolina, South Carolina, and Georgia. Large numbers of these settlers came from the southwestern part of England, an area different from both the East Anglican homeland of the Puritans and the northern Midland, northern English, Scottish, and Irish homelands of most of those who settled the middle colonies (Fischer, 1989).

Settlement in the southern colonies was distributed along rivers. There were few towns, and families tended to be separated by considerable distances. Under these conditions, it was difficult to gather sufficient numbers of children in one place to establish schools. Wealthy families hired tutors for their children. People in these colonies continued to identify very strongly with upper-class English values, and they often sent their sons to England to be educated in English schools. Education in these colonies was generally restricted to children of wealthy landowners; little schooling was available for those from less affluent families.

1800 to the Civil War

During the first 20 years of the nineteenth century, few educational innovations were introduced. American society was consumed with challenges such as settling the nation and providing workers for the nation's growing industries. There was more interest in getting young people into the workforce than in providing them with opportunities for extensive education. Schooling beyond rudimentary elementary instruction was generally available only to children of families who were able to pay for this privilege and who did not need the income that a young person could generate. Proposals for an educational system that was universal and free were only beginning to be discussed.

The Birth of the High School   In the early nineteenth century, only a few students attended secondary schools. The most popular secondary school continued to be the academy, which responded well to an American educational bias in favor of preparing learners for practical problem solving and work rather than for a life of scholarship. Many new academies came into being during the first half of the nineteenth century. By 1850, when the number of academies reached its peak, over six thousand were in operation (Barry, 1961).

Although the academies were highly regarded, they had an important drawback. Overwhelmingly, they were private tuition-charging institutions. This limited their learner population, as only young people from families that were relatively well off could attend. Gradually, people became convinced that larger numbers of young people than were being accommodated by the private academies could profit from secondary-level education. This recognition led to support for a new institution—the public high school.

The first public high school, the Boston English Classical School, was established in 1821. The school's courses closely paralleled the practical curriculum of most academies. The idea of public high schools did not catch on quickly, however. In 1860, there were only 40 in the entire country (Barry, 1961). It was not until 1900 that the number of public high schools surpassed the number of academies that had existed in 1850 (Barry, 1961).

Contributions of Horace Mann   During the 1820s, Horace Mann began to make his views known. Elected to the Massachusetts legislature in 1827, Mann was an eloquent speaker who took up the cause of the *common school* for the average Amer-

Horace Mann helped convince American taxpayers that it was in their best interests to support public schools.

ican. Mann's mission was to convince taxpayers that it was in their own interest to support the establishment of a system of public education. He pointed out that public schools would turn out educated young people whose skills would ultimately result in improved living standards for all. In Mann's view, the school was a springboard for opportunity and an institution capable of equalizing differences among people from different social classes.

Mann's arguments were persuasive. In 1837, Massachusetts established a State Board of Education. Horace Mann gave up his career in politics to become its first secretary. In time, Mann's views attracted the attention of people throughout the entire country.

In addition to his interest in encouraging people to get behind the idea of publicly supported schools, Mann also recognized the importance of improving teachers' qualifications. In response to this concern, the nation's first *normal school* (an institution specifically designed to train people to teach) was established in 1839. In the beginning, these normal schools provided only one or two years of formal education for those wishing to become teachers. Their importance is the precedent they set for formalizing the education of future teachers. Certification of teachers, a process that took years to develop, traces back to Mann's interest in setting standards for teachers. For more information, see Figure 11.2.

Prompted by Mann's work, public schools began to be established throughout the country. By 1860, 50.6% of the nation's children were enrolled in public school programs (U.S. Department of Commerce, 1975). A majority of states had formalized the development of free school systems, including elementary schools, secondary schools, and public universities. In 1867, a National Department of Education was established as part of the federal government. By the late 1860s, many of the basic patterns of American education were in place. That these patterns continue is a tribute to the vision, patience, and political skills of Horace Mann.

Horace Mann was a strong believer in normal schools, institutions specifically designed to prepare teachers. The first normal school was established in 1839. Even though many people supported the logic of providing special training for teachers and certifying them before they were allowed to work, these innovations were slow to be adopted. Stringent certification requirements did not become universal until the 1930s and 1940s.

All states had normal schools by the year 1900, but few required teachers to be graduates of these institutions. The state with the strictest regulations regarding teachers' entry into the profession was Massachusetts, which required them to have a high school diploma and two years of formal teacher training. Every other state had less stringent requirements.

As late as 1921, only four states required prospective teachers to have completed formal training programs. In that year, there were 14 states where people could qualify for a teaching credential with no more training than four years of high school. Some of these 14 states required teachers to have only an eighth-grade education. In 1921, there were 31 states with *no* official academic requirements for awarding a teaching credential (Bowen, 1981).

FIGURE 11.2 Certifying Teachers: An Innovation That Was Slow to Take Root

Civil War to 1900

The post–Civil War years were characterized by unparalleled industrial growth. Technological innovations reduced the need for unskilled labor. The resulting demand for workers who had knowledge that was of value in the workplace intensified interest in the vocational-preparation function of education.

Serving Immigrants and Financing Secondary Schools   Huge numbers of immigrants entered the United States during this period. These people needed both useful work skills and an orientation to the values of their new country. These needs placed new demands on educators, and there was a great increase in the number of schools. The schools these young people attended were eager to "Americanize" newcomers, and many immigrant learners were exposed to school programs that made light of or even fun of their native cultures and languages. There can be no doubt that American public schools exacted a psychological toll on many of the immigrant children who came into the country during this period.

In the realm of school financing, the famous Kalamazoo case (*Stuart v. School District No. 1 of the Village of Kalamazoo,* 30 Mich. 69 [1874]) resulted in a ruling that the state legislature had the right to pass laws levying taxes for the support of *both* elementary and secondary schools. This ruling established a legal precedent for public funding of secondary schools. As a result, there was a dramatic increase in the total number of schools and in the total number of learners who were enrolled as districts began to build many more secondary schools. Because of a widespread desire to provide older learners with "useful" educational experiences, many secondary schools broadened their curricula to include more practical, work-related subjects.

Influences of Professional Organizations   Organizational activity among teachers increased during this period. Prior to 1900, organizations that were the forerunners of today's American Federation of Teachers and National Education Association were established (see Chapter 2 for some more detailed information about these groups). Reports of such groups as the NEA's Committee of Ten and the Committee on College Entrance Requirements began to influence public school curricula. In the last decade of the nineteenth century, these groups acknowledged that schools should provide some services to learners with varied academic and career goals, but nevertheless suggested that preparation for college and university study was the primary purpose of high schools. This orientation represented a temporary reversal of a century-long trend to view secondary education as a provider of more practical kinds of learning experiences.

1900 to World War II

During the first two decades of the twentieth century, the conflict between those who viewed the high school as an institution to serve college-bound learners and those who viewed it as an institution to prepare young people for the workplace was resolved by a compromise. This compromise was a new conception of the high school as a "comprehensive" institution that would include curricula directed at pro-

Interiors of many schools in the late 19th century were very plain. Note the total absence of decoration in this classroom.

viding both academic and work-oriented instruction. Debate about how much weight should be given to each of these emphases continues even today.

Toward the end of the nineteenth century, there was a recognition that many of the increasing number of learners who were entering high schools were having difficulty doing the required work. Some individuals who studied this problem concluded that something needed to be done to ease learners' transition from elementary schools to high schools. A new institution that came to be known as the *junior high school* was the proposed solution.

The first junior high school was established in Berkeley, California in 1909. The Berkeley school district developed a 6-3-3 plan of school organization that, in time, came to be widely copied elsewhere (Popper, 1967). The first six grades comprised the elementary program, the next three grades the junior high school program, and the final three years the senior high school program.

The number of public schools and of learners attending them increased tremendously during the first four decades of the twentieth century. Schooling became almost universal during this period. In 1900, only 50.5 percent of young people in the 5- to 20-year-old age group were in school, but by 1940, 74.8 percent of this age group were enrolled (U.S. Department of Commerce, 1975). Given the tremendous growth in the total United States population between 1900 and 1940, these figures indicate that millions more children were served by schools in 1940 than in 1900.

John Dewey   An individual who had a tremendous influence on education during this period was John Dewey (1859–1952), whose work continues to affect educational thought and practice. Dewey viewed education as a process through which young people are brought to fully participate in society. He saw the primary goal of education as that of promoting growth and development of the individual. Hence, school should not set out to serve the goals of society (for example, turning out electrical engineers if the society is short of them) at the cost of overlooking the unique needs of individual learners. Schools, Dewey believed, should produce secure human beings who leave school committed to their own continuing self-education.

Dewey believed that every learner actively attempts to explore and understand the environment. Because of this, Dewey argued, learners need intellectual tools that they can use to make sound judgments about those things they encounter. They need to be familiar with thinking processes that can be applied to any unfamiliar situation. Dewey maintained that it was much more important for learners to master systematic thinking processes than to know specific items of information. Thinking processes can be applied universally, but a specific item of information often has little value beyond the context in which it is learned.

The thought process that Dewey felt learners should master was the scientific problem-solving method. He believed that familiarity with this method would give young people confidence in their abilities to develop rational responses to dilemmas they would face throughout their lives. Interest in teaching problem-solving techniques and a commitment to responding to individual differences still feature prominently in American schools today.

Testing Movement   Schools today also continue to be influenced by an early twentieth-century movement that first developed in France. Education in France became compulsory in 1904. At that time, a special commission was established there to identify those young people who might benefit from regular instruction in public schools and those who would be better off in special classes. To help with this identification, in 1905 Alfred Binet and his associates developed a test called the *intelligence quotient* (IQ) test that was designed to predict learners' likelihood of success in regular school classrooms. Soon educators from other countries, including the United States, were seeking information about ways to measure intelligence. It is interesting that a test designed to predict school success was viewed almost immediately as a test of intelligence. The presumption was that the school program had been designed so that the most intelligent would do the best. (Today, this idea is debated. Some people, for example, argue that the "most intelligent" learners resist school rules and procedures and do not do well.)

The testing movement in the United States grew during World War I. The military needed a system that could be used to identify individuals who would be suited to a variety of necessary tasks. Intelligence tests were developed that were believed to provide information that could be used to classify individuals by intelligence. At the time they were initially developed, few people doubted that the scores yielded by these tests represented a highly reliable measure of intelligence.

Some of these early intelligence tests were given to European immigrants. Immigrants from western Europe did better than immigrants from eastern Europe.

(This was hardly a surprising development because most tests were developed by western Europeans or Americans trained by western Europeans.) There is some evidence that laws passed by Congress restricting numbers of immigrants from eastern Europe resulted from dissemination of these score differences. This might be one of the first examples of the cultural bias that can be embedded within tests of this sort.

During and after World War I, the testing movement was embraced by educators. It became common for learners to be classified and counseled into certain courses on the basis of their IQ scores. There is evidence the patterns of interaction of some teachers with individual learners were affected by their perception of these learners' intelligence as revealed by IQ scores.

In recent years, the use of intelligence tests, particularly paper-and-pencil group intelligence tests, has been challenged. The issue of cultural bias has been raised by African Americans, Hispanics, and other minorities. Some people have argued that a factor as broad and diffuse as intelligence cannot possibly be measured by a single test. There have been instances in which perfectly normal young people have been assigned to institutions for the mentally retarded on the basis of a faulty IQ score obtained from a group intelligence test. The debate about intelligence testing continues. Although there is not a consensus on this issue, it is fair to say that educators are becoming increasingly hesitant to predict the educational futures of young people on the basis of a single measure such as an IQ score.

Cardinal Principles   As special circumstances and needs associated with the wartime situation expanded interest in the testing movement during the World War I years, people also became concerned about education's more general purposes. In particular, the last year of war, 1918, was a landmark one for education. In this year, the National Education Association's Commission on the Reorganization of Secondary Education identified seven specific goals for the public schools. These seven goals, which came to be known as education's "Cardinal Principles," are:

- health,
- command of fundamental processes,
- worthy home membership,
- vocational preparation,
- citizenship,
- worthy use of leisure time, and
- ethical character.

These principles laid the groundwork for the comprehensive high school. They implied that secondary schools should have a broader purpose than simply preparing learners for colleges and universities. In time, publication of the Cardinal Principles led to an expansion of course offerings in high schools. By no means, however, did all high schools give equal emphasis to each of the many subjects that came to be offered; in many, considerable attention (critics would say too much attention) continued to be given to college and university preparatory courses.

Changes in the schools wrought by both attention to the Cardinal Principles and actions taken by groups looking for a more practical emphasis in the curriculum suggested that ever more people were viewing education as a necessity for all young people. Compulsory attendance laws became common during the first two decades of the twentieth century. Increasingly, learners were being required to stay in school until they turned 16.

In the 1920s and 1930s, the influence of those who wanted schools to respond humanely to the needs and interests of individual learners was strong. The term *progressive education movement* has been applied to the general program of people who sought these goals. Supporters of the progressive education movement drew inspiration from the work of John Dewey. The installation of counseling programs in schools, for example, which developed at an especially rapid rate during the 1930s, represented a logical extension of Dewey's concern for individual development.

World War II to the Twenty-First Century

After World War II, the progressive education movement developed into a loosely knit group of people who supported school practices that came to be known as *life-adjustment education.* In some of its more extreme forms, life-adjustment education programs seemed to encourage learners to do whatever they pleased. Systematic attention to intellectual rigor or subject matter was avoided. Critics of such programs suggested that learners were being shortchanged by schools that failed to provide needed understandings and skills. These critics attracted many supporters, and by the middle 1950s, support for life-adjustment education had greatly diminished.

***Sputnik* and Rigor**   Rarely can change in education (or, indeed, in other social institutions) be attributed to a single event. But in the fall of 1957, the Soviet Union's launch of the first earth satellite, *Sputnik,* so changed the public's perception of education's role that many subsequent alterations in school curricula can be traced back to this single, seminal event. *Sputnik* shocked the nation by challenging America's presumed technological supremacy. Those people looking for an explanation for why the Soviet Union was first with such an accomplishment placed a great deal of blame on public education. Large audiences listened sympathetically to critics who told them that American schools had gone soft and that instruction in subject-matter content compared unfavorably with that provided to learners in other countries. Instruction in the sciences was identified as a particularly weak area of the curriculum.

Reacting to pressures to "do something" about the schools, the federal government passed the National Defense Education Act in 1958. This legislation provided federal funds to improve the quality of education. Large-scale curriculum reform projects were launched, first in mathematics and the sciences and later in the social sciences. Special summer workshops designed to upgrade teachers' skills were held on college campuses across the nation. There was a massive effort to improve the quality of textbooks and other instructional materials. People carried high hopes that this revolution in American school programming could be carried to a successful conclusion.

Cultural Change and Education in the 1960s   Although the curriculum reform movement of the 1960s did result in important changes, the modifications fell well short of the expectations of many who had supported passage of the

National Defense Education Act. Teachers who attended summer programs became proficient in the use of new techniques and materials, but only a small minority of all teachers participated in such programs. Others who did not take part found themselves ill at ease with many of the new programs, and a majority of teachers continued doing things much as they had always done them.

Another problem involved the new instructional materials themselves. Many were developed by subject-matter experts who had little experience working with public school learners. Consequently, some of the new materials were written at reading levels that were too difficult for many learners. Further, the issue of motivation was not addressed well. Many young people were simply not interested in some of the new instructional materials.

Probably the changing national culture of the 1960s did more than anything else to subvert those changes being pushed by people who wanted to introduce more "intellectual rigor" into school programs. With growing discontent over official governmental policies toward Vietnam and frustrations of minorities in the nation's large cities, the ground was not fertile for changes that appeared to critics to be an effort to push "establishment" values on the young. Increasingly, young people questioned the relevance of school curricula that seemed to favor esoteric intellectual subjects rather than topics of more immediate personal concern.

Junior High School versus Middle School

After World War II, concerns increased about the junior high school as an institution. Many people had originally hoped that junior high schools would be particularly sensitive to the emotional and developmental needs of early adolescents. Over time, however, a majority of junior high schools came to be organized as academic preparatory institutions for the high schools. In reaction to this trend, middle schools started to grow tremendously in popularity.

While the middle school movement first attracted large numbers of supporters during the 1960s, this interest continued throughout the 1970s, 1980s, and on into the 1990s. Individual middle schools often have one of several different grade-level organizational patterns. Generally, a middle school has three to five grades and almost always includes grades six and seven (Lounsbury & Vars, 1978). The National Middle School Association and other supporters of middle schools emphasize programs that are sensitive to the special characteristics of learners in the 11- to 14-year-old age group. Today, middle schools have displaced junior high schools as the dominant school type for learners between their elementary and high school years.

School Reform Efforts Since the 1980s

Beginning in the early 1980s, concerns about the quality of American schools led to a period of intense public scrutiny of school programs. There were concerns about the sophistication of thinking being developed by school programs, the readiness of graduates to assume jobs requiring ever more complex levels of technical proficiency, general reading and writing abilities of learners, patterns of scores on academic achievement tests, and unfavorable achievement comparisons between American learners and those in other nations.

A number of major themes have appeared consistently in recommendations to improve the schools that have been broadly circulated since the early 1980s. There has been a frequent call for school programs to become more rigorous. At the high school level, this recommendation has sometimes taken the form of a proposal to reduce the number of electives and to require all learners to take a common core of content drawn from the academic disciplines.

Recommendations have also addressed the issue of teacher quality. There have been suggestions of various ways to attract brighter, more committed people to teaching and to improve the duration and quality of their preparation (The Holmes Group, 1986). There also has been a recognition that quality people will not remain in the profession unless there are accompanying efforts to improve teachers' working conditions (including higher salaries and empowering teachers to make more decisions about how they discharge their responsibilities).

The issue of school administrative organization has also been addressed. There have been recommendations to decrease sizes of schools to allow for more personal attention to learners. There have also been suggestions that principals spend more time in their role as instructional leaders than in their role as business managers. Additionally, there have been proposals to lengthen the school year to make it conform more to those in countries where learners are doing better on content achievement tests than their United States counterparts.

In the past decade, discussion of educational improvement has been stimulated by reports of interested national groups and federal government action as well as by increased local interest in providing parents with more choices regarding how and where their children are educated. National efforts have included work of members of The Education Commission of the States and the National Governors' Association. Their work has focused attention on such issues as kinds of school programming that should be provided for students not going on to colleges and universities, improving the technological literacy of graduates of American schools, and enhancing student learning of traditional academic subjects.

These efforts have spawned an interest in many issues. These include (1) attempts to involve local communities and schools in implementing programs responsive to various federal initiatives; (2) emphasis on various approaches to school choice, including voucher plans, open-enrollment plans, magnet schools, and charter schools; (3) increased interest in school-business partnerships; and (4) recognition that it may be necessary to establish full-service schools to respond to the varied needs many learners bring with them to school. A theme running through all of these proposals is that reform needs to be *systemic*. That is, problems are multiple and diverse, and no single one can be solved without careful attention to the entire spectrum of difficulties facing schools and children.

Professional-development schools represent an example of an attempt to respond simultaneously to several pressing educational issues. Specifically, they are designed to house activities that bring building-level teachers, building-level administrators, university teacher-education specialists, and prospective teachers together for the purposes of:

- preparing prospective teachers in realistic environments that will enable them to move smoothly from the world of the university to the world of public school teaching;

- establishing policies and procedures related to teacher preparation, staff development, and general school improvement that are framed collaboratively by administrators, teachers, and university specialists;
- developing and implementing staff-development programs that are responsive to an individual school's special needs; and
- generating and pursuing school-based research agendas that result in the study and solution of problems of individual schools.

Prospective teachers in professional-development schools typically spend more time working in the schools than those who enrolled in the more traditional student-teaching programs that were the norm a decade ago (Innerst, 1998). Teachers and administrators in these programs play much more active roles in shaping experiences of future educators than was true in the past. Research studies are beginning to confirm that there are important benefits associated with the approach of professional-development schools. One recent study found that teachers in training who were prepared in professional-development schools performed better in three key areas at the end of their preparation programs than others prepared in more traditional programs. They (1) had better classroom-management skills, (2) used technology more effectively, and (3) engaged in more reflective classroom practice (Neubert & Binko, 1998). These results are beginning to build a case in support of the idea that professional-development schools are a systemic response to reform that works.

Professional-development schools and other attempts to achieve educational reform attest to a growing public interest in education. You will be entering the teaching profession during an exciting period when more and more people believe that the quality of public schools will determine the quality of our nation's future.

Key Ideas In Summary

- The history of American education, as is the case with all history, reflects values and biases of those who have written it. Since the majority of Americans are White and of European descent, it is not surprising that much educational history fails to question the appropriateness for *all* American children of educational practices rooted in traditions from Europe. In times past, some instruction in American schools failed to provide positive models for learners from minority cultures. Educators today are increasingly sensitive to this issue.
- Among educational practices and assumptions that trace their origins to Europe are (1) the idea that content should be organized under major headings, (2) the practice of dividing knowledge into separate subjects, (3) the tradition of dividing schools into an ordered sequence of grades, (4) the view that teachers should develop instructional plans that take learners' individual differences into account, (5) the idea that as many people as possible should be educated, (6) the practice of providing special training for teachers, and (7) the vision of schooling as a preparation for effective citizenship.
- In the American colonial period, the New England Puritans were motivated by desires to reform policies of the Church of England and raise their children in an

Following the Web 11.2

History of American Education

There are large numbers of Web sites that feature information about various aspects of the history of American education. Some of them treat general topics, and others focus on more specific issues.

For hot links to these sites, visit the companion Web site, located at *http://www. prenhall.com/armstrong.* Select Chapter 11 from the front page of the Web site, then choose the Following the Web module on the navigation bar on the left side of the page.

History of the American Public School System

- *http://www.greatbook.com/homepage/history.htm*

  This site features an outstanding compilation of links that tie to numerous topics of interest to students of American educational history. For example, you will find information relevant to such diverse topics as (1) the first American Textbooks, (2) the work of Horace Mann, (3) key court cases related to establishing and funding public schools, (4) early kindergartens, (5) dividing schools into grades, (6) development of the high schools, and (7) the Cardinal Principles of secondary education.

History of American Education Web Project

- *http://oit.iusb.edu/eduweb01/*

  This regularly updated site features numerous links to topics associated with the development of American education. Most links are to particular time periods. For example, you will find material here related to such periods as (1) the Colonial Period of American Education—1600–1776, (2) the Early National Period of American Education—1776–1840, (3) the Common School Period of American Education—1840–1880, (4) the Progressive Period of American Education—1880–1920, and (5) the Modern Period of American Education—1920–present.

History of Education in the United States

- *http://www.indiana.edu/~eric_rec/ieo/bibs/histedus.html*

  This site features a number of citations and brief abstracts of materials from the ERIC database that focus on the history of education. Individual items focus on diverse topics, including material on the history of education of women in American schools and on efforts through time to reform school practices. In addition to the ERIC citations, you will also find links to other Internet sites with material related to the history of education.

History of Education on the Internet

- *http://library.gcsu.edu/~sc/magelink.html*

  Maintained by Georgia State University, this site contains a number of links to Web sites that feature information about American educational history. You will find this a particularly useful place to identify sites with material on the history of the education of women in American schools.

Electronic Research and the Educational Historian

- *http://oit.iusb.edu/~rbarger/electronic_research.html*

This site provides excellent information for people who are interested in using Web-based resources to conduct research on the history of education. You will find references to useful listservs, databases, online newspapers, special projects, and other resources of interest to people who want to investigate topics in educational history. The site also contains useful information about copyright issues as they pertain to information obtained from electronic sources.

Colonial Children

- *http://etext.lib.virginia.edu/etcbin/toccer-new?id=HarColo&tag=public&images= images/modeng&data=/texts/english/modeng/parsed&part=0*

This extraordinarily useful site lists a huge numbers of work focusing on lives of children in the colonial period. You will find materials organized under broad topical areas. One of these features items organized under the heading "Colonial Schools." Some materials found here would be excellent additions to lessons. For example, many of today's learners might be interested in the short article written by Peter Kalm in 1748 about colonial pets. This is a site you should visit.

Education in the Twentieth Century: Selected Moments

- *http://fcis.oise.utoronto.ca/~daniel_schugurensky/assignment1/index.html*

This site features a huge number of links to significant events in educational history. Materials are organized chronologically, with individual items clustered under ten-year periods (1900–1909, 1910–1919, 1920–1929, and so forth).

The Center for Dewey Studies

- *http://www.siu.edu/~deweyctr/index2.html*

John Dewey was a remarkable educational thinker whose ideas continue to influence present-day practices in the schools. The Center for Dewey Studies at Southern Illinois University at Carbondale is a repository of materials relating to all aspects of Dewey's work. Links at this site tie to numerous topics associated with Dewey's contributions to education.

[Note: Web addresses change frequently. If you are unable to locate one of these sites using the listed URL, try putting the site name in a standard search engine.]

environment free from "religious error." This required a society of people capable of reading the Bible, and hence there was an interest in teaching a larger proportion of the population to read.

- Settlers in the middle colonies came from more diverse backgrounds than early residents of New England. In New York, many early private schools sought to prepare young people for commercial careers. In Pennsylvania, Quakers established schools that were open to all children.

- Settlements in the southern colonies tended to be along major rivers. Because there were few towns and cities, it was difficult for children to be brought together in sufficient numbers to support a school. Wealthy people hired tutors to educate their children, and some young people were sent to England for at least part of their education. Little schooling was available to children from less prosperous families.

- The first high school was established in Boston in 1821. Unlike academies, which were mostly private institutions, most high schools were publicly supported. At first, the growth of high schools proceeded slowly. In 1860, for example, there were only 40 high schools in the entire country.

- Horace Mann championed the common school in the 1820s and 1830s. He believed that it was in the taxpayers' interest to support a strong system of public education. He saw schools as vehicles for equalizing differences among people from different social classes and as engines for the future economic growth of the nation. Mann also supported the development of normal schools, formal institutions dedicated to the preparation of teachers.

- The post–Civil War period witnessed many changes in education. The famous Kalamazoo case established a legal precedent for public support of secondary as well as elementary education. Teachers began to organize in professional organizations. The large number of immigrants entering the country challenged educators to develop programs responsive to their needs and to the needs of American employers. Toward the end of the nineteenth century, there was interest in narrowing the focus of the school curriculum in the direction of placing more emphasis on knowledge students would need to succeed in colleges and universities.

- During the first 20 years of the twentieth century, one conflict regarding the purpose of the American high school was resolved. Arguments between those seeing high schools as college-preparatory institutions and those regarding them as vocational-preparatory institutions were accommodated in a new view of the high school as a comprehensive institution having multiple objectives.

- John Dewey had a significant influence on twentieth-century American education. Dewey believed that education should primarily focus on the development of the individual. He was especially interested in providing learners with the kinds of problem-solving abilities they would need to successfully confront the challenges they would face throughout their lives.

- Originating in France and developing rapidly during World War I, the testing movement led to American schools' extensive use of intelligence testing of learners by the second and third decades of the twentieth century. In recent years, much skepticism has been generated regarding the idea that an IQ represents an accurate measure of something as complex and sophisticated as human intelligence.

- After World War II, there was interest in life-adjustment education. Critics felt that this view of education encouraged learners to do only what pleased them and that school programs lacked needed intellectual substance. By the 1950s, much enthusiasm for life-adjustment education had faded.
- In the late 1950s, following the launch of the earth satellite *Sputnik* and continuing into the very early 1960s, there was a push to place heavier emphasis in schools on challenging academic content. There were particular efforts to strengthen programs in mathematics and the sciences. As public disaffection with the nation's Vietnam policy increased, suspicions began to be directed at leaders of many public institutions, including the schools. In time, these suspicions led to widespread rejection of narrow school programs with strong focuses on traditional academic subjects; increasingly, young people questioned the relevance of such programs.
- Beginning in the 1960s, concerns about junior high schools prompted a great deal of interest in middle schools. This interest continues to the present time. Supporters of middle schools believe that their programs tend to be more responsive than junior high school programs to special needs of learners in the 11- to 14-year-old age group.
- Beginning in the 1980s, a large number of proposals to reform the schools were made. These were prompted by concerns about the intellectual levels of school graduates, unfavorable achievement comparisons between American and foreign learners, and perceived learner deficiencies in such key areas as reading and writing.
- Recent proposals to improve education have been characterized by a recognition that real change requires systemic reform. An example of a systemic school-improvement approach is the professional-development school. The professional-development school brings together and encourages collaboration among school teachers, school administrators, university-level education specialists, and prospective teachers.

Chapter 11 Self Test

 To review terms and concepts in this chapter, take the Chapter 11 Self Test on the companion Web site, located at *http://www.prenhall.com/armstrong*. Select Chapter 11 from the front page of the Web site, then choose the Self Test module on the navigation bar on the left side of the page. Feedback for the Self Test is immediate. You can keep track of your Self Test scores yourself, or you can choose to submit your scores via e-mail to your instructor.

Reflections

 To respond to these questions online, and to save or submit your response electronically, visit the companion Web site, located at *http://www.prenhall.com/armstrong*. Select Chapter 11 from the front page of the Web site, then choose the Reflections module on the navigation bar on the left side of the page. Instructors and students may also wish to use these questions as discussion topics on the Message Board for the companion Web site.

1. What are your views on the issue that American schooling has been set up to benefit individuals of European descent more than to benefit others? What evidence do you have to support your views? Should schools try to develop both a common and shared set of values and an appreciation for values of individual cultural groups that might differ from those common and shared values? Why or why not?

2. Some people allege that certain school programs and instructional materials have demeaned learners from some groups. Do you think this continues to be a problem? What might you do in your own classroom to help each learner develop a positive self-concept?

3. You were introduced in this chapter to a number of commonplace educational practices that were adopted by American educators from European precedents. (Recall such things as the practice of dividing knowledge into separate subjects, division of schools into grades, and so forth.) Suppose early on we had decided not to do these things. How might our schools be different? Why do you think they might be more effective or less effective than they are today?

4. Why were colonial educational patterns different in New England, the middle colonies, and the southern colonies? Which patterns do you think had the most lasting influence on American education and why?

5. Why do you think Americans were much more quick to agree to support elementary schools with their tax dollars than secondary schools?

6. Why do you think American educators were so quick to use intelligence tests in schools once such tests became available?

7. Today, some critics argue that curricula in our schools should place more emphasis on specific technical skills high school graduates will need when they enter the job market. How do you think John Dewey would have reacted to this proposal? What differences do you see between Dewey's values and those favoring more technical skills training? What do you think about this issue, and how do your views reflect your own thoughts about what is really important?

8. In some parts of the country, a backlash to federal initiatives to improve education has developed. Critics argued that the federal government should keep its hands off educational policy. Why might they have developed such an attitude? What are your views regarding the proper role for the federal government in the area of educational policy? What do your views tell you about your personal values?

9. What is implied by the term "systemic reform"? How might you go about involving yourself in systemic reform efforts?

10. What do you personally view as the most pressing problems facing schools today? What are some of your ideas regarding how these problems might be productively approached? Describe some barriers that will need to be overcome if your ideas are to be implemented.

Field Experiences, Projects, and Enrichment

1. In the Middle Ages, many people in charge of teaching young people felt that certain kinds of information had to be kept secret.

For example, information about the religious practices of the ancient Greeks and Romans was considered particularly dangerous. Do we face any similar situations in education today? Together with several other people from your class, organize a symposium on the topic, "What Learners Should *Not* Be Taught in School."

2. Many lingering influences from European precedents remain in our schools today. As you look ahead to schools during the first quarter of the twenty-first century, which of these influences will weaken? Which will grow stronger? Who stands to benefit from any changes you foresee? Prepare a chart that summarizes your ideas, and share it with your class as you briefly summarize your position.

3. Some people argue that the comprehensive high school has outlived its usefulness. They suggest that it would be better to have separate schools for separate purposes. Organize a debate on this topic: "Has the Comprehensive High School Outlived its Usefulness?"

4. Do some research on minority-group dropouts. Is this situation improving or getting worse? Are there different patterns from one minority group to another? Is there evidence that the inappropriateness of the school curriculum influences minority-group learners to leave school before graduating from high school? Based on your research, draft a letter that might be sent to editors of newspapers in your state that explains the problem and suggests possible solutions. Ask your instructor to react to your letter.

5. The Goals 2000: Educate America Act of 1993 is an example of federal school improvement legislation. Review its various titles. Then prepare a research paper in which you provide examples of specific actions taken to implement provisions associated with each title. You may also wish to discuss some criticisms that have been made of some parts of this legislation. Present your paper to the course instructor. You may also wish to make a brief oral summary of your findings to your class.

References

Barry, T. N. (1961). *Origin and development of the American public high school in the 19th century.* Unpublished doctoral dissertation, Stanford University.

Bowen, J. A. (1981). *A history of Western education: Vol. 3. The modern West, Europe, and the New World.* New York: St. Martin's Press.

Coleman, M. (1993). *American Indian children at school, 1850–1930.* Jackson, MS: University of Mississippi Press.

Commissioner of Indian Affairs. (1888). *Annual report.* Washington, DC: U.S. Government Printing Office.

Fischer, D. H. (1989). *Albion's seed.* New York: Oxford University Press.

Gordon, P., & Szreter, R. (Eds.). (1989). *History of education: The making of a discipline.* London: The Woburn Press.

The Holmes Group. (1986). *Tomorrow's teachers.* East Lansing, MI: Author.

Innerst, C. (1998, May 10). Uniting the theory, reality of teaching: New programs link universities to public schools. *The Washington Times, 12*(87), p. 2.

Lounsbury, J. H., & Vars, G. E. (1978). *Curriculum for the middle years.* New York: Harper and Row.

Neubert, G. A., & Binko, J. B. (1998). Professional development schools—The proof is in performance. *Educational Leadership, 55*(5), 44–46.

Nieto, S. (1992). *Affirming diversity: The sociopolitical context of multicultural education.* New York: Longman.

Popper, S. H. (1967). *The American middle school.* Waltham, MA: Blaisdell.

Stuart v. School District No. 1 of the Village of Kalamazoo, 30 Mich. 69 (1874).

U.S. Department of Commerce. (1975). *Historical statistics of the United States, colonial times to 1970: Part I.* Washington, DC: Bureau of the Census.

12

Practical Influences of Philosophy

OBJECTIVES

This chapter will help you to

- state the importance of philosophy for a teacher.
- identify practical applications of philosophical ideas to the classroom.
- define basic categories addressed in philosophy.
- describe different educational philosophic systems.
- develop a personal philosophy.

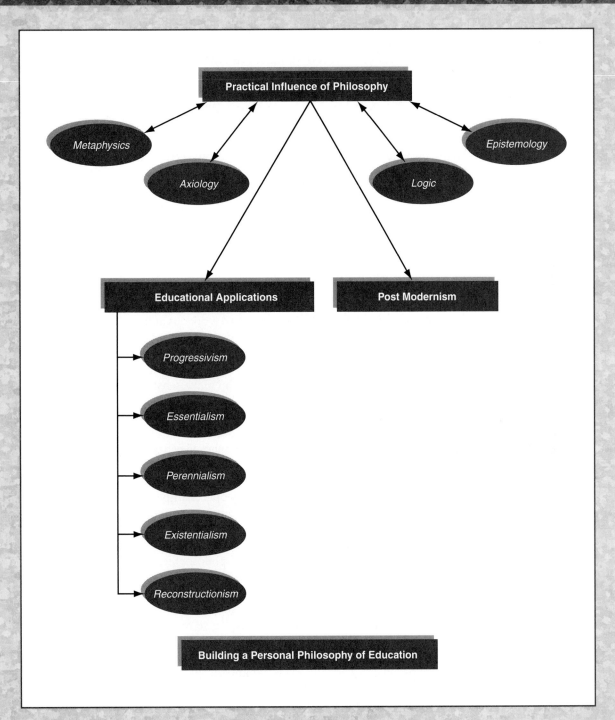

FIGURE 12.1 Practical Influences of Philosophy

INTRODUCTION

What comes to your mind when you hear the term *philosophy*? You may get an image of an arcane subject that deals with issues far removed from the realm of the practical. Some of you may recall unpleasant experiences in undergraduate philosophy courses that required you to confront difficult abstractions. Frustrations in dealing with this kind of content may lurk behind some anxieties you may experience when, during a job interview, the representative of the school district asks, "What is your philosophy of education?"

Philosophy's reputation as a subject that is unconnected to the "real" world is undeserved. Your philosophical positions help explain your personal reactions to what you confront in your daily life. Philosophy explains your own responses to such questions as:

- Are people basically good or bad?
- What is right, and what is wrong?
- How is truth determined?
- What is beauty?
- What is worth knowing?
- How should other people be treated?

Your experiences in living have helped you to work out at least informal answers to these questions. In fact, your responses to many of them have become so automatic that you probably rarely think about them. Your reactions have simply become part of you because of your interactions with our society's customs and traditions. You just assume that your patterns of behavior "make sense" and are a natural response to the world you live in.

Many of your philosophical assumptions influence how you see education. At this point in your life, you probably have some quite specific ideas about what should be taught, how it should be taught, how learners should behave, and what the proper relationship between teachers and learners should be. You probably only rarely think about your own assumptions. In fact, in times when few people challenge prevailing attitudes, you may go years without hearing people champion views different from your own. However, in times of change and uncertainty, you probably will find other people raising serious questions about educational practices that might seem perfectly reasonable to you.

There are several ways that your personal philosophical positions affect what you will do in the classroom. For example, consider decisions you make about the content to be taught. Researchers find that teachers vary significantly in the amount of time that they allocate to teaching different subjects. Even within a subject, teachers differ in the amount of time they designate to certain topics and the time they spend teaching ideas and concepts or involving learners in drill and practice activities (Good & Brophy, 1997). This variation is due in part to their differing responses to two basic philosophical questions: (1) What knowledge is worth knowing? and (2) Is knowledge fixed or constantly changing?

This teacher-to-teacher variation in content taught prompts another philosophical question that is also an ethical one—Is it right? What is your ethical obligation to present a broad base of information and content to learners?

Video Viewpoint

Making the Grade

WATCH: In the ABC News video segment, we meet Kathy Morgan, a guidance counselor at All Hallows School, an all-boys school in the South Bronx. When Kathy Morgan came to the inner-city school in 1997, less than 20% of the students there went on to college. Drugs, gangs, and street violence claimed the lives of many. Several years later, with Kathy Morgan's help, virtually 100% of the graduating seniors enroll in college programs.

THINK: With your classmates or in your teaching journal, consider these questions:

1. How can Kathy Morgan's approach to her work be considered a philosophy of education?
2. What is your philosophy of education? How can you put your philosophical beliefs into action in the classrooms?

LINK: Why is it important to have high expectations for your students?

Another way that personal philosophy will connect to your day-to-day reality in the classroom is that you will work with learners. How you will interact with members of your class reflects greatly on your general philosophical position regarding the nature of human beings. Do you see people as basically good or basically evil? Teachers who see people as essentially good work with their learners in ways that differ from those who see people as inherently bad.

Your personal philosophies will also influence your view of what conduct is moral or right and of what constitutes ethical conduct for teachers. Further, you likely have some perspectives on how you should deal with the issues of teaching values and morality.

Still another philosophical factor that will influence your teaching is your position regarding what constitutes correct thinking. For example, how will you ask your learners to defend their conclusions? Is intuition enough, or must there be some reliance on evidence? If so, what kinds of evidence are appropriate, and how must your learners organize the evidence?

Many teachers make decisions based on philosophical ideas that are grounded in the Western tradition. Indeed, the Western tradition may well have influenced your own thinking. With an increased diversity of learners in today's classrooms—many of whom come from non-Western philosophic traditions—you need to realize that other cultures may place less emphasis on what you define as reason and logic and place more emphasis on intuition and feeling. You have to be sensitive to these differences in perspectives if you hope to build bridges of understanding to learners who may be perplexed by patterns of logic that make sense to you.

Today, educators face many challenges. These include proposals to reform education through school choice, voucher plans, national certification of teachers, and other interventions. Changes in the linguistic and ethnic makeup of learners

Proposals to change curricula often result in lengthy discussions. People differ in their assumptions about characteristics of a "good" educational program.

present even experienced teachers with conditions that differ from what they experienced in the past. A few people even challenge the idea that public schools should exist at all. Members of this fringe group often argue that schools are nothing more than lackeys of a hostile government that increasingly acts to undermine individual liberties.

All of these challenges present you with a need to understand diverse philosophical perspectives. If you lack such knowledge, you will not be able to understand the premises from which critics of school practices argue their cases.

Though change and controversy often are frustrating, they also provide opportunities for you to become familiar with alternative answers to basic philosophical questions. As you work to appreciate bases of positions taken by people with differing views on educational issues, you need to become familiar with some basic categories of philosophical questions. These categories are introduced in the sections that follow.

METAPHYSICS (OR ONTOLOGY)

Metaphysics focuses on the nature of reality. Metaphysics is defined in the dictionary as "beyond the physical or the material." In essence, it deals with questions that go beyond those that can be answered by reference to scientific investigation. Metaphysical questions are speculative, and they focus on such issues as the nature of cause-and-effect relationships. Some examples are as follows:

- Do cause and effect exist in reality, or are they simply a creation of our mind?
- Is there a purpose to the universe, or is life basically meaningless?
- Are humans essentially spiritual beings, or are they creatures who exist in a particular time and space with no meaning beyond self?
- Is there a set of constant and unchanging principles that guides the operation of things and that, therefore, can be discovered?
- Is reality a constantly changing entity that is always relative, thus rendering any search for truth fruitless?

Obviously, these are not questions that can be answered by referring to results of scientific experiments.

Practical Implications

You may think that metaphysical questions are remote from the everyday world of the teacher, but they are not. Many serious debates and efforts to change the schools are based on alternative answers to these questions. For example, *theism* is a belief that the universe was created by God. Meaning in life is found by serving God and learning an established set of unchanging principles that God has provided to guide existence. Someone who accepts the premises of theism believes that the proper role of education is to help individuals in their search for God and for these unchanging principles. In fact, some theists would contend that there can be no real education that ignores God. If such an education cannot be delivered in public schools, theists would argue that parents should be allowed to send their children to private schools where such content is a regular part of the program. Not surprisingly, there is widespread support for private schools and for school choice among theists.

Certainly not all critics of prevailing school practices are theists. For example, there are others who are convinced that the primary purpose of education is to help learners achieve a well-adjusted or satisfying life. This implies that satisfaction or "happiness" is the answer to this important metaphysical question: What is the central purpose of life? People with this orientation may well contend that there is no subject matter worth knowing that is not of clear and pressing interest to the individual learner. They argue that schools should permit learners to determine what they will study and that, above all, schools should provide for learners' freedom and individual choice.

In addition to their commitment to "maximizing happiness," people with this view make a number of other philosophical assumptions. They reject the idea that known principles exist that explain reality that should be mastered by all learners. Furthermore, they perceive human beings to be essentially good and trustworthy. Basic to this position is an assumption that if people are given freedom, they will intuitively do what is good.

Many educational issues are divisive because people have arrived at different answers to basic metaphysical questions. If you are familiar with the nature of metaphysical questions—and more particularly with the reality that answers to such

questions cannot be tested against scientific evidence—you will understand the assumptions supporting views about school practices that differ from your own. You
will know when an argument is based on metaphysics (and cannot, therefore, be
proved with scientific evidence) and when an argument is not (and thus can be challenged or defended with this kind of information).

EPISTEMOLOGY

A second major category of philosophical theory is *epistemology.* Epistemological questions are concerned with the nature of knowledge. Since educators are interested in the
discovery and transmission of knowledge, you should have a special interest in this category. Answers to epistemological questions provide a rationale for selecting material
that is worth teaching and learning and suggest how information should be taught.

Two basic epistemological questions are:

- What constitutes knowledge? and
- Is knowledge fixed or changing?

Some people maintain that there is no possibility of obtaining knowledge about
ultimate reality. Others counter that it is possible to identify a set of principles that
represents "true" knowledge. Still others argue that there are no principles that are
true under all sets of conditions, but there is knowledge that is true in certain circumstances. (In other words, these people contend that knowledge functions in a
particular situation, and all we can know is what is "functional.")

In the past, the dominant philosophical orientation to the mind and knowledge led
most educators to help individuals acquire true knowledge of the world external to themselves (Soltis, 1981). However, the shift today is toward viewing knowledge as "cultural"
and, therefore, as a human construction. This conception has important implications. It
suggests that most knowledge is relative and that there are very few absolute truths.

If knowledge is a cultural construction, then how does one judge which construction is correct? This concern leads to another fundamental epistemological
question centering on ways of knowing and the reliability of these ways. How can
you be sure that what you claim to know is true? Basically, the issue involves what
you are willing to accept as a "test" of the truth of knowledge. Revelation, authority,
intuition, the senses, reason, and experimentation represent some options that are
open to you. Today, American culture has a bias favoring the position that knowledge comes from scientific experimentation. Indeed, this idea is so firmly rooted
among some people that they cannot imagine it being challenged. But even people
who are extremely committed to scientific experimentations sometimes take actions
based only on intuition. They do some things just because they "feel" right.

Practical Implications

Many things you will do as a teacher will tie to specific assumptions about how
young people learn. Philosophical positions form the intellectual scaffolding for orientations to teaching and learning such as *constructivism,* which assumes that indi-

viduals construct their own knowledge. Whether you embrace constructivism or any other orientation, you should consider what the orientation presumes about the nature of knowledge. For example, you might want to know whether the constructivist perspective that each person constructs his or her own reality of means that there are no universal principles that all should know.

As a teacher, how can you claim to know what is right or appropriate for young people to learn? In thinking about this issue, you need to recognize that education has a responsibility not only to transmit knowledge, but also to help learners think about and critically test alternative knowledge claims. This implies that a central focus in education ought to be critical and creative thinking. This does not mean that you should not transmit any specific information. Your learners need to start with something before they can construct their own knowledge through the application of sophisticated thinking skills. But you need to be careful that you do not suggest that the specific knowledge you introduce is taught as a set of fixed truths that are to be accepted and never challenged.

This shift toward the view that knowledge is a cultural construction is reflected in many multicultural programs. James Banks (1994) includes knowledge construction as a key element in multicultural education. He states that it is important for all learners to understand that certain common experiences, perspectives, and values influence the knowledge construction of a given culture and that knowledge is dynamic and changing. He advocates making the classroom a forum for debates about different knowledge constructions.

People in many other world cultures place a lower premium on scientific experimentation than we do. Because people in other parts of the world may have views about how knowledge is best acquired that differ from your own, you may sometimes find it difficult to understand the perspectives of people who live in unfamiliar cultural settings. When learners lack such understandings, they may conclude that other cultures are strange or even funny. An important objective of the school program is to help them understand that they see the world through "cultural blinders" of their own. One of your tasks as a teacher is to help them recognize that there is nothing correct in any absolute sense in the way that they think knowledge is best acquired. Their views simply reflect how American culture has decided to view reality (Oliver & Gersham, 1989).

Arguments about the content of the curriculum often are heated. These debates frequently stem from different philosophical views about the nature of knowledge, and they reflect a diversity of opinion about what should be central to the school instructional program. For example, some people believe the curriculum should feature the so-called classics of Western thought. Others favor a school program dedicated to developing learners' sophisticated thinking skills. Still others support school programs with heavy emphases on preparing learners for the world of work.

When you begin teaching, your approaches to introducing content will reveal much about your own answers to epistemological questions. For example, if you insist that learners master basic facts and principles, you will be operating on the assumption that there is such a thing as true knowledge. Some of your colleagues, on the other hand, may be more interested in teaching the processes of learning rather than specific content information. Their actions would signal their assumption that there are few, if any, ultimate truths learners need to master and that their time is best spent helping learners master problem-solving skills that can be applied to diverse situations.

Some school subjects feature instructional practices that derive from differing conclusions regarding the source of knowledge. For example, instruction in the humanities frequently assumes that knowledge results at least as much from intuition, feeling, and reason as from scientific experimentation. Critics who do not understand the appropriateness of an approach to truth through any process except scientific experimentation have sometimes labeled the humanities as "soft" subjects; that is, they are soft compared with the "hard" sciences that rely more heavily on scientific experimentation.

The labels hard and soft have nothing to do with the difficulty of the subjects. Rather, they relate to the sources of knowledge deemed appropriate within each discipline. Debates over the worthiness of soft subjects and hard subjects have important curricular implications. For example, people who believe that only scientifically verifiable knowledge is important tend to place a much heavier emphasis on the sciences than on the humanities. On the other hand, those advocating the cultural construction of knowledge point out that other modes of inquiry have a high status. For example, the methodologies used to assess the relative excellence of examples of art are very different from those used by the scientific community.

A comprehensive education includes learning experiences derived from different sources of knowledge and ways of knowing. This suggests that as a teacher, you should be open to helping young people view the world from different perspectives (Soltis, 1981).

AXIOLOGY

In the classroom, should you stress the acquisition of knowledge or the moral and character development of learners? Is there a particular standard of moral behavior that you should emphasize? Are there moral or ethical standards that you should follow? These questions relate to the area of *axiology*. Axiology focuses on questions about what "ought to be." The topics of morality, ethics, and aesthetics fall into this philosophical category. Some questions associated with axiology are:

- How should life be lived?
- What is the nature of existence?
- Does life have any meaning?
- What is the highest good?
- What is moral and immoral?
- What is beauty?

As a teacher, you should be particularly interested in how your learners answer these questions. For example, the rate of suicide among young people suggests that many of them have concluded that life has no meaning (or at least not a meaning worth living for). In recent years, there have been a distressing number of incidents where students have taken the lives of others with little apparent remorse. These events have led people to ask whether contemporary education has done an adequate job of addressing the basic questions of right and wrong that flow from axiology.

Your patterns of interacting with learners reflect your own answers to axiological questions.

Drug problems in schools also tie to issues of the value and worth of life. Many people who use drugs are acting on the assumption that the highest good features seeking immediate pleasure and living for the moment. In traditional philosophy, such attitudes, collectively, are referred to as *hedonism.* Even though many learners would be unable to define this term, their actions suggest that hedonism is their basic philosophy of life.

Hedonism is only one perspective that results from a consideration of axiological questions. Another perspective takes the optimistic view that life is absolutely worth living over the long term and that the highest good involves something other than short-term pleasure. For example, many people see the highest good as featuring self-realization or self-perfection. Star athletes in the schools often have this orientation, and social reformers of all kinds who believe in the perfectibility of the human condition also reflect this general position.

Theists find life's purpose through religion. They believe there is an ultimate purpose to life and that every human being has a divine reason for being. In their view, the highest good is served when people strive to understand God's will and meet God's expectations.

An important axiological question of a different kind concerns the nature of "right" conduct. How should a person behave? What is moral behavior? How do individuals know when they are doing the right thing? In answering these questions, some argue that there are universal principles or guidelines that can be followed. For example, there are people who cite the Ten Commandments as an example of a universal guide to appropriate behavior. Others reject the idea that there are guidelines that fit every set of circumstances. They contend that "appropriateness" of behavior is situation-specific. An example of this latter point of view occurred during the late 1960s, when some people argued that America's fight against Hitler during World War II was moral but that America's participation in the Vietnam War was not.

Practical Implications

Questions and issues related to axiology have important applications to education. For example, in recent years, many politicians and others have promoted the goal of making American learners the first in the world in math and science achievement. Is the competition between nations of the world on standardized mathematics tests of such importance that significant resources should be devoted to achieve it? Why are science and mathematics specifically identified? Does this mean that they are the most important subjects? Should we not want to be first in the world in terms of an understanding of democratic processes or in treating all individuals humanely? Attention to these kinds of axiological questions can help you to clarify your thinking and assist you in making decisions about the purposes of education and the use of resources to support your priorities.

When you begin teaching, you will find yourself constantly confronted by axiological questions. Every decision about what to teach, how much time to spend on specific content, and how to teach ties back to a value decision. Your views about the purposes of education or the highest good will strongly influence your decisions. If you believe that the highest good is citizenship and the preservation of the state, then much of what you do will be directed toward helping learners assume that role. If you believe that the highest purpose is preparing individuals for a productive career, then much of your teaching will be slanted to providing individuals with skills that will help them achieve success in the world of work.

Another important application of axiology in the classroom is evident in the way teachers relate to learners. In establishing relationships with learners, you will find yourself guided by your sense of ethics. You may find yourself seeking answers to questions such as:

- What is my moral responsibility toward those I teach?
- Should I make an effort to ensure that all of the young people in my classroom have an opportunity for success, or should I devote most of my time to the academically talented who are likely to benefit most from my efforts?
- Is my discipline plan fair and just, and does it communicate a sense of respect for the dignity of all humans?

When you were in school, you may have encountered teachers who you felt viewed their work as nothing more than a job to be done as easily and quickly as possible. Such teachers probably had poorly developed senses of moral responsibility, and they may have had a marginal (or totally absent) commitment to a code of professional teaching ethics. You may also have had teachers who dealt with discipline problems in harsh and uncaring ways. Such insensitive treatment of young people is indicative of a more general disrespect for the inherent dignity of human beings.

The content of the curriculum also relates to the area of axiology. In the classroom, you will often be faced with the need to help learners make value choices. Many polls of public attitudes toward education indicate that the public thinks that the teaching of values and morality is an important responsibility of education, and many Americans indicate a preference for more emphasis on these issues in schools. Recent national attempts to promote "character education" and best-selling books such as William Bennett's *Book of Virtues* are indications of public interest in the importance of dealing with values and morality in school programs.

When it comes to values, educators face difficult questions. Consider your own answers to these questions:

- What values or virtues should be taught, and how should they be taught?
- If I choose to try to indoctrinate someone in a given value or virtue, what am I saying about the nature of values and morality?
- What statement am I making about what I value in terms of individual rights and freedoms?
- What does this indicate about my values and ethics as a teacher?

Questions associated with axiology do not have easy answers. However, because these issues touch the very essence of what you will do as a teacher, you need to give them serious consideration.

LOGIC

Logic, the science of exact thought, is a subfield of philosophy. Logic deals with the relationships among ideas and with the procedures used to differentiate between valid and fallacious thinking.

There are several reasons why you will find a knowledge of logic useful. First, logic can help you to communicate more effectively by encouraging a careful, systematic arrangement of your thoughts. Second, logic can assist you as you work to evaluate the consistency of learners' reasoning. Third, logic contributes to your ability to assess the reliability of new information you encounter.

There are two basic types of logic—*deductive* logic and *inductive* logic. Deductive logic begins with a general conclusion and then elucidates this conclusion by citing examples and particulars that logically flow from it. Inductive logic begins with particulars, then reasoning focuses on these particulars and proceeds to a general conclusion that explains them.

Practical Implications

The choice of a deductive or an inductive approach has implications for how you organize and present material. When a deductive approach is selected, great care must be taken to ensure that learners acquire a solid grasp of the major principle or idea before you move on to illustrate it through the use of examples. Teaching methods such as direct instruction, the use of advance organizers, and the lecture method are basically deductive teaching approaches.

A choice of an inductive approach requires you to locate a large number of examples before instruction can begin. Further, these examples must be selected with great care. It is essential that they accurately represent the larger principle that, it is hoped, learners will come to understand. Inquiry approaches and discovery learning are teaching strategies based on the inductive approach.

There has been much professional discussion about the relative effectiveness of deductive and inductive instruction. Research suggests that neither approach is demonstrably superior to the other. The key issue seems to be how the teacher leads learners through a lesson, regardless of whether it is organized deductively or inductively. Clever teachers who help their learners grasp relationships between ideas and distinguish between valid and invalid arguments find that their learners do well regardless of whether content is sequenced deductively or inductively.

POSTMODERN PHILOSOPHY

Proponents of *postmodern* philosophy reject the traditional questions and philosophical theories (Jacobsen, 1999). For example, postmodernists contend that metaphysical questions are meaningless and that there is no need for this category of philosophical inquiry. In addition, they believe that epistemological questions regarding the nature of knowledge that are considered in isolation from the nature of learners are inappropriate. Their view is that knowledge is created by people. The linkage between knowledge and "knower" is so tight that they cannot be separated from each other. This conception is fundamental to *relational epistemology,* the idea that the social context within which people live exercises a tremendous influence over their view of the nature of knowledge and how it is attained. How people make sense of the world depends on the contexts within which they live, including their social setting and their personal histories (Thayer-Bacon & Bacon, 1998).

Supporters of relational epistemology contend that using traditional logic as a means of discriminating between valid and fallacious thinking is inappropriate. They suggest that traditional approaches to discerning "truth" have been encumbered political agendas and various kinds of cultural baggage that are rooted in Western thought. As a result, what has been presented by traditional philosophy as objective truth, good, or beauty is not objective at all. Rather, it has been shaped by the values, biases, and cultural assumptions of the creators (Jacobsen, 1999).

Postmodernists view reality as more complex than it has traditionally been assumed to be. They view it as a human creation, something that is molded in accordance with individual needs, interests, and prejudices (Beck, 1993). For them, reality is something that shifts constantly and is very individual. As a result, the focus of postmodernism is on the self and on how individuals in a community or culture construct a reality. They see the search for reality as pursued in many ways, including careful study of narratives such as legends and myths (Jacobsen, 1999). The search for reality is not directed at identifying something permanent or static but rather at identifying ongoing, interactive processes of knowledge creation. The quest is highly individualized, and each person who engages in it develops a "working understanding" of life that suits his or her individual purpose. Because the purposes and understandings of life and reality vary from individual to individual, reality is autobiographical and reflects a "personal narrative" (Beck, 1993). Arriving at an understanding of life and reality, therefore, is best approached through dialogue and conversation, where there is a mutual sharing rather than a simple transmission of ideas or information from an "expert" to a less informed individual.

A key principle associated with postmodern thought is that there is no one scholarly tradition, such as Western European, that is "right." Traditions associated with other groups including Native Americans, Asians, followers of Islam, and feminists all help members of these groups find meaning in life (Beck, 1993).

Practical Implications

There are several important implications of postmodernism for the schools. First of all, the perspectives of postmodernism are consistent with constructivist views of learning. Constructivists believe that knowledge is built by each individual and that what people put together as new insights relate to their previous knowledge and existing schema. Hence, construction of knowledge is perceived to be an individual enterprise, and the exact understandings developed by different people will vary. To achieve new knowledge, learners must interact with others and the environment in which they live. This feature of constructivism suggests that knowledge is culture dependent, value dependent, and subject to revision as circumstances change.

Postmodernism also has implications for the curriculum. Rather than a fixed curriculum of "truth" that is to be transmitted to all, postmodernists believe the curriculum should become less abstract and theoretical and should emphasize individual concerns and concrete applications. Because of the huge variety of people and conditions today's learners will encounter during their lives, this perspective supports expansion of multicultural and multidimensional aspects of the curriculum. In particular, postmodernists argue that learners' experiences in schools should not be drawn exclusively from the traditions of Western European culture. Lessons should help learners to develop ways of questioning the motives of authorities to make sure that political agendas are not being pushed under the name of "truth." The understanding that knowledge is related to values and culture means that young people should encounter alternative interpretations of events and alternative interpretations of reality.

Postsmodernists question the heavy reliance American society has placed on science in the search for knowledge. The use of stories, narratives, myths, and legends are also seen as legitimate ways to seek knowledge. The use of these approaches is consistent with postmodernists' contention that valuable knowledge is constructed in dialogue among members of the community. This implies a need for learners to encounter literature, music, art, and the humanities as they search for understanding and meaning in life.

Supporters of postmodernism reject the view that "official" authorities are the exclusive holders of correct knowledge. This suggests that teachers, rather than functioning as the source of information for learners, should see themselves involved in an enterprise where both they and the young people they serve are learners. This perspective assumes that, while the teacher may possess more knowledge in some areas, learners also possess valuable knowledge. Hence, learners' values and experiences deserve respect. Lessons should be delivered democratically in ways that keep possible conclusions open and that emphasize dialogue and inquiry.

Following the Web **12.1**

General Information Sources

Many Web sites feature information focusing on various aspects of educational philosophy. Interest in this subject is worldwide, and these sites are maintained by individuals and organizations in the United States and in many other countries. You may be interested in visiting some of the sites we have listed here.

For hot links to these sites, visit the companion Web site, located at *http://www. prenhall.com/armstrong*. Select Chapter 12 from the front page of the Web site, then choose the Following the Web module on the navigation bar on the left side of the page.

Stanford Encyclopedia of Philosophy: Abridged Table of Contents

- *http://plato.stanford.edu/contents.html*

  Are you ever unsure of meanings of some specialized terms used in discussions of philosophy? If so, this site is for you. You will find an easy-to-access and comprehensive listing of terms and their definitions provided here.

Philosophy of Education Society

- *http://www.ed.uiuc.edu/eps/pes/*

  This is the home page of the Philosophy of Education Society. You will find general information about this society and its publications, as well as links to other Internet sources of information about educational philosophy.

Course Materials in Philosophy

- *http://antioch-college.edu/~andrewc/pedagogy.html*

  A professor at Antioch College maintains this interesting site that features a vast collection of syllabi from various philosophy courses of universities around the

Certainly not everyone subscribes to positions taken by the postmodernists. For example, many state-level authorities increasingly are prescribing content of the curriculum, a trend more consistent with a "constituted-authority-knows-best" view than with postmodernism. However, even if you find yourself at odds with many positions of the postmodernists, the very presence of their views may prompt you to question assumptions that underlie your own instructional approaches and the prevailing assumptions in your school district.

EDUCATIONAL APPLICATIONS OF PHILOSOPHICAL IDEAS

Systems of philosophy address basic philosophical questions and their applications to education in logical and consistent ways. You can refer to philosophical systems as you attempt to clarify your beliefs about what the goals of education should be, what individuals should be taught, and what methods should be used to teach them. They can also help you to construct a personal philosophy.

country. These deal with a vast array of topics, and the site should be visited by anyone interested in how various aspects of philosophy are presented in university courses. Some of these are quite specialized. For example, you will find several syllabi for courses on Japanese Philosophy, Chinese Philosophy, and Philosophy of India.

Reinstating Emotion in Educational Thinking

- *http://www.ed.uiuc.edu/PES/97_docs/oloughlin.html*

  Thinkers associated with postmodernism are particularly interested in approaches to knowledge that do not depend on rational, scientific approaches. In this article, author Marjorie O'Loughlin discusses the role of emotion in educational thinking.

Midwest Philosophy of Education Society

- *http://www.ecnet.net/users/big0ama/mpes/journals/journals.html*

  This home page is maintained by the Midwest Philosophy of Education Society. At this site, you will find a listing of many other links to Internet resources dealing with educational philosophy.

Philosophy of Education: A Publication of the Philosophy of Education Society

- *http://www.ed.uiuc.edu/PES/*

  Each year the Philosophy of Education Society publishes the *Philosophy of Education Yearbook*. At this site, you can download articles from all yearbooks published since 1992.

[Note: Web addresses change frequently. If you are unable to locate one of these sites using the listed URL, try putting the site name in a standard search engine.]

No single philosophical system has been "proven" to be true. For one person, a given alternative may appear to be based on solid assumptions and sound arguments, whereas someone else may view it as weak and poorly reasoned. As you read the next section, you need to consider the assumptions and arguments of each system and consider which ones you perceive as strong and which ones you believe to be weak. This exercise will be valuable as you consider educational programs and educational changes. Most arguments and disagreements about education and educational policy are rooted in philosophical disagreements.

Progressivism

As applied to education, *progressivism* has its roots in the work of John Dewey (1902, 1910, 1916, 1938) and in the spirit of progress that characterized the close of the nineteenth century and the beginning years of the twentieth century. Progressivism emphasizes change as the essence of reality. It views knowledge as something tentative

John Dewey, one of the giants of American educational thought, developed much of the intellectual foundation for progressivism.

that may explain present reality adequately but has no claim to being true forever. Reality is seen as undergoing continuous change.

Progressives consider an educated person to be someone who has the insights needed to adapt to change. Dewey viewed problem solving according to the scientific method as the proper way to think and the most effective teaching method (Gutek, 1997). Dewey opposed the existing pattern of formal education that featured memorization of abstract information and ideas. He was distressed that this approach inappropriately acted to separate schools from the realities of society (Gutek, 1997).

Dewey and the progressives emphasized that schools should teach learners how to solve problems and inquire about their natural and social environments. Laboratory or experimental methods were favored as instructional approaches, and there was strong support for field trips to places around the community that would help young people relate learning to broad social, political, and economic issues (Gutek, 1997).

Progressives reject the idea that there are large numbers of unchanging truths that must be taught. For them, knowledge that is of value is that which can help people think about and respond to problems associated with their need to adjust to change. Progressives believe that human beings are basically good and that people who are free to choose generally will select a course of action that is best for them. Applied to schools, this perspective suggests that learners be given some choices regarding what and how they will study. Some principles of education that are consistent with progressivism include the following:

- Direct experience with the environment is the best stimulus for learning.
- Reliance on authoritarian textbooks and methods of teaching is inappropriate for the education of free people.
- Teachers should be instructional managers who establish the learning environment, ask stimulating questions, and guide learners' interests in productive directions.
- Individuals need to learn how to inquire about their environment.
- Schools should not be isolated from the social world outside of the school.

Dewey did not object to the introduction of new content to learners; however, he believed that the content should be presented so that the interest of learners was stimulated through an interaction with the environment. Dewey recommended that subject matter be organized in ways that would take advantage of learners' enthusiasms. By using personal interests as a point of reference, teachers could impart valuable problem-solving skills to learners.

Some educators understood or adopted only parts of the philosophy of Dewey. Extreme examples of these practices seriously distorted Dewey's views and led to educational practices of dubious significance. Some educators irresponsibly reduced Dewey's thinking to a simplistic, the "experience is the thing" slogan, which suggested involving learners in enjoyable classroom activities was all right even in the absence of evidence that they were directed at promoting serious new learning. Irresponsible classroom practices stemming from an inaccurate understanding of Dewey's work contributed to the development of some suspicions about the entire approach of the progressives.

In addition to a concern about an overemphasis on "experience," other individuals objected to Dewey's work on the grounds that his ideas promoted dangerous "relativism." They believed that enduring bodies of knowledge and truth exist and that Dewey's ideas were contrary to Judeo-Christian beliefs (Gutek, 1997). These individuals argued that certain truths and values are universally applicable and valid and that teachers should deliver this fixed body of content to learners.

Criticisms of progressivism, particularly since the end of World War II, have acted to reduce the number of educators who actively support this perspective. However, even today many of the principles and approaches that educators take for granted are rooted in the philosophy of Dewey and the progressives. For example, the practice of requiring learners to solve problems and engaging in experiments as opposed to memorizing conclusions of others clearly traces to the work of Dewey and his followers.

Essentialism

Essentialism, which began as an organized tradition in education in the 1930s, owes much to the work of William C. Bagley (1941). It began as a reaction against some of the more extreme variants of progressivism.

Essentialism is based on several important propositions. First, the school program should not be diluted by trivial and nonessential courses. Second, the academic rigor of American education is threatened by many of the perspectives of the progressives. Third, schools should not lose sight of their fundamental purpose—the provision of sound practical and intellectual training.

Essentialists hold that there is a core of knowledge and skills that should be taught to all learners. This common core includes those subjects that are essential for preparing a person to function as a productive adult in society. For example, the basic subjects of reading, writing, and arithmetic should form the main body of content taught at the elementary level. At the secondary level, science, mathematics, English, and history should be among the core requirements. Essentialists perceive serious knowledge as residing primarily in the sciences and the technical fields. Vocational subjects are favored because they meet the important criteria of practicality and usefulness.

Essentialists believe the arts and humanities are fine for personal pleasure, but they argue that content related to these subjects is not what learners need to prepare them for adulthood. Many of them view these subjects as frills and suggest that they should be the first courses cut when budgets are tight. Essentialists are convinced that the schools should not waste time dealing with topics that are of little practical utility.

Essentialists believe the teacher's job is to impart information to learners. For their part, learners are expected to learn and retain this factual information. Teacher-centered techniques such as the lecture are favored, as are any new technologies that are thought to be capable of transmitting new information quickly and efficiently.

Essentialists tend to believe that people are not basically good and that individuals who are left to their own devices will not develop the habits and knowledge necessary for them to become good people. Therefore, the authority of the teacher, hard work, and discipline are important values. Because essentialists believe that character development is important and that teachers instruct by example, they are convinced that the character and habits of the teacher must be above reproach.

Essentialism reflects the hard-work and can-do spirit of Americans. These perspectives can be traced to the earliest days of our country. Recall, for example, that Benjamin Franklin was interested in making the school a "more practical" place. Essentialism continues to be a potent force in American education.

Perennialism

Perennialism views truth as unchanging, or perennial. Perennialists such as Mortimer Adler (1982), Arthur Bestor (1955), and Robert Hutchins (1936) contended that education should focus on the search for and dissemination of these unchanging principles. Although perennialists grant that changing times bring some surface-level alterations in the problems that people face, they believe that the real substance of life remains unaltered over time. Furthermore, they argue that the experiences of human beings through the centuries have established which truths are worth knowing.

Perennialists believe that Western society lost its way several centuries ago. They decry what they see as a trend to rely too much on experimental science and technology and, thus, ignore enduring truths. They suggest that the growing status of scientific experimentation has led to a denial of the power and importance of human reason.

Perennialists favor schools that develop the intellect of all learners and prepare them for life. This preparation is best accomplished when individuals master the truths discovered through the centuries. Such wisdom is seen as important regardless of the career or vocation a person ultimately chooses to follow.

Because perennialists view knowledge as consisting of unified and unchanging principles, they condemn essentialists' emphasis on so-called "practical" information. The perennialist points out that what the essentialist considers "essential" is constantly changing. Therefore, a school program focused on the essentials runs the risk of teaching learners information that, in time, will have little relevance for their lives.

Perennialists are particularly vocal in their opposition to vocational training in the schools. They believe that vocational education represents a sellout of educational purposes of the school to the narrow interests of business and government. This concern is directed not only at public schools, but at colleges and universities as well.

Perennialists believe that higher education has developed entirely inappropriate emphases on developing students' research skills and on preparing them for future careers. In their view, such courses divert students away from a "genuine education" that would emphasize a mastery of lasting truth. If they could, perennialists would ban research and practical training from colleges and universities and turn these responsibilities over to technical institutes.

The perennialist shares with the essentialist the idea that the primary goal of education is to develop the intellect. In the perennialist view, however, learners should pursue truth for its own sake, not because it happens to be useful for some vocation. This pursuit of truth can best be accomplished through the study of the great literary works of civilization. Courses in the humanities and literature are particularly favored because they deal with universal issues and themes that are as contemporary today as when they were written.

One branch of perennialism is relevant to some current debate about school curricula. Supporters of this variant contend that universal truths flow from God. They see education as distorted and incomplete unless theology and religious instruction accompany the study of other topics. The protests of some religious groups about schools and schooling are manifestations of this point of view.

Existentialism

Existentialism, a philosophical position of relatively recent origin, is difficult to characterize in general terms. Many individuals associated with the existentialist position reject the view that existentialism is an all-embracing philosophy with widely agreed-upon tenets. However, one theme running through most descriptions of existentialism is that people come into this world facing only one ultimate constraint—the inevitability of their own death. In all other areas, they should have freedom to make choices and identify their own reasons for existing. Existentialism suggests that people do not fit into any grand design of God or nature. There is no logic in the events of the world. People are seen as being born into a world devoid of any universal meanings, and each person has an individual responsibility to define truth, beauty, right, and wrong. Education should challenge people to create personal meanings of their own design (Morris, 1966).

Existentialism has influenced education less than the other basic philosophies. In part, this may be true because schools, as institutions designed to provide at least some common experiences to learners, promote goals that are inconsistent with the existentialists' commitment to personal freedom. Today's emphases on accountability and on measuring common educational outcomes across schools, states, and even the nation are contrary to the tenets of existentialism. Present trends in American political thought and practice suggest that existentialism's influence on education is waning.

A good illustration of existentialism applied to education was the Summerhill program established by A. S. Neill (1960). The educational practices established at Summerhill have been applied in a few private schools in the United States. They are organized around the idea that children have a natural tendency to want to mature, to be competent, and to be like older children and adults. Such schools tend not to have a fixed curriculum. Instead, learning activities are organized around learners' questions and requests. Generally, programs feature lots of options for learners that emphasize field trips and experiential learning. The intent is to help young people explore the world and seek their own meaning and to avoid imposing on them the interpretations of others.

Participatory governance is another key characteristic of schools that have been influenced by existentialism. Learners participate in a democratic form of governance that allows learners a significant voice in the operation of the school. The traditional view that adults know what is best for young people is rejected.

Reconstructionism

Reconstructionists, similar to the perennialists, believe that society has lost its way. A classic work laying out this basic position is George Counts' 1932 work, *Dare the Schools Build a New Social Order?* Whereas perennialists seek answers from the past, reconstructionists propose to build a new kind of society. They believe that schools should serve as an important catalyst in the effort to improve the human condition through reform. For reconstructionists, education should lead people to critically appraise all elements of society. Graduates should be people who are in control of their own destinies and capable of promoting social reform.

Reconstructionists favor curricula that emphasize creating a world of economic abundance, equality, fairness, and democratic decision making. They see this social reconstruction as necessary for the survival of humankind. The school program should teach learners to analyze all aspects of life and to question rather than accept the pronouncements of those who hold political power. The reconstructionist curriculum draws heavily on insights from the behavioral sciences, which reconstructionists believe can be used as the basis for creating a society where individuals can attain their fullest potentials.

Following the Web 12.2

Information About the "Isms"

If you are interested in learning more about progressivism, essentialism, perennialism, existentialism, and reconstructionism, you will find much information on the Web. The specific sites we mention here will give you an idea about the range of available material.

 For hot links to these sites, visit the companion Web site, located at *http://www.prenhall.com/armstrong*. Select Chapter 12 from the front page of the Web site, then choose the Following the Web module on the navigation bar on the left side of the page.

Works about John Dewey, 1886–1995

- *http://www.siu.edu/~deweyctr/cdromsup.html*

  If you want to know more about progressivism, you will need to become more familiar with the work of John Dewey. At this Web site, you will find a huge listing of books and articles that focus on Dewey and his work.

Essentialism

- *http://www.soe.purdue.edu/fac/georgeoff/phil_am_ed/ESSENTIALISM.html*

  You will find a succinct explanation of essentialism at this site. This includes both basic tenets of essentialism as well as positions taken by those who have criticized essentialist views.

General Education vs. Vocational Education

- *http://www.harborside.com/home/r/radix/adlervoceducation.htm*

  You may recall that perennialists strongly oppose including vocational courses in school programs. In this essay, Mortimer Adler makes a case in support of this traditional perennialist position.

Existentialism: An Introduction

- *http://userzweb.lightspeed.net/~tameri/exist.html*

  As the title suggests, this material provides a general overview of existential thought. You will find alternative definitions, names of individuals associated with this perspective, and links to other resources with information related to the topic.

George Counts (1889–1974)

- *http://www.ux1.eiu.edu/~cfrnb/gcounts.html*

  George Counts is the name most frequently associated with reconstructionism in education. At this site, you will find a brief description of his life. There are also references to other materials related to Counts' work.

Four Twentieth-Century Theories of Education

- *http://www.morehead-st.edu/people/w.willis/fourtheories.html*

  This site provides brief descriptions of progressivism, perennialism, essentialism, and reconstructionism. Implications of each for instructional practices are provided.

[Note: Web addresses change frequently. If you are unable to locate one of these sites using the listed URL, try putting the site name in a standard search engine.]

Critical Incident

What's the Problem?

For his first two years as a teacher, Roberto Lopez taught sixth graders in an inner-city school. This year, he moved to another sixth grade position in an affluent suburban school district in the same county. Roberto has continued to use the same general approach to teaching that served him well during his first two years in the profession. He has been pleased by comments he has received from parents in the new school district. Many of them have told him their children have become quite excited about what is going on at school.

Roberto is convinced that young people need to be actively involved in their own education and that they are most interested in learning when they have a voice in deciding what to study. He works hard to build his program around the questions and interests of the learners in his class. He helps them identify pressing problems that people are facing in the real world. Then he assists them to learn what they need to know to understand the problems and think about possible solutions. All of this has resulted in lessons that integrate content from many subject areas.

For example, the class considered some of the problems created when large corporations influence political decisions. Learners' conducted investigations and had debated the roles of government and of citizens. They examined how past civilizations made decisions. They looked at some of the values inherent in some business practices that seemed to consider human beings as pieces of a machine that could be discarded when no longer needed. Members of the class drew on content from science as they looked at negative environmental side effects of practices of some irresponsible corporations. Language arts lessons related to this topic involved class members in writing letters supporting their points of view to state and federal regulatory officials. Members of the class got very involved in this learning activity, and they were particularly pleased when they received thoughtful responses to some of their letters from government officials.

Because of the positive reactions of his learners, Roberto—until today—would have responded with an enthusiastic Great! if anyone had asked him how things were going. However, after this afternoon's conference with the school principal, he is angry and confused. The principal, Ms. Fifer, visited Roberto's classroom for an observation and asked him to stop by for a debriefing at the end of the day.

Ms. Fifer told him that although she was pleased with his teaching skills and the ease with which he related to the young people in his class, she was very concerned about what he was teaching. She pointed out that he was straying too far from the prescribed curriculum. Ms. Fifer emphasized that the adopted curriculum included certain key knowledge that young people

Reconstructionists want teachers to see their role not as transmitters of knowledge, but instead as raisers of issues and as guides who direct learners to relevant resources. Young people should be actively engaged in the learning process. Ideally, the classroom should reflect the values of equality and social justice.

BUILDING A PERSONAL PHILOSOPHY OF EDUCATION

We began this chapter by pointing out that applicants for teaching positions are often asked what their philosophy of education is. Now we want to ask you a question of our own: Why is the question about your philosophy of education an important one?

need to master. If they do not learn this information, they will not do well on the state tests. Should this happen, parents will become angry.

Ms. Fifer went on to point out that sixth graders are too young and immature to deal with the problems they were discussing in any meaningful manner. She said the discussions she observed in Roberto's class were simply a sharing of ignorance. To be able to handle this kind of an activity, young people first must develop an adequate understanding of basic information. She pointed out that lessons based on the adopted textbooks would help learners build the needed information base and would ensure that when these learners became older, they would be able to engage in productive consideration of difficult issues. She concluded by suggesting that Roberto's instruction bordered on the unethical in that he was denying his young people access to content in the textbooks that had been carefully selected by experts. If he continued his present instructional program, members of his class would be denied the foundation of information that would help them in later years of education and in their life.

Roberto left this meeting very confused. He thought he was doing an excellent job. Now, Ms. Fifer has essentially told him that he is being irresponsible and, possibly, is even on the verge of harming his learners. Roberto finds this difficult to accept. He has seen the enthusiasm of the students, and he believes that helping young people learn how to make our society better is one of the most important outcomes of education. He's not sure what he should do next.

. . .

What do you think is the root of the problem between Roberto and his principal? What philosophical orientation does Roberto seem to have? Explain some differences in fundamental values between Roberto and Ms. Fifer. How would you characterize the philosophical orientation of Ms. Fifer? What do you see as the strong points in each of their arguments? What do you think ought to be done now? What does this situation suggest to you as you think about your future as a teacher?

ᏀᎳ To respond to this Critical Incident online, and to save or submit your response electronically, visit the companion Web site, located at *http://www.prenhall.com/armstrong*. Select Chapter 12 from the front page of the Web site, then choose the Critical Incidents module on the navigation bar on the left side of the page. Instructors and students may also wish to use these scenarios as discussion topics on the Message Board for the companion Web site.

Before you respond, take some time to consider the purposes of books like this text and purposes of the instructors that assign them. You might conclude that these courses and the required learning materials seek to prompt research-based thinking about educational practices in the hope you will gain knowledge that you can apply when you begin to teach. However, what you take away from your encounters with your courses and your texts depends on what we might call a "personal filter." This is a shorthand way of acknowledging that you have certain prior information, experiences, attitudes, and values that affect how you react to new learning experiences.

Your personal filter influences your visions about the purposes of education. It affects your beliefs about the nature of learners, the content you will select, and the

What Do You Think?

Philosophy and Educational Issues

Education has become a popular reform target. People regularly ask questions such as these:

- What should be taught?
- Who should decide what is taught?
- How should students be taught?
- When should they enter school?
- What is the authority of the school?
- How should educational outcomes be measured?
- What is the role of the teacher?
- How much choice should be provided?

As you reflect on your own experiences with these issues and the discussion of different educational philosophies, think about the following questions.

What Do You Think?

1. Which of the philosophical positions explained in this chapter seems to have the most support from politicians and policy makers? What evidence can you cite to support your conclusion?
2. Which of the educational philosophies is most consistent with your beliefs about the purpose of education, the nature of knowledge, and what is of most value?
3. Based on your experience as a student and on your classroom observation experiences, which educational philosophies seem to have been most influential in shaping school programs? What are some specific practices that support your conclusion?
4. Are there conflicts between your personal views and what you see happening in schools or being promoted by politicians and policy makers? If so, what are the implications for you? How might you respond to these conflicts?

kinds of conduct you will be willing to accept. It helps shape the types of interpretations you will make of the behaviors of others and the personal view you will have regarding your sense of morality and ethics as a teacher.

Your personal filter is an expression of your philosophy of education. Because it is so important, we want you to think about your personal philosophy. It will have an impact on what you learn about being a teacher and on your behavior once you join the teaching profession. It is because your personal perspectives are so important that employers ask the question of your philosophy of education. They want to know how your beliefs correspond with the goals and purposes of the school district and the community.

The culture in which you were reared, the socioeconomic background from which you come, the experiences you have had in your schools, and other factors have shaped your personal philosophy. If you never have taken time to reflect consciously on many of your fundamental convictions, we urge you to do so. This kind of philosophic self-understanding will contribute to your development as a teacher.

As you think about your own philosophy, review some of the questions raised in this chapter. Re-examine the different philosophical systems. Identify those positions and ideas that you think are strong or reasonable and those you think are weak and not so reasonable. How sound are your arguments for the positions with which you agree? What merit can you find in those positions with which you disagree? What points do they make that you consider valid? You may find that there is no one system that you agree with totally. You may find that there are elements of different systems that make sense to you. If so, you have what is termed an *eclectic philosophy,* one that includes different elements of different philosophical systems.

Once you have identified the basic elements of your personal philosophy, you need to think about their implications. What does your philosophy mean in terms of the content that you think is important? How will it affect how you interact with and treat learners? How does it relate to the methods that you will select for use with the learners you will teach? Think about these questions as you go about the business of identifying your personal philosophy of education.

Key Ideas In Summary

- Most people operate on a set of assumptions about what is right that is the product of our culture and our past experiences. Individuals need to make these assumptions and ideals explicit so that they can investigate and clarify them.
- Most of the debates and disagreements about the direction education should take and about how it should be reformed are basically disagreements over philosophical issues.
- *Metaphysics* deals with the nature of reality. Answers to metaphysical questions have implications for the identification of educational goals, the selection of appropriate content, and the formation of attitudes regarding the general nature of learners.
- *Epistemology* is concerned with the nature of knowledge. It has relevance for such educational issues as determining the types of knowledge to be taught and deciding on the reliability of alternative ways of learning content.
- *Axiology* deals with the nature of values. It has implications for teachers in identifying what is believed to be important, in deciding on a code of ethics for how they relate to learners, and in defining the contents of moral or character education.
- *Logic* centers on the clarity of thought and on the relationships between ideas. It provides people with a process they can use to make clear distinctions between valid and fallacious thinking. For this reason, educators should be concerned that learners develop a solid grounding in logical thinking.
- Most teachers have been reared in the Western philosophical tradition. There are other philosophical traditions that view the nature of reality, knowledge, and values very differently than Western philosophy. Postmodernism is a philosophical perspective that rejects traditional philosophical categories. Postmodernism is based on the idea that typical philosophical questions reflect the culture and the politics of Western civilization. It views reality as constantly changing and related to culture.

- Several systematic philosophies have developed that help guide educational thought. These philosophies of education include *progressivism, essentialism, perennialism, existentialism,* and *reconstructionism.* None of these philosophical systems has been proven to be true. They need to be evaluated based on the soundness of their assumptions and arguments.
- Clarifying one's personal philosophy is an important step in becoming a teacher in times of change. There are many and varied proposals about what education ought to be and how teachers ought to teach. A sound personal philosophy will help teachers sort through these proposals and make decisions.

Chapter 12 Self Test

To review terms and concepts in this chapter, take the Chapter 12 Self Test on the companion Web site, located at *http://www.prenhall.com/armstrong.* Select Chapter 12 from the front page of the Web site, then choose the Self Test module on the navigation bar on the left side of the page. Feedback for the Self Test is immediate. You can keep track of your Self Test scores yourself, or you can choose to submit your scores via e-mail to your instructor.

Reflections

To respond to these questions online, and to save or submit your response electronically, visit the companion Web site, located at *http://www.prenhall.com/armstrong.* Select Chapter 12 from the front page of the Web site, then choose the Reflections module on the navigation bar on the left side of the page. Instructors and students may also wish to use these questions as discussion topics on the Message Board for the companion Web site.

1. What are some examples of ways that philosophy influences teacher decisions?
2. Why is it that school personnel officials so often ask prospective teachers about their personal philosophy of education?
3. What are some arguments that have been made in support of the view that an understanding of knowledge construction should be a key element in multicultural programs in the schools?
4. What are some examples of ways that an unexamined personal filter or personal philosophy might hinder a person learning to be a teacher?
5. What philosophy of education seems to have the most current support?
6. What contemporary issues in education are related to axiological questions?
7. How would a person who subscribes to postmodern ideas approach teaching and learning?
8. What instructional emphases would you expect from a school that is strongly committed to perennialism?
9. How would the curriculum of a school organized around social reconstructionism differ from that of a school organized around essentialism?
10. What evidence can be seen of the influence of Dewey and progressivism in the schools?

▰▰▰▰ Field Experiences, Projects, and Enrichment ▰▰▰▰

1. Review some of the trends in education mentioned in earlier chapters. What are the philosophical foundations of these trends?
2. Sketch out the elements of your personal philosophy. What do they imply in terms of the kind of school and the kind of classroom where you would be most comfortable? Define a list of questions you might ask or things you might observe when looking for a school that would be consistent with your philosophy.
3. Review either state curriculum guidelines or a local school district curriculum. See if you can identify elements of the different philosophical systems in the guidelines.
4. Observe in a classroom and pay close attention to what is emphasized and how the class is conducted. What elements of different philosophies can you note?
5. Interview a school personnel officer. Ask what patterns people who are responsible for hiring new teachers are looking for when they listen to how candidates respond to the question of their philosophy of education. Ask this person whether he or she believes all districts are looking for the same kinds of answers or whether expectations will vary from school district to school district.

▰▰▰▰ References ▰▰▰▰

Adler, M. (1982). *The Paideia proposal.* New York: Macmillan.

Bagley, W. (1941). The case for essentialism in education. *National Education Association Journal, 30*(7), 202–220.

Banks, J. (1994). *Multiethnic education* (3rd ed.). Boston: Allyn & Bacon.

Beck, C. (1993). *Postmodernism, pedagogy, and philosophy of education.* Champaign, IL: University of Illinois at Urbana Champaign, Philosophy of Education Society.

Bestor, A. (1955). *The restoration of learning.* New York: Knopf.

Counts, G. (1932). *Dare the schools build a new social order?* New York: John Day.

Dewey, J. (1902). *The child and the curriculum.* Chicago: University of Chicago Press.

Dewey, J. (1910). *How we think.* Boston: D. C. Heath.

Dewey, J. (1916). *Democracy and education.* New York: Macmillan.

Dewey, J. (1938). *Experience and education.* New York: Macmillan.

Good, T., & Brophy, J. (1997). *Looking in classrooms* (7th ed.). New York: HarperCollins.

Gutek, G. L. (1997). *Historical and philosophical foundations of education: A biographical introduction,* (2nd ed.) Columbus, OH: Merrill/Prentice Hall.

Hutchins, R. (1936). *The higher learning in America.* New Haven: Yale University Press.

Jacobsen, D. A. (1999). *Philosophy in classroom teaching: Bridging the gap.* Columbus, OH: Merrill/Prentice Hall.

Morris, V. (1966). *Existentialism in education.* New York: Harper and Row.

Neill, A. (1960). *Summerhill: A radical approach to child rearing.* New York: Hart.

Nieto, S. (1992). *Affirming diversity.* New York: Longman.

Oliver, D., & Gersham, K. (1989). *Education, modernity, and fractured meaning.* Albany: State University of New York Press.

Soltis, J. (1981). Education and the concept of knowledge. In J. Soltis (Ed.), *Philosophy and education: Eightieth yearbook of the National Society for the Study of Education.* Chicago: University of Chicago Press.

Thayer-Bacon, B. J., & Bacon, C. S. (1998). *Philosophy applied to education: Nurturing a democratic community in the classroom.* Columbus, OH: Merrill/Prentice Hall.

Part Five

Contexts of Teaching

CHAPTERS

13

Challenges of School Reform

OBJECTIVES

This chapter will help you to

- recognize characteristics of systemic reform.

- identify the responsibilities of schools as developers of social capital.

- describe principles developed by the Interstate New Teacher Assessment and Support Consortium (INTASC).

- describe activities of the National Board for Professional Teaching Standards (NBPTS), and discuss some issues associated with national certification of teachers.

- explain purposes of the NBPTS.

- describe varied features of different responses to the idea of school choice, including voucher plans, open-enrollment plans, magnet schools, and charter schools.

- describe some alternative approaches to school-business partnerships.

- point out some reasons for the growing interest in establishing full-service schools.

- suggest questions that might be used as a focus for a personal professional-development plan.

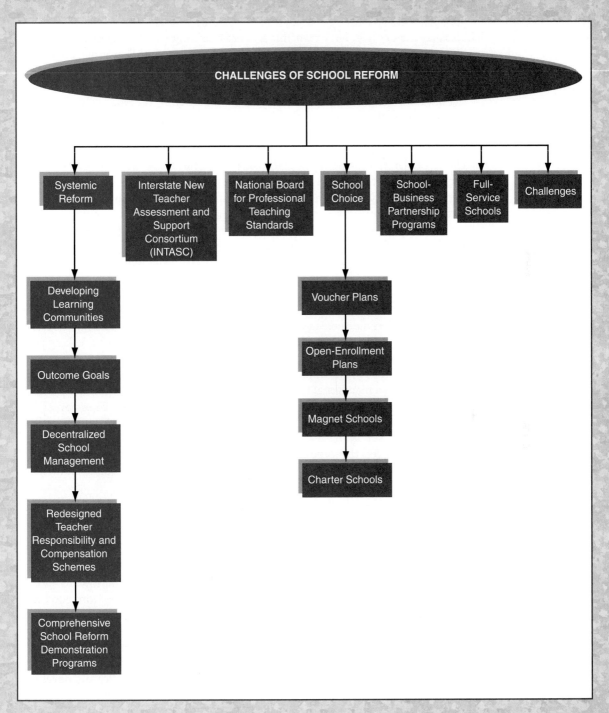

FIGURE 13.1 Challenges of School Reform

INTRODUCTION

Schools play many roles. They transmit academic content from one generation to another. They provide opportunities for learners to develop useful interpersonal relations skills and help them prepare for the world of work. Perhaps most significant of all, schools nurture development of social capital.

Social capital refers to the propensity of people to work cooperatively in groups and organizations that include individuals who are not members of their own families. The willingness of Americans to join and participate actively in voluntary groups has long been recognized as one of our nation's strengths. Alexis de Tocqueville, who traveled in the United States in the 1830s, was struck by this behavior of Americans—something he noted that differed markedly from prevalent social practices in Europe.

American society's large supply of social capital makes maximum use of individual talents. As a result, businesses, governments, and social service organizations draw on the expertise of an extraordinarily bright and gifted population. Social capital ensures a continuity in the nation's private and public institutions, which is in sharp contrast with circumstances in some other parts of the world.

In China, for example, social and business organizations have been built largely around families. This feature has made it particularly difficult for enterprises to be maintained across generations. Although expertise within a given family may exist for a few years, once the leaders die, there may not be similarly talented members within the same family group to take their places. In China, there has been little tradition of seeking professional managers outside the ranks of the family controlling the enterprise. This varies significantly from the American practice of voluntary, non-family-based organizations in which professional managerial talent is the norm and in which it is common practice to go outside of the organization to find new leadership talent when the need arises.

The success of this system depends on a willingness of people to work together voluntarily and to subordinate at least some personal priorities for the good of the group. Some people feel this type of commitment is not as strong today as it once was. For example, economic dislocations resulting from downsizing of basic industries have uprooted many people from their traditional places of residence. Unexpected and unwelcome moves have diminished people's willingness to establish strong voluntary ties with groups such as churches, PTAs, political associations, and social organizations. Also, the electronic revolution that has furnished homes with televisions, VCRs, and modem-equipped computers has made it convenient for people to spend their leisure hours at home rather than in public gathering places such as court house squares and parks. Finally, there has been a movement in recent years toward an exceptionally rigorous defense of individual rights (ranging across themes from gun control to euthanasia). As a result, compromises that place limits on individuals for the purpose of promoting the general good of society have been difficult to achieve.

These challenges establish the importance of work you will do as a teacher. Throughout your career, you will be called upon to shape programs that strike an acceptable balance between developing learners' individual characteristics and developing citizens who will willingly associate with, trust, and support others. Developing and reacting to reform initiatives that attempt to respond to these competing needs will be career-long obligations.

Voluntary groups, such as PTAs, attract leadership talent from a broad cross-section of citizens. The ability of voluntary groups to find capable people to manage their affairs gives American organizations such as PTAs an extraordinarily large pool of talent to draw from.

SYSTEMIC REFORM

Publication of *A Nation at Risk: The Imperative for Educational Reform* (National Commission on Excellence in Education, 1983) triggered the present wave of educational change. This document detailed potential threats to the nation that logically might follow declines in test scores and increases in drop-out rates. This report and others that followed proposed that schools could be "made better" by increasing the rigor of academic programs, stiffening requirements for teacher preparation, and introducing more sophisticated school-management practices.

Reform efforts of the 1980s, 1990s, and early 2000s led to calls for schools to present more public information about how well learners were doing. This pressure led to increased use of standardized tests and wider reporting of scores. When you begin teaching, you will be affected by this trend, and you may worry about how test performance of your learners will be interpreted by parents and other community members. If you have such concerns, you will have company. As Vars (1997) observes, "Most of American teachers today are anxious, if not paranoid, about

What Do You Think?

Quality of Local Schools

Public-opinion surveys regularly find that people rate their local schools higher than they rate schools in general. This may result, for example, from media coverage that highlights negative school situations, or it may simply be a matter of people being more willing to accept what they know well as "good" and to be suspect of those things that are less familiar.

What Do You Think?

1. What were the best features of the schools you attended?
2. In general, do you think your teachers were competent?
3. What are some weaknesses of schools you attended?
4. Think about general criticisms you have heard about American schools. Could any of these logically be applied to schools you attended?
5. Why do you think we tend to think schools in our local areas are better than American schools in general?

preparing their students for state proficiency exams and other externally-exposed assessments" (p. 44).

Although many people believe that low test scores are a reliable indicator of a "problem" school, the reality is more complex. By themselves, scores indicate almost nothing about the conditions that led to them. Was there inappropriate teaching? Were learners exposed to a curriculum that varied markedly from what was tested? Did learners come to school without eating a good breakfast? Were the tests given to excited youngsters just before dismissal on the last school day before a holiday? Low scores are a concern, and they do suggest that something may need attention. However, they provide only a restricted view of reality and are poor criteria to use if the intent is to judge the general worth of a school.

Today, more and more people with interests in improving the schools have come to recognize that many variables affect learners' performance. Real improvement comes from comprehensive programs that attack a number of problem areas at the same time. These may include outdated administrative arrangements, inappropriate instructional materials, insufficient family support for learners, denying teachers opportunities to make decisions about how to teach their own learners, and negative features of the general school environment. The term that is being applied to the effort to respond proactively to multiple problems is *systemic reform.* Examples of attempts to implement systemic reform include:

- establishing "learning communities,"
- emphasizing "outcome goals,"
- providing for decentralized school management,
- redesigning teacher responsibility and compensation schemes, and
- implementing federal Comprehensive School Reform Demonstration Programs.

Developing Learning Communities

Specialists who have studied organizations have found that those that prosper avoid complacency (Shaffer & Amundsen, 1993). More specifically, they engage in ongoing challenges to their operating assumptions, and they involve employees at all levels in examining present practices with a view to providing better alternatives. Today, leaders in education recognize that schools must become learning organizations or communities. Schools should engage in careful study of present practices, involve many different kinds of people in decision making, and implement instructional and managerial practices that are quite different from what many of you experienced as clients of the schools (Henson, in press).

Learning communities are proactive. They embark on change in anticipation of problems rather than in response to concerns raised by others. Traditionally, school practices have been slow to change. Schools that reconstitute themselves as learning communities are able to modify deficient practices quickly and, thereby, avoid situations that often have led dissatisfied groups to adopt highly negative views of educators and schools.

Outcome Goals

Outcome goals are goals that emphasize the results or effects of instruction. Today, educational reformers place a heavy emphasis on outcome goals. This trend represents a shift away from a focus on *input goals,* or goals that describe various components of the school program that, collectively, are thought to produce outcomes. In the past, for example, comparisons among schools were sometimes made using such evidence as the number of computers in the classrooms, the percentage of teachers with advanced degrees, and the availability of recently published texts and other instructional materials. The problem with input information is that it says little about what learners are gaining from their experiences in school programs. For example, if a school had a large up-to-date library, an observer using input goals might conclude this was a "good" school. An observer who was committed to looking at outcome measures might say, "Wait a minute. What evidence is there that learners are profiting from the library and everything else going on in this building?"

Part of the effort to focus on outcome goals has been directed at identifying high-quality learning outcomes for all subject areas. For example, excellent work of this kind has been done by the National Council of Teachers of Mathematics (NCTM) and the National Council for Geographic Education (NCGE). New curriculum standards developed by these groups are now being reflected in published material, and efforts are under way to prepare teachers to emphasize the upgraded standards in their instruction. Many other professional groups are also working to upgrade curriculum standards in their respective subject areas.

Another trend in efforts to reform schools is the attention being given to the development of rigorous assessment procedures. In general, evaluation techniques that require learners to demonstrate sophisticated thinking skills are replacing older forced-choice techniques such as true-false and matching tests that lack the capacity to assess

Asking children to perform is an example of how music teachers use authentic assessment.

higher-order learning. One approach to evaluating learners' performances that is now attracting much interest is *authentic assessment* (Wiggins, 1989; Spady, 1994).

Authentic assessment requires learners to demonstrate what they have learned in a way that has much in common with how a proficient adult might deal with the content that has been learned. In a traditional class, for example, you might ask learners to write an essay about possible consequences of locating a new factory close to a residential neighborhood. In authentic assessment, you might ask learners to provide documentation and testimony to a committee playing the role of a zoning board (and you might actually invite a zoning board member or two to participate in the exercise).

Decentralized School Management

In the past, some efforts to improve the quality of our schools have suffered because highly centralized administrative arrangements in school districts have not responded well to conditions faced by principals and teachers at individual schools. To remedy this situation, many supporters of systemic reform favor decentralizing decision-making power. The idea is to greatly expand the authority of teachers and administrators at the individual building level to make many kinds of decisions related to the operation of the school. The term *site-based management* is one that is used to describe the decentralization of decision-making power to professionals at the individual school level.

The idea of site-based decision making is to trust critical decisions to the people who will actually be delivering educational services to learners. Often a team approach is used. Leadership team members from an individual school may include teachers, administrators, parents or guardians, representatives from the local community, and a few learners. Teacher participation has been identified as a variable associated with highly successful site-based management approaches (Clark, Clark, & Irvin, 1997).

More and more frequently, site-based leadership teams are being given authority over such issues as budgeting, personnel selection, school curriculum, and in-service planning. Therefore, as you prepare for a career in teaching, you should take advantage of opportunities to gain expertise in areas related to school budgets, community relations, state curriculum guidelines, and personnel selection and hiring. As a teacher today, you will be assuming responsibilities that go well beyond instructing learners.

Redesigned Teacher Responsibility and Compensation Schemes

The expansion of teachers' responsibilities that has been encouraged by the trend toward site-based management has led to new interest in the old idea of *differentiated staffing*. Differentiated staffing refers to the idea that not all teachers should have exactly the same set of responsibilities. For example, if you are a teacher who is particularly good at working with student teachers, you might be allocated time to work exclusively with a group of these prospective members of the profession. On the other hand, if you are especially adept at wrestling with issues associated with school budgets, you might be allocated time to work out alternative financial scenarios for presentation to the school's management team. Depending on your own special talents, you might be assigned other roles associated with such tasks as mentoring new teachers, helping to organize school clubs, contacting parents or guardians, or talking about school issues to community groups.

The "professional life space" of a teacher may last 40 or more years, and most of the formal preparation for teaching takes place at the very beginning of this period of time. While some staff-development expectations have been part of teachers' professional lives for many years, they traditionally have not been expected to demonstrate a level of expertise in the middle and later years of their professional lives that varied much from what they were able to do at the beginning of their careers. Differentiated staffing challenges this pattern. It assumes that you will grow in terms of what you can do as a teacher as you mature in the profession. As your expertise increases, there is an expectation that you will assume new and more challenging roles.

Successful differentiated staffing programs ensure that teachers who perform more challenging roles receive some kind of recognition. In some places, titles such as *lead teacher, teacher curriculum specialist,* and *team leader* denote individuals who have earned the right to play specialized roles. Increasingly, there is a trend toward providing additional compensation to teachers who have been assigned to discharge special responsibilities.

Various compensation schemes have been devised. These differ somewhat from traditional merit-pay plans, which provide salary supplements for teachers who are identified as being outstanding faculty members. While pay increases are not usually tied to any special, nontraditional responsibilities, merit pay is designed to provide extra compensation to "good" teachers so they will stay in the classroom.

Merit-pay plans generally have not been popular with teachers. There have often been suspicions that individuals identified as meritorious may be selected because of their personal compatibility with raters rather than because they are more effective practitioners than others. Compensation plans associated with differentiated staffing have been somewhat less controversial, because the additional money is paid to individuals who are required to discharge specific, demanding responsibilities. Since these responsibilities clearly go well beyond those demanded of typical classroom teachers, there has not been so much concern that personality factors have played a role in the decision to award these increases as has been the case in many traditional merit-pay plans.

Comprehensive School Reform Demonstration Program

Traditionally, federal programs designed to improve education have been targeted for support of limited-purpose programs. For example, there have been federal monies allocated to support a mathematics program, a literacy program, and a program for learners in districts with high levels of poverty. These "add-on" programs have not sought simultaneous improvement of an entire school. Because of concerns that these narrowly focused programs were not having as much impact on the overall quality of schools, Congress in 1998 passed Public Law 105-78. This legislation established the Comprehensive School Reform Demonstration (CSRD) program.

CSRD focuses on school-wide reform that is designed to help schools improve their entire operation. There must be changes in basic academics, professional development of teachers, levels of involvement of parents and guardians, uses of analyses of local needs, and attention to research-based ideas for improvement. The attempt is to develop programs that will allow all learners to achieve challenging academic standards. Program funds flow from the federal governments to the states. State-level authorities pass on funds to individual school districts that, in turn, pass them on to eligible schools. States must meet certain criteria to qualify for the funds.

To be eligible for CSRD funds, a school must have a plan for comprehensive school reform that includes each of the following nine components (Comprehensive School Reform Demonstration Program, 1998):

- effective, research-based methods and strategies;
- comprehensive design with aligned components (with the intent of meeting the needs of *all* enrolled learners);
- professional development (for teachers and staff members);
- measurable goals and benchmarks;
- support within the school (to include a strong commitment of faculty, administrators, and staff);

- parental and community involvement;
- external technical support and assistance (with available assistance from an outside group experienced in supporting school reforms);
- evaluation strategies; and
- coordination of resources (suggests how money from various sources will be utilized to support the comprehensive improvement program).

The intent of CSRD to pay for reforms that will benefit *all* learners in a school represents a shift in the nature of federal support for school-improvement initiatives. In the past, much federal money was targeted at specific subgroups within the total school population. If CSRD programs succeed in improving achievement levels of all learners, it is probable that more federal funding in the future will be directed to other systemic, comprehensive reform efforts.

INTERSTATE NEW TEACHER ASSESSMENT AND SUPPORT CONSORTIUM

Organized in 1987, the Interstate New Teacher Assessment and Support Consortium (INTASC) is an example of an education reform initiative that seeks to improve the schools by ensuring that new teachers meet high standards. The group is an alliance of state education offices, colleges and universities, and several national organizations dedicated to educational reform and to career-long development of teachers. INTASC is committed to the view that "an effective teacher must be able to integrate content knowledge with pedagogical understanding to ensure that *all* students learn and perform at high levels."(Interstate New Teacher Assessment and Support Consortium, 1999).

The group has developed a set of principles, *INTASC Model Core Standards,* that should be represented in effective teaching regardless of subject or grade level. It is hoped that these standards will be used as a framework for planning developmental experiences for students in teacher-preparation programs. The ten principles that support the *Model Core Standards* are (Interstate New Teacher Assessment and Support Consortium, 1999):

1. The teacher understands the central concepts, tools of inquiry, and structures of the discipline(s) he or she teaches and can create learning experiences that make these aspects of the subject matter meaningful for students.
2. The teacher understands how children learn and develop and provides learning opportunities that support their intellectual, social, and personal development.
3. The teacher understands how students differ in their approaches to learning and creates instructional opportunities that are adapted to diverse learners.
4. The teacher understands and uses a variety of instructional strategies to encourage students' development of critical-thinking, problem-solving, and performance skills.
5. The teacher uses an understanding of individual and group motivation and behavior to create a learning environment that encourages positive social interaction, active engagement in learning, and self-motivation.

Following the Web 13.1

National School Reform Programs

In addition to numerous local initiatives, many national school reform models have been developed. Increasingly, these are oriented toward providing comprehensive, systemic school improvement. To develop an appreciation for the scope and diversity of these national reform efforts, you may wish to visit some of the following Web sites.

For hot links to these sites, visit the companion Web site, located at *http://www. prenhall.com/armstrong.* Select Chapter 13 from the front page of the Web site, then choose the Following the Web module on the navigation bar on the left side of the page.

Accelerated Schools Project

- *http://www.stanford.edu/group/ASP/*

  This research project of the Stanford University School of Education seeks to develop schools where children excel, regardless of their backgrounds. All learners are expected to be provided with enrichment, to engage in independent research, and to be supported by a nurturing, collaborative environment. You will find links here that provide information about locations of accelerated schools, costs of the program, accomplishments of participating schools, and other issues related to the program.

New American Schools

- *http://www.naschools.org/*

  New American Schools (NAS) involves a coalition of teachers, administrators, parents, policy makers, and community and business leaders. NAS seeks to achieve improvement by reorganizing an entire school rather than changing practices within a given subject or at a single grade level. "Blueprints" for change are provided to schools that wish to participate.

Different Ways of Knowing

- *http://www.dwoknet.galef.org/dwok.html*

  Different Ways of Knowing is a program sponsored by the Galef Institute. It provides a comprehensive philosophy of education, a model curriculum, a design for good instruction, and a mechanism for sharing information about sound

6. The teacher uses knowledge of effective verbal, nonverbal, and media communication techniques to foster active inquiry, collaboration, and supportive interaction in the classroom.
7. The teacher plans instruction based upon knowledge of subject matter, students, the community, and curriculum goals.
8. The teacher understands and uses formal and informal assessment strategies to evaluate and ensure the continuous intellectual, social, and physical development of the learner.
9. The teacher is a reflective practitioner who continually evaluates the effects of his/her choices and actions on others (such as students, parents,

teaching practices. This project has a particular concern for integrating content from the visual, performing, literary, and media arts into school programs.

National Paideia Center

- *http://www.paideia.org*

  This national reform initiative, headquartered at the University of North Carolina at Greensboro, disseminates a whole-school reform model that emphasizes a rigorous liberal arts education in grades K–12. The purpose is to give learners the requisite knowledge to earn a living, think and act critically as citizens, and continue learning throughout their lives. The program promotes three modes of instruction: didactic teaching (based on textbooks, lectures, and videos), coaching (learning by doing), and seminar teaching.

Introducing America's Choice for School Design

- *http://www.ncee.org/ac/intro.html*

  The America's Choice School Network promotes a research-based design for schools and school districts that are committed to education based on rigorous achievement standards. At this site, you will find information regarding the five design tasks for all schools that adopt the America's Choice design. In addition, there is specific information regarding special designs for use in K–8 and 9–12 schools.

North American Montessori Teachers' Association

- *http://www.Montessori-namta.org/NAMTA.html*

  This site provides a wealth of information about Montessori education. This approach is based on the work of the famous Italian educator, Maria Montessori. You will find information here about special Montessori environments, Montessori programs throughout the world, and about books and articles you can read that describe Montessori-based education.

[Note: Web addresses change frequently. If you are unable to locate one of these sites using the listed URL, try putting the site name in a standard search engine.]

and other professionals in the learning community) and who actively seeks out opportunities to grow professionally.

10. The teacher fosters relationships with school colleagues, parents, and agencies in the larger community to support students' learning and well-being.

At the present time, INTASC is developing performance assessment methodologies and content-related standards for individual school subjects. A portfolio-evaluation system is being devised, and special "academies" are being held around the country to help professionals who prepare teachers to better understand how INTASC portfolios can improve the quality of preparation programs and, ultimately, the quality of teaching in the schools.

Critical Incident

"Improving Quality": Is My Subject Now a Frill?!

My name is Sook-ja Kim. I'm about eight months through my second year of teaching at Centennial Middle School. I direct the school orchestra and teach orchestra classes. For the most part, I've had a great experience.

Last month, I took my students on a two-day trip to the state orchestra competition. We went to the state capital, about 100 miles away. The students raised money for the trip, and we had plenty of parents along to help. These kids had really worked hard for this contest experience, and I was absolutely thrilled when we received a "1" rating, the highest awarded.

As soon as the award ceremony was over, I hurried back to the hotel and called my principal. She was delighted at the good news. Centennial's orchestra had never before received such a high rating. In fact, the principal was so excited that she immediately called the superintendent. It turns out that our superintendent has been concerned for some time that our district's music program was not as strong as it should be, and the news about our top rating was very welcome.

A few days after I returned to school, I got a nice letter from the superintendent, congratulating me and all of the kids in the orchestra for our hard work. The letter went on to invite me to a school board meeting where I was to receive some public congratulations for the honor brought to the district by our orchestra's high rating. The school board meeting was last night.

It was fairly late into the evening when the board president asked me to stand. Some very nice words were said about what had been accomplished by the Centennial orchestra kids, and I heard some nice comments about how much the district appreciated what I had accomplished in just two years in the district. At the conclusion of these remarks, each member of the school board came over to shake my hand. I felt I had arrived at some kind of professional pinnacle.

The next item on the agenda was an open forum for citizens' comments. The first speaker deflated my fine feelings in a hurry. He said that the school district was spending too much money on frivolous nonacademic subjects such as music. He said that he and other people in

NATIONAL BOARD FOR PROFESSIONAL TEACHING STANDARDS

Based on recommendations of the Carnegie Forum on Education and the Economy, the National Board for Professional Teaching Standards (NBPTS) was established in 1987. Sixty-three people, representing teachers, administrators, members of the public, and other stakeholders in education, govern the board. Most members are teachers, and NBPTS is a private, nonprofit group. Financial support comes from foundations, grants from large businesses, and federal funding sources.

NBPTS has organized its work around the following five core propositions (NBPTS, 1999):

1. Teachers are committed to students and their learning.
2. Teachers know the subjects they teach and how to teach those subjects to students.
3. Teachers are responsible for managing and monitoring student learning.

the district were "sick and tired" of not being able to hire high school graduates who could write a grammatical sentence or make accurate change. He indicated that the two days my orchestra kids had spent participating in the state contest had robbed them of two days of serious instruction in English and mathematics. He said this kind of thing provided just one more reason in support of an effort he and another group of citizens were mounting to replace the present school board with people who would emphasize what he called *serious* academics.

I left the meeting feeling depressed. I've worked so hard this year, but now I know that there are people in town who think my entire function is unnecessary. I have a really bad taste in my mouth about this. I just don't know what I'm going to do.

. . .

What are differences in how Sook-ja Kim probably describes "excellence" in school programming and how the person who spoke at the school board meeting describes it? What do these differences say about what is important to each? What do you think Sook-ja should do next? Do the school principal and the superintendent have roles to play here? If so, what are they? What advice would you give to this teacher? Do you think other teachers have faced similar circumstances? If you know of any particular instances, how did these teachers resolve their difficulties? How might other schools in this district be affected if a new school board is elected that announces its first priority will be to establish "serious" academics in the schools?

℞ To respond to this Critical Incident online, and to save or submit your response electronically, visit the companion Web site, located at *http://www.prenhall.com/armstrong*. Select Chapter 13 from the front page of the Web site, then choose the Critical Incidents module on the navigation bar on the left side of the page. Instructors and students may also wish to use these scenarios as discussion topics on the Message Board for the companion Web site.

4. Teachers think systematically about their practice and learn from experience.
5. Teachers are members of learning communities.

NBPTS has identified high and rigorous standards regarding what teachers should know and be able to demonstrate to help learners achieve. The group has developed rigorous assessment processes that candidates must meet to qualify for National Board certificates. Candidates for these certificates are observed both in actual classroom teaching situations and at special assessment centers. In addition, they must prepare extensive portfolios to document their instructional procedures and their effectiveness with learners. The process requires about five months to complete, and the fee for assessment is currently $2,000. NBPTS is developing standards for certificates in approximately 30 fields.

National Board certificates do not replace teaching credentials, certificates, or licenses issued by states. State certificates typically indicate that individuals have met minimum requirements necessary to work with learners in the classroom. National

Board certificates recognize people who have met much higher standards. State certificates signal that holders have met requirements established by a single state. National Board certificates will verify that holders have met a standard of excellence that will be applied uniformly to applicants from all over the country. In essence, National Board certificates aim to provide school districts throughout the country with evidence that holders are outstanding classroom practitioners.

Some states have aggressively encouraged teachers to pursue National Board certification. With more National Board certificate holders than any other state, North Carolina provides a higher salary to teachers who hold this prestigious certification. Local school districts actively encourage teachers to seek National Board certification, and many of them provide financial assistance to teachers interested in doing so. The hope is that these teachers not only will be superior performers in the classroom, but that they will commit many years of their lives to the profession.

Although many school districts support it, National Board certification has generated controversy. Some critics argue that the idea of national certification runs counter to our long-standing practice of certifying teachers at the state level. Even though National Board certification is not intended to replace state certification, some people suggest that it is a first step in that direction. Supporters, on the other hand, point out that the high NBPTS standards will prompt states to impose more rigorous certification requirements and that this trend will, in time, improve the quality of teachers in all of our nation's classrooms.

For additional information, visit the National Board's Web site at *http://www.hbpts.org/nbpts/*

SCHOOL CHOICE

An important thread running through the fabric of school reform discussions is the idea of school choice, which allows parents and learners to choose from among a variety of schools. School choice contrasts with traditional practices that obligate children to attend schools lying within attendance zones prescribed by local school districts. Proponents of school choice point out that learners have many different needs and also note that views of parents about what constitutes "good school practice" vary tremendously. It is unlikely that any one school lying within a single attendance zone can accommodate wishes of all parents and characteristics of all learners living within the zone. School choice allows parents and learners to consider many different schools and to select one that they believe represents a best fit with priorities of each family.

A number of benefits have been claimed for school-choice policies. Among claimed advantages for these policies are the following (Wells, 1990):

- School-choice policies have the potential to allow learners from low-income families to avoid mediocre, overcrowded inner-city schools.
- Families' interest in education may increase because they play an active role in selecting schools their children attend.
- Competition among schools to attract learners may result in a general improvement in the quality of all schools.

- Children attending schools that have been selected from among several alternatives potentially will find themselves in learning environments better matched to their needs than schools within their traditional mandatory attendance areas.

Many different approaches to school choice have been tried in various parts of the country. These include voucher plans, open-enrollment plans, magnet schools, and charter schools.

Voucher Plans

In a *voucher plan,* tax money is provided to parents, which they can use to pay for the education of their children at a school of their choice. One possible scenario is that if a state pays individual schools $4,500 per year for each child in attendance, a parent or guardian will receive a voucher in this amount for each school-aged child in the household. Once the parent or guardian decides what school the child will attend, this voucher is turned over to officials at that school. The officials deposit the money in the school's account and use it as part of the school's instructional and operational budget.

The voucher plan is an idea that has been discussed for many years. Supporters believe it will promote healthy competition among schools. School programs will improve as administrators and teachers work to attract additional learners. Some critics suggest that voucher plans have no provision for helping schools that are not perceived to be good and that might fail to attract learners. Such schools may become worse, because as learners and their support vouchers depart for other schools, the deserted schools will have to deliver instructional services with less money than they had before. Although leaders in such schools may want to do a better job, they will lack the financial resources to make needed improvements.

There also have been concerns about whether voucher plans will serve the needs of learners from economically impoverished families. If a selected school is out of a learner's usual attendance zone, transportation to the school may be expensive or highly inconvenient. Well-to-do families may be able to drive their children to these schools; less affluent families may not be able to. If students must rely on public transportation, families may find it difficult to handle the added expense. Some voucher plans that have been proposed make special financial provisions to help parents or guardians who may have concerns about transporting their children to these schools.

Open-Enrollment Plans

Open-enrollment plans vary from voucher plans in that they do not issue tax funds directly to parents or guardians. Rather, a system is established that permits them to select the school their child wishes to attend. The child attends that school, and the state, with the advice of the local district, sees to it that support money is diverted to the budget of the chosen school. Most open-enrollment plans limit learners' choices to schools within a given school district. A few allow learners to cross district lines.

Sometimes open-enrollment plans are described as *controlled-choice* plans. Even though these plans place great stock in preferences of parents or guardians in assigning learners to individual schools, other considerations do come into play, and the central school district administrators retain some final control over assignment of pupils and students to particular schools. Typically there are provisions that allow administrators to ensure that acceptable racial balances will be maintained in individual schools.

Supporters of open enrollment have suggested that this policy will encourage parents and guardians to look carefully at the quality of academic programs in individual schools. The idea is that they will choose to send their children to those schools that they believe provide more rigorous learning experiences for their children. Critics point out that some parents or guardians have chosen schools for reasons having little to do with the quality of the educational program. It is alleged that some children are placed in individual schools because the schools are closer to where parents or guardians work than the school in the traditional attendance zone. There also are suspicions that a few parents or guardians have chosen one school over another because of a feeling that their athletically inclined son or daughter could make the team easier at the chosen school.

Magnet Schools

Magnet schools, most of which are secondary schools, are located within a single school district and draw learners from throughout the district. Many large cities, including Houston, Chicago, Boston, New York, and Philadelphia, have had magnet schools for many years. Often individual magnet schools have a specific theme for which they are especially well known; for example, there may be a magnet school specializing in the sciences or one specializing in the performing arts. In addition to serving the special interest of learners they enroll, they also provide urban school districts with a means of achieving acceptable levels of racial integration. Integration in magnet schools can be accomplished because, unlike zones drawing on learners living in residential areas that may not have racially mixed populations, magnet schools enroll learners from all residential areas in a city.

Magnet schools provide outstanding learning experiences for many of the students they enroll. They do pose certain problems, however. The issue of transportation is a particular concern. Some critics allege that transportation problems facing learners from economically impoverished families have made it easier for learners from more affluent families to attend magnet schools. In response to this difficulty, many districts with magnet schools provide transportation subsidies to learners from low-income families.

Admission to many magnet schools requires a record of excellent academic performance in schools previously attended. Some argue that this practice results in a skimming of the learner population that deprives other schools in the district of needed academic talent. Further, there have been suspicions that magnet schools have received funding at levels that have placed other schools in their districts at a disadvantage.

Video Viewpoint

Charter School Debate

WATCH: In this ABC News video segment, Amy Stuart Wells (a professor of education at UCLA) and Jeanne Allen (President of the Center for Education Reform) discuss the issue of charter schools. According to news anchor Kevin Newman, President Clinton advocates charter schools because they are "open to all students regardless of background or ability" and they "give great flexibility in exchange for high levels of accountability."

THINK: With your classmates or in your teaching journal, consider these questions:

1. According to the experts featured in the video and your own research, do charter schools deliver on the President's claims?
2. According to the experts featured in the video and your own research, what are the advantages of charter schools? What are the disadvantages?
3. On what criteria would you judge the success and effectiveness of a charter school?

LINK: What impact do you think charter schools have on public schools?

Charter Schools

Charter schools are schools that are exempted from important rules to provide for more flexibility of operation and management. These schools typically pursue a specific set of objectives that are approved by the chartering agency, typically an arm of state government. Supporters of charter schools believe that problems most public schools face today result from excessive state and local regulation.

Charter school proponents make some arguments that are similar to those favoring voucher plans and open-enrollment plans. They hope that since they are freed from regulatory burdens, charter schools will develop outstanding instructional programs that will become models for other schools to emulate. Charter schools often seek to meet special needs of particular categories of learners. In California, for example, charter schools have been created specifically to help Latino learners who do not know English.

Many arguments have been made both in support of and in opposition to charter schools. Some people argue that charter schools are cost-effective because they do not have to tolerate the bureaucratic inefficiencies characterizing typical public schools. Supporters also contend that outstanding teachers who are frustrated by constraints imposed on them in traditional public schools will be attracted to charter schools and that these teachers will introduce exciting, innovative kinds of instruction.

Detractors point out some negatives associated with charter schools. Among other things, they suggest that charter schools have the potential to divert money away from schools already in existence. Any improvements in education that are seen at a charter school may come at the expense of a decrease in quality at other schools. Others argue that bureaucratic constraint as an obstacle to innovation in existing public schools has been overstated by charter school supporters. They point

Following the Web 13.2

Charter Schools

The movement to establish charter schools continues to gather momentum. A majority of states now have authorized establishment of charter schools, and more states are considering adopting the necessary enabling legislation. Many Web sites now feature information about issues related to charter schools. You may wish to visit some of the following examples.

 For hot links to these sites, visit the companion Web site, located at *http://www. prenhall.com/armstrong*. Select Chapter 13 from the front page of the Web site, then choose the Following the Web module on the navigation bar on the left side of the page.

About Charter Schools

- *http://edreform.com/charters.htm*

  This Web site is maintained by the Center for Education Reform. You will find a large number of links to other sites with information related to topics such as charter school laws, research on charter schools, and books and periodicals of interest to individuals who wish to establish them.

Charter School Web Community

- *http://www.uscharterschools.org/csr_1/visit?x-a=v&x-id=3026*

  This site provides a number of extraordinarily useful links to a wide range of information about charter schools. A particularly interesting feature is the lengthy synopsis of content that will be found at each link. This information allows users to decide upon the relevance of information at listed sites without requiring them to actually follow the link. Information here includes material on research on charter schools and on some support mechanisms for charter schools that have been established in individual states.

out that many innovative schools exist that have not asked for the kinds of relief from existing state and local regulations that have been given to charter schools.

Although interest in charter schools remains high, these schools are not yet being established in large numbers even in states that have approved enabling legislation. Specifics in individual state legislation account for some of this slow growth. For example, in Kansas and New Mexico, a charter school must make a separate request for every regulation it wishes to have waived. In states such as Georgia and Wisconsin, applications for charter schools have to be initiated by local school boards. These may be composed of people who have few quarrels with many existing regulations and school practices. Still other states require that charters be issued only to existing public schools so that scarce educational dollars are not encumbered to build new schools.

Despite some problems supporters have experienced in states where charter schools have been authorized, strong interest continues in this approach to school

Vaughn Next Century Learning Center: The Lessons of Experience

- *http://edreform.com/press/vaughn.htm*

   If you would like to read a case study that focuses on successes of one school that converted to a charter school, you should visit this site. You will find a detailed account of what happened when Vaughn Street School in the Los Angeles Unified School District took advantage of California's charter schools law.

The Business-Linked Charter Schools Project

- *http://www.nab.com/schooltowork/charterschools/project.cfm*

   This site includes information about attempts to link school-to-work programs with charter schools. It reports a project supported by the U.S. Department of Education that involves the National Alliance of Business, Public Policy Associates, and Michigan Future, Inc.

Welcome to the Charter School Research (CSR) Project

- *http://csr.syr.edu/*

   The Information Institute of Syracuse maintains this site, which contains numerous links to sources of research findings related to charter schools.

United States Charter Schools

- *http://www.uscharterschools.org/*

   This site is maintained by the Center for Education Reform. It includes excellent links to information focusing on topics such as (a) starting and running a charter school, (b) state information and contacts regarding charter schools, (c) profiles of individual charter schools, and (d) general resources and information sources regarding charter schools.

[Note: Web addresses change frequently. If you are unable to locate one of these sites using the listed URL, try putting the site name in a standard search engine.]

choice. For example, the U.S. Department of Education has established a "Charter School Demonstration Program" that is designed to generate and disseminate knowledge about how effective charter schools operate. Discussion of charter schools seems certain to remain a hot topic among educators.

SCHOOL-BUSINESS PARTNERSHIP PROGRAMS

Because our entire society benefits when learners have productive experiences in school, many outside our profession have a keen interest in what goes on in the schools. This interest has led to many efforts over the years to establish partnerships of various kinds between public schools and other agencies and organizations. For example, many colleges and universities around the country have linked with specific schools for the purpose of helping them develop academic programs that will adequately prepare graduates

These business and school leaders are working together to identify ways in which a school-business partnership might be established. The aim of such programs is to make school programs better.

for the demands of higher education. In some places, social agencies have established ties with schools that are designed to make their services more readily available to learners. (More about this kind of cooperative activity is introduced in the next section, which focuses on full-service schools.) In recent years, corporations and businesses of all kinds have actively sought to establish formal partnership arrangements with schools.

One important effect of the interest of business in the schools has been the establishment of *tech prep programs* throughout the country. Tech prep programs came about because there were fears that many efforts to reform the schools were promoting academic experiences having little practical value to students once they left school. For the most part, tech prep programs are 2 + 2 models, which means that they focus on the last two years of high school and two additional years of training, most often in community and junior colleges.

The intent of tech prep programs is to provide rigorous, integrated experiences that will smooth the transition from school to the world of the contributing adult citizen. To this end, the Carl D. Perkins Vocational and Applied Technology Act of 1990 defines tech prep as a program that

- leads to an associate degree or two-year certificate;
- provides technical preparation in at least one field of engineering technology, applied science, mechanical, industrial, or practical art, or trade, or agriculture, health, or business;

- builds student competence in mathematics, science, and communication (including applied academics) through a sequential course of study; and
- leads to placement in employment.

Proliferation of programs designed to foster school programs that help students make a smooth transition to the workplace led to passage of the federal School-to-Work Opportunities Act in 1994. This act provides grants to states and communities to develop systems and partnerships designed to better prepare young people for additional education and careers. The intent is for students to experience the workplace as an active learning environment and to ensure that learners see relationships between what they experience in school and what they will need to know to earn a living.

Business interest in school programs has taken many forms other than supporting legislation such as the Carl D. Perkins Act and the School-to-Work Opportunities Act. In some cases, schools have been helped in somewhat indirect ways. For example, companies have initiated child-care services and programs for employees that have encouraged them to play active roles in their children's education. Often these initiatives have offered employees flexible work schedules to enable parents or guardians to visit schools during the day.

Other school-business partnerships have been much more ambitious and have encouraged partnerships as a way of improving entire systems of schools. One of the most notable efforts has occurred in Kentucky where leaders of The Business Roundtable, which is a national group including chief executive officers of 200 of the nation's largest corporations, have established The Partnership for Kentucky School Reform. This coalition of people from business, government, labor, and education has been formed to support efforts to reform and improve public education throughout the state of Kentucky.

In Wisconsin, leaders of the Milwaukee Public Schools have instituted a system-wide school-to-work emphasis. Elements of this approach are found in curricula at every grade from kindergarten through grade 12. For example, children in early-childhood programs engage in activities that are designed to develop their problem-solving abilities. Children in elementary grades receive basic training in various aspects of the world of work and engage in lessons involving classroom businesses. Middle school learners engage in out-of-school experiences with various organizations and businesses in the city. High school students have opportunities to become involved in a variety of apprenticeship programs (System-Wide School-to-Work Transition and Parental Choice, 1999).

In New York City, the Chamber of Commerce has established a Department of Education and Workforce Development. The department's Partnership for Leadership program has established a way for school principals to seek out and receive assistance from experienced leaders in the business community. The Summer Jobs program provides opportunities for public school students to gain work experience and learn skills that will help them obtain positions when they leave the school system (Education and Workforce Development, 1999).

Some school-business partnerships have been developed between businesses and a single school. For example, at Everett Elementary School in Lincoln, Nebraska, a program called Ventures in Partnerships has been established. Among other things, this involves a "school buddies" program for children who have been identified as being at risk. Many buddies come from businesses who have agreed to be involved in the program. The idea is to provide at-risk learners with some attention from a caring, supportive adult. The buddies come to school and get involved in such things as eating lunch with their assigned child, participating with the child during recess, and talking about schoolwork. Some participating firms send letters to the child commending such things as good classroom performance and perfect attendance.

Interest in school-business partnerships is increasing, but not everyone agrees that they are a good idea. There are fears that some businesses are not so much interested in helping children as they are in promoting their own products. Supporters argue that schools can develop guidelines to prevent this sort of thing from happening and that it is in the interest of educators to encourage an interest in public education of people outside of the profession. Discussions about this issue are continuing.

FULL-SERVICE SCHOOLS

Individual human services professions that serve our nation's education, health, legal, and social support needs have developed huge bodies of sophisticated knowledge over the past half century. Training of specialists in these professions has never been better. What has not happened is a bringing together of these professions in ways that build on strengths of each and that bring their diverse understandings to bear on common problems. This is particularly true in the public-education arena. Difficulties children face cannot be neatly sorted into categories labeled as educational problems, health problems, legal problems, and social problems. What children experience as individuals are difficulties that cross all of these lines.

Full-service schools are beginning to emerge that attempt to bring all human-support activities together under one roof. The need to do this was recognized over 20 years ago when the Bicentennial Commission of the American Association of Colleges of Teacher Education devoted fully 40 pages to the need to link education and human services (Howsam, Corrigan, Denemark, & Nash, 1976). In its mid-1990s publication, *The State of America's Children* (1994), the Children's Defense Fund highlighted the intractability of problems facing our young people and the need to engage multiple human services professions in the effort to solve them.

Many full-service schools have been established to help learners from economically or educationally impoverished backgrounds. There is evidence that some families in these circumstances are unable to take advantage of some of the support services various social agencies provide. When these services are gathered together in one place—the school becomes more user-friendly. Full-service schools are in operation in many parts of the country. The Options School in McAllen, Texas, has social workers, nurses, and various other social service professionals on hand as well as classroom teachers. Students there receive specialized job training in addition to their regular academic classes.

Elk Elementary School in Charleston, West Virginia is a full-service school that offers a variety of services to learners and their families. Among other things, these services include literacy counseling, home-buying assistance, child care, and immunization help. In Waco, Texas, the local school district's Lighted Schools program provides middle school learners and their families with routine health-care checkups. In addition, many after-school activities, including sports, cultural enrichment, and career explanation, are offered (Pew Partnership for Civic Change, 1999). Project SAFE is an interesting county-wide effort to provide a full range of services to learners and families in Garfield County, Oklahoma. It provides services in individual schools that are designed to identify and respond to social, emotional, and health needs of children and their families (Poole, 1997).

Some critics of full-service schools argue that they usurp responsibilities that properly belong to families. Supporters contend that families play important roles in determining what goes on in these schools and that learners who are enrolled would not be able to access many services were they not available at the school site. At the present time, many national organizations representing the interests of different human-support services organizations are expressing interest in expanding the number of full-service schools. Any expansion will have implications for training of future social service professionals.

Traditionally, prospective teachers have been introduced to information about such issues as learning styles, instructional design, psychological development of young people, classroom management, assessment of learners, administrative arrangements of schools, and so forth. Very little time has been spent focusing on content related to public health, social work, law enforcement, and other areas that have always been discharged by social service professionals working in other settings. This situation has led to recommendations for cross-professional training.

Supporters of this idea argue that prospective teachers should have formal exposure in their preparation programs to content related to what pediatricians, social workers, law enforcement officials, and public health workers do. Similarly, training programs for these professionals should expose them to at least some of the kinds of training that typically is provided to beginning teachers. Today, a number of colleges and universities around the country are beginning to provide some cross-professional training to prospective teachers (Corrigan & Udas, 1996; Gonzalez & Garcia, 1997). It seems likely that more will be doing so in the future.

CHALLENGES AND PROSPECTIVE TEACHERS

In this chapter, you have been introduced to just a few challenges that are now percolating within the education community, and we hope you have concluded that this is a particularly fine time to be entering the teaching profession. Interest in improving the schools is widespread. Today, the discussion has moved well beyond the wringing-of-the-hands stage, and schools are implementing many exciting new approaches. The impetus to make schools better presents you with a wonderful opportunity to join the reform movement and help shape schools in ways that will better serve learners.

As you look forward to becoming a teacher, consider engaging in a personal professional-development program that goes beyond what you will be able to gain from your courses and your field work in the schools. Read widely, talk to people in the field, and ask questions. Think about your own responses to questions such as these:

- What are some reasonable learning outcomes for pupils and students in areas I want to teach, and what might I do to measure them?
- What can I do to prepare myself to participate in making management decisions as a member of a school leadership team that might include administrators, other teachers, parents, guardians, and community members?
- What should I learn about other human service professions and how their services can best be accessed by my learners and their families?
- What valuable new knowledge might I apply to my own teaching situation from experiences of charter schools and voucher plans?
- How can links be established between schools and businesses in ways that promote legitimate educational interests but do not allow for a co-option of the school program?

Key Ideas In Summary

- One key obligation of schools is to help build our nation's store of social capital. Social capital refers to people's willingness to work cooperatively and voluntarily with groups and organizations that include individuals who are not members of their own family. This commitment to work with and support others is thought to have contributed importantly to the development of our country.
- Change is under way in education. Proposals for doing things in different ways come from many quarters. It behooves prospective teachers to become familiar with school reform initiatives and to engage in the national discussion related to this important issue. Those who become involved may affect the direction of change; those who do not may find themselves working in school environments that are shaped in ways that dismay professional educators.
- Because problems of schools are so complex, many critics of present practices are convinced that the only successful reforms will be those that will attack many variables at the same time. This effort is known as *systemic reform.* Many systemic reform efforts include a concern for developing schools that are learning communities, an emphasis on outcomes of education rather than inputs, an emphasis on decentralized school management, an emphasis on redesigned teacher responsibility and compensation schemes, and Comprehensive School Reform Demonstration (CSRD) projects.
- The Interstate New Teacher Assessment and Support Consortium (INTASC) seeks to improve the quality of the schools by ensuring that new teachers meet high standards. Work of this group is greatly influencing teacher-preparation practices throughout the nation.
- The National Board for Professional Teaching Standards (NBPTS) is attempting to identify high and rigorous standards regarding what teachers should know and be able to demonstrate to help learners achieve. There are plans for NBPTS to issue National Board certificates to teachers meeting appropriate standards. These certificates will not replace local certificates but rather will be recogni-

tions for outstanding teachers who have met extraordinarily high national standards of excellence.

- An important idea running through discussions of school improvement is *school choice.* School choice allows parents or guardians and learners to select a school from among a number of alternatives. This represents a change from traditional arrangements where learners were assigned to specific schools based on their home addresses. Among school choice approaches that have been tried are *voucher plans, open-enrollment plans, magnet schools,* and *charter schools.*

- Many businesses and corporations have been interested in improving the quality of public education. This interest has been reflected in a number of ways. Private-sector support has been an important factor in supporting the spread of tech prep programs. These are programs designed to integrate training during the last two years of high school and two years in a post–high school institution, typically a community or junior college. The idea is to provide rigorous academic work that is tied in practical ways to the demands these young people will face at the end of the program. In addition to their support of tech prep, businesses have also been involved in many other kinds of partnerships with schools. These range from efforts to improve the quality of education within an entire state to efforts centered on a single school.

- Many different professions are involved in important human service activities. In addition to education, these include professionals trained in health care, social welfare, law, and law enforcement. There is evidence that professionals in these respective areas do not know much about what professionals in other human services areas are doing. Further, some people in our society find it difficult to access all of the human services to which they are entitled. One response to this problem has been the establishment of *full-service schools.* These schools bring together at a common location professionals from a variety of human service professions. They encourage communication among professionals from different human service backgrounds and make it easier for learners and their families to access their expertise.

- Professional courses and field experience opportunities are important contributors to the development of prospective teachers. However, it also makes sense for individuals preparing for teaching to develop personal professional-development plans. A series of focus questions can be developed to guide reading, interviews, and other actions taken to broaden understanding of the many issues facing educators today.

Chapter 13 Self Test

CW To review terms and concepts in this chapter, take the Chapter 13 Self Test on the companion Web site, located at *http://www.prenhall.com/armstrong.* Select Chapter 13 from the front page of the Web site, then choose the Self Test module on the navigation bar on the left side of the page. Feedback for the Self Test is immediate. You can keep track of your Self Test scores yourself, or you can choose to submit your scores via e-mail to your instructor.

Reflections

To respond to these questions online, and to save or submit your response electronically, visit the companion Web site, located at *http://www.prenhall.com/armstrong.* Select Chapter 13 from the front page of the Web site, then choose the Reflections module on the navigation bar on the left side of the page. Instructors and students may also wish to use these questions as discussion topics on the Message Board for the companion Web site.

1. What is the importance of having schools that seek to develop social capital?
2. What are some components of systemic reform, and why do its supporters believe this kind of reform is necessary to improve our schools?
3. What are key features of Comprehensive School Reform Demonstration programs?
4. What are the objectives of the Interstate New Teacher Assessment and Support Consortium? In what ways do you think work of this group might change ways in which teachers are prepared?
5. Some critics of the National Board for Professional Teaching Standards are concerned that National Board certification is a first step toward moving certification authority from the states to the federal government. Suppose this were to happen. Would this have good or bad effects on the effort to make our schools better?
6. What are voucher plans? Suppose a voucher system were in place everywhere. What changes would there be in how

schools operate? What problems might teachers and administrators face? Would such a policy improve our schools? Why or why not?

7. Proponents of charter schools argue that existing state and local regulations are important barriers to educational reform. How valid are these arguments? What do you see as strengths and weaknesses of points made by those who would like to see more charter schools?
8. Should school-business partnership programs be encouraged? What negatives and positives might be associated with an effort to dramatically increase the number of such relationships?
9. Full-service schools attempt to bring together at one place a range of educational, health, legal, and social welfare services. Professionals from these various human-support-services organizations work cooperatively to help learners and their families. How do you feel about such arrangements?
10. Today many different approaches to delivering educational services to the young are being tried. We are in the middle of an effort to reform American education that has been accelerating rapidly since the middle 1980s. How do you think some changes you already know about might change teacher-preparation programs in the future? What are some things you can be doing to prepare yourself for the educational world of the twenty-first century?

Field Experiences, Projects, and Enrichment

1. In a few places around the country, local citizens have lost so much faith in the abilities of public school officials to manage local school programs that they have

turned over operation of their schools to private corporations or to a local university. The term *contract school* sometimes is applied to a school that has been placed under the authority of this kind of external contracting agency. In essence, the private corporation or university contracts with the local citizens to improve the quality of educational services. Do some reading about how these arrangements have worked out. Prepare a report to share with others in your class.

2. Most states now have legislation allowing the establishment of charter schools. If your state has or is considering such legislation, find out what requirements must be met to establish a charter school. If your state legislature has not considered this issue, gather information about the situation in a neighboring state. Prepare a short paper in which you make reference to such issues as (1) kinds of groups that can request authority to establish a charter school, (2) limitations on numbers of charter schools that can be established, and (3) provisions relating to funding of charter schools. See Following the Web 13.2 as a possible source of information.

3. Attempts to establish full-service schools have sometimes been thwarted because of objections from parents or guardians who do not want public health officials and social welfare officials working with their children. They worry that information may be disseminated to their children about issues such as birth control that are inconsistent with values taught at home. Organize a debate on this topic: "Resolved that full-service schools are a threat to the authority of the family."

4. Ask your instructor if there have been efforts to decentralize decision making in your area through such mechanisms as site-based management. If this has been done, interview some teachers who are participating as members of school leadership teams. Ask them whether they were prepared for these kinds of management responsibilities when they were preparing to become teachers. What advice do they wish to share with future teachers who might find themselves working in schools with site-based management?

5. Help organize a panel of six to eight teachers from local area schools. Ask them to comment on the kinds of things they do every day for which they had little formal preparation. Take notes on their remarks and consider them as bases for some questions you might wish to pursue as part of your personal professional-development plan.

References

Children's Defense Fund. (1994). *The state of America's children yearbook 1994: Leave no child behind.* Washington, DC: Author.

Clark, S. N., Clark, D. C., & Irvin, J. I. (1997). Collaborative decision making. *Middle School Journal, 28*(5), 54–56.

Comprehensive School Reform Demonstration Program (1998). *Guidance on the comprehensive school reform demonstration program: U.S. Department of Education.* [http://www.ed.gov/offices/OESE/compreform/csrdgui.html]

Corrigan, D., & Udas, K. (1996). Creating collaborative, child and family centered, education, health, and human services systems. In J. Sikula, T. Buttery, & E. Guyton (Eds.), *Handbook of research on teacher education* (pp. 893–921). New York: Macmillan Publishing.

Education and workforce development (1999). [http://www.nycp.org/buckets/yeep.html]

Gonzalez, B., & Garcia, B. (1997). CSU, Fresno interprofessional collaboration project. *Services Bridges: Higher Education Curricula for Integrated Services Providers, 2*(2), 1–2.

Henson, K. T. (in press). *Curriculum Development for Education Reform.* 2nd edition, New York: McGraw-Hill.

Howsam, R. B., Corrigan, D. C., Denemark, G. W., & Nash, R. J. (1976). *Educating a profession: Relating to human services education.* Washington, DC: American Association of Colleges for Teacher Education.

Interstate New Teacher Assessment and Support Consortium (1999). *Interstate new teacher assessment and support consortium.* [*http://www.ccsso.org/intasc.html*]

National Board for Professional Teaching Standards (NBPTS) (1999). *The five propositions of accomplished teaching.* [*http://www.nbpts.org/nbpts.standards/five-props.html*]

National Commission on Excellence in Education. (1983). *A nation at risk: The imperative for educational reform.* Washington, DC: U.S. Department of Education.

Pew Partnership for Civic Change (1999). *Full-service schools reach out to children and parents.* [*http://www.pew-partnership.org/bestpract/schools.html*]

Poole, D. L. (1997). The safe project: Community-driven partnerships in health, mental health, and education to prevent early school failure. *Health & Social Work, 22*(4), 282–287.

Shaffer, C. R., & Amundsen, K. (1993). *Creating community anywhere.* New York: Jeremy P. Tarcher/Putnam Sons.

Spady, W. G. (1994). Choosing outcomes of significance. *Educational Leadership, 51*(6), 18–22.

System-wide school-to-work transition and parental choice (1999). [*http://www.aypf.org/tripreports/1995/tr101995.htm*]

Vars, G. F. (1997). Student concerns and standards too. *Middle School Journal, 28*(4), 44–49.

Wells, A. S. (1990, March). *Public school choice: Issues and concerns for urban educators. ERIC/CUE Digest,* No. 63. (ERIC Clearinghouse on Urban Education No. ED 322275)

Wiggins, G. (1989). A true test: Toward more authentic and equitable measurement. *Phi Delta Kappan, 70*(9), 703–713.

14

The Influence of Curriculum

OBJECTIVES

This chapter will help you to

- point out some basic characteristics of curricula that reflect a needs-of-learners orientation.

- summarize several advantages and disadvantages of planning curricula that are consistent with a needs-of-learners orientation.

- describe characteristics of an academic-subject-matter orientation to curriculum planning.

- point out some advantages and disadvantages of academic-subject-centered curricula.

- explain features of broad-fields curricula.

- describe characteristics of a needs-of-society orientation to curriculum planning.

- point out some advantages and disadvantages of using a needs-of-society orientation as a basis for curriculum planning.

- describe typical content patterns in elementary and secondary schools.

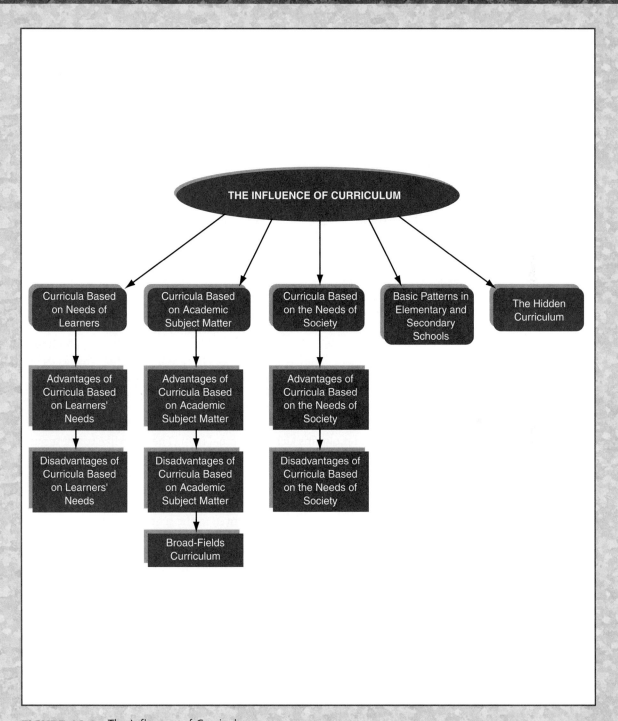

FIGURE 14.1   The Influence of Curriculum

INTRODUCTION

The term *curriculum* comes from a Latin word that refers to a track for running. Over the years, the term has come to mean a running sequence of learning experiences. In a modern school setting, the curriculum reflects decisions that have been made relating to the selection and organization of content and learning experiences. The nature of these decisions varies from place to place. Even within individual buildings, not all teachers agree about the characteristics of a good school program.

A school's curriculum acts as a kind of screen or filter. Because the time required for possible information that might be taught far exceeds the time available for us to teach it, there is a need for a mechanism to establish priorities. That is what a curriculum does—it reflects decisions about the goals of education and the kinds of content and learning experiences that should be provided to help our learners achieve them. It serves as the primary vehicle for achieving the goals and objectives of a school (Thompson & Gregg, 1997). Because different people have different values, their educational priorities differ. Larry Cuban (1993), a leading historian of school practices, has pointed out that debates about what should be included in curricula "fire passions, grab headlines, and lead off the evening news" (p. 183).

Some educators favor a learner-centered approach that emphasizes individual needs more than subject-matter content. Those who subscribe to this position see personal development as the most important obligation of the school.

Others believe that schools should be devoted to helping young people move smoothly into the workplace. They want educators to carefully analyze the needs of society and develop instructional programs that will prepare learners to meet them. Many supporters of this view are concerned that learner-centered programs may not provide young people with useful employment skills.

Still others reject both learner-centered and needs-of-society approaches. They fear that learner-centered programs lack intellectual rigor. They also like to point out that the needs of society change frequently and, hence, do not provide dependable guidelines for planning and organizing school learning experiences. Many educators who reject these two approaches argue that school programs should be built around the traditional academic disciplines (such as English, history, and mathematics).

These three basic views are widely represented in the schools today. Partisans of each position are sincere in believing their view to be the best or the most responsible. Differences in priorities reflected in these positions underscore the difficulties that policy makers face when they make decisions about what must be taught. Whatever approaches they take will likely be applauded by some people and attacked by others.

CURRICULA BASED ON NEEDS OF LEARNERS

An early proponent of focusing on the needs of individual learners was the eighteenth-century philosopher Jean-Jacques Rousseau. As he studied the world, Rousseau concluded that human civilization was corrupt. He rejected the idea that learners should be educated to meet the needs of society. In his view, this would result in an irresponsible transmission of corrupt social values from generation to generation.

Rousseau believed that children were born good, and whatever evil might come to characterize them later in life was imposed by society's negative influences. To remedy this situation, he felt schools should protect children from society and let children's naturally good instincts unfold with minimum disruption.

Rousseau believed that people pass through four distinct growth phases on the way to maturity. From birth to age 5, perceptual skills and muscle coordination develop. At this stage, Rousseau recommended that educators protect children from social restraints and allow them to experience directly the consequences of their own actions.

During the next stage, from ages 8 through 12, Rousseau recommended that there be no formal education. The child should simply be allowed to do what comes naturally. Rousseau felt that personal experience alone was a sufficient teacher for young people in this age group.

Rousseau argued that education should become a formal enterprise during the next chronological stage. During the years from ages 12 to 15, children should be exposed to teachers who would make learning opportunities available to them. Instruction should not be heavy-handed or prescriptive. Teachers should function primarily as motivators, and their roles should be to stimulate learners' curiosity to the extent that they would want to study such subjects as astronomy, geography, and agriculture.

This teacher examines a curriculum guide supplied by a commercial publisher of textbooks.

Rousseau saw the final stage of development occurring between the ages of 15 and 20. During this time, he believed that individuals developed refined human-relations skills, an appreciation of beauty, and a sense of personal and religious values. He thought young people in this age group should be encouraged, but certainly not forced, to study such subjects as religion and ethics.

The needs-of-learners orientation to curriculum has influenced the development of educational programs for many years. For example, many curricular innovations directed at "humanizing" school programs are linear descendants of the beliefs of Rousseau. Perhaps the best known American to be associated with learner-centered education was the eminent American educational philosopher John Dewey. Dewey believed that the curriculum should be constructed out of the actual experience and curiosity of the child. However, Dewey did not reject inclusion of traditional subject matter; he believed this academic content, when included, should be organized in such a way that it related to learners' life experiences.

Some contemporary educators strongly support curricula that are learner oriented. For example, Valerie Polakow (1999) contends that the trend of our society to become increasingly more culturally diverse and more complex makes a compelling case in support of learner-centered school programs.

Advantages of Curricula Based on Learners' Needs

Probably the most important strength of needs-of-learners programs is that they place concern for individual learners at the heart of the planning process. Such programs remind educators of their responsibility to serve young people and provide experiences that will help them to live rich and fulfilling lives.

Learning experiences associated with this orientation have the potential to break down artificial barriers among subject areas. For example, when you use the interests of young people as the basis for planning and organizing courses, then you are able to draw specific information from a wide selection of academic specialties. This approach frees knowledge from its artificial compartmentalization into the traditional disciplines. It can also support your efforts to develop highly motivating learning environments.

Disadvantages of Curricula Based on Learners' Needs

Critics of curricula based on learners' needs often focus on the issue of efficiency. They point out that efforts you might undertake to diagnose and respond to special needs of each member of your class are not cost-effective. These same critics would argue that it would not be practical for you to create unique programs designed to meet the special needs of each learner. In addition, people who challenge the appropriateness of curricula based on characteristics of individual learners feel that some content should be mastered by all young people, regardless of their levels of initial interest.

There is some concern, too, that learners may be poor judges of their own real needs and will opt for academic experiences that are shallow. If, as a teacher, you pander to poor decisions of immature learners, the net result may be graduates who are ill-equipped for the demands of living in a complex, technological society.

CURRICULA BASED ON ACADEMIC SUBJECT MATTER

Throughout history, one of the most common ways to organize the curriculum has been to divide it along the lines of academic subjects. Even in Roman times, educational programs were separated into subjects based on the assumption that there were disciplines (or bodies of knowledge) that grouped together elements of content that were related in some natural way. Learning was thought to be easier when young people were introduced to knowledge that had been organized into academic subjects such as mathematics or music.

Many people who organize school curricula around academic subjects believe that scholars in individual disciplines have developed reliable, responsible, and precise ways of knowing about the world. They contend that, as a teacher, you should insist that learners master certain kinds of information. It is alleged that mastery of this content will enable young people to gain control of their own destinies. Subjects that have frequently been denoted as essential for all learners include English, history, science, and mathematics. Usually, courses dealing with these major subject areas are mandated by state law.

Exactly *which* subjects should be mandatory for our learners has been the subject of considerable debate. Perhaps not surprisingly, scholars in each subject have found compelling reasons for placing a very heavy emphasis on their own specializations. (Mathematicians bemoan the public's lack of mathematical literacy, geographers decry the public's lack of geographic literacy, economists despair over the public's lack of economic literacy, and on and on.) Conflicts among supporters of different academic subjects have become familiar events in state capitols throughout the nation, as legislators have called on expert witnesses to help them define the essential elements of a "basic education."

Some people have suggested that teachers should not place too much emphasis on the need for learners to master factual content associated with each subject. Instead, they should introduce learners to the organizational features of each discipline. Initial interest in the *structure of the disciplines* (the organization of the individual academic subjects and how professionals in these disciplines ask and answer questions) developed after the former Soviet Union launched the earth satellite *Sputnik* in 1957.

Supporters of the structure-of-the-disciplines emphasis believed that many school practices featured too much attention on isolated facts. They favored instead new programs that would help young people to recognize basic principles associated with each major subject area. The idea was to develop learners' thinking abilities and engage them in learning activities that, to the extent possible, paralleled problem-solving procedures used by professional academic scholars in each subject area. There was great interest in this approach through the 1960s and into the early 1970s. An underlying theme was that learners who became thoroughly familiar with the structures of the academic disciplines during their school years would enter college ready to do more advanced work.

Beginning in the 1970s, concerns about the Vietnam War, treatment of minorities at home, and other social issues eroded support for a strong structure-of-the-disciplines emphasis. Mandates for academic programs emphasizing equity and fairness dominated much of the educational debate in the 1970s.

In the 1980s, there was renewed interest in programs with a traditional academic subject focus, but the reform reports of the 1980s tended to promote school programs that sought to familiarize learners with the findings of academic specialists, not with the structures of their disciplines. Concerns about the nation's relative intellectual and economic competitiveness prompted critics to call for school programs that would produce graduates who were well-grounded in academics, particularly in content associated with mathematics and the sciences.

During the 1980s and 1990s and continuing into first years of the twenty-first century, some critics of school practices expressed increasing concern about whether teachers had adequate preparation in the academic subjects they were teaching. In response to these concerns, many teacher-preparation programs have extended the length of their programs. While continuing to offer traditional four-year teacher-certification schedules, others have increased content requirements in the fields students have been preparing to teach.

Advantages of Curricula Organized Around Academic Subject Matter

Individual subjects tend to organize content that contains many common elements. For example, mathematics courses of all kinds have much more common content than would be found in a course that contained content blended from English and French. The common focus of each academic discipline is thought to make learning easier, as exposure to information in a single discipline introduces your learners to content that is limited in scope and logically related.

As the most traditional form of organizing school programs, this pattern enjoys a certain respectability because of its long familiarity to parents and other patrons of the school. School programs organized in this way provide an aura of stability and continuity that many people find attractive. As a teacher, you may appreciate the security of knowing that you will be teaching familiar subjects. Administrators generally feel confident in explaining this kind of organizational pattern to parents.

The vast majority of school textbooks are organized on the assumption that they will be used in programs based on traditional academic subjects; for example, there are separate books for classes in mathematics, English, and biology. Textbooks that represent a fusion of content from several academic disciplines are less common. Since the textbook continues to be a widely used instructional resource, it acts as an influence to support an academic-subject-matter orientation throughout the school program.

Today, there is great interest in holding schools and teachers accountable for their performance. Often learners' scores on standardized tests of achievement are used by people who are interested in making comparisons of the relative excellence of individual schools. Though testing specialists often decry this practice, pointing out that many variables other than the quality of the instructional program can affect test scores, the political reality is that these scores are scrutinized with great interest by the general public. For the most part, standardized tests are organized around traditional academic subjects. Hence, school curricula that reflect an academic-subject-matter organizational pattern may deliver information to learners in ways similar to how it appears on standardized tests.

Disadvantages of Curricula Organized Around Academic Subject Matter

Even though individual academic subjects have a certain internal consistency, it is by no means clear that the world is organized into history, mathematics, English, biology, and other separate subjects. The young people you will teach do not encounter a reality that is neatly sliced and filed into individual disciplines. Since reality is not divided into individual subject areas, some critics of the academic-subject-matter orientation suggest that the school curriculum should be more interdisciplinary in character. That is, individual courses should be organized in a way that allows content to be drawn from many sources.

Other critics argue that dividing school programs into packages associated with academic disciplines inhibits transfer and integration of knowledge. For instance,

School programs built around traditional academic disciplines are familiar to parents. This familiarity often makes them less controversial than programs constructed around other approaches.

Critical Incident

Is Relevance Irrelevant?

Sondra McPhee put down the report from the National Center for Educational Statistics. She nodded her head in agreement with its finding that eighth graders believed their social studies classes to have much less relevance for their future lives than their classes in English, mathematics, and science. As a second-year eighth-grade social studies teacher, Sondra's own observations squared perfectly with this conclusion. She had frequently told anyone who would listen, "My kids just don't seem to care. I think I'm simply boring them to death."

The national report convinced Sondra that her problem was not unique and something needed to be done. She spent weeks reading everything she could find about motivation, eighth graders, junior high school social studies, and, most particularly, ideas for inspiring the Hispanic and African American young people who accounted for about 70% of her learners. Late one Saturday afternoon, after several nonproductive hours in the library, she stumbled onto some information about oral history lessons. She dug into the material with increasing enthusiasm. "This is it," she said to herself.

A few weeks later, she went to visit her principal, Viola Gutierrez. She told Dr. Gutierrez that she had some ideas for changing the eighth-grade social studies program, explaining that she wanted to orient the course around the use of oral history techniques. She wanted her Hispanic students to interview their parents and relatives about experiences that they and their ancestors had had during the bloody Mexican revolution of the early twentieth century. She wanted her African American students to gather information on such issues as patterns of living in the days before the civil rights movement. She pointed out to Dr. Gutierrez that her students would see the topics as relevant, and researchers had found oral history lessons to be highly motivating.

Dr. Gutierrez, a cautious administrator, was noncommittal but told Sondra that she would think about her ideas. Three weeks later, Sondra found a note in her box from Dr. Gutierrez, asking her to come in during her planning period to talk about the oral history proposal.

Dr. Gutierrez expressed appreciation to Sondra for her willingness to innovate and for her professionalism in searching out pertinent research literature to support her case. Then she went on to say that she was going to deny permission for the oral history project. She proceeded to explain her reasons.

First of all, Dr. Gutierrez pointed out, the course text did not emphasize the Mexican Revolution, nor did it deal much with the lives of African Americans in the years before 1960. She went on to remind Sondra that the state tested all eighth graders at the end of the school year, and test items tended to be drawn from content covered in the adopted textbook.

some of your learners may produce flawless prose in their English classes but in other classes turn in papers with many mistakes, assuming the attitude: "This is history. We aren't supposed to write perfect papers here. That's for English. Here we learn names and dates."

Some learners complain that the learning experiences they encounter in the traditional academic subjects are irrelevant. For example, a student studying algebra might ask, "Why should I study this stuff? What good is it?" Although content from algebra certainly does have some important links to real life, many learners fail to

Dr. Gutierrez also emphasized that very few parents had experienced an oral history approach when they were in school, and many of them might be skeptical of the technique. It was her experience that most parents seemed to prefer textbook-based reading assignments accompanied by traditional homework. If she started the oral history project, some influential parents might view it as an attempt to "water down" the social studies program.

Finally, Dr. Gutierrez pointed out that the administrators at the district's high school continued to be concerned about the lack of subject-matter preparation junior high school graduates had when they entered ninth grade. She indicated that the school simply could not take a chance that an oral history approach would make students appear to be even less prepared for high school than they currently were.

. . .

What does Sondra view as one of the most important problems she faces as a teacher? Does her sense of priorities tell us anything about her values? In light of her view of her problems in the classroom, what does Sondra see as appropriate and professional responses to them? What do we learn about the kinds of information Sondra believes are relevant to a decision about her proposal to introduce oral history into her instructional program? How do others mentioned in this discussion weigh the relative importance of the information Sondra values?

What does Dr. Gutierrez view as the primary responsibilities of teachers in her building? How do her perceptions differ from Sondra's? What forces in her professional life might have acted to shape her world view? We do not get direct evidence here of parents' feelings. We get only Dr. Gutierrez's opinions regarding what these feelings might be. Is Dr. Gutierrez accurately reporting how parents feel, or is she consciously or unconsciously biasing her reports of their feelings because of her own personal attitudes?

What do you think Sondra should do now? Are there others she should involve? Are there ways to bridge differences in perceptions of the various "players" in this situation?

To respond to this Critical Incident online, and to save or submit your response electronically, visit the companion Web site, located at *http://www.prenhall.com/armstrong*. Select Chapter 14 from the front page of the Web site, then choose the Critical Incidents module on the navigation bar on the left side of the page. Instructors and students may also wish to use these scenarios as discussion topics on the Message Board for the companion Web site.

make the connection between the content of the course and the demands of life beyond the school.

Broad-Fields Curriculum

An approach that seeks to respond to certain criticisms of curricula that have been organized around academic subjects is the broad-fields curriculum. In this scheme, two or more traditional subjects are combined into a broad area. These areas sometimes center on large themes such as industrialism or evolution. As a teacher, you can use these themes to prepare lessons that draw on knowledge from several subject areas. This approach has been promoted as a means of breaking down barriers that separate knowledge into individual academic disciplines. Thompson & Gregg (1997) warn that attempts to break down the discipline barriers often fail because teachers have been trained to separate content into individual disciplines. As a result, they find it difficult to meld together content from several subjects into a new, broad-fields "whole." However, when teachers succeed in doing this, resulting programs are said to have important benefits for learners. Among other things, broad-fields instruction is said to enhance young people's ability to transfer what they have learned to new situations.

This approach is not without its problems. One major difficulty is that few educators possess a breadth of knowledge in multiple academic disciplines. Few college and university courses that prepare teachers are organized according to a broad-fields approach. If this has been true of your own academic preparation, you may find it a real challenge to identify and utilize relevant content from a wide variety of sources. Efforts to blend content from several disciplines can also lead to trivialized treatment of important subject matter (Harrison, 1990).

CURRICULA BASED ON THE NEEDS OF SOCIETY

According to W. H. Schubert (1986), "Part of the reason for the existence of schools is that they fulfill social needs. Societies ostensibly establish schools to help further their goals and promote their values in successive generations" (p. 217). Curricula developed from this perspective may be one of several basic types. Among them are curricula organized according to a *problems approach* and those designed to promote *citizenship development.*

The problems approach has been favored by educators who believe that schools should provide experiences designed to help learners develop skills and insights relevant to solving pressing social problems. Supporters contend that the schools are institutions charged with ensuring social survival. They maintain that to accomplish this objective, young people should be introduced during their school years to problems that challenge our social order. Such exposure seeks to produce future citizens who will be willing to confront problems and work for their solution.

Proponents of citizenship development point out that adult members of our society need certain basic skills in order to make a contribution. Programs consistent with this emphasis place a high priority on teaching what will be useful to learners in their adult years. Vocational education of all kinds is assigned a high priority. Some partisans of this view are suspicious of school experiences that do not have a clear relationship to what young people will be encountering as working adults.

The citizenship-development approach has appealed to many pragmatically oriented Americans. Frequently, attacks on so-called frills in school programs are reflections of the concerns of people who want schools to concentrate more heavily on providing learning experiences more clearly relevant to their future careers.

Advantages of Curricula Organized Around the Needs of Society

Content of school programs associated with this perspective is drawn from a variety of academic subjects. This arrangement helps break down the idea that knowledge must be compartmentalized into artificial categories with labels such as history, English, mathematics, or physics. Needs-of-society curricula help young people integrate knowledge from a variety of sources as they use this knowledge to make sense of the world as it really is.

Supporters also point to the motivational advantages of organizing programs around reality. For example, if a class you are teaching is oriented toward a career in which some of your learners are interested, they are likely to have a personal desire to learn the material. A learner might find it much easier to master mathematics in the context of studying to become a pilot than by plodding through a traditional mathematics textbook page by page. Reinstein (1998) found that an assignment requiring students to locate and interview someone in the community who uses high-level math skills did more to motivate students than any action the school could take.

Clearly, a focus on important problems can be an important incentive for young people. For example, you may find that your learners see the relevance of a topic such as consumer rights more easily than one such as decision making in ancient Sparta. Since social problems often are discussed in learners' homes, it is not surprising that many of them prefer to study issues of concern to their parents, friends, and others in the community beyond the school.

Disadvantages of Curricula Organized Around the Needs of Society

A major problem of the needs-of-society emphasis is the difficulty you can face as a teacher in identifying just which needs to address in school programs. There is a danger that these will be identified in haste and that the programs you develop will be excessively narrow in scope and nonsubstantive in content.

The rapidity with which needs change also poses difficulties. Some problems pass away; new problems emerge. Over time, technical changes alter job requirements tremendously. When educators view needs too narrowly, there is a danger that instruction will provide learners with information that will be obsolete by the time they leave school. Poorly conceived programs may also produce school graduates who lack the flexibility needed to adapt easily to changing conditions.

Some critics of programs organized around needs of society contend that they encourage young people to make career choices too early in their school years. Learners who express a personal interest based on a whim or enthusiasm of the moment may find themselves tracked into a set of courses relevant for only a limited number of career options. It may prove difficult for them to switch to another preparation sequence when their interests change.

What Do You Think?

Relative Attractiveness of Different Teaching Assignments

Assume you are a newly certified teacher faced with the task of deciding which of two job offers to accept. Salaries and general working conditions are about the same in each place, and in both positions, you will be expected to teach five classes a day at the high school level. Your assignments for each district would be as follows:

School District One	*School District Two*
American history	Technology and society
American history	Technology and society
World history	(Planning period)
(Planning period)	Militarism
World history	Militarism
World geography	Dynamics of leadership

How would you feel about accepting a position in either of these districts given these prospective teaching assignments?

What Do You Think?

1. In general, would you prefer district one or district two?
2. For which teaching assignments do you have the better college or university preparation? Why do you think so?
3. In which situation do you think you would experience the most difficulty in locating appropriate instructional materials? Why?
4. How do you think learners would react to the courses in the two districts?

Needs-of-society programs that focus heavily on social problems sometimes draw criticism from parents and other community members. They may fear that this kind of instruction will impose what they believe to be inappropriate values or perspectives. These concerns have made school authorities in some places hesitant to organize school programs around a social-problems emphasis.

BASIC PATTERNS IN ELEMENTARY AND SECONDARY SCHOOLS

Although there are some place-to-place differences, much uniformity can be found among the basic programs offered in most of the nation's elementary, middle, junior high, and senior high schools. Guidelines governing general categories of information to be taught are often included in state regulations governing education.

Elementary school programs nearly always include instruction in the areas of:

- reading and language arts,
- mathematics,
- social studies,
- science,
- health,

The belief that students should develop leadership skills as part of the school experience is consistent with the needs-of-society orientation.

- physical education, and
- fine arts.

It is very common in elementary schools for reading instruction to occur at the beginning of the day. Reading is considered to be a critically important subject, and many educators believe that pupils should be exposed to its instruction when they are well rested and ready to learn.

The amount of time devoted to each subject area in elementary schools varies from place to place. In some parts of the country, there are strict state regulations mandating that minimum amounts of time be devoted each day to certain high-priority areas of the curriculum. In other areas, no such guidelines exist, and time-allocation decisions are left to local districts, principals, and individual teachers. Because proficiency in reading is a key to academic success in so many other areas, nearly all elementary school teachers devote a great deal of time to reading instruction. Some unfavorable comparisons of United States learners' proficiency in mathematics and science as compared to learners in other countries have tended to prompt increased emphases on these subjects in elementary school programs. Increasingly, too, elementary schools are providing basic instruction in computers.

Following the Web 14.1

Diversity of Curriculum-Related Web Sites

If you type the word *curriculum* into any Web search engine, you will find thousands of matches. Religious groups, university departments, school districts, commercial publishers, professional organizations, and business groups have sites with content that deal with some aspects of this broad topic. In fact, virtually any group with an interest in training and education has a legitimate interest in program organization, content, and sequencing. The sites listed here represent a small sample of the kinds of organizations and groups that post curriculum-related information on their Web pages.

 For hot links to these sites, visit the companion Web site, located at *http://www. prenhall.com/armstrong*. Select Chapter 14 from the front page of the Web site, then choose the Following the Web module on the navigation bar on the left side of the page.

The Regional Laboratory Network

- *http://www.mcrel.org/about/network.asp*

    This site provides links to each of the 10 federally funded Regional Education Laboratories. At Web sites for the individual laboratories, you will find an abundance of curriculum-related information. Each Regional Education Laboratory has a special focus, as noted in this list:
    - Appalachian Region (AEL): specialty area—rural education
    - Western Region (WestEd): specialty area—assessment and accountability
    - Central Region (McREL): specialty area—curriculum, learning, and instruction
    - Midwestern Region (NCREL): specialty area—technology
    - Northwestern Region (NWREL): specialty area—school change process
    - Pacific Region (PREL): specialty area—language and cultural diversity
    - Northeastern Region (LAB): specialty area—language and cultural diversity
    - Mid-Atlantic Region (LSS): specialty area—urban education
    - Southeastern Region (SERVE): specialty area—early childhood education
    - Southwestern Region (SEDL): specialty area—language and cultural diversity

Middle school and junior high school programs tend to feature many of the same subjects taught in elementary schools. Particularly in seventh and eighth grades, options for students with different interests and abilities are available. Several mathematics options may be available; for example, some students may take algebra, others may choose a less rigorous course, and still others may enroll in a more challenging class. Unlike the situation that prevails in most elementary schools, students at the junior high school level are allowed to take some elective courses.

State and local high school graduation requirements largely drive the programs at the senior high school level. While these requirements vary somewhat from place to place, patterns tend to converge around a set that prescribes a minimum number of years or semesters of high school instruction in English/language arts, mathematics, science, and physical education. Many places now have minimum computer-literacy requirements. However, large numbers of electives are also available to high school students.

Many school reform reports have recommended that more work be required for high school graduation in certain so-called basic subjects, including English, mathe-

Association for Supervision and Curriculum Development's

- *http://titen.educ.utas.edu.au/HTML/roles/plan1.html*

  This is the home page of the Association for Supervision and Curriculum Development (ASCD). ASCD is the largest professional organization for people interested in curriculum development. Members include individuals from school districts and universities and colleges. You will find links here to sample lessons as well as much other curriculum-related information.

Australian Curriculum Studies Association

- *http://www.acsa.edu.au/publications/publications.htm*

  This is the home page of the Australian Curriculum Studies Association (ACSA). You will find many links to curriculum-related content focusing on such topics as (1) integrated curriculum, (2) early childhood education, (3) literacy, and (4) professional development. It also provides a listing of contents of issues of ACSA's quarterly journal, *Curriculum Perspectives.*

A Child-Centered Philosophy of Teaching and Learning

- *http://www.brighthorizons.com/new/educational_philosphy/text1.htm*

  This site is maintained by Bright Horizons, a commercial firm that specializes in providing child-care services in the workplace. Material on this site is an example of a learner-centered approach to curriculum that is promoted by private-sector businesses whose clients are young children.

[Note: Web addresses change frequently. If you are unable to locate one of these sites using the listed URL, try putting the site name in a standard search engine.]

matics, social studies, and science. For example, in its report *A Nation at Risk: The Imperative for Educational Reform,* the National Commission on Excellence in Education (1983) called for changes in high school graduation requirements. The report pointed to the need for all students to complete a minimum of four years of English, three years of science, three years of social studies, and three years of mathematics. Over the past 20 years, larger numbers of students have been enrolling in these so-called "basics." However, this trend does not reveal much about the nature of the content that learners have been encountering in these courses. At best, displays of curricular programs provide a sketchy outline of what goes on in schools. The real school program continues to be shaped by the actions of teachers as they work with young people in their individual classrooms.

The explosion of knowledge, the ready access to information via technology, and improved understanding of how individuals learn suggest a need for continuous curriculum evaluation and revision. Content that was considered indispensable in the

Video Viewpoint

Failing Grade

WATCH: In this ABC News video segment, researcher Bill Schmidt explains why he believes students in America did not perform very well when their math and science scores on a comprehensive examination were compared to the scores of students in 40 other countries. According to Schmidt, the difference lies in "what we teach and how we teach it." Students in Japan, for example, scored much higher, and the approach their schools take is to study fewer subjects in greater depth, and to take a problem-solving approach rather than one that emphasizes procedure and memorization.

THINK: With your classmates or in your teaching journal, consider these questions:

1. Does the approach and curriculum that Bill Schmidt describes as ideal have a needs-of-learners orientation, an academic-subject-matter orientation, or a needs-of-society orientation? Support your answer.
2. How are teaching techniques and curricula interrelated?

LINK: Given Bill Schmidt's assertion that the two key issues are what we teach and how we teach it, how would you describe and rate the curricula you experienced as a K-12 student?

past may have to be replaced with newer content. In time, even the basic patterns of school curricula you remember from your own school days will be forced to give way to new patterns that respond to changes in knowledge, technology, and insights into the learning process.

There is evidence that such changes will not come easily. Tradition exerts a powerful force, and schools have proved to be among the most change-resistant of our institutions (Renzulli, 1998; Callan, 1998). Despite these difficulties, however, pressures on schools to modify programs in light of new conditions continue to mount. It is probable that curricula you encounter early in your teaching career will vary markedly from those that will seem commonplace in your later years in the profession.

THE HIDDEN CURRICULUM

Young people learn more at school than the topics introduced in the formal, written curriculum. They are also influenced by their exposure to what experts have variously described as the "implicit" or "hidden" curriculum. The hidden curriculum includes all of those things in the school setting that send our learners messages regarding what they ought to be doing and even how they should be thinking. Curriculum researcher Decker Walker (1990) points out three key features of the hidden curriculum. These include (1) teachers' general expectations about how learners should control their emotions in class, (2) what learners should do when there is a need to move from one area of the classroom to another, and (3) how learners should act when they wish to participate in a discussion. Gail McCutcheon (1988), who has also studied the hidden curriculum, points out that much of its content is "transmitted through the everyday, normal goings-on in schools" (p. 191). Patterns vary

from school to school and are influenced in varying degrees by administrators, teachers, and parents and guardians (Henson, 2000).

Your actions as a teacher will help shape the hidden curriculum in your own school. What you do signals to learners what you consider important. If you are unconscious of your hidden-curriculum actions, you may not realize that you are sending unintended messages to members of your class. For example, suppose you are teaching social studies at the high school level. You might have made a point of telling students that they should read articles on the front page of the newspaper every day because good citizens keep up on current events. If your students see you during morning, lunch, or after-school breaks reading only the sports section, they may well conclude that you are insincere. You may say the hard news on the front page is important, but they see that you really only pay attention to sports. The "lesson" these students take away from this experience is the kind of thing young people learn from their exposure to the hidden curriculum. In the case of this social studies example, this kind of learning has little to do with either the formal, prescribed curriculum or with what you believe your real academic intentions to be.

Some authorities who have studied the hidden curriculum fear that it sometimes sends messages to learners that are inconsistent with the values of their own cultural or social group. For example, curriculum experts Michael Apple and Landon Beyer (1988) note that the hidden curriculum in many schools emphasizes deference to authority and an attitude that competence in school subjects will result in high status and lucrative jobs for graduates. Many learners find these perspectives inconsistent with the attitudes of their parents, families, and friends, and hence they may reject the entire school program as irrelevant.

Nearly all authorities agree that the hidden curriculum influences learners' attitudes toward the school program. There is a consensus that teachers need to be sensitive to all the messages that learners may be getting from both the school program and the general school environment. What learners take away from exposure to the hidden curriculum can importantly influence their attitudes toward teachers and the academic offerings of the school.

Following the Web 14.2

Examples of Some Specialized Curriculum-Related Web Sites

Many curriculum-related Web sites specialize in providing specific kinds of information. For example, some of them focus on lesson plans and other instructional support materials, some feature content of interest to people in particular subject areas, and others summarize information related to some major challenges teachers face, regardless of grade levels or subjects they teach (such as assessing learners, motivation, or classroom management). Examples of curriculum Web sites that feature specialized content are provided here.

 For hot links to these sites, visit the companion Web site, located at *http://www. prenhall.com/armstrong*. Select Chapter 14 from the front page of the Web site, then choose the Following the Web module on the navigation bar on the left side of the page.

Understanding the Keys to Motivation to Learn

- *http://www.mcrel.org/resources/noteworthy/barbaram.asp*

  The problem of motivating learners challenges teachers everywhere. This site includes an excellent summary of research-based guidelines that you can use to establish conditions that promise to motivate members of your class to learn. An extensive set of references on motivation is provided.

Curriculum Resources

- *http://k12.bellsouth.net//curriculum/*

  Maintained by BellSouth, this site includes numerous links to materials that can be used in instructional programs that make extensive use of the Internet. Many links are provided for use in (1) elementary schools, (2) middle schools, and (3) senior high schools. If you are looking for resources for Web-based lessons, this site should be one of your first stops.

Curriculum Associates

- *http://www.curriculumassociates.com/*

  This is an example of a site maintained by a commercial firm that is in the business of selling supplementary instructional materials to educators. You will find examples of lesson plans, materials for homeschool programs, software, and many other instructional support items.

Key Ideas In Summary

- The term *curriculum* refers to the selection and organization of content and learning experiences. Because different people use different criteria in making decisions about selection and organization of content, there are important place-to-place variations in elementary and secondary school curricula.
- Curricula that reflect a needs-of-learners orientation are developed as a result of program planners' perceptions of learners' needs and interests. Jean-Jacques

Curriculum Resource Center of Maine

- *http://www.crcom.org/*

  Though not apparent from the title of this Web page, this site specializes in information related to technical education. Contents are designed for use by people in technical colleges, applied technology centers, adult vocational education programs, family and consumer science programs, and by tech prep programs offered in secondary schools. You will also find good links to other Web sites containing materials of interest to technical-education specialists.

Connections+

- *http://www.mcrel.org/resources/plus/index.asp*

  Maintained by a federally funded Regional Education Laboratory, this site features an enormous number of Internet resources (lesson plans, activities, and support materials) that are organized under specific subject areas. There is a vast quantity of material accessible through this site. If you are interested in exploring the scope of instructional support materials available on a good Web site, this would be a fine place to start.

Curriculum Studio

- *http://artsedge.kennedy-center.org/cs.html*

  This site is maintained by ArtsEdge, a joint project of the John F. Kennedy Center for the Performing Arts and the National Endowment for the Arts. It includes links to curriculum design frameworks, to model curricula in the arts, and to units and lesson plans with an arts emphasis. If you are interested in any aspects of the arts in grades K–12, this is a site you should visit.

Philosophy of Curriculum Modification

- *http://silver.skiles.gatech.edu/gallery/barrierfree/curric/CPVA-01.HTML*

  This site includes excellent information related to modifications that can be made to assist learners with disabilities of various kinds. You will find ideas for modifying your instructional program to assist learners having vision, mobility, hearing, or cognitive disabilities.

[Note: Web addresses change frequently. If you are unable to locate one of these sites using the listed URL, try putting the site name in a standard search engine.]

Rousseau was an early proponent of this perspective. In this approach, learners are placed at the center of the planning process. These curricula are alleged to motivate learners and avoid unnecessary fragmentation of content. Critics argue that it is impractical to prepare separate academic experiences for each learner's needs and interests. They are also concerned about whether learners are the best judges of their own and society's needs.

- The academic-subject-matter approach to curriculum development divides content into individual disciplines such as mathematics, history, and English. This approach is based on the assumption that material contained within an individual discipline shares certain similarities. These commonalities, it is alleged, make it easier for learners to master the material. Critics of the approach point out that the real world is not divided into separate academic disciplines. They also note that division of content into packages associated with separate subjects fragments learning and makes it difficult for young people to transfer information to situations beyond the setting in which it was learned.

- There have been two general approaches to preparing programs using an academic-subject-matter orientation. The most common of these has featured the development of learning experiences designed to familiarize learners with the findings of subject-matter specialists. A second approach has favored familiarizing learners with the "structure" of the disciplines. Programs designed in this way seek to introduce young people to the processes that professionals in the disciplines use as they study data and arrive at conclusions.

- Broad-fields curricula attempt to respond to some criticisms that have been made of programs organized around traditional academic disciplines. Broad-fields approaches combine two or more traditional subjects into a single broad area or theme. This theme is used as a basis for planning, and programs are developed that draw content from several disciplines. Broad-fields curricula are promoted on the basis of their capacity for helping learners break down boundaries between and among individual subjects. Problems with the approach include (1) a lack of instructional materials of an interdisciplinary nature and (2) difficulty in finding individual teachers who have enough depth of knowledge in a variety of disciplines to draw materials responsibly from a wide selection of content areas.

- Curricula developed according to a needs-of-society orientation are designed to produce learners capable of maintaining and extending broad social goals. These curricula sort into two basic types: some programs focus on content designed to help learners recognize and respond to important problems, and others center on citizenship development. Many of the latter emphasize providing young people with the kinds of skills they will need to make a living. Supporters of these programs suggest that they promote learners' levels of interest because the content is highly relevant to their own lives. Critics suggest that identification of so-called problems may bring teachers into unproductive conflicts with parents and other community members who have different perspectives on these issues. These critics also maintain that vocationally oriented programs may not be responsive to rapid changes in the job market, and school programs may be providing learners with training experiences that will not match up well with the real needs of the employment market they will enter when they leave school.

- Even though there are important place-to-place differences, certain common patterns are found in many elementary and secondary schools. Large numbers of elementary schools require learners to be exposed to instruction focusing on reading and language arts, mathematics, social studies, science, health, and physical education. Increasingly, elementary pupils are also being introduced to the use of computers. In secondary schools (particularly in senior high schools), learners have a number of electives from which to choose. However, they are usually still obligated to take a certain number of courses in such areas as English, social studies, mathematics, science, and physical education. At the secondary level, there is also an increasing tendency to require students to take at least one computer course.

Chapter 14 Self Test

To review terms and concepts in this chapter, take the Chapter 14 Self Test on the companion Web site, located at *http://www.prenhall.com/armstrong*. Select Chapter 14 from the front page of the Web site, then choose the Self Test module on the navigation bar on the left side of the page. Feedback for the Self Test is immediate. You can keep track of your Self Test scores yourself, or you can choose to submit your scores via e-mail to your instructor.

Reflections

To respond to these questions online, and to save or submit your response electronically, visit the companion Web site, located at *http://www. prenhall.com/armstrong*. Select Chapter 14 from the front page of the Web site, then choose the Reflections module on the navigation bar on the left side of the page. Instructors and students may also wish to use these questions as discussion topics on the Message Board for the companion Web site.

1. To what does the term *curriculum* refer?
2. What are some characteristics of the needs-of-learners orientation?
3. What are some characteristics of the academic-subject-matter orientation?
4. What are some features of a broad-fields curriculum?
5. What are some characteristics of a needs-of-society orientation?
6. Think about some characteristics of the school programs you experienced during your elementary and secondary school years. Can you identify some aspects of these programs that reflected a needs-of-learners orientation?
7. Some people argue that the entire school program should reflect an academic-subject-matter orientation. What are some strengths and weaknesses of this idea? Today's learners represent a very diverse group. Are there some learners who would profit more

than others from such a program? Are there some learners who would be hurt? What is your own position regarding this suggestion?

8. Certain critics argue that our schools are doing a poor job of preparing young people for work in an increasingly technologically complex society. How do you react to this view? If you accept the validity of this contention, what specific changes would you make in the present grades K–12 school program?

9. Supporters of the needs-of-learners orientation point out that learners tend to be motivated by school programs based on this point of view. By implication, are they suggesting that programs developed from the perspectives of the academic-subject-matter orientation and needs-of-society orientation are less motivating? If you agree with these people, what do you think might be done to make school programs based on these orientations more interesting to learners?

10. Some of the reform proposals of the 1980s recommended that students should take more courses in English, mathematics, science, and social studies as requirements for graduation. Does requiring students to take more courses ensure that they will necessarily know more about these subject areas? Why or why not?

▮▮▮▮▮   **Field Experiences, Projects, and Enrichment**   ▮▮▮▮▮

1. With the assistance of a school principal or your course instructor, locate in your library a list of subjects taught at two or more grade levels within a given school. From titles and descriptions of these subjects, decide whether they are based on a needs-of-learners orientation, an academic-subject-matter orientation, a needs-of-society orientation, or whether they reflect a combination of two or even all three of these perspectives. Prepare a written report that summarizes your findings.

2. Write a position paper focusing on one of these topics:
   • School programs need to reflect more of a needs-of-learners orientation.
   • School programs need to reflect more of an academic-subject-matter orientation.
   • School programs need to reflect more of a needs-of-society orientation.

3. Examine two or more reform proposals that appeared during the 1980s. (Ask your instructor for suggestions.) Note at least three recommendations for changes in school curricula made in each proposal. Then interview a school principal or a school district curriculum director about changes in local programs made in the last decade. Determine whether any of these changes paralleled those suggested in the national reform proposals. Share your findings with members of the class.

4. Interview several teachers within a single building who teach a subject or grade level that interests you. Ask them about state, district, or school requirements for learners who take this subject or who are enrolled at this grade level. Also ask whether these requirements are well suited to learners' needs. Finally, ask these teachers what specific changes in requirements for students they would recommend. Prepare an oral report of your findings to share with members of your class.

5. Join together with three or four others in your class to prepare a report on one of these topics:
   • What should a "good" elementary school program look like today?
   • What should a "good" middle school or junior high school program look like today?
   • What should a "good" senior high school program look like today?

   Present your conclusions in the form of a symposium, and then use them as the basis for a short article. Consider sending it to the features editor of your local newspaper.

▮▮▮▮   **References**   ▮▮▮▮

Apple, M. W., & Beyer, L. E. (1988). Social evaluation. In L. E. Beyer & M. W. Apple (Eds.), *The curriculum: Problems, politics, and possibilities* (pp. 33–49). Albany, NY: State University of New York Press.

Callan, R. J. (1998). Giving students the (right) time of day. *Educational Leadership, 55*(4), 84–87.

Cuban, L. (1993). The lure of curriculum reform and its pitiful history. *Phi Delta Kappan, 75*(2), 182–185.

Harrison, C. J. (1990). Concepts, operational definitions, and case studies in instruction. *Education, 110,* 502–505.

Henson, K. T. (2000). *Curriculum development for education reform* (2nd ed.). New York: McGraw-Hill.

McCutcheon, G. (1988). Curriculum and the work of teachers. In L. E. Beyer & M. W. Apple (Eds.), *The curriculum: Problems, politics, and possibilities* (pp. 191–203). Albany, NY: State University of New York Press.

National Commission on Excellence in Education. (1983). *A nation at risk: The imperative for educational reform.* Washington, DC: U.S. Department of Education.

Polakow, V. (1999). A view from the field. In Henson, K. T. & Eller, B. F. (Eds.), *Educational Psychology for Effective Teaching.* Belmont, CA: Wadsworth.

Reinstein, D. (1998). Crossing the economic divide. *Educational Leadership, 55*(4), 28–29.

Renzulli, J. S. (1998). A rising tide lifts all ships: Developing the gifts and talents of all students. *Phi Delta Kappan, 80*(2), 105–111.

Schubert, W. H. (1986). *Curriculum: Perspective, paradigm, and possibility.* New York: Macmillan.

Thompson, S., & Gregg, L. (1997). Reculturing middle schools for meaningful change. *Middle School Journal, 28*(5), 27–31.

Walker, D. F. (1990). *Fundamentals of curriculum.* Orlando, FL: Harcourt Brace Jovanovich.

15

School Funding, Staffing, and Organization

OBJECTIVES

This chapter will help you to

- describe traditional ways in which public education is funded.

- explain some issues associated with school funding.

- point out basic patterns of school district organization.

- identify some of the kinds of professionals who work in school districts.

- describe some basic organizational patterns of individual schools.

- identify responsibilities of different categories of employees who work in individual school buildings.

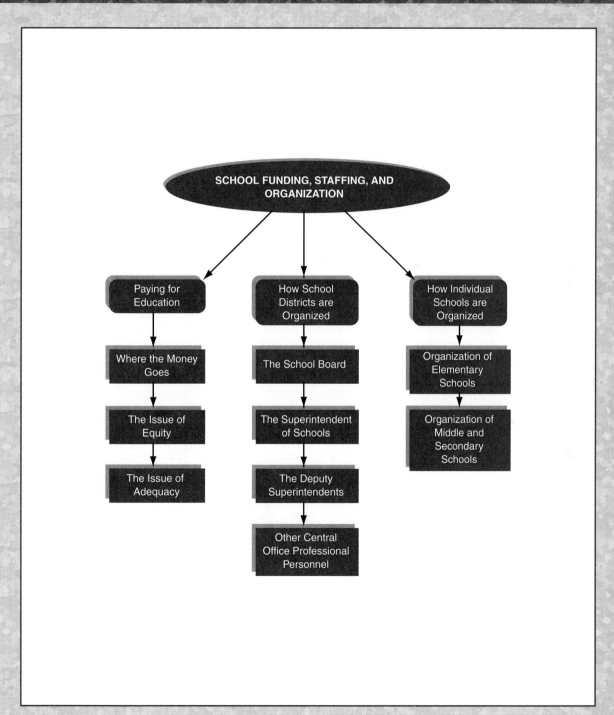

FIGURE 15.1 School Funding, Staffing, and Organization

INTRODUCTION

In recent years, discussion of school-related issues has prompted commitment of more financial resources to support public education. You may be surprised to know that more money than ever before is now used for this purpose. In statistical terms, the dollar amount that is provided to support each child's education is now 40 percent higher (in terms of noninflated dollars) than it was in 1980 (*Mini-Digest of Education Statistics,* 1998).

Though debates continue about whether much higher levels of support are needed to improve the schools, much discussion about school financing today focuses on *how* school money is distributed. For some years, there have been concerns that existing funding arrangements have allocated much more money to support education in some school districts than others. Numerous plans have been proposed to address this inequity.

More recently, critics of prevailing funding patterns have pointed out that simply providing equitable ways to support education in individual school districts does not ensure that high-quality learning is occurring in the schools. They favor fiscal reform that ties allocation of dollars to well-defined programs of study that allow learners to master important content. Reformers interested in this approach have attempted to define characteristics of an "adequate" education and have devised ways for distributing funds to support delivery of this kind of instruction.

Regardless of how they are funded, all school districts have employees who fit into many categories. You may be surprised to know that only about half of the people who work in school districts are teachers. Support staff, including personnel for administrative offices, transportation, food service, plant and maintenance, health, and other assorted categories, account for about 30 percent of all school employees. Instructional staff other than teachers (such as classroom aides, instructional media specialists, guidance counselors, and psychological personnel) represent about 12 percent of the total school employment force. The final category of principals and district administrators accounts for between 4 percent and 5 percent of the total (Snyder, 1994).

Leaders of school districts have had to develop sophisticated organizational plans to manage the educational enterprise. Larger school districts have more complex organizational schemes than smaller ones. Similarly, individual schools with many learners also have more intricate organizations than those that enroll fewer learners.

Teachers' contacts with individuals who play various roles within school districts and buildings vary with district and school-enrollment size. For example, if you accept a teaching position in a small elementary school, you will have frequent (often daily) conversations with the school principal. On the other hand, if you work in a large high school, days or weeks may go by without your having occasion to speak to the principal. Indeed, in the latter situation, the principal may never step into your classroom during an entire school year. If you teach in a large school, you will be much more likely to see a vice principal, an assistant principal, or some other administrative subordinate of the principal.

As a teacher, you will have infrequent personal contact with many employees of the school district. For example, much of the custodial work in the district where you work may be completed after you have left for the day, and you probably will have

Video Viewpoint

Aging Public Schools in Dire Need of Repair

WATCH: In this ABC News video segment, we learn that more than $112 billion is needed to repair America's aging public school buildings, three-fourths of which are more than 25 years old. President Clinton has said "we cannot expect our children to raise themselves up in schools that are literally falling down," but both state and federal funding for school repairs, renovations, and rebuilding are contentious issues.

THINK: With your classmates or in your teaching journal, consider these questions:

1. Currently, the federal government does not provide funding for renovation of school buildings, except in emergencies like natural disasters, so many school districts rely on local taxes and bond measures to finance such projects. Where do you think the money for repairs to school buildings should come from?
2. How important is the addition of technology infrastructure (e.g. wiring that allows for Internet access and networking) to America's schools, most of which were built before 1955?

LINK: How are students affected by the physical environment of the school they attend?

very few occasions to meet with school nurses during the working day. Central administrative office support personnel (for example, people assigned to manage the district's transportation system) spend little time in the district's schools. Hence, you are not apt to meet many of these individuals.

PAYING FOR EDUCATION

Schooling is expensive. In one recent year, expenditures on elementary and secondary education in the United States totaled about $340 billion (*Mini-Digest of Education Statistics,* 1998). This amounts to between $7,000 and $8,000 for every learner enrolled in grades K through 12 (*Condition of Education,* 1998). From where does this money come? You may be surprised at the answer.

Today, elected federal officials assert that educational reform is a top national priority. It has become commonplace for the president to put forward quite specific proposals for improving the schools in the annual State of the Union address. Given the rhetorical attention to education by elected federal officials, you might suppose that the federal government has become a major financial supporter of public education. Or, at the very least, you might expect that there would have been a great increase in the percentage of federal financial support for schools in recent years. While these assumptions may be logical, neither is true. In terms of its financial support for the nation's schools, the federal government is a small player. In recent years, only about 7 percent of public school revenue has come from the federal government. In fact, this represents a decline from 20 years ago, when federal money represented nearly 10 percent of total public school expenditures (CPRE, 1999b).

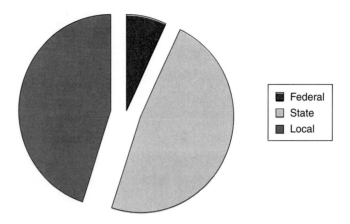

Federal contributions = 7 percent
State contributions = 48 percent
Local contributions = 45 percent

FIGURE 15.2   Relative Contributions of Federal, State, and Local Governments to the Support of Public Education

State and local governments represent far more significant sources of financial support for the schools than the federal government. For the past 40 years, there has been a trend toward shifting more financial responsibility for education from local sources to state sources. Part of this change can be explained by the desire for state governments to increase their levels of financial assistance to less wealthy local school districts. As a result of this trend, state governments today provide about 48 percent of total school revenues, and local governments provide about 45 percent (CPRE, 1999b). As noted above, the federal government accounts for the remaining 7 percent. (See Figure 15.2 for a graphic representation of contributions from federal, state, and local sources.)

Where the Money Goes

There are hundreds of school districts in the United States, and they differ greatly in terms of wealth, nature of the learners they serve, levels of community support, and in other characteristics. Despite these variations, patterns of distributions of school funds are surprisingly similar from place to place.

About 60 percent of funds needed to support the schools goes to support instruction, including regular teaching in traditional classrooms as well as instructional services for learners with special needs. Despite frequently public concerns about "high administrative costs," actual expenditures for administration are relatively low, a little over 8 percent of the total. This figure is well below the 10.2 percent spent on maintenance of buildings and general operations. Transportation services and food services each account for a little over 4 percent of the typical school district budget (CPRE, 1999c).

The Issue of Equity

Debates about school financing often have centered around the issue of *equity*. As applied to public school districts, the principle of equity holds that there should not be tremendous disparity between the financial resources available to support learners in one school district as compared to another. Traditional funding arrangements have not always served this principle well.

Historically, state governments gave local school districts the right to raise money by levying property taxes. The difficulty with this approach is that individual school districts vary tremendously in the taxable value of property within their boundaries. In one state, for example, a carefully designed study found that there was 10 times as much taxable wealth available to support each learner in the wealthiest school district than in the poorest school district (CPRE, 1999d). Variations in the amount of taxable property has made it relatively easy for school districts with high property valuations to generate adequate funds. Indeed, often these districts have so much wealth that they can raise needed school funds with a relatively low rate of taxes. This is especially likely to be the case in a school district with relatively few children to serve that has within its boundaries some extremely valuable commercial and industrial properties. Taxes on these commercial properties generate a tremendous amount of income for schools. As a result, tax rates, particularly those on private houses, can be kept quite low.

On the other hand, school districts with less valuable taxable property have found it difficult to raise money to support schools. Such districts frequently have higher than average tax rates; however, because the value of the district's property is not high, the high tax rates may not provide enough money to adequately support the schools. Often these districts have little valuable commercial property. As a result, high tax rates hit individual homeowners hard.

Debates about the equity issue often point out that learners have little personal choice about where they live. With some exceptions, most must attend school in their home school districts. Since this is the case, some advocates of funding reform feel that a young person should not be penalized by being forced to attend an inadequately funded school simply because he or she lives in a community with little taxable property.

They suggest that states should do something to make the taxable property available to all school districts more equal. A common approach to this problem has been for states to provide what often is called a *foundation program* for their schools. Foundation programs seek to provide additional funds for less wealthy districts to enable them to provide educational services of a quality that meets a minimal standard set by the state. The difficulty has been that many foundation programs have established levels of support that are too low to provide significant help to the poorest school districts.

A more controversial plan has been the *guaranteed tax base* (GTB) approach. Though there are variations on this theme, the basic idea is for state governments to pool all taxable property in the state. The value of this property is divided among the state's school districts based on their enrollments. The purpose is to provide an equal amount of taxable property behind every learner in the state, regardless of where he or she lives. If adopted, a GTB approach might allow a less wealthy school district to lower its previous tax rate while, at the same time, enabling it to take in as much or even more money to support educational programs.

What Do You Think?

School Support Up, but Parents Still Pay More

Over the past two decades, there has been a substantial increase in total spending to support public schools. In fact, the total price of public education has increased faster than prices in general. At the same time, parents and guardians of learners are being asked to write personal checks to pay for more and more of the school program. They are billed for such things as rental of musical instruments, insurance to cover sports injuries, and parking. Fees in some school districts now are so numerous that parents and guardians find themselves writing checks for several hundred dollars for each child enrolled in school.

What Do You Think?

1. What might be some explanations for there being an increase in fees paid by parents at the same time public funding for education has been rising?
2. Is it appropriate for public schools to impose special fees on parents and guardians of learners? Why or why not?
3. As you look ahead, do you foresee a trend for more fees to be paid by parents and guardians, or have these fees pretty much "topped out" at this point? Explain your answer?

The Issue of Adequacy

Increasingly, critics of school financing practices suggest that reforms to address equity are insufficient. The problem with a focus on equity, they allege, is that responses do little more than ensure that per-pupil spending in districts with less wealth does not remain irresponsibly lower than that in districts with more wealth. They believe that a more appropriate goal is to concentrate on the issue of learner achievement. What is needed is a clear idea of what young people should learn and a well-articulated plan to help them master designated content and skills at an appropriate level. Once these matters are defined, then experts can determine a cost of an *adequate spending level* that will provide resources necessary to allow learners to reach the designated achievement levels.

Several approaches are being tried to identify an adequate spending level. One scheme looks at how learners in individual school districts have performed on standardized state tests (CPRE, 1999a). Districts with learner scores at levels believed to be high enough to signal satisfactory achievement are identified. Then an average per-pupil funding level of these successful districts is computed. This figure is identified as the minimum necessary for school districts to provide an "adequate" program for learners. Additional funds are directed to school districts below this level to bring their per-pupil spending up to the level of the successful districts.

The issue of adequate funding continues to evolve. In fact, the whole area of school funding represents a thicket of tricky policy alternatives where value judgments often play as important a role as dispassionate consideration of data. A consensus solution to school funding challenges is not imminent. Indeed, you probably

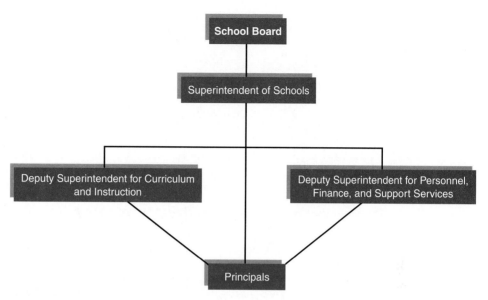

FIGURE 15.3   Example of the Basic Administrative Organization of a School District

will be hearing (and possibly participating in) heated debates about school funding throughout your career in education.

HOW SCHOOL DISTRICTS ARE ORGANIZED

There are more than 15,000 school districts in the United States. These vary from small operations in isolated rural areas to districts encompassing the densely popu-lated core areas of the nation's major cities. The kind of management scheme needed to oversee the operation of a given district depends, in large measure, on the number of learners enrolled in the district's schools.

Even districts that enroll roughly equivalent numbers of learners reflect some differences in their administrative organizational schemes. These variations result from unique local conditions, special requirements imposed by state education au-thorities, and long-standing traditions. An example of an organizational scheme for a school district is provided in Figure 15.3.

The School Board

The school board is the basic policy-making body of a school district. In some dis-tricts, it may be known by other names such as board of education, board of trustees, or school council. School boards represent a link between the local school district and the state department of education. Because the state department of education im-plements mandates of the state legislature, local school boards are also indirectly

Following the Web **15.1**

Financing Education

Interest in school programs spawns an accompanying concern about how educational resources are being spent. Different groups have different priorities regarding how money for school should be spent, and these varying perspectives give rise to debates about spending priorities. The sample Web sites that follow contain information that often plays a role in these discussions.

 For hot links to these sites, visit the companion Web site, located at *http://www. prenhall.com/armstrong*. Select Chapter 15 from the front page of the Web site, then choose the Following the Web module on the navigation bar on the left side of the page.

Welcome to the Consortium for Policy Research in Education

* *http://www.wcer.wisc.edu/cpre/*

  The Consortium for Policy Research in Education (CPRE), headquartered at the University of Wisconsin-Madison, links five top national research universities interested in improving student learning through educational reform, policy, and finance initiatives. At this highly recommended site, you will find connections to outstanding discussions of policy issues related to finance.

Study Group Links School Finance with Standards-Based Reform

* *http://www.nasbe.org/fincerpt.htm*

  Much discussion of school financing today focuses on how various approaches that receive monetary support tie to student learning. This Web site features a discussion of findings of a study group commissioned by a national professional organization for school board members to explore the relationship between achievement-based school reform and commitment of financial resources.

Spending and Revenue for Children's Programs

* *http://www.financeproject.org/spending.html*

  This site features an excellent article commissioned by The Finance Project. It features a discussion of various sources of financial support for children both in the area of education and in the area of general social services.

linked to the legislature. The state legislature, in fact, exercises ultimate control over local school districts. In most states, the legislature has the right to create, modify, eliminate, and otherwise affect the operation of local school districts.

School boards vary in size, usually containing from five to nine members. Members are elected in most districts; in a few, they are appointed. Members of elected school boards are supposed to reflect general community sentiment regarding the schools. In reality, though, school board members are often well-established community members who reflect mainstream and somewhat conservative thinking. People who agree to serve on school boards often do so as a matter of public service. While school board members in many parts of the country receive no compensation, they are paid for their work in some places.

Legal Issues and Constraints Affecting Finance Reform for Education and Related Services

- *http://www.financeproject.org/legal.html*

  If you are interested in the relationship between proposals to reform education and dollars available to fund suggested improvements, you will find material at this site useful. The article was commissioned by The Finance Project.

Behind the Numbers: When States Spend More

- *http://epn.org/prospect/36/36rothf.html*

  What happens when states *do* spend more money on education. In this article prepared for *The American Prospect, Inc.,* Richard Rothstein provides some interesting answers.

Financing Schools

- *http://www.futureofchildren.org/sch/*

  This material, which was published by the David and Lucile Packard Foundation, features a number of articles that focus on various aspects of school financing. Diverse topics range from the history of funding of school programs to nontraditional ways of supporting education involving the use of chargers, private contracts, and charters.

Financing Schools Equitably: Expanding the Debate to Encompass Achievement

- *http://www.ascd.org/issue/finance.html*

  This article is published by the American Society for Supervision and Curriculum Development (ASCD). You will find it a good source of information about the recent focus on the relationship between school funding and learner achievement.

[Note: Web addresses change frequently. If you are unable to locate one of these sites using the listed URL, try putting the site name in a standard search engine.]

The school board's primary responsibility is to establish basic policy for the district. Part of its role is to oversee implementation of state requirements. The school board adopts the budget and reacts to recommendations regarding personnel and curriculum that it receives from the district superintendent and his or her staff.

School board members are among the unheralded heroes of American education. They put in long hours on school-related work. They receive telephone calls late into the night from school patrons who have grievances to air. Their decisions are watched closely by the local media, and their actions sometimes draw negative comments on the editorial pages of local newspapers. Letters to the editor and editorials often question the motives of school board members (and sometimes even their integrity). Angry taxpayers freely let school board members know their displeasure when tax rates must

Members of this school board are engaged in making basic policy for the school district.

be hiked to fund school budgets. In short, school board members find themselves torn between the competing perspectives of many contending interest groups, each of which is certain that it holds the key to a policy decision that will improve the schools.

Given the pressures they face, it is a wonder that people want to fill vacancies on school boards. But they do, and in many communities, school board service confers an important status on board members. Schools everywhere are beneficiaries of the willingness of these good people to serve.

Many citizens in local communities believe that school board members are intimately involved in the day-to-day operations of the school, but this generally is not the case. The board directs the superintendent to oversee the running of the school. Its own task is to frame policy and hold the superintendent responsible for implementing it. In some districts, board members do try to involve themselves in operational decisions (see this chapter's Critical Incident). This invariably leads to conflict between the board and the superintendent, which sometimes results in a change of superintendents. Neither the school board nor the superintendent can discharge responsibilities appropriate to each function unless there is trust and confidence on both sides.

Most school board meetings are open to the public. State laws vary from place to place regarding the kinds of circumstances that allow boards to meet in private (usually called "executive") sessions. Boards often have the right to do so when they are considering sensitive personnel matters.

At one time, many school boards scheduled their meetings during the day, but this practice is dying out. Increasingly, school boards meet at night to allow members of the community with daytime jobs to attend. It is common practice for school boards to set aside some time after the formal agenda has been completed for members of the public to speak briefly about issues of concern to them. When the board is considering a controversial policy issue (such as whether to implement a busing program to establish a racial balance in the district's schools), board meetings are very well attended.

In summary, the school board acts as the district's major policy-making body. It functions as a political entity that allows members of the public to make their influence on school policy decisions felt. At the same time, it represents the broader interests of the state legislature and the state department of education.

The Superintendent of Schools

The superintendent is the chief executive officer (CEO) of a school district. A school district superintendency is a challenging position, particularly in a large school district. In such a setting, executive responsibilities of the superintendent parallel those of top corporate administrators.

Often the superintendent is hired by the school board, but some are chosen in other ways (for example, some superintendents are publicly elected officials). The superintendent usually attends all school board sessions except for those where his or her own performance is being evaluated. The superintendent, who may argue against a certain course of action when it is being considered by the school board, is obligated to support and implement all school board policies once they have been adopted.

The superintendent exercises some control over the school district's workforce, because the superintendent in most places officially recommends candidates for employment to the school board. All other employees of the school district are directly or indirectly accountable to the superintendent. Even though specific responsibilities may be delegated to others, ultimately the superintendent is held accountable for their performance.

The superintendent is responsible for all aspects of the school program. For example, he or she monitors all academic programs and arranges for periodic status reports to the school board. The superintendent oversees the maintenance of all school buildings and equipment and approves expenditures of funds within the general guidelines authorized by the school board.

The superintendent works closely with administrative subordinates to ensure smooth functioning of the entire district operation. One of the superintendent's most important jobs is overseeing the preparation of the annual budget, which must be submitted to the school board for review and approval. Budget proposals always attract a great deal of scrutiny from board members and from the public at large.

As the chief public relations officer of the school district, the superintendent must defend school policies in many public forums. Superintendents are often called upon to speak before civic groups and other citizens' organizations. They tend to be individuals who are comfortable with many different kinds of people. Because public relations is such an important part of the job, many superintendents have exemplary writing and speaking skills.

Critical Incident

A Visit from the School Board

Woong Kim teaches second grade in a suburban district outside of a major West Coast city. He is in his second year of teaching and is particularly interested in teaching reading. As an undergraduate, he was influenced by several of his professors who believed in a whole-language approach to reading instruction. This method builds on learners' natural patterns of oral language, and Woong has found it to be effective in working with his own pupils. Members of his class are a diverse group representing many ethnic groups, some of whom do not speak English at home. Large numbers of families in the area have incomes below the official poverty level.

Loretta Robinson, a newly elected member of the local school board, recently sent a letter to all of the district's elementary school teachers. In the letter, she pointed to some research studies that strongly support the use of a phonics approach to reading. Ms. Robinson went on to note that standardized reading test scores of children in the district are well below national averages and recommended that teachers adopt the phonics approach to teaching reading. Ms. Robinson indicated that she would be contacting selected teachers in the district later in the year regarding what they were doing to improve their reading programs.

Woong recalled that the university professors who favored the whole-language approach had not had many good things to say about phonics-based reading instruction. Many of them had cited research supporting whole-language instruction that seemed to say quite different things from those studies mentioned in Ms. Robinson's letter.

To get another point of view, Woong checked with his grade-level leader and principal. Both of them said that district policy prescribes no specific method of reading instruction. Teachers are assumed to be professionals who are expected to make instructional decisions that are appropriate for the children in their own classrooms. The principal also pointed out that the superintendent has an excellent working relationship with most members of the school board and that it is very unusual for a school board member to make a direct appeal to teachers regarding a specific instructional approach.

After thinking about the situation, Woong initially decided to keep using the whole-language approach. But yesterday something happened that has made him uneasy. He received a letter

The Deputy Superintendents

In medium- and large-sized school districts, the superintendent has several subordinate administrators to whom responsibilities for specific managerial tasks are delegated. These people have titles such as deputy superintendent, associate superintendent, or assistant superintendent. The administrative scheme illustrated in Figure 15.3 provides for two deputy superintendents: the deputy superintendent for curriculum and instruction and the deputy superintendent for personnel, finance, and support services.

Each of these deputies is responsible for a major component of the district's operation. As the title suggests, the deputy superintendent for curriculum and instruction has responsibility for managing the district's academic programs. This person oversees a number of other administrators. Three key subordinates include the executive director of elementary education (responsible for programs in grades pre-kindergarten

from the president of the school board announcing that the entire board will spend a day visiting his school. Although it is not clear which board members will visit which classrooms, Woong is worried that Ms. Robinson may visit his. He is afraid she might notice that he is not using a phonics approach and is wondering whether she might make negative comments about his teaching that could hurt his career.

. . .

Specifically, what does Woong see as the problem? What past experiences have conditioned his views? In what ways might they differ from experiences of others who may become involved? How might these experiences have led these people to develop opinions about the whole-language approach that differ from Woong's? What negatives might there be for a school board member in deciding to complain about Woong's approach? What positives? What do you think the most probable result will be?

Is there someone specific to whom he should talk? What might happen if Ms. Robinson asks him about his commitment to phonics-based instruction and he gives her an honest response? Will this honesty hurt his career? Is Ms. Robinson justified in questioning a teacher's instructional approach? How might other school board members react to her actions?

Are there pressures on teachers to conform to wishes of people in positions of authority? Who exerts these pressures? Have you ever been in a situation where you have felt yourself forced to adopt a position that runs contrary to your true feelings? How did you react? Do you think these kinds of pressures interfere with efforts to introduce changes into school programs? Can people who are "change agents" survive long in public education? Why or why not?

To respond to this Critical Incident online, and to save or submit your response electronically, visit the companion Web site, located at *http://www.prenhall.com/armstrong*. Select Chapter 15 from the front page of the Web site, then choose the Critical Incidents module on the navigation bar on the left side of the page. Instructors and students may also wish to use these scenarios as discussion topics on the Message Board for the companion Web site.

through 6), the executive director of secondary education (responsible for programs in grades 7 through 12), and the executive director of student support services.

The executive director of elementary education and the executive director of secondary education supervise a number of people who have specialized responsibilities for maintaining and enhancing the quality of the instructional program. Many of these people are specialists in teaching specific academic subjects. The executive director of student support services oversees leaders of the district's psychological services, counseling, and guidance programs; its special education programs; its health service operations; its school-attendance monitoring function; and its federal programs. Figure 15.4 illustrates an example of an organizational plan for that part of a district's operation falling under the jurisdiction of the deputy superintendent for curriculum and instruction.

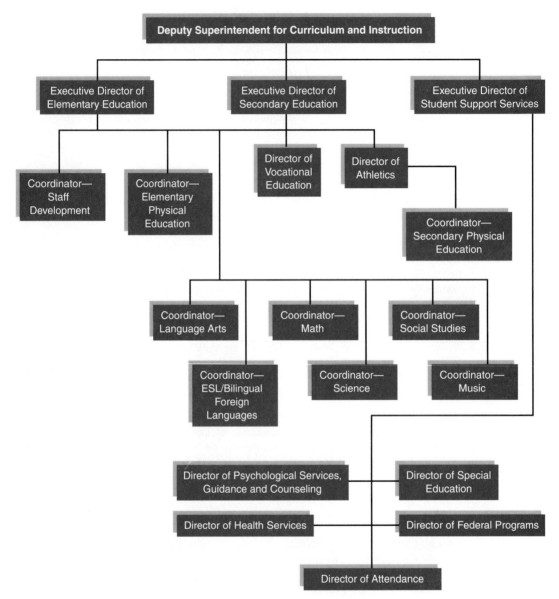

FIGURE 15.4   Example of the Administrative Jurisdiction of a Deputy Superintendent for Curriculum and Instruction

Note that Figure 15.4 does not provide a separate leadership structure for junior high schools or middle schools. These schools are administered by personnel charged with responsibilities for either elementary education or secondary education.

Even the terms *elementary education* and *secondary education* are not interpreted in the same ways in all places. For example, in some areas, elementary education is often thought of as embracing grades K through 6, whereas in other places, grades K through

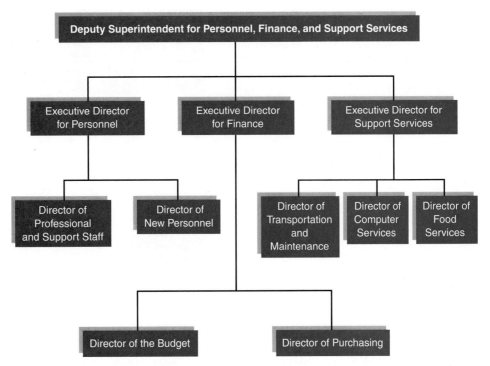

FIGURE 15.5 Example of the Administrative Jurisdiction of a Deputy Superintendent for Personnel, Finance, and Support

8 comprise the elementary program. Similarly, in some districts, secondary education is often interpreted to mean grades 7 through 12, but other districts consider it to be grades 6 through 12, 9 through 12, or some other set of grades. (Grades 10, 11, and 12 are almost always included within the secondary education designation.)

The pattern becomes even more confusing in districts that identify separate organizational structures for junior high schools and middle schools. The term *middle school* has been particularly difficult to pin down in terms of the grade levels it embraces. Where middle schools exist, they ordinarily include grades 6 and 7. Beyond these two grades, middle school grade configurations vary tremendously from place to place. For example, some middle schools have grades 5, 6, and 7; some have grades 5, 6, 7, and 8; some have grades 6, 7, and 8; some have grades 6, 7, 8, and 9; and some have still other arrangements.

The deputy superintendent for personnel, finance, and support services has a wide range of responsibilities. Subordinate administrators who assist this person may have responsibilities in such areas as personnel, finance, and support services. An example of an organizational plan for the part of a district's operations that is the responsibility of the deputy superintendent for personnel, finance, and support services is provided in Figure 15.5.

The executive director for personnel is responsible for screening candidates and making hiring recommendations. These decisions often involve cooperation with

Many school districts have bus routes that extend great distances. They own large numbers of buses and employ many drivers. Managing school transportation services is an important responsibility of a central school district administrative office.

other district administrators. For example, it may be necessary to get the concurrence of the principal in the building to which a prospective new employee is to be assigned. The executive director of personnel's office also often monitors all records of existing faculty and staff members, keeps track of where each person is on the salary scale, monitors employee benefits programs, and takes charge of many other duties having to do with employee relations.

As the title implies, the executive director for finance has broad authority in areas related to budgeting and purchasing. This office is often responsible for drafting initial versions of the proposed annual budget. This administrator is responsible for overseeing expenditures to ensure that they are in line with what has been authorized. School purchases of all kinds are often executed and monitored by personnel attached to the executive director for finance.

The executive director for support services oversees a variety of important functions. For example, this office will often manage all transportation and maintenance operations. Food services provided by the schools frequently come under the jurisdiction of this executive director as well. The executive director for support services and this person's subordinates may also manage other support services such as printing and computer services.

Other Central Office Professional Personnel

Some school districts, particularly large ones, have many professionals with specialized skills who are headquartered in the district's central administrative offices. (A number of these people are referenced on the charts in Figure 15.4 and Figure 15.5.) Typically, they have responsibilities that are either district-wide in scope or that serve at least some of the district's schools.

Figure 15.4 identifies a number of "coordinators." These are individuals responsible for instruction in the area under their jurisdiction. Some districts use different terms to describe these individuals; for example, they may be called consultants, directors, or district program chairs. Often, these positions are held by former teachers who proved to be exemplary performers in the classroom and have gone on to do advanced study in their specializations and in curriculum. Some states and districts require coordinators to hold special kinds of certificates.

Many school districts have several people attached to an office who are responsible for overseeing guidance and counseling activities throughout the district. For example, there may be one or more professional psychologists attached to this office, as well as other people with advanced training in specialized areas related to the counseling and guidance function.

Many districts employ *psychometrists*. Psychometrists are people who have had advanced training in the construction and administration of sophisticated tests that are designed to measure mental abilities of various kinds. These individuals frequently have advanced degrees and must qualify for a special certificate in many places.

There may also be some special kinds of teachers attached to the central administrative offices. These include specialists in such areas as reading who work with teachers and learners in several of the district's schools. Additionally, there may be homebound teachers who are assigned to work with learners in the district who are unable to attend regular school classes. Many teachers in these specialty areas have advanced academic training in their fields.

Some districts have research and evaluation specialists who are charged with monitoring innovations and overseeing the administration of standardized testing programs. Many of these people tend to hold advanced degrees, and some districts require them to hold special certificates as well.

These are just some examples of the kinds of professionals who often work out of a district's central administrative offices. Today's school districts employ large numbers of people besides school principals and regular classroom teachers.

HOW INDIVIDUAL SCHOOLS ARE ORGANIZED

Administrative organizational schemes for schools are varied, although some features are quite common. Most school-to-school differences result because of variations in enrollment. Elementary schools tend to have organizational patterns that distinguish them from secondary schools, which draw learners from several "feeder" elementary schools. This means that, typically, an elementary school enrolls fewer learners than a secondary school. Hence, in most cases, administrative organizational schemes in elementary schools are somewhat less complex than those in secondary schools.

Organization of Elementary Schools

Building Administrators   The school principal is the chief executive officer of an elementary school and is responsible for all aspects of the school's operation. The principal oversees the academic program and ensures that it is in compliance with state and local regulations. The welfare of individual pupils is another important

Following the Web **15.2**

Developing School Leaders

The quality of leadership in schools affects the quality of the their programs. For this reason, people concerned about improving education often place a heavy emphasis on enhancing the quality of school personnel. Abundant information is available on the Web that relates to developing the capacity of school leaders. Examples of sites that you might wish to visit follow.

For hot links to these sites, visit the companion Web site, located at *http://www. prenhall.com/armstrong*. Select Chapter 15 from the front page of the Web site, then choose the following Web module on the navigation bar on the left side of the page.

Educational Leadership

- *http://odie.ascd.org/pubs/el/elintro.html*

  Educational Leadership is a journal published eight times a year by the Association for Supervision and Curriculum Development (ASCD). At this site, you will find links to articles that have appeared in recent issues. Many of them focus on school leadership issues.

Publications: Governance & Leadership

- *http://www.educ.msu.edu/epfp/iel/pubs/govt.html*

  This site is maintained by the Institute for Educational Leadership, Inc. You will find annotated bibliographies of several books focusing on leadership of the schools.

ELC—Executive Leadership Center

- *http://www.csla.org/CSLA/elc.html*

  Many states have their own programs for development of top school leaders. This site is maintained by The Executive Leadership Center, a partnership between the Association of California School Administrators (ACSA) and the California Department of Education. You will find information related to the nature of professional development programs ELC offers to superintendents in our most populous state.

School Leadership

- *http://middleweb.com/ContntsLead.html*

  Leadership needs vary somewhat depending on the type of school being served. This Web site provides numerous links to leadership-improvement ideas for administrators who work in middle schools.

References

- *http://www.sedl.org/change/leadership/references.html*

  Much has been written about school leadership. This site contains an extensive bibliography of books and articles that treat this topic. About 100 individual titles are listed.

responsibility of the principal. Except in the very largest of elementary schools, principals often know the names of a great number of pupils in every grade.

As a rule, parents of elementary school children take an active interest in the operation of the school. The principal is charged with winning parental support for school programs and encouraging active parental participation in parent-teacher groups and other school activities.

Principals are also responsible for the performance of each teacher in their building. Teachers look to the principal for guidance and support, and the principal is expected to provide leadership in assisting teachers who may be experiencing difficulty in the classroom. Scholars Sharon Feiman-Nemser and Robert E. Floden (1986), after an extensive review of research studies focusing on teachers' attitudes toward principals, found the following common feelings:

- Teachers do not want the principal to interfere with their daily instructional decisions.
- Teachers expect the principal to act as a buffer between themselves and their critics.
- Teachers expect the principal to take the lead in establishing and maintaining a disciplined learning environment.
- Teachers cooperate best with a principal who is perceived to be properly discharging the legitimate professional role of the principal.
- The most important lever a principal has to achieve high academic standards is the good will of the teachers in the building.

Principals also oversee the work of other professional and staff employees. Depending on the size of the school, other employees might include assistant principals, counselors, individual subject specialists (for example, in reading), special education teachers, nurses, and custodians. Because of their broad-ranging responsibilities, most principals are issued contracts that call for them to be on the job more days during the year than are classroom teachers. Often, principals are expected to be in their buildings for at least 11 months of the year.

Larger elementary schools have one or more assistant principals who oversee certain aspects of the school program as directed by the principal. Assistant principals' contracts also typically require them to work a longer school year than do classroom teachers.

An example of an administrative organizational plan for a medium-sized elementary school (approximately 450 pupils) is provided in Figure 15.6.

Grade-Level Leaders   Larger elementary schools often have teachers who are assigned to play special leadership roles as grade-level leaders. Grade-level leaders are found in schools where two (and often three or more) classes exist at each grade level. Teachers who fill these positions represent the concerns of all teachers at their grade level in meetings with the principal. They work with all teachers at their grade level to plan and coordinate learning experiences for children. They sometimes take the lead in introducing new techniques and in modeling their use in the classroom. They are often responsible for ordering materials for all teachers at their grade level. Grade-level leaders usually are selected on the basis of their years of successful teaching, interpersonal relations skills, and advanced academic training.

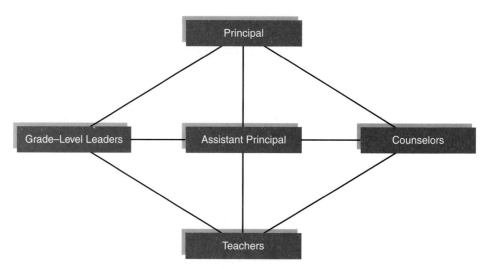

FIGURE 15.6   Example of the Administrative Organization of a Medium-Sized Elementary School

Specialty Teachers   Elementary schools often include a few teachers who have received some type of specialized training. Among them are teachers who are specialists in working with learners who have emotional or physical handicaps. There may be one or more reading specialists assigned to a single building, and/or there may be several teachers who are trained to work with gifted and talented learners. Some schools have teachers who have been hired to work with other categories of learners for whom special educational support money is available (for example, children of migrant workers).

Other Professionals   Several categories of nonteaching professional employees often are employed in elementary schools. For example, a school nurse may be in attendance for at least part of the school day. This person's responsibility is to deal with minor health problems and to oversee the management of learners' health records.

A school may have one or more counselors. Counselors typically are professionals who taught several years then went on to complete advanced coursework leading to special counseling certification. Their role is to help learners work through personal and academic problems. They frequently also have responsibilities for administering standardized tests. Counselors often are issued contracts that require them to work two or three weeks longer each school year than do regular classroom teachers.

A title such as "learning resource specialist" increasingly is being used to describe professionals who formerly were known as librarians. The change in title reflects the broadening range of these employees' responsibilities. In addition to managing all aspects of the school library (including teaching classes in library skills), they are often responsible for managing instructional support equipment such as VCRs, film projectors, tape recorders, audiocassette players, television sets, and computers. Many of them have special training in instructional technology as well as in library science. Because of the need to process books, inventory equipment, and take care of other

Many elementary schools are served by reading specialists. These professional staff members work with individual children with reading difficulties. They often also assist regular classroom teachers with materials and instructional methodologies associated with reading.

job-related matters, some learning resource specialists work a longer school year than do regular classroom teachers.

Other Staff Members   Elementary schools have employees who perform many other important functions. One or more secretaries may work in the principal's office. In larger schools, there may also be secretaries assigned to work with the assistant principals and counselors. There may be a supply room clerk who takes charge of ordering and distributing materials. Sometimes this person also is in charge of managing and maintaining duplicating equipment.

Paraprofessionals are people who, although lacking formal professional training as teachers, are hired to assist teachers in various ways. They may work with individual learners who experience problems, help teachers prepare instructional materials, monitor learners when they take tests, and complete other tasks to support the work of classroom teachers.

Many elementary schools prepare lunches for pupils. A kitchen staff headed by a chief cook is responsible for this activity. In addition, virtually every school has a custodial staff that is responsible for cleaning the building and taking care of routine maintenance tasks. In small schools, there may be only one custodian; larger schools employ several.

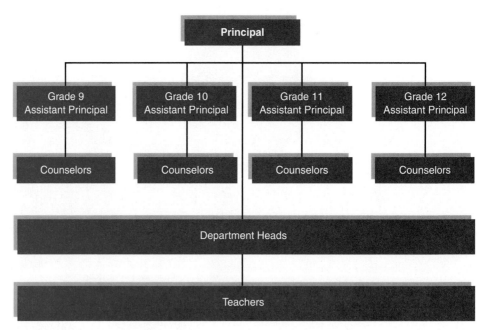

FIGURE 15.7   Example of an Administrative Organizational Plan for a High School of Education

Organization of Middle and Secondary Schools

Because middle schools have a variety of possible administrative arrangements, it is difficult to point to a general pattern. We have elected to treat middle schools and secondary schools together, because large numbers of middle schools are organized into academic departments much as high schools are. Those middle schools that are not organized in this manner have patterns more closely reflecting those found in elementary school buildings.

Building Administrators   Secondary schools vary greatly in size. The complexity of the administrative arrangement tends to increase as school enrollment increases. An example of an administrative arrangement for a high school enrolling between 1,500 and 2,000 students is provided in Figure 15.7.

The principal of a large secondary school has the demanding job of supervising a huge teaching and support staff. A school with 2,000 students, for example, may have more than 75 teachers. The principal also has to manage a large budget and has a challenging public relations role. He or she must deal effectively with parents and other citizens who have different views about what a good school should provide. This requires the principal to be visible in the local community, which includes attendance at all major school events as well as participation in service and other community organizations. Finally, the principal must exercise leadership over the school program and ensure that all federal, state, and local requirements are met.

In most secondary schools, the principal has one or more assistants. In the example provided in Figure 15.7, the principal has four assistant principals, one to work with each class (grade 9, grade 10, grade 11, and grade 12). Individual assistant principals are responsible for instruction, guidance, scheduling, and other functions as they relate to students at their assigned grade level. This arrangement is only one of several that are commonly found in secondary schools.

An alternate scheme followed in many high schools assigns responsibilities for one or more functions to each assistant principal. Each assistant works with students and teachers in all grades, but only in a limited number of areas of responsibility. For example, there may be an assistant principal for scheduling and discipline; an assistant principal for curriculum; an assistant principal for budget, computing, maintenance, and food services; and an assistant principal for guidance and student services. Whatever the administrative arrangement, however, the principal and the assistant principals typically work a much longer school year than do teachers.

In addition to the principal and the assistant principals, a large secondary school may have other administrators. For example, there may be a head counselor, who is responsible for assigning responsibilities to members of the counseling staff. There may also be an athletic director, who oversees budgets and personnel associated with interschool and intramural athletics. Another sort of director found in many secondary schools is the finance director, who oversees a small staff of people monitoring the school budget and managing accounts for student organizations.

There may be a vocational-programs director, who monitors mandated federal and state programs designed to prepare high school graduates for specific kinds of jobs. This individual manages the required paperwork and often makes contacts with employers in the local community who cooperate in school-based training programs of various kinds.

The head custodian is an important administrator in large secondary schools. This person supervises a considerable staff of people who clean the building and take care of routine maintenance. Classroom teachers may never encounter some members of the head custodian's staff. In many large buildings, a night shift comes on duty after teachers and students leave for the day.

There often is a head dietitian, who is responsible for planning lunch menus and overseeing a large kitchen and cafeteria staff. The school lunch program is a large and complex activity, and the head dietitian must handle a great deal of paperwork as well as direct the activities of food-service employees.

Large schools may also have a head resource specialist. This person oversees the work of school library personnel as well as the staff responsible for maintaining media equipment. Identifying learning resource needs, ordering, and processing new material and equipment also fall under this person's jurisdiction.

Department Heads   Department heads are teachers who lead the individual academic departments. They report either directly to the school principal or indirectly to the school principal through one of the assistant principals. Department heads often are relieved of one instructional period a day to allow them time to take care of departmental business. Their employment contracts often require them to work two or more weeks longer than do other teachers.

Department heads are experienced, respected teachers. Their duties include:

- activities as informing members of their departments about important administrative policies,
- working with teachers new to their staffs,
- passing on concerns of department members to the principal,
- making recommendations for assigning department members to individual courses,
- allocating the materials' budget among department members,
- arranging for textbook distribution, and
- representing the department at district-level curriculum meetings.

Specialty Teachers   As is the case with elementary schools, secondary schools also include some teachers who have received specialized training. Because the average secondary school is larger than the average elementary school, secondary schools frequently employ more specialty teachers than elementary schools. Groups served by these individuals are emotionally disturbed learners and learners with physical disabilities, gifted and talented students, learners with reading problems, and learners in a variety of other special programs.

Other Professionals   Most secondary schools have several counselors who have had advanced coursework in guidance and counseling. Many of them have advanced academic degrees. In most places, they hold special counseling certificates, although this pattern varies somewhat from state to state and from place to place within some states. Many counselors handle both academic and personal counseling. In very large schools, some counselors may have specific responsibilities. For example, there may be a counselor who works only with college and university placement issues. Another may be concerned only with vocational counseling and aptitude testing. Another may work exclusively with managing the standardized-testing program.

There may also be several school nurses in a large secondary school. These individuals are responsible for maintaining health records and dealing with minor health-related situations that arise during the school day.

There likely are a number of learning resource specialists within a large secondary school. Some of them work full-time in the library, and others may be assigned to work exclusively with specialized instructional support equipment.

Other Staff Members   Secondary schools often have large secretarial staffs. There may even be a head secretary charged with overseeing the work of all other secretaries in the building. Individual secretaries may be assigned to the principal, the assistant principals, the counselors, the finance office, and the main-office reception area. There may be one secretary who is assigned to do nothing but handle incoming telephone calls. Telephones often ring frequently at larger secondary schools, and answering them and directing the call to the appropriate party is a time-consuming activity.

Custodial staffs in many secondary schools are large. This also tends to be true for kitchen staffs. Not all kitchen-staff employees work a full eight-hour day, however. Some come in for only a few hours during the middle of the day.

There may be one or two supply room clerks. These people are responsible for maintaining an inventory of paper, pens, pencils, and other items. Teachers contact these clerks when they need supplies. Because of the nature of their responsibilities, supply room clerks are individuals with whom teachers come into frequent contact.

Paraprofessionals are not quite so numerous in middle schools and secondary schools as in elementary schools. In the middle and secondary schools that employ them, they function much as they do in elementary schools; that is, they are assigned to help individual teachers, and they perform many different kinds of duties in discharging this responsibility.

Key Ideas In Summary

- For over 20 years, there has been a trend toward increasing the amount of funds committed to educating each child. Most money spent on public education, about 60 percent, goes to support classroom instruction. Administrative costs consume about 8 percent of the total spent each year on the public schools.

- Concerns about *equity* (that is, concerns about the fairness of established ways for paying for public education) have been an important theme of debates about school funding. The issue arises because the value of taxable property varies greatly from one school district to another. Hence, less wealthy school districts have a harder time raising money to support programs and often must adopt higher tax rates than wealthier districts in order to secure sufficient operating money.

- In recent years, there has been a trend to move away from discussions focusing on the equity issue and to look more directly on the components of an *adequate* school program. The idea is to identify (and provide) a level of funding necessary to support the delivery of instruction that has a demonstrated capacity to help learners master specified content.

- School districts have developed sophisticated organizational plans for managing their activities. In general, administrative schemes are more complex in larger school districts than in smaller ones. Similarly, school buildings enrolling larger numbers of learners tend to feature administrative organizations that are more complex than those serving smaller numbers of learners.

- The specific categories of school personnel with whom teachers are likely to have frequent daily contact vary from place to place. In part, these variations are related to the numbers of learners attending the school. For example, while a teacher in a small elementary school may interact with the principal every day, several days may pass without the teacher in a large school even seeing the principal.

- The school board (sometimes known by names such as board of education, board of trustees, or school council) is the basic policy-making body of a school district. It represents a link between the local district and the state department of education. In most places, school board members are elected. The school board hires and monitors the work of the district's superintendent.

- The superintendent is the chief executive officer of a school district and is responsible for all aspects of the district's day-to-day operations. Among other responsibilities, the superintendent is the ultimate supervisor of all employees, is responsible for ensuring that academic programs are in compliance with federal and state regulations, is charged with preparing budget proposals for the school board, and is the top professional public-relations spokesperson for the district. Depending on the size of the district, the superintendent may be assisted by one or more deputies, associates, or assistants.

- As chief executive officers of individual schools, principals are responsible for all aspects of their school's operation. Among other things, they oversee the academic program, monitor learners' progress, check on teachers' performances, manage budgets, and work to maintain good public relations with parents and other citizens. In larger buildings, assistant principals aid them.

- In some elementary schools, the principal and assistant principals may be assisted by grade-level leaders. These teachers represent the interests of other teachers at the grade level they teach in interactions with the principals and, sometimes, in meetings with central-office personnel. Other professionals in larger elementary schools include school nurses, counselors, and learning resource specialists. There often are other support personnel, including secretaries, food-service workers, and paraprofessionals.

- Administrative arrangements in secondary schools vary somewhat from those in elementary schools. Secondary schools typically enroll more students and generally have more elaborate administrative management schemes than do elementary schools. In addition to the principal and assistant principals, administrators in a medium- to large-sized high school might include a head counselor, an athletic director, a finance director, a vocational-programs director, a head custodian, a head dietitian, and a head learning resource specialist.

- Department heads in secondary schools lead the departments with which they are affiliated. They inform department members of important policy decisions. Also, they meet frequently with the principal or an assistant principal and, hence, function as an important conduit between the school administrative office and teachers in the departments they represent. Often, department heads represent the school in district-wide meetings of subject-area specialists. They typically work a slightly longer academic year than do other teachers, and they often have one nonteaching period a day reserved for their departmental administrative responsibilities.

- There are many support personnel in secondary schools. Among these are food-service workers, custodians, secretaries, clerks, and paraprofessionals.

Chapter 15 Self Test

To review terms and concepts in this chapter, take the Chapter 15 Self Test on the companion Web site, located at *http://www.prenhall.com/armstrong*. Select Chapter 15 from the front page of the Web site, then choose the Self Test module on the navigation bar on the left side of the page. Feedback for the Self Test is immediate. You can keep track of your Self Test scores yourself, or you can choose to submit your scores via e-mail to your instructor.

Reflections

To respond to these questions online, and to save or submit your response electronically, visit the companion Web site, located at *http://www. prenhall.com/armstrong.* Select Chapter 15 from the front page of the Web site, then choose the Reflections module on the navigation bar on the left side of the page. Instructors and students may also wish to use these questions as discussion topics on the Message Board for the companion Web site.

1. How would you explain differences between (a) a school finance-reform approach designed to address the "equity" issue and (b) a school finance-reform approach designed to provide for educational "adequacy." Which would you prefer and why?

2. For two decades, there have been increases in the amount of money spent to support public education. Do you think this trend will continue? Why or why not?

3. What are some of the basic responsibilities of the superintendent?

4. Describe some of the duties of grade-level leaders in an elementary school.

5. In addition to the principal and his or her assistants, a number of other administrators are often found in larger secondary schools. Who are these people and what do they do?

6. Who are some of the professionals who might be assigned to a specific school building for purposes other than teaching regular classes?

7. Should the superintendent try to sell the local community on innovative new programs, or should he or she attempt to read the local community and provide programs that do not need to be sold?

8. Individuals who have studied school board members agree that serving on the school board is a taxing, demanding responsibility. Yet few districts have any difficulty finding candidates to run for vacancies. How can this be explained?

9. Many elementary schools have grade-level leaders and many secondary schools have department heads. Do you think that a grade-level leader is likely to have more influence on a beginning elementary teacher than a department head is likely to have on a beginning secondary-school teacher? Why do you think so?

10. Some critics argue that principals in large high schools are so consumed by basic management issues that they cannot adequately monitor the quality of instruction being delivered in their classrooms. Do you agree or disagree with this position? Why?

Field Experiences, Projects, and Enrichment

1. Conduct some research to find out how schools are funded in your state. You may wish to talk with some officials in local public school districts. Your instructor may also provide you with some leads. Prepare a short talk on these funding patterns for delivery to your class. You may wish to discuss any debates or pending changes in funding practices in your state.

2. Attend a local school board meeting. What kinds of topics were on the agenda? How was time allocated among topics to be covered? What kinds of people were invited to speak at the meeting? What sorts of controversial issues were discussed? What role did the superintendent play in the meeting? Were citizens invited to speak on any topics of interest (including those not on the agenda)? If possible, ask a school official how a given issue gets added to a meeting's agenda. Prepare a short written report that summarizes your findings.

3. Invite a superintendent to visit your class. Ask this person to describe a typical week on the job. Specifically, ask about what percentage of time is devoted to (a) curriculum and instructional matters, (b) personnel matters, (c) budgetary matters, and (d) public-relations matters. What does the superintendent do to ensure that policies are being carried out in the individual buildings? How do administrators in the buildings communicate their concerns to the superintendent? What kinds of contact, if any, does the superintendent have with beginning teachers? (Devise other questions designed to provide class members with insights about the superintendent's role.)

4. If you are planning to teach elementary school, interview one or more grade-level leaders. If you are planning to teach secondary school, interview one or more department heads. Ask these people what their general responsibilities are, whether they are released from any teaching obligations as a result of their appointment to the position of grade-level leader or department head, and to whom they report. If you are a future elementary teacher, get together with three or four others in the class who also interviewed grade-level leaders. If you are a future secondary teacher, get together with three or four others from the class who also interviewed department heads. In your groups, try to write a formal job description for either a grade-level leader or a department head. Share your work with the course instructor, and ask for comments.

5. Select a school district either where you might like to teach or that is located near your college or university. Call the district's central administrative offices and ask whether any charts or descriptive materials are available that show the district's basic administrative organizational material. (Many districts have this kind of information on hand.) Look at the organizational scheme of the district you select. How is it similar and how does it differ from the examples of organizational plans displayed in this chapter? How do you explain any differences?

References

The Condition of Education, 1998 (1998). Washington, DC: National Center for Educational Statistics.

CPRE [Consortium for Policy Research in Education at the University of Wisconsin-Madison]. (1999a). *Determining an adequate spending level: Methods of tying funding to educational adequacy.* [http://www.wcer.wisc.edu/cpre/Finance/adequacy/spending.htm]

CPRE [Consortium for Policy Research in Education at the University of Wisconsin-Madison]. (1999b). *Sources and levels of education revenues and changes over time.* [http://www.wcer.wisc.edu/cpre/Finance/Finance/revenue.htm]

CPRE [Consortium for Policy Research in Education at the University of Wisconsin-Madison]. (1999c). *Traditional resource reallocation and use: Uses of the educational dollar—expenditure patterns.* [http://www.wcer.wisc.edu/cpre/Finance/Finance/tradresource.htm]

CPRE [Consortium for Policy Research in Education at the University of Wisconsin-Madison]. (1999d). *Traditional school finance inequities: Spending differences and local property wealth.* [http://www.wcer.wisc.edu/cpre/Finance/Finance/inequities.htm]

Feiman-Nemser, S., & Floden, R. E. (1986). The cultures of teaching. In M. C. Wittrock (Ed.), *Handbook of research on teaching* (3rd ed., pp. 505–526). New York: Macmillan.

Mini-Digest of Education Statistics (May 5, 1998 update). Finance: Overall expenditures. Washington, DC: National Center for Education Statistics. [http://nces.ed.gov/pubs98/MiniDigest97/98020-5.html]

Snyder, T. D. (Project Ed.). (1994). *Digest of education statistics, 1994.* Washington, DC: National Center for Education Statistics.

Academic Freedom   Refers to teachers' rights to speak freely about their subject, experiment with new ideas, select materials they use in the classroom, and decide on teaching methods.

Academic Learning Time   That portion of total engaged time when the learner is experiencing a high degree of academic success while working on the assigned task. *See also* Engaged Time.

Academic-Subject-Matter Curriculum A curriculum orientation that assumes the primary purpose of education should be to develop learners' mastery of content from academic disciplines.

Academy   A term applied to private secondary schools that became popular in the middle years of the nineteenth century. In time, most academies were displaced by publicly supported high schools.

Acceleration Program   An approach to serving gifted learners that increases the pace at which they complete their schooling through such practices as skipping grades and/or courses. *See also* Subject-Matter Acceleration, Grade-Level Acceleration.

Accountability   Refers to the idea that schools and teachers should be held responsible for ensuring that learners in school master what is specified in the curriculum.

Active Teaching   Teaching that is characterized by the teacher directly leading the class playing such roles as (a) presenter of new information, (b) monitor of learner progress, (c) planner of opportunities for learners to apply content, and (d) reteacher of content (as necessary).

ADD   *See.* Attention Deficit Disorder.

Adequacy Approach to School Funding An approach that identifies a certain desired level of achievement, identifies costs required to get learners to perform at this level, and allocates funds at a level consistent with these identified costs.

Administrative Law   Guidelines used to implement legislative intents as they are expressed in statute law. *See also* Statute Law.

Advance Organizer   An organizing framework presented to learners in preparation for their mastering new content that is designed to help them sort out fragmented pieces of information and organize them into specified categories.

Affective Domain   Domain of learning that focuses on attitudes, feelings, interests, and values.

Alienated Learners   Term applied to learners who do not see school work as personally important and who have not experienced success at school even when they have worked hard.

Allocated Time   Time that is assigned for the purpose of helping students to learn specific subjects or materials.

American Federation of Teachers (AFT) A large national teacher organization that is affiliated with organized labor (the AFL-CIO).

American Society for Training and Development (ASTD)   A professional organization for educators in private industry.

Anticipatory Set   A step in the Hunter and Russell sequencing model that is designed to focus learners' attention on the instruction that is about to begin.

Assessment The purposeful gathering of data from a variety of sources regarding the attainment of educational outcomes.

Assessment Plan An overall scheme for assessment developed by a teacher that identifies various sources of data that are relevant to a specified set of learning outcomes he or she has identified.

Attention Deficit Disorder (ADD) A serious form of learning disability that makes it difficult for affected children to stay organized and complete assigned tasks. Many youngsters with this condition appear to be hyperactive.

Authentic Assessment Assessment that takes place in a situation allowing the learner to replicate "real world" conditions to the maximum extent possible.

Axiology A branch of philosophy concerned with what ought to be that pays particular attention to the topics of morality, ethics, and aesthetics.

Behavioral Setting A physical space with unique characteristics that affects the behavior of individuals who live and act within it.

Bell-Shaped Curve A graphical plot whose shape results from an assumption about how a given characteristic is distributed among members of a total population.

Bilingual Education An approach in which learners are taught for at least part of the day in English and part of the day in their home language.

Bloom's Taxonomy Shorthand for the *Taxonomy of Educational Objectives: The Classification of Educational Goals. Handbook 1: The Cognitive Domain,* a work developed by a group of educators headed by Benjamin Bloom.

Boston English Classical School Established in 1821, this was the nation's first public high school.

Boston Latin Grammar School A famous early secondary school established in 1635 that was designed to prepare boys for Harvard.

Broad-Fields Curriculum A curriculum approach that seeks to blend two or more traditional subject areas into a single broad area.

Cardinal Principles of Secondary Education Developed in 1918 by the National Education Association's Commission on the Reorganization of Secondary Education, they embrace seven goals. They became a rationale for the establishment of the comprehensive high school.

Carl D. Perkins Vocational and Applied Technology Act Federal legislation passed in 1990 that supports the establishment of tech prep programs. *See also* Tech Prep Program.

Certificate *See* Teaching Certificate.

Charter School A school that, as a result of special state legislation, has been exempted from many rules affecting other schools to maximize its flexibility of operation.

Citizenship Curriculum An approach to curriculum that operates on the assumption that schools' primary purpose is to prepare learners for the roles they will play as adults, with particular emphasis on their vocational roles.

Clarity A defining characteristic of effective teachers that includes variables such as the teacher's verbal and nonverbal style, lesson-presentation structure, and proficiency in providing cogent explanations.

Class-Conflict View of Schools A subset of the more general economic-class conflict view. It holds that school programs arise out of disputes that often feature pressures for change from identifiable, disadvantaged groups such as ethnic and cultural minorities. *See also* Economic-Class Conflict View of Schools.

Class-Reproduction View of Schools A subset of the more general economic-class conflict view. It holds that school programs are shaped primarily by desires of economic elites to produce adult citizens who will serve the elites' economic interests. *See also* Economic-Class Conflict View of Schools.

Coding-System Approach to Classroom Observation An approach to classroom observation that features the use of codes or symbols to represent behaviors that are of interest to the observer.

Coercive Power Power that comes to a person because he or she has the authority to administer punishment.

Cognitive Domain Domain of learning that focuses on intellectual dimensions of learning, including remembering and processing information.

Comer-Model School A school that follows principles consistent with the work of a prominent school reform leader, Dr. James Comer.

Common School A term popularized by Horace Mann, this was to be a school open to all children. Mann believed that education in the common school would produce an educated population and that, over time, this would result in improved living standards for all.

Componential Intelligence Refers to the ability to acquire information by separating the relevant from the irrelevant, thinking abstractly, and determining what needs to be done. *See also* Triarchic Theory of Intelligence.

Comprehensive High School A term applied to high schools to imply that they have purposes broader than preparing students for entrance to colleges and universities. The rationale for the comprehensive high school was spelled out in a series of "Cardinal Principles" that were developed in 1918 by the National Education Association's Commission on the Reorganization of Secondary Education.

Comprehensive School Reform Demonstration (CSRD) Program A systemic school reform program authorized by Public Law 105-78 that provides federal funds for schools that establish an approved comprehensive school reform plan.

Compulsory Attendance The requirement by a state that all learners must attend school, whether public or private.

Constitution A written document that expresses basic principles that will be used as reference points as cases within its jurisdiction are decided by the courts.

Constructivism A perspective that holds that knowledge is constructed in the minds of learners based on their prior knowledge and previous experiences.

Content Standards Describe what teachers are supposed to teach and what learners are expected to learn.

Contextual Intelligence Refers to the ability to adapt to new experiences and to solve problems in a specific situation or context. *See also* Triarchic Theory of Intelligence.

Controlled-Choice Plan A type of open-enrollment plan in which a school district places some restrictions on schools where an individual child can enroll. *See also* Open-Enrollment Plan.

Copyright Regulations Laws and rules designed to protect the creative work of others.

Court-Decisional Law Legal principles arising from the collective impact of court decisions.

Credential *See* Teaching Certificate.

Criterion-Referenced Evaluation Assessment in which the performance of someone is judged against a preestablished criterion or set of preestablished criteria.

Cultural-Deficit View   A discredited view of minorities that held poor school performance on the part of minority-group learners could be explained by a failure of their parents to provide them with an intellectually stimulating home atmosphere.

Curriculum   The result of decisions made relating to the selection and organization of content and learning experiences.

Curriculum Coordinator   *See* Curriculum Leader.

Curriculum Director   *See* Curriculum Leader.

Curriculum Leader   An individual charged with leadership responsibilities for academic programs in a given subject area or areas or for a given grade level or grade levels.

Curriculum Supervisor   *See* Curriculum Leader.

Decentralized School Management   A school-management approach that shifts power away from central school district authorities into the hands of leadership teams (including teachers, administrators, community members, and others) at the individual building level.

Deductive Logic   A pattern of reasoning that begins with general conclusions and moves on to illustrate them with reference to specific examples. *See also* Inductive Logic.

Department Chair   A person who is the leader of teachers within a given academic department in a middle school, junior high school, or senior high school.

Developmental Portfolio   A specialized teaching portfolio that features evidence designed to document improved proficiency of a teacher in a narrowly defined area of interest.

Differentiated Staffing   The idea that not all teachers should have the same responsibilities. Individuals are assigned to discharge

different functions based on their particular kinds of expertise.

Direct Assessment   *See* Performance Measurement.

Direct Instruction   *See* Active Teaching.

Diagnostic Assessment   A variety of assessment that is designed to identify causes of a learner's failures.

Dress Code   A requirement of a school or school district that requires learners to abide by certain dress guidelines when in the school.

Due Process   A guarantee provided to United States citizens by the Fourteenth Amendment to the U.S. Constitution that requires that certain specified procedures be followed in any action that might put a citizen's rights in jeopardy.

Dyslexia   A term used to describe a learning disability. It is a condition affecting some children who have difficulty understanding written or oral language.

Economic-Class Conflict View of Schools A perspective based on the idea that our society is a battleground where people and groups with different values contest for supremacy. School policies are seen as the result of conflicts between groups having different economic interests.

Educable Learner   As used in reference to mental retardation, the category of learners who deviate least from the so-called normal range of mental functioning and who often spend all or most of their time at school as members of regular classrooms.

Education for All Handicapped Children Act   1975 legislation that put the force of federal law behind the effort to educate learners with disabilities in regular classrooms (Public Law 94-142).

Education Code   A term used to describe the total collection of a state's laws, rules, and regulations governing education.

Educational Outcomes   The goals of instruction that focus on what learners will learn as a result of the instruction.

Emotional Intelligence   Refers to the ability to exercise self-control, remain persistent, and be self-motivating.

Emotionally Disturbed Learner   A learner whose behavior deviates from that expected of learners in his or her age group that interferes with individual development and creates difficulty in establishing and maintaining harmonious relationships with others.

Employment Portfolio   A portfolio prepared by a teacher that documents areas of potential interest to employers such as proficiencies in the areas of lesson planning, assessment of learners, and classroom management.

Engaged Time   The part of allocated time when instructional activities actually related to the focus subject are occurring. *See also* Allocated Time.

Enrichment Program   A category of programming for gifted learners that (1) seeks to provide them with educational experiences that go beyond those provided to nongifted learners and (2) keeps these young people in contact with the entire spectrum of school learners by maintaining their membership within classes that include both gifted and nongifted learners.

Epistemology   A branch of philosophy concerned with the nature of knowledge. *See also* Relational Epistemology.

Equity principle   As applied to public schools, this principle holds that there should not be tremendous variations in the amount of education money available per learner in different school districts, even though individual districts may vary enormously in their wealth.

Essentialism   As applied to education, this perspective holds that there is a core of essential knowledge, mostly derived from scientific and technical fields, that all learners should master. The most valued knowledge is knowledge that is practical and useful.

Estranged Learners   Term applied to learners who believe the content of the school program is important but who, for a variety of possible reasons, fail to do well in school.

Evaluation   The process of making a judgment about the worth or the value of something.

Event Sampling   A term used to describe a type of classroom observation characterized by an observer recording information about one or more categories of events that might be of interest to the teacher during a debriefing session.

Exceptional Learner   A general term to describe a learner who has special or unusual characteristics such as a learner with one or more disabilities or a learner who is gifted.

Existentialism   A view that people come into the world facing only one constraint—the inevitability of their own deaths. In the absence of any "grand design," people are expected to discover their own reasons for existing. In school programs, this perspective places much emphasis on learner's abilities to choose what they study.

Experiential Intelligence   Refers to the ability to cope with new experiences by formulating new ideas and combining unrelated facts to solve new problems. *See also* Triarchic Theory of Intelligence.

Expert Power   Power that comes to a person because he or she possesses specialized knowledge.

Expulsion   This is the permanent separation of a learner from a school.

Factory Model of Education   A view that sees educational enterprises operating along the same lines as factories and that prizes standardization.

Fair Employment Regulations   Regulations designed to prevent discrimination in the employment process.

Fair Use   A doctrine associated with copyrights that recognizes that sometimes it is in the public interest to allow for reasonable use of copyrighted material without first securing permission from its developers. *See also* Copyright Regulations.

Family Educational Rights and Privacy Act   This 1974 legislation requires schools to provide parents and guardians free access to their children's school records. Further, it grants rights to learners over 18 years old to view their records themselves.

Formative Assessment   The process of gathering data during instruction in order to determine if learners are making satisfactory progress and to adjust instruction if necessary.

Foundation Program   Term applied to arrangements in many states to provide additional funds to support education in less wealthy school districts to pay for educational services of a quality consistent with an established minimum state standard.

Franklin Academy   An institution established by Benjamin Franklin in 1751 that was free from religious ties and that included a curriculum that focused on practical subjects such as mathematics, astronomy, navigation, and bookkeeping.

Free and Appropriate Education   Refers to the rights of learners with disabilities to (1) receive an education and required related services free and to (2) have them in an appropriate setting, usually a regular school classroom.

Free-Response Measure   Category of test that requires the test taker to construct a response to the question or questions.

Freedom of Conscience   This is the freedom guaranteed by the Constitution to be free from state interference in matters of religion and conscience.

Freedom of Expression   This is the freedom guaranteed by the Constitution to freely encounter and express ideas and opinions, even those that might be unpopular.

Frequency Count Approach to Classroom Observation   An approach in which the observer notes the number of occurrences of a behavior of interest.

Full Inclusion   Term used to describe a school in which there are virtually no special classes for exceptional learners; all modifications for learners with special needs take place within regular classrooms. *See also* Inclusion.

Full-Service School   School that makes available to learners and their families a whole range of human-support services that may include services designed to respond to health, emotional, social, and legal needs.

Functionalist View of Schools   A perspective based on the idea that the vast majority of people in society share common values. Schools are seen as places designed to prepare young people for roles in the specialized institutions that keep society going.

Fundamental School   A special type of magnet school that emphasizes "back to the basics." *See also* Magnet School.

Genetic-Deficit View   A discredited view of minorities that held that school achievement problems of children from minority groups resulted because they lacked the needed intellectual tools essential for academic success.

Gifted Learner A learner category that includes those who have outstanding intellectual ability or creative talent.

Goals 2000 Initiative Begun under President Bush and continued under President Clinton, this program includes a comprehensive set of initiatives designed to improve the quality of American schools with a view to having them compare favorably with the world's best schools.

Grade-Level Acceleration A kind of acceleration that occurs when a learner skips an entire grade and enrolls as a regular class member of a group comprised of older learners *See also* Acceleration.

Grade-Level Chair A person in an elementary school with leadership responsibilities for all teachers assigned to a given grade level.

Grades Symbols that are part of a system for communicating the results of an evaluation to other interested parties.

Guaranteed Tax Base (GTB) Approach A scheme to promote equitable support for education in all areas of a state. It establishes a system whereby each school district in the state has the same value of taxable property available to support educational services for each learner within its service area.

Guided Practice Work that learners do after learning new material and that features close monitoring by the teacher to assure that new information is being properly applied.

Hearing-Impaired Learner A learner who is markedly different from so-called normal learners in his or her ability to produce speech and to acquire language skills.

Hedonism A belief that the highest good is characterized by a search for immediate pleasure and living for the moment.

Hidden Curriculum The impact of all elements of the school setting that send

learners messages regarding what they ought to be doing and how they should be thinking.

High Adapters Term applied to learners who believe the content of the school program is important and who generally experience success in their classes.

High-Stakes Assessment Refers to assessment procedures with results that may have serious consequences for those whose proficiencies are being measured and judged.

Higher Level Questions Questions that require learners to apply, analyze, integrate, create, or synthesize and use relatively complex thinking processes.

Human Resource Development (HRD) A term frequently used to describe the training function in large businesses and corporations.

Hunter and Russell Model A seven-step approach to sequencing instruction that was developed by Madeline Hunter and Douglas Russell.

IDEA *See* Individuals with Disabilities Education Act of 1997.

IEP *See* Individualized Education Program.

Immediacy Refers to the idea that events in the classroom often require the immediate attention of the teacher.

In Loco Parentis A traditional legal doctrine governing the relationship of the school and learners that held school authorities (teachers and administrators) acted "in place of the parent." This doctrine held that children in the schools were essentially in the custody of school authorities and did not enjoy constitutionally protected rights of citizenship.

Inclusion A concept that extends the idea of mainstreaming to embrace the idea that schools should not place learners with disabilities in regular classrooms simply because federal law obligates them to do so, but rather because these learners are *wanted* as members of these regular classrooms. *See also* Full Inclusion.

Independent Practice   Practice with new content that learners accomplish under conditions where no direct teacher assistance is available.

Individualized Education Program (IEP)   First required by the Education for All Handicapped Children Act, these programs must be planned for a child with disabilities by teams of individuals with representatives of various constituencies, including parents and guardians and regular classroom teachers who work with the learner.

Individuals with Disabilities Education Act of 1997   Legislation that extended provisions of the Education for All Handicapped Children Act in the direction of adding more support for programs featuring full inclusion of learners in regular school classrooms (Public Law 105-117). *See also* Inclusion, Full Inclusion.

Induction Years   A term often applied to a newcomer's first few years in the teaching profession.

Inductive Logic   A pattern of reasoning that begins with specifics or particulars and moves on to explanatory generalizations or principles. *See also* Deductive Logic.

Input Goals   Goals that describe various components of the school program that, collectively, are thought to produce desired outcomes.

Inservice Education   Staff-development activities for teachers.

Intelligence Quotient (IQ) Test   A kind of test, originally developed by Alfred Binet and his associates in 1905, that was designed to assess individuals' prospects for success in regular school classrooms.

Interstate New Teacher Assessment and Support Consortium (INTASC)   A cooperative alliance of state education offices, colleges and universities, and national organizations that seeks to improve schools by assuring new teachers meet high standards.

Kalamazoo Case   The court case that established the legal right of states to use tax money in support of secondary education. Previously, taxing authority to support elementary education had a clear legal basis but not authority to use public expenditures in support of secondary schools.

Irrelevant Perceivers   Term applied to learners who have the capacity to succeed in school but who do not see school work as important.

Jacob K. Javits Gifted and Talented Students Education Act of 1994   Federal legislation that awarded grants, provided leadership, and sponsored a national center focusing on the educational needs of gifted and talented learners.

Lead Teacher   Term used to denote a teacher who has been assigned to play a specific role that involves directing or coordinating the work of others.

Learner-Centered Curriculum   A curriculum orientation that emphasizes individual needs in planning, organizing, and delivering instructional programs.

Learning Community   An organization in which all are committed to examining present practices with a view to identifying and implementing particular strategies and policies that are designed to enhance the organization's overall quality.

Learning Intention   A specification of what learners are supposed to be able to explain or do as a consequence of their exposure to a lesson or series of related lessons. Sometimes it is referred to as an "objective."

Least Restrictive Environment   Provision of the Education for All Handicapped Children

Act that required school districts to extend every possible effort to teach learners with disabilities in regular classrooms alongside nondisabled learners.

Legitimate Power   Power that comes to a person because of the position he or she holds.

Lesson Pacing   Term used to describe the rate at which instruction moves along during a lesson.

Libel   A false *written* statement about another person that exposes this individual to contempt, ridicule, or disgrace. *See also* Slander.

Liberty Right   A right of a citizen to be free from all restraints except those imposed by law.

Licensure   *See* Teaching Certificate.

Life-Adjustment Education   A term applied to a perspective with roots in progressive education that developed after World War II that placed an extremely heavy emphasis on responding to learners' personal needs and interests, even at the expense of avoiding systematic attention to rigorous academic content in some of its more extreme manifestations.

Logic   A sub-field of philosophy that deals with the relationships among ideas and with procedures used to differentiate between valid and fallacious thinking. *See also* Deductive Logic, Inductive Logic.

Lower Level Questions   Questions that call on learners to recall specific items of previously introduced information and that do not require them to engage in sophisticated thinking.

Magnet School   A school that draws its enrollments from throughout the entire extent of a school district. Many have special themes, such as mathematics and science, and most are secondary schools.

Malfeasance   A variety of negligence that occurs when a teacher acts deliberately and knowingly to harm someone else (typically a learner). *See also* Negligence.

Malpractice   As applied to education, an action that is either unprofessional or an action that is inappropriate for the receiving individual and has some negative consequences for this person.

Management   As used in reference to classroom control, a term referring to a pattern in which a teacher exercises top-down control with the expectation that learners' roles will be limited to following the teacher's directives.

Marker Expression   A statement a teacher makes to highlight the importance of something that has been said so that learners will understand they need to pay particular attention to it.

Massachusetts School Law of 1642   Though this legislation did not provide for the establishment of schools, it placed a legal obligation on parents to make sure their children's education would not be neglected.

Measurement   The process of quantifying the presence or absence of a quality, trait, or attribute.

Merit-Pay Plan   Label given to a compensation arrangement whereby individuals who have been identified as outstanding teachers receive salary supplements.

Metaphysics   A branch of philosophy concerned with the nature of reality that asks questions that go beyond those than can be answered through the application of scientific processes. The term *ontology* is sometimes used as a synonym.

Minimal Brain Dysfunction   A term used to describe a learning disability. It is a condition affecting some children who have difficulty understanding written or oral language.

Misfeasance   A variety of negligence that occurs when a teacher acts unwisely or without taking proper safeguards. *See also* Negligence.

Modeling   A teacher action designed to provide learners with examples or demonstrations of competencies associated with a lesson.

Motivational Activities   Activities designed to stimulate and maintain learners' interest in what is being taught. They need to be provided at the beginning of a learning sequence, during a learning sequence, and at the conclusion of a learning sequence.

Multicultural Education   Educational programming that seeks educational equity for all learners by incorporating information from history, the social sciences, the behavioral sciences, ethnic studies, and women's studies.

Multidimensionality   Refers to the idea that classrooms are complex environments.

Multiple Intelligences   A learning theory propounded by Howard Gardner that holds that intelligence is not a unitary trait but rather is divided into a number of distinct categories.

Narrative Approach to Classroom Observation   In this approach, the observer attempts to write down as much as possible about everything that goes on during the observation period. The term *scripting* is also used to describe this approach.

National Board for Professional Teaching Standards (NBPTS)   A body that has developed a certification process to recognize with special "National Board" certificates teachers who have met a particularly rigorous set of professional standards.

National Council for Accreditation of Teacher Education (NCATE)   A national organization that accredits teacher-education programs.

National Defense Education Act of 1958   Passed in part because of concerns about the quality of American schools after the Soviet Union's launch of the earth satellite *Sputnik,* this law provided funds to improve education. Projects included large-scale curriculum reform initiatives as well as special training programs for teachers.

National Education Association (NEA)   The nation's largest professional organization for teachers.

Needs-of-Society Curriculum   A curriculum orientation that emphasizes equipping learners with the expertise required to respond effectively to society's needs.

Negligence   A failure to use reasonable or due care to prevent harm.

Negotiation   As used in reference to classroom control, a term that sees the teacher and learners operating as parts of a community characterized by shared decision making and group problem solving.

Nonfeasance   A variety of negligence that occurs when a teacher fails to act when there was a duty to do so. *See also* Negligence.

Norm-Referenced Evaluation   Judging the performance of a person with how well others in the reference group performed.

Objective   *See* Learning Intention.

"Old Deluder Satan" Act of 1647   Law requiring every town of 50 or more inhabitants to hire a teacher of reading or writing. The name comes from language in the law that implies that education will be for the purpose of defeating Satan's wiles.

Ontology   *See* Metaphysics.

Open-Enrollment Plan   Term applied to a system whereby a parent or guardian can decide which school his or her child will attend. Often, such plans allow enrollment at any schools in a district. Some allow learners to cross district lines to attend a school in another administrative jurisdiction.

Orthopedically Impaired Learner   Term applied to a learner who may suffer from one or more conditions that limit his or her physical abilities.

Outcome goals   Goals that emphasize the results or effects of instruction. *See also* Input Goals.

Pacing   The rate or speed of instruction provided in a lesson.

Percentile Ranking   This ranking indicates how an individual compares to the norming group. For example, scoring at the 50th percentile means that the individual scored better than 49 percent of the norming group and lower than 49 percent of the group.

Perceptual Handicap   A term used to describe a learning disability. It is a condition affecting some children who have difficulty understanding written or oral language.

Perennialism   As applied to education, this refers to the view that important truth and knowledge does not change over time. Educational programs should promote an understanding of unchanging principles and should avoid emphasizing vocational training.

Performance Dimensions   *See* Rubric.

Performance Measurement   Assessment procedure that requires the evaluator to directly observe and measure a learner engaged in the performance of a task.

Performance Standards   These reference levels of proficiency that are expected of a particular group or category of learners.

Placement Assessment   Gathering data before beginning instruction in order to determine the appropriate place to begin.

Portfolio   A purposeful collection of products and performances that tells a story about a learner's effort, progress, or achievement. *See also* Teaching Portfolio.

Postmodernism   A perspective that rejects traditional questions and philosophical theories because they have been too heavily influenced by narrow political agendas and other cultural baggage and, as a consequence, have failed to consider non-Western, nonscientific, nonintuitive ways of knowing.

Probable Cause   Evidence of wrongdoing that is sufficiently convincing to support the view that a person is guilty of illegal behavior. *See also* Reasonable Suspicion.

Problems-Approach Curriculum   An approach to curriculum that assumes schools should prepare learners to solve pressing social problems.

Procedural Component of Due Process   Guidelines that specify procedures that must be followed to ensure that a person's due-process rights have not been violated. *See also* Due Process.

Product Measurement   Used in evaluation that is based on the actual products or materials that learners have produced.

Professional-Development School   A term referring to a school-based approach designed to respond simultaneously to several pressing educational issues. A professional-development school involves teachers, administrators, university-based professionals, and future educators in tasks related to such diverse purposes as preparing future teachers in realistic environments, planning and implementing worthwhile staff-development programs, and generating and pursuing answers to research questions that are meaningful at the individual school site.

Professional Life Space   Term used to refer to the total period of time an individual works in a professional capacity (for example, as a classroom teacher).

Program-Approval Approach   A scheme used in identifying people eligible to receive a teaching certificate that is based on state examination of elements of a teacher-preparation program. If the program is approved, candidates successfully completing it are eligible for a teaching certificate.

Progressive Education Movement   Founded on the ideas of John Dewey, this perspective held that the focus of schooling should be on meeting needs of individual learners in a humane way.

Progressivism   As applied to education, this perspective sees change as the essence of reality and promotes the view that schools should develop learners' problem-solving abilities to help them cope with it.

Property Right   A right to specific property, whether tangible or intangible.

Proximity Control   Term applied to an approach to classroom control that seeks to deal with episodes of misbehavior by having the teacher approach the area of the classroom where it is occurring.

Psychometrist   A professional who has had advanced training in the construction and administration of sophisticated tests that are used to measure various kinds of mental abilities.

Psychomotor Domain   Domain of learning that focuses on physical abilities, muscle, coordination, and motor skills.

Public Law 94-142   *See* Education for All Handicapped Children Act.

Public Law 105-117   *See* Individuals with Disabilities Education Act of 1997.

Publicness   Refers to the idea that teachers' actions in the classroom occur in an observable setting.

Reasonable Suspicion   A less rigorous standard of evidence than "probable cause," it requires only that there be a reasonable suspicion that someone is guilty of an offense. *See also* Probable Cause.

Reconstructionism   As applied to education, this perspective presumes that the schools should play an important role in the effort to reform society.

Record Keeping Portfolio   A portfolio that is used to keep material that might be passed on to another teacher to help this person develop an instructional program well-suited to this learner's needs.

Referent Power   Power that comes to a person as a result of a warm, positive relationship that has been established with others.

Relational Epistemology   A view that holds that the social context within which people live exercises a tremendous influence on their view of knowledge and how it is attained.

Reliability   As used in measurement, this term refers to the ability of an assessment procedure to produce consistent results when applied to similar situations.

Reward Power   Power that comes to a person as a result of his or her ability to provide to others something they want.

Rubric   Guideline or set of guidelines designed to tell an assessor what he or she should look at in making judgments about the quality of learner performance on a given task or set of tasks.

School Board   The basic policy-making body of a school district.

School-Business Partnership   General term applied to cooperative work of businesses and schools to promote improvement of educational programs.

School Choice   A principle that establishes as a priority the rights of consumers of educational services (such as parents, guardians and learners) to choose the school that members of a family will attend.

School-to-Work Opportunities Act   Federal legislation passed in 1994 that provides grants to states and communities to develop mechanisms for better preparing learners for careers.

School Voucher   *See* Voucher Plan.

Scoring Criteria   *See* Rubric.

Scoring Rubric   *See* Rubric.

Scripting   *See* Narrative Approach to Classroom Observation.

Search and Seizure   Refers to a constitutional guarantee that citizens shall not be subject to unreasonable searches and seizure of property. This especially refers to items that might be seized and later used as evidence in a trial or disciplinary proceeding.

Seating-Chart Approach to Classroom Observation   An approach to classroom observation that is useful when the purpose is to focus on behaviors of individual learners. It features use of seating charts and data-gathering schemes that make it possible to associate particular behaviors with particular learners.

Selected-Response Measure   Category of tests in which responses are provided and the test taker must choose the best from among the given options.

Selective Verbatim Record   Term used to describe an approach to classroom observation that focuses on everything a teacher says that falls within a predetermined category such as "praise statements."

Sequencing   The act of arranging components of the instructional act in such a way as to maximize the potential that learners will master the material.

Sexual Harassment   A condition resulting when a a hostile environment is created because of actions taken that relate to the gender of an individual.

Showcase Portfolio   Portfolio that features only a learner's most notable accomplishments.

Simultaneity   Refers to the idea that in school classrooms, many things are occurring at the same time.

Site-Based Management   *See* Decentralized School Management.

Slander   A false *spoken* statement about another person that exposes this individual to contempt, ridicule, or disgrace. *See also* Libel.

Special Education   Term referring to a cluster of services for learners with special needs that increasingly are delivered to them as members of regular school classrooms.

Sputnik   The name of an earth satellite orbited in 1957 by the Soviet Union. This event shocked American citizens and prompted a reexamination of schools that resulted in a heavier emphasis on more rigorous academic content.

Standardized Tests   Tests that are constructed by assessments of groups (for example, from scientifically selected samples of all third graders) for the purpose of establishing norms (expected scores).

Standards-Based Education   A movement in education dedicated to establishing clear, measurable descriptions of what learners should know as a result of their educational experiences.

Status-Group Conflict View of Schools   A perspective based on the idea that society features conflict among status groups in our society. Disputes among these status groups drive efforts to change school policies and practices.

Statute Law   Law that is comprised of enactments of legislatures.

Subject-Matter Acceleration   An approach to acceleration that allows learners to take courses earlier than would be typical.

See also Acceleration.

Substantive Component of Due Process
The basic set of principles upon which due process is based.

Summative Assessment   Assessment that takes place at the conclusion of an instructional sequence.

Superintendent   The title of the chief executive officer of a school district.

Suspension   The temporary separation of a learner from school.

Systemic Reform   The idea that improvement will not result from changing one or two components of the educational system. Rather, simultaneous attention to multiple components is required.

Task Analysis   The process of examining a body of content a teacher proposes to teach with a view to breaking it down into component subtasks and, thereby, making it easier for learners to master the material.

Taxonomy   A category system that classifies according to certain criteria.

Teacher Curriculum Specialist   A teacher with expertise in a particular aspect of the school curriculum who has been assigned to play a role where this knowledge can be put to effective use.

Teacher-Made Tests   Tests that teachers make to administer to their class on a specific unit of study.

Teaching Certificate   Document that gives the holder a legal right to hold appointment as a teacher in the schools of the jurisdiction that issues it (usually a state).

Teaching Contract   A document spelling out conditions of employment for a teacher that includes responsibilities to be assumed by the teacher and responsibilities to be assumed by the hiring school district.

Teaching Portfolio   A collection of evidence that documents a teacher's accomplishments over time, in a variety of situations, and that displays evidence of his or her competence.

Team Leader   *See* Lead Teacher.

Tech Prep Program   Programs that typically involve two years of senior high school training that are followed by two years of additional training, usually in community or junior colleges. The purpose is to provide relevant training and to smooth the transition from the world of the school to the world of work.

Tenure   A condition that allows a teacher who holds it to have a right to reemployment provided certain stipulated conditions are met. Typically, teachers in districts that offer tenure must work several years before it is awarded.

Theism   A belief system premised on the belief that there is a God who created the universe.

Time Sampling   A term used to describe an approach to classroom observation that features an observer noting what goes on in a classroom at time intervals (for example, every 15 seconds).

Tort   Civil as opposed to criminal wrongdoing.

Traditional Measurement Techniques
Measurement techniques that have typically been used in classrooms. These include essay, multiple choice, and matching types of measurement items.

Training and Development   A journal serving educators and trainers who work in private industry.

Transition   Term used to describe the point at which one part of a lesson or activity ends and another part begins.

Triarchic Theory of Intelligence Propounded by Robert Sternberg, this theory identifies characteristics of componential, experiential, and contextual intelligence.

Unpredictability   Refers to the unique constellation of people in each classroom and how these place-to-place differences produce quite varied patterns of interaction in individual classrooms.

Validity   Term used to describe the extent to which a measurement tool measures what it is intended to measure.

Visually Impaired Learner   Learner with an ability to see that is markedly inferior to that of people who are not characterized by this condition.

Voucher Plan   A plan that gives a voucher for funds needed to support the education of a child to his or her parent or guardian who then can select a school for the child. When this is done, the voucher is turned over to the selected school. The school uses the funds to pay for educational services delivered to the child.

Wait Time   Term applied to describe the interval between the time a teacher asks a question and a learner responds

Yearly Contract   Contract offered to a nontenured teacher. There are no rights to reemployment at the conclusion of the term specified in the contract. *See also* Tenure.

Subject Index